CREATING A UNIVERSITY

CREATING A UNIVERSITY
The Newfoundland Experience

EDITED BY

Stephen Harold Riggins and Roberta Buchanan

Foreword by Dr. Noreen Golfman, Provost and Vice-President (Academic)

ISER Books

LIBRARY AND ARCHIVES CANADA CATALOGUING IN PUBLICATION
Title: Creating a university : the Newfoundland experience / edited by Stephen Harold
    Riggins and Roberta Buchanan ; foreword by Noreen Golfman, provost and vice-president
    (academic).
Names: Riggins, Stephen Harold, 1946- editor. | Buchanan, Roberta, editor.
Series: Social and economic papers ; no. 36.
Description: Series statement: Social and economic papers ; no.36 | Includes index.
Identifiers: Canadiana (print) 20190061669 | Canadiana (ebook) 2019006370X | ISBN
    9781894725521 (softcover) | ISBN 9781894725583 (PDF)
Subjects: LCSH: Memorial University of Newfoundland—Faculty—Biography. | LCSH:
    Memorial University of Newfoundland—History. | LCSH: College teachers—Newfound-
    land and Labrador—Biography. | LCSH: Public universities and colleges—Newfoundland
    and Labrador—History. | LCSH: Education, Higher—Newfoundland and Labrador—
    History.
Classification: LCC LE3.N45 C74 2019 | DDC 378.718/1—dc23

Cover image: Students walk past the reviewing stand during the opening ceremonies for the
new Memorial University of Newfoundland campus, 1961. (Photographer: Frank Kennedy,
courtesy of Memorial University Libraries).

Cover design: Alison Carr
Page design and typesetting: Alison Carr
Copy editing: Richard Tallman

Published by ISER Books
Institute of Social and Economic Research
Memorial University of Newfoundland
PO Box 4200
St. John's, NL A1C 5S7
www.hss.mun.ca/iserbooks/

Printed in Canada
25 24 23 22 21 20 19   1 2 3 4 5 6 7 8

Publication of this book is supported by grants from the Provost and Vice-President (Academic)
of Memorial University, Dr. Noreen Golfman; by the Memorial University of Newfoundland
Pensioners' Association; and by the Memorial University Publications Subvention Program.

CONTENTS

V GROWING PAINS

Aerial view of the campus in the early 1970s showing the temporary buildings. (Photo from *Celebrate Memorial: A Pictorial History of Memorial University of Newfoundland*, originals held at Memorial University Library Archives and Special Collections.)

Foreword

Dr. Noreen Golfman

Provost and Vice-President (Academic), Memorial University

My own experience of Memorial is both similar to and different from many of the authors in this collection of essays. In 1984 I was an Assistant Professor in a tenure-track position at the University of Maine in Orono when my then husband, Ronald Rompkey, was informed about an unusually large number of positions opening up in the Memorial University English Department to accommodate an expected surge in enrolment. Ron, who sadly passed away a couple of years ago, was born in St. John's, did his undergraduate degree in English at Memorial, and had accompanied me to Maine via Alberta without any immediate employment prospects. I was the one with the working visa. He was (merely) a spouse, albeit one with a University of London PhD, a hard-working scholar who did most of the research and a lot of the writing for his acclaimed biography of Sir Wilfred Grenfell when we lived in Orono. But by the time his former mentor and supervisor and head of the English Department, Dr. Patrick O'Flaherty, called to urge him to apply, Ron was pretty keen to respond. "I have a wife who is on a tenure-track here in Maine," Ron informed Pat. "Sure, that's fine, b'y," Pat replied, "tell her to apply, too." And so I did.

And so here I am, some 34 years later, writing the Foreword to this lovely collection of memories about the early decades of the Newfoundland experiment in post-secondary education. Ron would have loved to have contributed to this collection, I am sure, and I have thought about him on almost every page. Editors and authors Stephen Riggins and Roberta Buchanan have done a very fine job of herding some stray cats to produce a largely affectionate social history of Memorial's evolution from a twinkle in Premier Joey Smallwood's eye to a full-born institution, albeit one in a near-constant state of growth and change. Roughly, the period covered in this collection spans 1949 to the early 1990s, from the birth of the university through an Act of legislation to its emergence as a comprehensive institution with more bricks and mortar than even

Joey himself likely ever imagined.

The authors included in this volume — professors and partners of professors — were all part of the noble experiment of establishing a university in and for Newfoundland and Labrador. Some seemed to understand, however vaguely, that they were partaking of something new and exciting. Others were just grateful to have a job offer, even in a place they could neither pronounce nor recognize on a map. Almost all were from away — mostly from the United Kingdom and a few from the United States. All were young, open to new adventure, and grateful for professional employment. What emerges from their accounts all these years later is a shared set of themes having to do with the unknown: both the town of St. John's, especially for those from away, and the generally unscripted, unbaked idea of a university they would help to realize.

Encountering this new land and this fledgling project posed unique challenges. The essays collected in this volume are all deeply personal reflections. For those of us who have been acquainted with many of the authors in this collection it is comforting to hear their voices on these pages, and, in some cases, even to get to know them a bit better. In his candid memoir, new Physics hire Chung-Won Cho, conspicuously the only person around at the time of non-European origin, notes, "there were some faculty members whose views on the future of the institution were stiflingly parochial and provincial. . . . Nine years of being Canadians did not seem to heal the strong resentment by some citizens against Confederation with Canada." Sandra Djwa vividly remembers the English Department head, the Englishman E.R. Seary, as a "caricature of an absent-minded professor, wearing a mouldy and decrepit gown, much in need of repair." Elsewhere Neil V. Rosenberg reflects on the huge influence of renowned American scholar Herbert Halpert on his own career in the Folklore Department. Rosenberg recalls what has become a fond and time-honoured cliché in these parts — that is, Halpert telling his townie students who thought folklore only existed around the bay that "St. John's is the biggest outport." I especially enjoy the drollery of the Medical School's Brian Payton, who describes the application process in the late sixties, when the university started to expand with gusto: "I sent a letter expressing interest in 1968, and was interviewed in late May 1969," he observes. "I awoke to see snow falling outside my window." Having shown his wife some photos he had snapped when he came for his interview, she wanted to know "why all the children were wearing parkas!" There is a lot of this sort of thing here, as is to be expected. Freshly hired outsiders from New York, the American Midwest, Scotland, and England well remember being surprised by the inhospitable weather, but also by the lack of infrastructure, unpaved roads, and far too modest accommodations. As French professor Tony Chadwick notes, "[w]hat little I knew of the province was restricted to the stamps I had collected as a child." Indeed, as a young stamp collector Chadwick was already well ahead of most of the newcomers who did not yet have a clue about their new-found-land.

Offsetting the strangeness, even the alienation, of such newness and unsettling weather was the opportunity to build something new, literally from the ground up. Many of these essays recall the excitement of setting a curriculum in place, of teaching for the first time, becoming a colleague, educating a whole new generation of Newfoundlanders who were hungry for knowledge and inspiration, watching buildings rise up from the rocky soil — creating something out of nothing. And not to be ignored is the recurring observance of the beauty of the landscape, the intense pleasure of berry-picking or of walking by the sea, so close and so cold. For almost all of these newcomers St. John's was, as it remains for us all, maddeningly paradoxical, at once annoying and gorgeously irresistible. For most, it quickly became home.

Creating a University is a labour of love, to be sure. Reading it, anyone already familiar with even a little of the history of Memorial or with favourite stories passed around at dinner parties through the years will likely bathe in a great warm wash of nostalgia. Anyone unfamiliar with any of the above should nonetheless delight in the drawing of a vivid portrait of early university life. The Memorial University enacted by a famously uncompromising Premier emerges here as a character in its own right, an awkward, hopeful personality with raw, innocent charm and much potential. It is easy to say that Memorial has come a long way since those early days in the twentieth century. True, one or two of those paper-thin "temporary" buildings described in these pages still dot the campus like menacing reminders of our ongoing infrastructure challenges. But Memorial now occupies an expansive piece of property in the centre of the city, straddles a busy, divided highway, and is, at the time of this writing, witnessing the construction of a massive state-of-the-art Core Sciences Facility that will change, well, just about everything.

Nostalgic reminiscences can lead to melancholy, and I would be remiss if I did not acknowledge a bittersweet pleasure in reading through the essays in this collection. That is the inevitable effect of comparing then and now. Although in their introductory essay Riggins and Buchanan describe the Memorial of 1990 as a "multiversity," a term made famous by former University of California at Berkeley President Clark Kerr to describe a large, modern, complex, and multi-faceted institution, it is not even close to the sprawling, research-intensive university of 2018. As I said at the outset, I came to Memorial in 1984. For more than three decades I have been witness and party to its evolution. Much of that growth and change has been necessary and fruitful. I firmly believe this university is one of the absolutely best things Joey Smallwood ever did and the province should be consistently proud of the contributions its graduates have made to the social and economic well-being of its people and beyond. But among other attributes, what goes missing in the multiversity of the twenty-first century is that strong sense of community captured in the essays here. When Memorial was still raw and open to its own experimentation, people were more intimate with each other, consciously committed to building an intellectual project for the future. It is not that the times were perfect, but they were certainly not preoccupied with the deadening instrumentality of modern institutional life. They were idealistic and expectant, growing something of which they would be proud. I can hear that pride between many of the lines in these essays. It is heartening.

There isn't an essay in this collection from which I have not learned something either about the university's origins or the person recollecting them or both. But I would be remiss if I did not point the reader to the piece that arguably inspired the title of this collection, a masterfully written slice of autobiography, social history, and witty reportage. "The Creation of the Memorial University of Newfoundland" by David G. Pitt is a brilliant, often hilarious account of the author's fateful return to the province from which he had cheerfully exiled himself. There was no resisting the last living Father of Confederation, however, and before he could even think of refusing Joey's direct offer, Pitt was leaving the University of Toronto to help set up the English Department at Memorial.

The rest is history, of course, but what an informative, humorous account of that experience this is. Professor Pitt passed away only a little while ago, but it is so especially gratifying to know he composed his essay in time to be included in this collection, obviously keeping his wry sense of humour intact to the end. Pitt lived it all. The early founders who had hired him, such as Presidents "Bertie" Hatcher, A.C. Hunter, and Moses Morgan, were the patriarchal titans of the day. They ran the original Memorial College on Parade Street and set the tone for the foreseeable future. Pitt, who was almost overwhelmed with the challenge thrust upon him at the time, paints these men large and colourfully. One can hear echoes of Jane Austen in the prose, Dr. Johnson, too. Pitt was shrewdly disciplined to have kept detailed diaries of his experience. We are all well rewarded for such diligence. "The Creation of the Memorial University of Newfoundland" is an utterly delicious read of a time we shall not see again.

I am grateful to the editors for managing to achieve this wonderful collection in the first place, and for giving me the opportunity to reflect on the essays that follow. I applaud their persistence: editing a volume of essays is often a tedious task. But I also recognize they share the same fondness for the Newfoundland experiment that was and remains Memorial University.

Students on parade at the opening of the new campus. (Photo from *Celebrate Memorial: A Pictorial History of Memorial University of Newfoundland*, originals held at Memorial University Library Archives and Special Collections.)

Introduction: The "MUNographies"

Roberta Buchanan and Stephen Harold Riggins

1

This is the "Age of the Autobiography." According to literary scholar Roger J. Porter, "we have made self-revelation endemic to our culture."[1] Life writings of all kinds pour from the press or are posted on social networks. Memoirs often dominate the bestseller list. There are celebrity memoirs and nobody memoirs; misery memoirs of substance abuse, alcoholism, child abuse; autoethnographies; autopathographies — memoirs about illnesses such as AIDS or cancer; slave narratives and captivity narratives and conversion narratives; "frautobiographies" about invented selves and lives; and, if you get tired of reading words, there are graphic memoirs in pictures. If any reader should become bewildered by this proliferation of life writing, there are an *Encyclopedia of Life Writing* edited by Margaretta Jolly, *Memoir: An Introduction* by G. Thomas Couser, and *Memoir: A History* by Ben Yagoda, as well as scholarly periodicals: *a/b: Auto/Biography Studies* and *Life Writing*. It was only to be expected that academics should jump on the memoir bandwagon.

New subgenres of life writing keep appearing. G. Thomas Couser, who wrote a memoir about his father, invented the term *patriographies* to distinguish "writing the father" as a genre worthy of study.[2] Perhaps we could coin the term *MUNographies*, memoir writing about Memorial University of Newfoundland, to describe the present book. It started with a little group of pensioners who formed the Memorial University Pensioners' Association Memoir Group, back in 2003. The idea for the group came from Raoul Andersen, anthropology; Don Steele, biology; and Bill Marshall, medicine.

Roberta Buchanan was interested in the Memoir Group because she had started writing her autobiography some time ago and then it languished in her files. Now that she was retired, perhaps she could finish it at last, she thought. Roberta was always fascinated by autobiographies and diaries. She had taught a course on Writing Our Lives for Memorial University Extension, and also conducted many journal-writing workshops for various different groups — feminists, writers, artists, poets, gays; and also taught a graduate course in autobiography in the English Department. She wrote an article on "Journal Writing for Writers" for the Writers' Alliance of Newfoundland and Labrador's *Resources for Writers*.[3] She has been the key organizational leader of the Memoir Group since its inception. She assumed it would be like a writers' workshop, where we would polish our writing efforts — but she was soon disabused of that notion. Her fellow members had spent a lifetime teaching and marking students' efforts, and now that they were retired they wanted to enjoy themselves and have a good time! They looked upon the group as an enjoyable social occasion. Two of our members stated they were not at all interested in writing about themselves. Howard Clase wanted to write about his family, and the family of his Finnish wife, Leila, so that his grandchildren would have some knowledge of their roots. Ingeborg Marshall wanted to translate the diary of her German mother, also for her family. Bill Marshall and Brian Payton produced family diaries they wanted to transcribe: Bill had two diaries, one by his father in World War I; and the other a travel journal of his mother who took a trip around the world when she was a young woman. Brian had the post-World War II diary of Christa, his German wife.

We met once a month at lunch time, in the sociable Faculty and Staff Club. The atmosphere was relaxed. Each member of the group read some short piece of writing while the others listened, munching on their sandwiches. As it happened we were all non-Newfoundlanders, so we decided to start by writing about how we came to be at Memorial, which was also a good way of getting to know each other. Then we wrote about other experiences. Some were fixated on a particular period of life: Bill Allderdice wrote about ranching in Montana, and usually brought one of his paintings as an illustration. Raoul Andersen described growing up in a working-class area of Chicago. Bill Marshall wrote about his schoolteachers. Don Steele wrote about his boyhood in Ontario. The interdisciplinary nature of the group made it interesting. Bill Marshall, Brian Payton, and Sharon Buehler were from the Medical School; Howard Clase was a chemist; Chung-Won Cho a physicist; Raoul Andersen an anthropologist; Don Steele a biologist. Ingeborg Marshall was the distinguished historian of the Beothuks. Bill Allderdice was a geographer. Later we were joined by Jo Shawyer, also from Geography; Dorothy Milne, a librarian; Joan Scott, Biology/Women's

Studies; Kjellrun Hestekin, School of Music; and Tony Chadwick, French. These were the regulars, but others joined from time to time.

The memoirs were so interesting and entertaining that the idea of collecting them into a little book was proposed. But it was not until Stephen Riggins joined the group in 2010 — he was then not retired but was writing a history of the Sociology Department — and offered to become an editor that the book became a serious undertaking. Stephen had already published an autobiography, *The Pleasures of Time: Two Men, a Life*.[4] We decided to focus on our memories of Memorial University of Newfoundland: the MUNographies. We were all part of an "occupational community" after all, that is, a group of people engaged in the same kind of work, whose identity is drawn from their work.[5] A general appeal was made to other pensioners to write their recollections of Memorial, and other contributions began to arrive. Contributions were also solicited from a wide range of departments and faculties to give a more balanced view of the rapid development of the university in the previous half-century. Thirteen members of the Memoir Group have contributed to this anthology.

Other Canadian anthologies written by academics about university life have preceded this one: *A Fair Shake: Autobiographical Essays by McGill Women* (1984);[6] *Echoes in the Halls: An Unofficial History of the University of Alberta* (1999);[7] *Women in the Academic Tundra: Challenging the Chill* (2002);[8] *I Remember Laurier: Reflections by Retirees on Life at WLU* (2011);[9] *Back in the Day 1963 to 2013: The University of Windsor as We Knew It* (2013).[10] There is also an ongoing series of memoirs by historians in the *Canadian Historical Review*, "A Life in History," which includes two former Memorial University professors, Gregory Kealey and Linda Kealey.[11]

Stephen and Roberta had different ideas about what their book should be. Roberta envisaged it as an anthology of entertaining pieces about our experiences of the university. She found some of the memoirs in some of the former collections factual but lacking in emotion. Stephen, however, took a more serious view. He more ambitiously envisaged the book as containing a (necessarily piecemeal) history of Memorial told through the various individual chapters. He energetically solicited contributions that would reflect the whole spectrum of departments, faculties, and schools. Some responded; some didn't. Some promised, but never delivered. Stephen saw the book as primarily a scholarly work. Some kind of historical context for these piecemeal contributions was needed, and we asked Melvin Baker, historian and archivist, to provide a brief overview of the university from 1949 to 1990, and Newfoundland historian Jeff Webb to write about the university's Extension Service. (This volume excludes Sir Wilfred Grenfell College in Corner Brook, which was established in 1975.)

Stephen wanted solid, well-researched chapters, not short amusing anecdotes. The book reflects both approaches. And Roberta must confess that she was instigated to put more research and thought into the contributions she wrote for the book, which she thinks gave them more depth than the light-hearted off-the-cuff approach she initially took. However, Roberta in her turn would ask "Where is the 'I' in this piece?" After all, it was a book of memoirs. Stephen learned from Roberta that his identification with the cause of feminism was more superficial than he had realized.

The autobiographies that attract the largest readership tend to be stories about extreme situations or stories by celebrities.[12] Obviously this is a collection of stories about more ordinary lives. The editors shaped these chapters in that we wanted, above all, an accessible book for general readers interested in Newfoundland; and second, a book for readers interested in the history of higher education. The situation in which this book was written naturally resulted in an "organizational saga,"[13] that is, a book contributing to pride and identity. However, both editors have written chapters rather critical of the university. As editors, we were concerned that our contributors concentrate on the uniqueness of Memorial and Newfoundland rather than the features common with universities in the rest of Canada. But the former also seemed to be what our contributors really wanted to write about. Characteristics of Memorial, such as the rapidly expanding job market in the 1960s, occurred across Canada. But they were more spectacular in St. John's when Newfoundland lacked a degree-granting university until 1949 despite being Britain's first North American colony.

If autobiographical writing is, by definition, "a work of personal justification,"[14] it would have been counterproductive for the editors to have been very controlling. Initially, we let contributors put their careers in perspective as they wanted. However, we did shape the chapters to some extent if we felt that the authors had made factual errors, were not saying enough about their colleagues, or were too modest about their own achievements. We encouraged contributors to emphasize events before 1990 but let them write about more recent events as long as they were not the major topic in their chapter. Why 1990? By that date Memorial had become the university that it is today, a research-oriented "multiversity."[15] It was no longer a small provincial institution. In its early years as a university, the faculty at Memorial was international in scope, although the majority of Memorial professors who arrived in the 1960s and 1970s were either American or British. Canadians were less tempted to travel to the eastern extremities of their country. The federal Department of Immigration and Employment, beginning in 1981, required that Canadian universities advertise for Canadian candidates first. Their suitability had to be evaluated before seeking foreign candidates.[16] Consequently, the second generation of professors at Memorial University was quite different from the first.

In the years covered by this volume, primarily 1950 to 1990, few Memorial faculty were Canadians, let alone native-born Newfoundlanders. Only the chapter by F.L. (Lin) Jackson explicitly raises the question of whether being American or British — or even Canadian — was (and still is) a liability for social scientists studying the province's population. This issue was debated in public in the 1960s because this was the beginning of the social science literature on Newfoundland. The first generation of students writing what are now considered classic studies of outports were PhD students in anthropology and sociology from American and British universities. These young men — Tom Philbrook, John Szwed, Shmuel Ben-Dor, Melvin Firestone, Louis Chiaramonte, James Faris, and Gerald Mars — were at the beginning of their careers.[17] None visited the island prior to arriving for their research. Would Newfoundlanders have come to the same conclusions as they did? Probably not. But one hopes that the reactions of the two groups would not have been completely different. Readers of this volume will occasionally find chapters in which passing remarks by authors exoticize the province. Most of the contributors to this book have now resided in Newfoundland and Labrador for many years. They no longer have these reactions. We thought it was important to record the initial reactions of the come from aways.[18]

Most of us had no idea of the complexity of Newfoundland history. We knew about Sir Humphrey Gilbert proclaiming Newfoundland a part of England, and of the fishing admirals, and about Newfoundland being Britain's oldest colony. But we had no idea of the fluctuations of government, of Legislative Assembly, Amalgamated Assembly, the Colonial Office granting Representative Government and Responsible Government, the change from colony to independent Dominion, the humiliating surrender of Responsible Government in return for financial rescue and the appointment of a Commission of Government. And many of us had little or no awareness of the furious debates of the National Convention and the narrow victory of Confederation with Canada in the second referendum of 1948.[19] Some Newfoundlanders looked back with nostalgia to the time when they were the nation of Newfoundland, instead of the weakest "have-not" province of Canada. Jeff Webb comments: "Those who grew up in the self-governing colony felt something had been lost, even as they welcomed the benefits of Confederation, and many newcomers to the island embraced the study of the place as well. It was as if, having relinquished the path towards being a nation state, Newfoundland-born intellectuals now wanted to preserve something of the national ethos."[20]

The CFAs (come from aways) who invaded the university arrived in the middle of this intellectual ferment. Some of us owed our jobs to it, hired to do specifically Newfoundland research and contribute to the new interdisciplinary Newfoundland studies. Others performed a species of cultural imperialism. Roberta remembers the English Department teaching the "canon" of "great" literature, almost exclusively the DWEMs (Dead White English Males), with a few Americans thrown in. When a departmental meeting was asked to discuss a proposal for courses in Canadian literature, a British colleague stated, "There is no Canadian literature." It was both an ignorant and an arrogant statement. (He afterwards changed his mind.) Courses in Newfoundland literature were also introduced. We found ourselves in the middle of a post-colonial cultural renaissance.

Memorial University has never been a place for the faint-hearted who want to enjoy balmy weather. Readers will discover that some of our contributors instantly liked Newfoundland. Others warmed to the province more slowly. But as come from aways, almost all of the contributors to this volume stayed despite some genuine personal hardships caused by living on the very edge of North America, far from everyone they knew. Some contributors discovered the city of St. John's and the university community through non-academic activities: amateur participation in the fine arts and social activism of various sorts; or they discovered a new perspective on their academic discipline by living in a region that is unique and whose history, dialect, arts, and institutions had been poorly documented. In retrospect, how little we CFAs knew about Newfoundland — and Canada — at the time of our arrival is astonishing.

After two introductory survey chapters by Melvin Baker and Jeff Webb, the book is divided into four additional parts: "The Old Parade Street Campus"; "New Developments"; "New Adventures – Arriving"; and "Growing Pains." Malcolm MacLeod has written an excellent history of Memorial University College: *A Bridge Built Halfway: A History of Memorial University College, 1925–1950*.[21] But there has been no book-length continuation of the history describing the transformation of the two-year university college to a full-fledged university. Our first section, "The Old Parade Street Campus," has memoirs from those who taught at the old campus — e.g., physicist Chung-Won Cho — or who were students there, like Sandra (Drodge) Djwa. We also have a chapter about the experience of a young faculty wife in the 1950s: Elizabeth Willmott, partner of the university's only sociologist at the time. This section contains two of our oldest contributors: Norman Brown, who was hired as a one-person Philosophy Department, and David Pitt, the first faculty member hired when Memorial became a degree-granting institution, who had been a student at Memorial University College. Both men have since passed away, Professor Brown in his ninety-second year in 2014 and Professor Pitt in his ninety-seventh year in 2018, which highlights the importance of collecting our MUNographies in an aging demographic. (Other contributors to this volume have also passed away since completing their memoirs.) John Hewson describes the old campus in some detail, as well as his role in the creation of a new Linguistics Department. They were pioneers in creating the new university, and witnessed the move from the old, outdated, and inadequate campus to the newly built one on Elizabeth Avenue.

The next section, "New Developments," deals with the ferment of expansion and the creation of new departments, schools, and divisions:

Folklore, the School of Business, and the Division of Junior Studies. Three members of the Memoir Group have contributed: Howard Clase on the Botanical Garden; Dorothy Milne on the library; and Don Steele on the establishment of the Bonne Bay Marine Station.

The third section, "New Adventures: Arriving," is perhaps the heart and origin of the book in the Memoir Group: eight of its 10 contributions are from its members. We record the excitement of arriving in St. John's, the problems of dealing with a new culture, and the adventures of our first teaching experiences in the expanding university.

The final section, "Growing Pains," as its title suggests, concerns the challenges faced by a growing institution. Kjellrun Hestekin describes the difficult conditions of the new School of Music; Roberta Buchanan recounts the struggle for equality for faculty women. Steven Wolinetz gives an account of the student strike of 1972 and Lord Taylor's confrontational stance as university President. Joan Scott provides the long view: 50 years as faculty wife, mother, student, graduate, and faculty member.

Some European universities are among the few institutions (along with the Icelandic Parliament and the Catholic Church) to have survived since the Middle Ages. Whether in Europe or North America, the modern university is an odd institution. Highly bureaucratized at some level, its decentralized nature makes it a poor model of bureaucracy. The acclaimed scholar of higher education, Burton R. Clark, referred to the university as consisting of "different worlds, small worlds."[22] The university attracts and retains some of the most literate people in society and has extensive archives. Yet few of its residents bother to look at the archives. In some ways the university consequently functions as an oral culture with a shallow institutional memory. Everyone is so concerned about the hurly-burly of the immediate future (the next lecture, the next exam, next publication, next meeting, next grant) that they do not have time for the university's past. Almost all students are gone in four years. By the end of 25 or 30 years of teaching, professors may have spent more time with their colleagues than with their (new) spouse. Yet colleagues often know little about each other. As Robert Nisbet pointed out, universities are created to accomplish a task: scholarship and teaching. The resulting community is an afterthought.[23]

We don't have a survey to prove it, but we suspect that the sense of community among the MUN faculty has been reduced to the level of a department or even to a faction within a department. It is clear from some of the chapters in this volume that when Memorial was a small institution, with cramped office space, the faculty seemed to have been more interdependent. Due to administrative shortsightedness we have lost vital spaces for informal socializing such as the Faculty and Staff Club and the cafeteria in the Arts and Administration Building. Another factor contributing to a broader sense of community, according to some of our oldest contributors, is that the professional lives of Memorial University professors were relatively relaxed in the early years until a wave of hyper-professionalism swept North American universities beginning in the mid-1970s when the academic job market shrank. From the 1950s to the mid-1970s faculty members were younger and more energetic, when a completed PhD degree was not a requirement to get a tenure-stream teaching position. To imagine that this volume might substantially change a fragmented academic culture at Memorial is to impute too much power to ideas, a common mistake of intellectuals. Nonetheless, we continue to hope that this volume — a sort of Memorial University family reunion without a drunken uncle — will contribute in some modest way to a stronger sense of local traditions and solidarity. The success of a book of memoirs can be judged by the number of memoirs it provokes among readers. We hope that those who cannot find their own voices in this volume will be encouraged to write their own MUNography.

Acknowledgements: The publication of this book was made possible by the financial support of the Provost and Vice-President (Academic), Dr. Noreen Golfman; Memorial University of Newfoundland Pensioners' Association (MUNPA); and Memorial University Publication Subventions Program. Thanks to Steven Wolinetz for his advice.

   We would particularly like to thank Dr. Golfman for her encouragement of our project and for graciously writing the Foreword. ISER Books Academic Editors Dr. Sharon Roseman and Dr. Fiona Polack made detailed and valuable suggestions on the manuscript. We would like to acknowledge the invaluable assistance of novelist Lisa Moore.

   Roberta Buchanan would like to thank her friends Georgina Queller, Joan Scott, and Phyllis Artiss for help freely given. Stephen Riggins would like to thank Paul Bouissac for his assistance.

Notes

1.   Roger J. Porter, "Review of *Burdens of Proof: Faith, Doubt, and Identity in Autobiography*, by Susanna Egan," *a/b: Auto/Biography Studies* 26, no. 2 (2011): 372.

2.   Stephen Mansfield, "Fashioning Fathers: An Interview with G. Thomas Couser," *Life Writing* 11, no. 1 (2014): 5.

3.   Roberta Buchanan, "Journal Writing for Writers," in Catherine Hogan, Linda Russell, and Janet McNaughton, eds., *Resources for Writers* (St. John's: Writers' Alliance of Newfoundland and Labrador, 1994): 1–4.

4.   Stephen Harold Riggins, *The Pleasures of Time: Two Men, a Life* (Toronto: Insomniac Press, 2003).

5.   H.L. Goodall, Jr., "Casing the Academy for Community," *Communication Theory* 9, no. 4 (1999): 465–66.

6.   Margaret Gillett and Kay Sibbald, eds., *A Fair Shake: Autobiographical Essays by McGill Women* (Montreal: Eden Press, 1984).

7.   Mary Spencer, Kay Dier, and Gordon McIntosh, eds., *Echoes in the Halls: An Unofficial History of the University of Alberta*. Association of Professors Emeriti of the University of Alberta (Edmonton: Duval House and University of Alberta Press, 1999).

8.   Elena Hannah, Linda Paul, and Swani Vethamany-Globus, eds., *Women in the Academic Tundra: Challenging the Chill* (Montreal and Kingston: McGill-Queen's University Press, 2002).

9.   Harold Remus, general ed., Rose Blackmore and Boyd McDonald, eds., *I Remember Laurier: Reflections by Retirees on Life at WLU* (Waterloo, ON: Wilfrid Laurier University Press, 2011).

10.   Kathleen McCrone, general ed., Sheila Cameron, Ralph Johnson, Kenneth Pryke, and Lois Smethwick, eds., *Back in the Day 1963 to 2013: The University of Windsor as We Knew It* (Windsor, ON: Black Moss Press, 2013).

11.   Gregory Kealey, "Community, Politics, and History: My Life as a Historian," *Canadian Historical Review* 97, no. 3 (2016): 404–25; Linda Kealey, "Activism in Scholarship," *Canadian Historical Review* 95, no. 1 (2014): 78–96.

12.   Jeremy D. Popkin, *History, Historians, and Autobiography* (Chicago: University of Chicago Press, 2005), 6.

13.   Burton R. Clark, *On Higher Education: Selected Writings, 1956–2006* (Baltimore: Johns Hopkins University Press, 2008), 53.

14.   Popkin, *History, Historians, and Autobiography*, 25.

15.   A very large university with many component schools, colleges, or divisions and widely diverse functions (*Merriam-Webster Dictionary*, s.v. "multiversity"); proposed by Clark Kerr, "The Idea of a Multiversity," in *The Uses*

of the University (Cambridge, MA: Harvard University Press, 1963).

16. Jeffrey Cormier, *The Canadianization Movement: Emergence, Survival, and Success* (Toronto: University of Toronto Press, 2004), 187.

17. The research of most of these scholars was published by Memorial's Institute of Social and Economic Research. See Tom Philbrook, *Fisherman, Logger, Merchant, Miner: Social Change and Industrialism in Three Newfoundland Communities* (St. John's: ISER Books, 1966); John F. Szwed, *Private Cultures and Public Imagery: Interpersonal Relations in a Newfoundland Peasant Society* (St. John's: ISER Books, 1966); Shmuel Ben-Dor, *Makkovik: Eskimos and Settlers in a Labrador Community: A Contrastive Study in Adaptation* (St. John's: ISER Books, 1966); Melvin M. Firestone, *Brothers and Rivals: Patrilocality in Savage Cove* (St. John's: ISER Books, 1967); Louis Chiaramonte, *Craftsmen–Client Contracts: Interpersonal Relations in a Newfoundland Fishing Community* (St. John's: ISER Books, 1970); James C. Faris, *Cat Harbour: A Newfoundland Fishing Settlement* (St. John's: ISER Books, 1972). See also Gerald Mars, "An Anthropological Study of Longshoremen and of Industrial Relations in the Port of St. John's, Newfoundland, Canada," PhD thesis, Anthropology (University of London, 1972). For more information about the early years of the Institute of Social and Economic Research, see Jeff A. Webb, *Observing the Outports: Describing Newfoundland Culture, 1950–1980* (Toronto: University of Toronto Press, 2016); Stephen Harold Riggins, "Sociology by Anthropologists: A Chapter in the History of an Academic Discipline in Newfoundland during the 1960s," *Acadiensis* 46, no. 2 (2017): 119–42.

18. The phrase "come from away" is not in the *Dictionary of Newfoundland English*; "a person who is not from the Atlantic region generally" (*The Canadian Oxford Dictionary*, s.v. "come from away"). Folklorist Neil Rosenberg dates the expression to a joke current in Newfoundland in the early 1970s, when "new faculty members were arriving from all quarters of the globe. 'You can't get a job at Memorial,' the joke-teller would begin, 'unless you got your CFA.' Listeners would ask for an explanation of the acronym, which seemed to stand for some kind of academic degree, like 'Ph.D.' In a society still used to imposed colonial leadership, 'come from away' was self-explanatory" ("A Folklorist's Exploration of the Revival Metaphor," Oxford Handbooks Online, Oxford University Press, 2013. DOI:10.1093/oxfordhb/9780199765034.013.005). Now popularized as the title of a hit musical, *Come From Away*, by Irene Sankoff and David Hein (2013), about the American planes redirected to Gander after the 11 September 2001 terrorist attacks on the United States, which closed US airspace and airports for three days.

19. *Encyclopedia of Newfoundland and Labrador*, s.v. "Government," "Confederation."

20. Webb, *Observing the Outports*, 4.

21. Malcolm MacLeod, *A Bridge Built Halfway: A History of Memorial University College, 1925–1950* (Montreal and Kingston: McGill-Queen's University Press, 1990).

22. Clark, *On Higher Education*.

23. Robert Nisbet, *The Degradation of the Academic Dogma: The University in America, 1945–1970* (New York: Basic Books, 1971), 41–59.

I

HISTORICAL
BACKGROUND

Premier Smallwood paying an informal visit to the campus. (Photo from
*Memorial University of Newfoundland and its Environs: A Guide to Life
and Work at the University in St. John's,* courtesy of Memorial University
Libraries.)

Memorial University of Newfoundland at St. John's, 1949–1990

Melvin Baker

2

M emorial University of Newfoundland came into existence in 1949 when the Liberal government of Premier Joseph R. Small-wood elevated by statute Memorial University College to the status of a university to "encourage the preservation of the Newfoundland culture" and to be "an active and energetic means to the economic development of Newfoundland . . . more than merely a centre of culture and learning."[1] The college in St. John's dated from 1925, officially opening on 15 September as a two-year junior college with financial assistance from the Carnegie Corporation. Its first President (1925–33) was retired Manchester Grammar School High Master John Lewis Paton.[2] The college's opening was the result of several years of effort by educators to provide a non-denominational system of post-secondary education in the arts and sciences and to improve teacher training (long the responsibility of various church-affiliated schools). The Memorial building was first used by the Normal School, which had been officially opened on 29 September 1924 and offered a one-year teacher training program until 1932. In 1934 the Newfoundland Memorial University College (or Memorial College as it was generally known) began offering a teacher training program. The campus covered nearly two acres and was located at the intersection of Merrymeeting Road and Parade Street near the city's downtown core. The building culminated in the efforts of educators and citizens to honour those Newfoundlanders who lost their lives in the Great War.[3]

For several years prior to 1949, college officials had considered extending the college to university status, but Newfoundland's Confederation with Canada in 1949 hastened this process under the province's enthusiastic Premier Smallwood (1949–72). The 1949 legislation provided for a Chancellor, a Board of Regents, a President (appointed by the Board), a Senate, and faculty councils. The Board of Regents had oversight over the "management, administration, and control of the property, revenue, business and affairs of the University." Except for two members elected by convocation, all Board members were government appointees. Over the years, Board composition became larger with the inclusion of elected alumni and student representatives appointed by the government on the recommendation of the undergraduate and graduate students' unions. The Act gave responsibility for academic matters to the Senate, an appointed body initially consisting of the President, the Deputy Minister of Education, the deans of faculties, a representative of any college or institution affiliated with the university, and a maximum of six others appointed or elected under the authority of the Board of Regents (and later student representation). The three faculties formally recognized by the Board in 1950 were Arts and Science, Applied Science, and Education.

Dr. Albert Hatcher (1886–1954) was the college President from 1933 to 1949 and the first President of the university, before retiring in 1952. Born in Moreton's Harbour and educated at McGill, the University of Chicago, and Columbia University, the mathematics professor was part of the first teaching staff of the college in 1925. In such a small institution, former Dean of Arts and Science A.C. Hunter noted, Hatcher had an "intense interest in every student as a person. He trained and exercised his natural gift for remembering the names, native places, and circumstances of all his students."[4] St. John's lawyer Raymond Gushue (1900–80) succeeded him; he had a long association with the college, having been a member of the governing board of the college and vice-chairman of the Board of Regents before his appointment as President. Former President Moses Morgan has observed that Gushue saw his principal function as President as being a "good co-ordinator" who (Morgan said) "excelled in that.... He used the powers of his office not to impose a pattern but to encourage a process, immanent in the body academic."[5] Although the student base and research focus were mainly rooted in Newfoundland, Memorial recruited faculty from many universities and countries. A large percentage of new faculty members in the 1950s were British, but many were American and Canadian, including Newfoundlanders such as David Pitt,[6] Allison O'Reilly Feder, and George Story[7] in the English Department, Cater Andrews in Biology, Moses Morgan[8] in Political Science, William Summers in Geography,[9] and George Hickman in Education. A 1954 Columbia University graduate, Hickman (1909–2000) had joined the college in 1944 and was Dean of Education from 1950 to 1974. A long-term effect of this hiring practice was the broadening of the province's cultural and ethnic awareness.[10] In a small, informal setting, personal contacts were critical in hiring before the early 1970s; indeed, during his sabbatical year in 1965–66 taken at Oxford University, George Story played a prominent role on behalf of the university administration in interviewing potential candidates such as Robert Paine and Keith Matthews for employment at Memorial in the general area of Newfoundland Studies.

From 1949 Memorial University usually experienced annual increases in enrolment.[11] The number of students in 1949–50 was 307. By 1960–61 there were 1,234 full-time undergraduates and 30 graduate students. Students registered in the Faculty of Education comprised about 50 per cent of the total number in the 1950s. After 1949 the academic policy of the university was to slowly establish new programs and degrees on sound academic lines. The first emphasis was on a broadly based undergraduate program in the arts and sciences, followed later by graduate programs in selected disciplines. In early 1951 the Board of Regents appointed Robert Newton, a former President of the University of Alberta, to advise on the future development of the university. This included the site for a new campus. In 1951 the government chose an 80-acre area (later expanded to 120 acres) located in a planned suburb, which the St. John's Housing Corporation had commenced building in the mid-1940s.[12] In October 1952 the Rt. Hon. the Viscount Rothermere of Hemsted, the university Chancellor (1952–61), presided over an official ceremony to lay the cornerstone for the main building. For financial reasons, construction did not commence until 1959 when university and government officials had planned every aspect of the university's physical and academic needs.

In 1950 and 1951 Memorial adopted regulations for the Bachelor of Arts (Education), Bachelor of Arts, and Bachelor of Science degrees. In 1960 a separate Bachelor of Education degree was inaugurated. New courses were added during the 1950s, including philosophy (1952), physical education (1953), geology (1953), commerce (1954), linguistics (1956), sociology (1956),[13] pre-forestry (1956), and psychology (1957). The physical education and commerce courses were later expanded into full degree programs. Graduate programs were established in the 1950s.

The departments of Chemistry and English Language and Literature were the first to offer graduate programs, with four students receiving master's degrees at the 1956 Spring Convocation.[14] The departments of History, Geology, and Biology soon followed. As alumnus Peter Neary ('59) has recalled of his time at Memorial, the university on Parade Street was "compact, companionable and collegial. It was also a place of intellectual ferment and great opportunity. The electoral scholarships had just been introduced and these and other awards allowed the best students from across the province to gather on Parade Street. Many of us were the first members of our families to attend university. Newfoundland was very outward-looking in the years immediately after the Second World War, and my contemporaries imagined themselves in careers all over the world. Happily, their dreams came true."[15]

In 1959 the university adopted a more formal approach to its offering of non-credit courses with the appointment of John Colman as the first Director of Extension Service.[16] Oxford-educated, Colman had previously been the Director of Extra-Mural Studies at Makerere College, Kampala, Uganda. The Extension Service offered non-credit courses and educational television programs such as *Decks Awash* during the early 1960s; later in the decade the name was used for a monthly magazine published by the Extension Service dealing with history and current events in rural Newfoundland and Labrador. The Service also established the St. John's Orchestra and the St. John's Extension Choir (under the direction of Ignatius Rumboldt)[17] and began appointing fieldworkers in community development (the first, in Bonavista). In the 1960s the Extension Service under painters Christopher Pratt and later Peter Bell became responsible for the university's art collection,[18] while Murray Schafer was responsible for music.[19]

Student athletic, social, and other activities were controlled by the Students' Representative Council (SRC) elected annually by the student body to serve as a liaison with the President and faculty. In 1957 the SRC was replaced by the Council of the Students' Union (CSU). The student body was organized into a number of special interest groups such as the pre-medical, engineering, education, arts and science, radio, and the dramatic societies. On 11 December 1950, the first issue of the student newspaper *The Muse* was published. (Prior to *The Muse* the *Memorial Times* had been published since 1936, but on an irregular basis.)

From the beginning, the university and Premier Smallwood recognized the paramount role Memorial could play in promoting Newfoundland Studies, long the domain of amateur enthusiasts and popular writers, including Smallwood himself. In 1954 the university applied to the Carnegie Corporation for help in establishing provincial archives. Carnegie agreed to a three-year grant of $30,000 on condition that, once established, the archives would be passed over to the province. When the Carnegie grant expired in 1958, the university received financial assistance from the Canada Council until the archives were transferred to the province in 1960. As part of this project, librarian Agnes O'Dea later published a bibliography of Newfoundland and Labrador writings. Her efforts to collect and preserve publications on Newfoundland and Labrador eventually led to the establishment of the Centre for Newfoundland Studies.[20]

The official sod-turning ceremony for the new university was on 23 May 1959. Memorial then began to occupy its 120-acre campus on Elizabeth Avenue during the summer of 1961. Opening ceremonies were held with great fanfare in early October. The campus consisted of four buildings: Arts and Administration, Physical Education, Science and Engineering, and the Library. Funding for the second phase came from a campaign, known as the National Fund, undertaken in October 1960. The campaign raised funds for three residences and a dining hall (later named Gushue Hall). Funds were donated for two residences — Rothermere and Bowater — by the Anglo-Newfoundland Development Company and the Bowater Pulp and Paper Company. Other academic buildings were subsequently built: the Education Building (occupied in September 1966), the Chemistry-Physics Building (1968), and six new residences. A new Student Centre, financed in part by a gift of $500,000 from the university's Chancellor, Lord Thomson of Fleet, opened in May 1968. The Thomson Student Centre housed offices of the CSU, a gymnasium, a cafeteria, and various student services. In the late 1960s the Roman Catholic, Anglican, and United Church denominations each opened a college residence on the campus.[21]

In the 1960s new research and teaching programs were introduced. The Institute of Social and Economic Research (ISER) was established in 1961 to conduct research into the social and economic problems of the province. Under the direction of Ian Whitaker (1961–65) and Robert

Paine (1965–73), ISER gained an international reputation for scholarly research and publishing.[22] Diploma courses were first offered in Public Welfare in 1961, and a decade later as a degree program in Social Work. In 1965 the Senate approved social welfare as a major for the Bachelor of Arts degree and in 1968 approved a five-year Bachelor of Social Work. The first class graduated in 1970.[23] The university's first doctoral programs were established during the 1965-66 academic year in the departments of Chemistry and English. In 1967 the Marine Sciences Research Laboratory (MSRL) at Logy Bay, with American biologist Dr. Fred Aldrich as Director, was established with the financial assistance of the National Research Council of Canada and the Newfoundland government. Aldrich had joined Memorial's Biology Department in 1961 and became a specialist in the study of the giant squid. David Idler, Director of the Halifax branch of the Fisheries Research Board of Canada, succeeded Aldrich, who became the university's first Dean of Graduate Studies in 1970.

The new campus experienced explosive growth during the 1960s as Memorial evolved from a small, primarily undergraduate institution to a comprehensive university offering master's and doctoral degrees. When the new campus opened in 1961, enrolment stood at 1,907; by the end of the decade it had risen to 7,239. Despite the many new facilities, rapid growth in enrolment once again resulted in a shortage of classroom and office space. In 1968 the university opened several one-storey wooden "temporary" buildings, some of which were still in use in the 1990s. Student enrolment after 1965 was greatly boosted by Premier Smallwood's decision to provide free tuition and student allowances to all Newfoundland residents and to pay every student a salary over and above free tuition. This program lasted until 1969 when the province required all applicants for financial assistance to borrow a minimum of $400 from the new Canada Student Loan Program before being approved for free tuition.

In 1966 President Gushue retired and Dean of Arts and Science Moses O. Morgan (1917–95) stepped in to serve as President (pro tem) from February 1966 to June 1967, while the government searched for a permanent successor. Morgan was the faculty's choice for the position and, according to his biographer, would have accepted the position if offered it by the Premier.[24] The year 1966 was a milestone in the university's development. As President (pro tem), Morgan initiated Senate reviews of the university's administrative and academic programs, which led to the establishment of new programs in keeping with the needs of a growing student population and program diversity to suit the needs of the province. Within a year, the university had 17 new academic departments. To promote distance and continuing education, in 1966 the Educational Television Centre (ETV) was established and the following year the university hired Duane Starcher as Director; he joined Memorial from Western Michigan University where he had been the Assistant Director of Broadcasting. Other administrative changes included the Faculty of Education being divided into three new academic departments and instituting a graduate program. Several new departments were created in the Faculty of Arts and Science in 1967. The Department of Social Studies was replaced by five new departments: Sociology and Anthropology, Commerce, Economics, Political Science, and Social Welfare. Other new departments were Romance Languages and Literatures, German and Russian Language and Literature, Biochemistry, and Theology (later Religious Studies). The School of Nursing admitted its first class in 1966.

In the 1960s Memorial established professional degree programs in Nursing, Medicine, Social Work, and Engineering. Joyce Nevitt was appointed the first head of the Nursing Department, which began admitting students in 1966 and graduated its first Bachelor of Nursing degree recipients (four RNs) in 1969. The first basic students graduated in 1971. The British-born Nevitt had previously been head of Public Health Nursing at Wayne State University in Detroit.[25] In 1974 the department was elevated to the status of a school. The university approved the establishment of a School of Medicine in 1966 with the selection of Newfoundlander Dr. Ian Rusted as Dean in 1967.[26] The Medical School admitted its first class three years later. With instructors in place, undergraduates in medicine were admitted in 1969; the first graduating class was in 1973. In 1966 the Senate also approved a degree program in Engineering, having offered since 1930 a three-year diploma program. In 1967 the Senate approved an engineering co-operative program that allowed students to alternate academic and work terms, graduating with a healthy mix of the theoretical and the practical. In 1968 University of Waterloo engineering Professor Angus Bruneau was appointed Dean. Engineering degrees were then offered in four disciplines: civil, mechanical, mining, and electrical engineering. The first class graduated in 1973.

The 1960s also witnessed Memorial establishing research programs devoted to the social and economic needs of the province. In the arts and humanities, collaborative research was ongoing. The Department of English Language and Literature had been researching Newfoundland place names and language, with the encouragement of Canada Council grants, since the late 1950s; the chief researchers were Professors George Story and Ronald Seary (the Sheffield University graduate had come to Memorial in 1954 from the College of Arts and Science in Baghdad).[27] In 1959 and 1962 they were joined by William Kirwin, who came from Ripon College in Wisconsin, and Herbert Halpert, a leading American folklorist, as specialists in linguistics and folklore, respectively. Seary subsequently published several books on family names and place names, while Story with Kirwin and John Widdowson (of the University of Sheffield and a former Memorial folklorist) researched the *Dictionary of Newfoundland English*, which was published to great acclaim in 1982.

Premier Smallwood's search for an internationally known figure to be President resulted in his selection of the Rt. Hon. The Lord Taylor of Harlow (1910–88).[28] The 1949 University Act had given the Board of Regents the right to select and recommend a presidential nominee for approval to the government, but in 1959 the Smallwood government, following public disagreements over enrolment limits and the delay in establishing an Extension Service at Memorial, amended the legislation to give itself the right to do so.[29] A colourful figure, Taylor was a physician who had served as a British Labour MP from 1945 to 1954. After 1954 he was appointed a member of the Harlow Development Corporation and in 1958 he was named to the House of Lords as Lord Taylor of Harlow.[30] Taylor visited Newfoundland in May 1966 when the government confirmed its decision to hire Taylor, who earlier that month had met with a joint committee of the Board of Regents and the Senate to allow the government to have Memorial's views on the proposed appointment. The Senate representatives were Drs. E.R. Seary, J.D. Eaton, and G.M. Story. The committee's meeting with Taylor took place in the Premier's library of his Roaches Line residence. In their report, Story and Dr. Leslie Harris, Dean of Arts and Science (pro tem), observed that Taylor was a "man with a quick and agile mind, and possessed of supreme self-confidence," especially with regard to his medical qualifications and experience. He saw the role of President and Vice-Chancellor as "one concerned with broad strategy, long-range planning, and external relations on a high level. Indeed, from his vantage point in the House of Lords, he saw himself as ambassador extraordinary at Memorial."[31]

Taylor assumed office on 1 June 1967. In his 1988 memoir, Taylor acknowledged the significant roles and contributions of both Morgan and Harris to his presidency. Before agreeing to Morgan's appointment as Vice-President, Taylor acknowledged that as a political scientist Morgan specialized in "both political theory and practical power structure" and asked himself if he wanted a Vice-President "who held so superb a hand of cards." As Morgan was totally dedicated to the welfare of the university, Taylor considered Morgan to be an asset he had to have. He subsequently found that in interviewing candidates for employment: "our judgements were almost always identical." Despite the secretive nature with which Morgan conducted general university business, Taylor thus learned "as a rule to keep one jump ahead of him, but it was not easy and I did not always succeed."[32] As for Leslie Harris, Taylor wrote that he was a "first class administrator, with an outstanding academic intelligence. My only fear was that it might be wrong to waste so brilliant an historian and polymath on administration. . . . Les had superb judgement, and when there was a particularly horrible job to be done, I would sometimes pass it on to Mose, who in turn passed it on to Les. Les was less tortuous than Mose, but like Mose he played his hand close to his chest."[33]

Following Lord Taylor's assumption of the presidency in June 1967, Memorial established a residential campus at Harlow, England, for both undergraduates and graduates of Memorial requiring practical experience in engineering, social services, and teaching. There were also significant changes to Memorial's administration. The faculty council was divided into separate councils — science, education, engineering, and medicine. In 1969 provision was made for the election of faculty members and students to the Senate. Since the mid-1950s the university had been concerned about the academic performance of first-year students. Its solution was to establish Junior and Senior Divisions. The former, comprising first-year studies and a foundation program designed to prepare high school students for university, was instituted in the

1968–69 academic year. The next year the university changed the September–April academic year to a semester system. The Division of Summer Session and Extramural Studies was established in 1970. The university began to offer Engineering degrees at both the bachelor and the master's levels in 1969. A grant of $3 million was received from the Atlantic Development Board to help provide a building for the faculty.

In the late 1960s Memorial's coming of age as a university received recognition from a number of sources. In 1968 it was chosen by the World Health Organization as an International Reference Centre for Avian Malaria Parasites. Under the direction of Marshall Laird, the Centre conducted research into all aspects of avian blood parasites. The Institute of Social and Economic Research and anthropologists in the Department of Sociology and Anthropology received a four-year Canada Council Killam grant in 1968 to study the eastern Canadian Arctic, which led to several publications by ISER Books.[34] With the help of a three-year grant from the National Research Council of Canada in 1968, the Institute of Research in Human Abilities, under the directorship of Arthur Sullivan, started to co-ordinate and conduct research on learning disabilities among school students. Besides work on Newfoundland dialect and language and ISER studies on the economy and resettlement, in the late 1960s there was renewed emphasis on research in Newfoundland history and folklore at both the faculty and graduate levels. In Newfoundland history the impetus came from the research of Keith Matthews and David Alexander, who in 1971 formed the Maritime History Group to study the maritime and economic history of Newfoundland and the North Atlantic region.[35] Under the leadership of Herbert Halpert, the Department of Folklore became the first of its kind in English Canada, offering degrees at the bachelor's, master's, and doctoral levels.[36]

The period from 1967 to 1973 was one of increasing activity for the Extension Service under the leadership of its second Director, Donald Snowden. The Winnipeg native had previously been a consultant for the Extension Service on co-operative organizations, and from 1956 to 1964 had worked in co-operatives for the federal Department of Northern Affairs and Natural Resources. Snowden was a well-known expert on the Canadian North. In 1967 a Film Unit was established with the assistance of the National Film Board of Canada. The Extension's Film

Unit pioneered a technique of community involvement known as the "Fogo Process," which was followed in several countries.[37] The Centre for the Development of Community Initiatives began operations in 1973, offering a multidisciplinary degree in community and development studies, but closed in 1978 because of fiscal restraint at the university necessitated by provincial government policy.

Lord Taylor retired as President on 31 August 1973 and was succeeded by M.O. Morgan, whose association with Memorial began as a student in the 1930s and continued as a professor and administrator after 1950. (He was succeeded as Vice-President by Leslie Harris [1929–2008], another alumnus of Memorial.) The Blaketown native — and Newfoundland Rhodes Scholar for 1938 — was a graduate of Dalhousie and Oxford universities, whose education was interrupted by service in the Canadian Army during World War II. He joined the faculty at Dalhousie in 1948 and came to Memorial in 1950 to teach political science. In a 1995 tribute to Morgan, Leslie Harris observed that there was a "strong pragmatic streak" to him that was "coupled with an unyielding commitment to the idea that the special expertise that could be mobilized and brought to bear by the university was that which would . . . move the Newfoundland community towards appropriate development."[38]

Morgan viewed the university as a major instrument of development for the province, both directly through teaching and research and through the Extension Service. In the 1970s the university continued concentrating on Newfoundland-related studies — particularly in the areas of earth sciences, marine sciences, ocean engineering, folklore, history, anthropology, and linguistics. With the assistance of a grant from the Devonian Group of charitable foundations in Calgary, the university founded the Centre for Cold Ocean Resources Engineering (C-CORE). The Newfoundland Institute of Cold Ocean Science (NICOS) was established in 1979 in the Faculty of Science in order to co-ordinate research. To provide assistance to small businesses, the School of Business Administration and Commerce established the P.J. Gardiner Institute for Small Business Studies. The Department of Music, opened in 1975, was elevated to the status of a school in 1985. The Medical School during the 1970s became a major Atlantic centre for research in such areas as cancer, kidney disease, and hypertension. In

1979 the university launched a successful fundraising campaign for a commerce building and a library (which began service in 1982), named for Queen Elizabeth II.

Three departments were elevated to the status of schools: Business Administration and Commerce (which became a faculty in 1981), Social Work, and Nursing. In 1974 the university inaugurated an institute (later named the G.A. Frecker Institute) at St. Pierre, where students could spend a semester studying French language and literature. The Institute for Education, Research and Development was founded in the Faculty of Education in 1975 to undertake and sponsor research in Newfoundland's educational philosophy and practice. The Faculty of Education set up a program to train Indigenous Labradorians as teachers, while university activities in Labrador were co-ordinated through the Labrador Institute of Northern Studies, established in 1979 and based at Goose Bay.

President Morgan retired on 31 August 1981 and was succeeded by Leslie Harris, the first graduate of Memorial to be President.[39] As Public Orator Shane O'Dea has observed, Harris presided over a university that had gone from the "bricks and mortars" phase of the 1960s and 1970s to one that "matured in an intellectual and aesthetic manner."[40] In 2004 Memorial named its new Centre of Regional Policy and Development in his honour as recognition for his great devotion to the social and economic development of the province. During the 1980s Harris presided over a period of growth in academic programs at the undergraduate and graduate levels as enrolment soared annually, doubling from 9,000 students in 1978 to 18,000 in 1991. The university added extra classrooms and teaching staff but remained underfunded because the provincial grant, plus revenues from the lowest tuition fees in Atlantic Canada, failed to keep pace with increasing costs. When the campus moved to Elizabeth Avenue in 1961, Memorial was a small liberal arts institution with limited graduate programs, but by the 1980s it had grown into a significant research university with professional schools and provided high-level training and professional development in meeting the many social requirements of the province.[41] Restraint remained a dominant theme during the 1980s as the province experienced a downturn in its economy, while pressures on the university grew as student enrolment continued to rise sharply. However, some new programs were added, including Women's Studies and Pharmacy.[42] In 1985 the History Department began a PhD degree in Canadian, Maritime, and Newfoundland history. A master's degree was instituted in toxicology, and master's and doctoral degrees were offered in food science. During the 1983–84 academic year the Division of Junior Studies was merged with what had been the Senior Division and first-year programs became the responsibility of the newly created School of General Studies, which had responsibility for first-year students and senior students who had either declared a major or been accepted into a professional school or faculty. In 1982 the Department of Earth Sciences was created from the merger of the Geology Department and the Geophysics Section of the Physics Department. The geology program, under the headship of Ward Neale, had become one of the best-known in Canada. The Centre for Earth Resources Research (CERR) was set up in 1983 to co-ordinate and promote research in the Earth Sciences Department. In 1986 the provincial government made available $25 million from its offshore oil development fund to build a modern research facility to house the new department and CERR. The facility opened officially in 1990 as the Alexander Murray Building. In the mid-1980s the Natural Sciences and Engineering Research Council (NSERC) and Petro-Canada provided funding for a research chair in marine crustal seismology, Mobil (Canada) and NSERC funded a chair in ocean engineering, and Fisheries Products International and National Sea Products funded one in fisheries oceanography.

Fisheries research continued to be further enhanced with the creation in 1986 of the Canadian Centre for International Fisheries Training, in co-operation with the Institute of Fisheries and Marine Technology. The Centre's role was to provide and co-ordinate Canadian assistance to developing countries. In 1985 the National Research Council of Canada established the Institute for Marine Dynamics, a marine hydrodynamics facility dedicated to the study of marine vessels and offshore structures. The university's Seabright Corporation was set up in 1986 to stimulate economic development by a transfer of expertise in development to the private sector. In 1988 the research facilities of the Marine Sciences Research Laboratory and other marine-related units merged to become the Ocean Sciences Centre. A building program during the 1980s included extensions to the Health Sciences Centre to house the Schools of Nursing and Pharmacy and the medicine faculty's pioneering telemedicine facilities. A building to house the School of Music was opened in 1985 and named in honour of former President Morgan.

Academic life at Memorial since the 1970s has been described in several fictional accounts, three of them by members of the English Department: Gildas Roberts's 1974 novel *Chemical Eric*, which captures campus life at Memorial in the early 1970s; Lawrence Mathews's *The Artificial Newfoundlander: A Novel* (2010), about a professor from the mainland who studies an obscure Newfoundland writer; and a 1990 short story by Patrick O'Flaherty (also of the English Department) in which the author describes the 1980s bureaucratic nature of rising (or not rising) from the academic ranks to senior administrative positions. The portrait of the University of Atlantica in David J. Hawkin's novel *Pilgrims in a Barren Land* (2010) was based in part on experiences at Memorial.[43] Besides the departmental histories noted above, there have been several accounts by female professors of their experiences at Memorial in the 1970s and 1980s.[44] How they were paid less than their male counterparts was documented in a 1977 publication by William Schrank of the Economics Department.[45] The academic staff, organized as the Memorial University of Newfoundland Teachers' Association since 1952, became a collective bargaining unit in 1988 known as the Memorial University of Newfoundland Faculty Association (MUNFA).

During its first four decades as a university, Memorial evolved to meet the needs and expectations of the people of the province, thereby living up to Smallwood's 1949 hopes. It did this in a number of ways: through the development and expansion of academic programs and through the creation of community and outreach services in both St. John's and rural areas on the island and in Labrador. As former President Morgan remarked to the author in 1991 when the university closed its Extension Service, it had been the responsibility of Memorial to provide a service to the people when none existed and there was a public need for it, but it was necessary for Memorial to move out of the way when the people themselves were able to provide that service. As an individual who came of age in the 1930s when Newfoundland had voluntarily surrendered parliamentary democracy in 1934, and much influenced by the college's first president, John Lewis Paton, Morgan knew only too well that it was the university's paramount responsibility to give its citizens the necessary training and education to provide stewardship for generations of Newfoundlanders and Labradorians to come.

Notes

1.   Joseph R. Smallwood, "Memorial University of Newfoundland — 'A Live, Dynamic Centre of Learning [and] Culture,'" ed. Melvin Baker, *Newfoundland Quarterly* 93, no. 2 (2000): 4. An overview of the history of Memorial from 1949 to 1990 and its relationship to the community at large can be found in Melvin Baker, "Memorial University of Newfoundland," *Encyclopedia of Newfoundland and Labrador* 3 (1991), 503–10; and Melvin Baker and Jean Graham, *Celebrate Memorial! A Pictorial History of Memorial University of Newfoundland* (St. John's: Memorial University, 1999). Other historical information on Memorial can be found at http://www.mun.ca/memorial/history and http://collections.mun.ca/cdm/, Memorial's Digital Archives Initiative.

2.   Reminiscences of Paton can be found in Stan Carew, *J.L.P. — A Portrait of John Lewis Paton by His Friends* (St. John's: Memorial University, 1968).

3.   On the college's history, Presidents Paton and Hatcher, and some of its students, see Malcolm MacLeod, *A Bridge Built Halfway: A History of Memorial University College, 1925–1950* (Montreal and Kingston: McGill-Queen's University Press, 1990); MacLeod, *Crossroads Country: Memories of Pre-Confederation Newfoundland* (St. John's: Breakwater, 1999); MacLeod, "Saint and Survivor: The Presidents of Memorial University College," Part 1 (Paton), *Newfoundland Quarterly* 90, no. 2 (1996): 25–31, and Part 2 (Hatcher), *Newfoundland Quarterly* 90, no. 3 (1996): 25–30; MacLeod, "Making Friends & Enemies: Public Relations at Memorial University College, 1925–1950," *History of Intellectual Culture* 1, no. 1 (2001): 1–6. His unpublished manuscript, "Parade Street Personalities: Founders & Early Faculty of Memorial University, 1925-1950," is available in the Centre for Newfoundland Studies, Memorial University.

4.   Baker and Graham, *Celebrate Memorial!*, 6.

5.   Ibid., 36. Gushue's role as a public servant with the Newfoundland Fisheries Board before 1952 and later as Memorial President is worthy of a biographical study of its own.

6.   Pitt wrote a memoir of his student and faculty days at Memorial, which extended into the 1980s. It is being prepared for publication by his son, Robert D. Pitt.

7.   See George Story, *People of the Landwash: Essays on Newfoundland and Labrador*, eds. Melvin Baker, Helen Peters, and Shannon Ryan (St. John's: Harry Cuff Publications, 1997).

8.   See Cyril F. Poole, *Moses Morgan: A Life in Action* (St. John's: Harry Cuff Publications, 1998).

9. On geography at Memorial, see Alan Macpherson's 2000 history of the Geography Department at: http://www.mun.ca/geog/about/Goodridge_Summers.pdf

10. On the recruitment of faculty, see Malcolm MacLeod, "Crossroads Campus: Faculty Development at Memorial University of Newfoundland, 1950–1972," in Paul Stortz and Euthalia Lisa Panayotidis, eds., *Historical Identities: The Professoriate in Canada* (Toronto: University of Toronto Press, 2006), 131–57.

11. On Memorial in the 1950s, see Kenneth Brian Johnston, "Government and University: The Transition of Memorial University from a College to a University" (PhD thesis, University of Toronto, 1990); Stefan P.T. Jensen, "A History of Memorial University Students, 1949–1961" (MA thesis, Memorial University, 2002).

12. Christopher Sharpe of the Geography Department has written extensively on this corporation. For example, see "'... to prevent confused or over-optimistic thinking and possible disappointment': Brian Dunfield and the Slum Clearance Problem in St. John's, Newfoundland, 1944," *Newfoundland and Labrador Studies* 27, no. 1 (2012): 99–129.

13. See Stephen Harold Riggins, "Memorial's First Sociologist: The Dilemmas of a Bureaucratic Intellectual," *Newfoundland and Labrador Studies* 29, no. 1 (2014): 47–83.

14. On the history of the Chemistry Department, see Hugh Anderson, *Chemistry at Memorial* (St. John's: Memorial University, 1988). The history of Classics at Memorial since 1925 has been documented in Mark Joyal, *In Altum: Seventy-Five Years of Classical Studies in Newfoundland* (St. John's: Memorial University, 2001).

15. Baker and Graham, *Celebrate Memorial!*, 22.

16. See Jeff A. Webb, "The Rise and Fall of Memorial's University Extension Service, 1959–91," *Newfoundland and Labrador Studies* 29, no. 1 (2014): 84–116.

17. On Rumboldt, see Paul Woodford, *The Life and Contributions of Ignatius Rumboldt to Music in Newfoundland* (St. John's: Creative Publishers, 1984).

18. On this gallery, see Crystal Parsons, "Memorial Collects: Old Masters, Official Portraits, and the Early Beginnings of Art at MUN," *Newfoundland Quarterly* 105, no. 2 (2012): 18–23.

19. In 1998 Memorial honoured Schafer with an honorary degree for his contributions to music in Canada. He taught at Memorial from 1963 to 1965. See *Gazette* (Memorial University), 4 June 1998, and Shane O'Dea's oration.

20. See Melvin Baker, "Memorial University's Role in the Establishment of a Provincial Archive for Newfoundland in 1960," *Newfoundland Studies* 9,

no. 1 (1993): 81–102; and Baker, "Newfoundland Studies," in *Encyclopedia of Newfoundland and Labrador* 4 (1993), 66–69. On O'Dea, see Anne Hart, "Dr. Agnes C. O'Dea, 1911–1993," *Newfoundland Studies* 8, no. 2 (1992): 179–81. Impetus for the creation of a Centre for Newfoundland Studies followed from a 1968 paper prepared by George Story calling for a fully integrated academic, archival, and library facility at the university. See Memorial University Records, President's Office, Box E-10, file "Centre for Newfoundland Studies, 1968–1986," Story to Harris, 3 July 1968, with attachment "A Centre for Newfoundland Studies."

21. On the role of one provost at one of these colleges, see Cyril F. Poole, *George Halden Earle: A Concert unto Himself* (St. John's: Harry Cuff Publications, 2001), 107–24.

22. On ISER's history, see Leslie Harris, J.D. House, and M.O. Morgan, *Special Anniversary Edition, ISER: 30 Years (1961–1991); ISER Books:25 Years (1966–1991)*, ISER Research and Policy Papers 15 (St. John's: Institute of Social and Economic Research, 1992); Melvin Baker, "The Establishment of Memorial's Institute of Social and Economic Research in 1961," *Newfoundland Quarterly* 92, no. 3 (1999): 21–25.

23. See Ella Brett, "Development of Social Work Education at Memorial," in Gail Burford, ed., *Ties That Bind: An Anthology of Social Work and Social Welfare in Newfoundland and Labrador* (St. John's: Jesperson Publishing, 1997), 301–04.

24. Poole, *Mose Morgan*, 101–05.

25. In 1978 Nevitt published *White Caps and Black Bands: Nursing in Newfoundland to 1934* (St. John's: Jesperson Press).

26. See Ian Rusted, "Faculty of Medicine, Memorial University of Newfoundland," in John Bowers, ed., *New Medical Schools at Home and Abroad* (New York: Macy Foundation, 1978), 219–59. See also the historical information available at the Faculty of Medicine's Founders' archive web page at: http://www.library.mun.ca/hsl/archives/index.php.

27. On Seary, see G.M. Story, "Edgar Ronald Seary," in A.A. Macdonald, P.A. O'Flaherty, and G.M. Story, eds., *A Festschrift for Edgar Ronald Seary* (St. John's: Memorial University, 1975), 1–8.

28. Taylor wrote of his selection as President and his presidency in his memoir, *A Natural History of Everyday Life: A Biographical Guide for Would-be Doctors of Society*, Memoir Club Series (London: British Medical Journal, 1988).

29. Johnston, "Government and University," 177–86.

30. *London Gazette*, 8 Aug. 1958, at: https://www.thegazette.co.uk/London/issue/41467/page/4930. I thank Peter Neary for bringing this information to my attention.

31. Taylor, *A Natural History*, 409; Memorial University, Senate Minutes, 2 Feb., 15 Mar. 1965, 29 Mar. 1966; Memorial University Records, President's Office, Dean of Arts and Science Files, Box 4, file "Committee on the Presidency, 1966," Report of the Joint Senate-Board Committee on the Presidency by Dr. L. Harris and Dr. G.M. Story.

32. Taylor, *A Natural History*, 420–21.

33. Ibid., 421.

34. Robert Paine and Lawrence Felt, "Reflections on ISER Books," *Papers of the Bibliographical Society of Canada* 48, no. 1 (2010): 169–74.

35. See Eric W. Sager and Gerald E. Panting, *Maritime Capital: The Shipping Industry in Atlantic Canada, 1820–1914* (Montreal and Kingston: McGill-Queen's University Press, 1990), as well as the several publications of the Atlantic Canada Shipping Project. A biographical portrayal of Alexander is Stuart Pierson's "David Alexander: A Reminiscence," in David G. Alexander, *Atlantic Canada and Confederation, Essays in Canadian Political Economy*, comp. Eric W. Sager, Lewis R. Fischer, and Stuart O. Pierson (Toronto: University of Toronto Press, 1983), x–xviii. Keith Matthews's career at Memorial is discussed in Jeff Webb, "Revisiting Fence Building: Keith Matthews and Newfoundland Historiography," *Canadian Historical Review* 91, no. 2 (2010): 315–38.

36. For the career of Halpert, see Kenneth S. Goldstein and Neil V. Rosenberg, eds., *Folklore Studies in Honour of Herbert Halpert* (St. John's: Memorial University, 1980); Martin Lovelace, Paul Smith, and J.D.A. Widdowson, eds., *Folklore: An Emerging Discipline. Selected Essays of Herbert Halpert* (St. John's: Folklore and Language Publications, Memorial University, 2002). His career (and a number of other scholars) is also discussed in Jeff A. Webb, *Observing the Outports: Describing Newfoundland Culture, 1950–1980* (Toronto: University of Toronto Press, 2016).

37. On Snowden and the Fogo Process, see Sandra Gwyn, *Film, Video-Tape and Social Change* (St. John's: Memorial University, 1972); Jerry White, "Guys with Brylcreem Discussing Fish Processing: Form, Community, and Politics in the NFB's Newfoundland Project," in Darrell Varga, ed., *Rain/Drizzle/Fog: Film and Television in Atlantic Canada* (Calgary: University of Calgary Press, 2009), 101–30; Susan Newhook, "The Godfathers of Fogo: Donald Snowden, Fred Earle and the Roots of the Fogo Island Films, 1964–1967," *Newfoundland and Labrador Studies* 24, no. 2 (2009): 170–97; Susan Newhook, "Six Degrees of Film, Social, and Cultural History: The Fogo Island Film Project of 1967 and the 'Newfoundland Renaissance,'" *Acadiensis* 39, no. 2 (2010): 48–69.

38. Baker and Graham, *Celebrate Memorial!*, 52.

39. I would like to thank Bruce Woodland for his reminiscences of Presidents Taylor and Morgan presented 28 March 2010 and 29 October 2011 to the Holyrood History Club, an informal group of individuals interested in the history and culture of Newfoundland and Labrador. A member of the club, Bruce is an alumnus of Memorial University College and served in a number of senior administration positions between 1967 and 1983 with Presidents Taylor, Morgan, and Harris.

40. MUN *Gazette* 14, no.2 (2008).

41. An account of one academic's battles with both the university's research bureaucracy and that of federal granting agencies is Sam Revusky, *Battles with the Canadian Council on Animal Care: A Memoir* (St. John's: Yksuver Publishing, 1997).

42. On the early days of this program, see Linda Kealey, "A Life in History: Activism and Scholarship," *Canadian Historical Review* 95, no. 1 (2014): 78–96.

43. Gildas Roberts, *Chemical Eric: A Witches' Brew of Sex, Drugs, Phony Mass-Media Personalities, and Skullduggery at a Canadian University* (St. John's: Belvoir Books, 1974); Lawrence Mathews, *The Artificial Newfoundlander: A Novel* (St. John's: Breakwater, 2010); Patrick O'Flaherty, "The Inside Track," *Canadian Fiction Magazine* 72 (1990): 21–27; David J. Hawkin, *Pilgrims in a Barren Land: A Novel*, ([Raleigh, NC]: Lulu, 2010.)

44. Psychologist Elena Hannah, political scientist Susan McCorquodale, and biologist Joan Scott have written brief accounts of their academic life at Memorial in the 1970s and 1980s in Elena Hannah, Linda Paul, and Swani Vethamany-Globus, eds., *Women in the Canadian Academic Tundra: Challenging the Chill* (Montreal and Kingston: McGill-Queen's University Press, 2002).

45. William E. Schrank, "Sex Discrimination in Faculty Salaries: A Case Study," *Canadian Journal of Economics* 10, no. 3 (1977): 411–33.

3

The Many Roles of Memorial University Extension

Jeff A. Webb

Memorial has a long and distinguished history of public service that extended beyond its mission of educating students.[1] The first President of Memorial University College, J.L. Paton, had set a pattern of university outreach long before the college became a degree-granting institution. It offered adult students non-academic courses: for example, Muriel Hunter taught art appreciation, Ignatius Rumboldt music, and Edna Baird nutrition and home economics. Some of these faculty members also taught academic courses to the public.[2] All this activity did not come out of nowhere. People in Newfoundland in the 1940s knew of the role that the Antigonish Movement in Nova Scotia played in economic development in the Maritime provinces. Several community development fieldworkers, trained at the Extension Department of St. Francis Xavier University, worked for the Newfoundland government during the 1930s. The fieldworkers' efforts were supplemented by a radio program that promoted co-operatives as an alternative to an economic life dominated by merchants and the fishery.[3] So in the 1950s, both the government and university imagined a unit that did something more than teach academic subjects. An extension unit would encourage the co-operative movement and offer courses to the public. More than that, it would be a force helping rural communities and individuals to modernize.

In 1959 the university President, Raymond Gushue, hired S.J. Colman, an English-born and Oxford-trained educator who had directed an extension unit in East Africa, to create an Extension Division. With support from the Carnegie Corporation of New York, John Colman travelled widely on the island of Newfoundland to learn of local needs, and in both Canada and the United States to examine community development organizations in other jurisdictions.[4] The Extension Service Colman designed that year had two roles. It taught academic and cultural courses to the public, and it shaped the social and economic development of rural communities. While it was the latter for which Extension became the most celebrated, the part Memorial University Extension played in fostering a cultural sector of the province was equally important. Memorial University Extension excelled in two areas. It identified social and economic problems in rural Newfoundland, and it helped individuals and communities make the transitions to new conditions. From local government to professional associations, Extension was there to give people organizational skills. It also played a crucial role in developing an artistic industry in the province. Art, music, and theatre were all taught and supported by the university, creating the conditions in which a successful cultural sector developed.

The Extension Service was centralized in St. John's but had representatives located in other communities. Baird continued to teach home economics and nutrition, organized conferences, and served as Acting Director when Colman was travelling. In addition to the small full-time staff, part-time instructors were frequently hired to teach a range of courses on practical subjects as well as more artistic ones. The young artist Christopher Pratt was hired as Specialist in Art, for example, something that not only encouraged "art appreciation" among the public but also helped to launch the careers of a range of visual and performing artists. George Palmer, who served as Specialist in Drama, directed plays at the university and on television, and also worked to raise the level of professionalism among community theatrical groups. The Newfoundland government had long used radio broadcasting to inform and educate the broadly spread population, and Extension followed suit when it hired Gerald Ottenheimer as its director of media.[5]

Over time, Extension developed a varied use of mass media to respond to people's needs. Starting in the early 1960s and running into the 1970s Extension had its own television show, *Decks Awash*, which was broadcast by the privately owned CJON. Reproducing the scripts in print, for circulation to those who lacked access to television, soon evolved into a magazine of the same name that was published from 1968 to 1993. For many years the magazine circulated free to all households in the province. It is no exaggeration to say that for many people in rural communities *Decks Awash* was the principal way they had contact with their university. Its combination of information and profiles of communities and individuals in rural Newfoundland and Labrador was an important mirror held up to the province as it underwent significant changes. Edited by Susan Sherk and later by Sally LeMessurier, *Decks Awash* had a photographer and writer visit as many communities in the province as possible and profile hundreds of individuals. The magazine developed a loyal following, which lasted even after the university found itself having to charge a subscription and accept advertising. When Memorial closed the magazine to save money, several of its staff took it over as a co-operative — but it did not last long.[6] Extension offered courses in St. John's and used a mass media unit at the university to bring information to the public; it also employed fieldworkers who were based in rural communities. Two of the first fieldworkers, Julia Morgan and Vera Moore, had been trained in community development at the University of Wisconsin, and moved to Bonavista in November 1960, but Julia Morgan's illness a few months later necessitated their resignation.[7] Other fieldworkers were soon hired. D.J. MacEachern, a St. Francis Xavier University-trained fieldworker who had worked for the Newfoundland government's co-operative division during the 1930s, was assigned to work in Corner Brook.[8] He was later joined by Fred Earle, who was based in Lewisporte, and Tony Williamson, in Labrador. Earle had family connections to both Change Islands and Fogo, and knew from personal experience some of the needs of business and the fishing communities in his area. Williamson came to Memorial from the United States, trading a potential academic career for hands-on work among both newcomers and settlers, Inuit and Innu. Both Earle and Williamson, and their many counterparts in other regions, worked on community development in their areas and communicated to Memorial about the information and skills people needed.[9] The Extension office in St. John's could then organize a workshop, set up a course, prepare a film or video, or provide the information that people told the fieldworkers they needed.

Many other universities in North America taught courses in practical skills to the public, and some employed fieldworkers to help farmers, for example, learn scientific insights about working the land. A few universities also encouraged the organization of producers' co-operatives, but Memorial took these initiatives to another level. By having field representatives live in communities, Memorial University Extension listened to what rural people needed during the 1960s and 1970s, and decided governance was a primary challenge.

Since few Newfoundland communities had local government in the 1950s, Memorial University Extension often encouraged the first local development boards and local organizations. Workshops on how to organize and run a meeting spurred people to create municipal councils. Extension fieldworkers did more than offer courses on things such as accounting skills; they sometimes served as middlemen between government officials and rural people. Since Memorial had access to government funds and organizational expertise, at a time when few people in small communities had the skills that would enable them to apply for federal or provincial aid, Extension could help and have greater sensitivity to local conditions than officials in St. John's or Ottawa.[10] The foundation of most of Extension's activities was laid during Colman's tenure, but the unit reached the height of its influence under the leadership of his successor, Donald Snowden, who became almost synonymous with Extension's progressive role. Snowden came to Memorial in 1965 after establishing a name for himself in the Arctic, where he had helped establish co-operatives. The provincial government had hired Snowden to write a report on co-operatives in the province, which led to the offer to work at Memorial. After moving to St. John's, Snowden continued to have connections in Ottawa that made it easier for the university to gain federal government contracts. Many of the younger members of Extension saw Snowden as a dynamic leader whose personal qualities shaped the unit.[11]

Memorial's emerging use of media techniques as tools for social change received a transformative shot in the arm when Snowden and Earle, who had been working to revitalize the economy on Fogo Island, started working with Colin Low of the National Film Board (NFB). The Challenge for Change Program of the NFB pioneered the use of filmmaking as a technique to highlight the plight of the poor. The "Fogo Process" that emerged through the collaboration of Extension and the NFB aimed to help the powerless in society articulate their goals and problems both to themselves and to governments. It had a lasting effect on the island, and was emulated in the developing world. Memorial University Extension's media unit continued to develop film, and later videotape, production as community tools. Filmmakers would record individuals and groups discussing their lives and community problems, and the films would be shown to their neighbours as a way of identifying common challenges and working together. Successes in Fogo, including playing a role in establishing the Fogo Co-operative, were followed up on the west coast, and the media unit became the highest-profile part of Extension.[12]

In addition to its rural and economic development work, Extension fostered a cultural industry in the province, particularly in the provincial capital. Snowden hired George Lee, then a teacher in Labrador and someone involved in community theatre, to work on cultural programming. Lee soon became Snowden's right-hand man. Extension's operation of an art gallery in St. John's later formed the basis of a provincial gallery, and while led by Edith Goodridge it became a social centre for artists and musicians who worked in many media. At Extension's Bond Street facility, young creative people found a rehearsal space, equipment, and expertise that allowed them to develop their craft. Extension's media unit trained members of the nascent film and video industry, providing a foundation for the basis of an industry. Extension supported many individual artists by hiring them to teach, and founded a printmaking facility in the rural community of St. Michael's. St. Michael's Print Shop later moved to St. John's, and over the subsequent decades fostered a vibrant visual arts scene.[13]

By the mid-1970s, the widespread belief that, with expert knowledge, the state could solve nearly any social problem seemed to be past its peak of influence. That made it more difficult for Memorial University Extension to get government financial support for its activities. In 1974 Snowden's relationships at the university had become strained. He stepped down as director and was appointed as a special advisor (who was paid for only eight months per year).[14] After the departure of Snowden for development work in other parts of the world, Extension had a succession of short-lived directors and organizational structures. But never again did Memorial University Extension have the important role in rural communities or the sense of mission that had once animated it. Government cutbacks to Memorial's operating grants and swelling student numbers forced the university administration to make difficult decisions. In 1991 then university President Arthur May closed what remained of Memorial's Extension to focus the university on its core academic priorities. Many at the university saw this as retribution for the role that Extension had played in giving people the tools to protest government policy. It was a controversial decision, particularly among the artistic community that owed so much to Memorial University Extension, but May argued that it no longer served rural Newfoundland's needs.[15]

Notes

1. Much of this chapter draws upon Jeff A. Webb, "The Rise and Fall of Memorial University's Extension Service, 1959–91," *Newfoundland and Labrador Studies* 29, no. 1 (Spring 2014): 84–116.
2. Malcolm MacLeod, *A Bridge Built Halfway: A History of Memorial University College, 1925–1950* (Montreal and Kingston: McGill-Queen's University Press, 1990).
3. Jeff A. Webb, *The Voice of Newfoundland: A Social History of the Broadcasting Corporation of Newfoundland, 1939–49* (Toronto: University of Toronto Press, 2008), 58–65.
4. S.J. Colman to R. Gushue, 15 Sept. 1959, Extension – General, 1953–1960, President's Office Files, Memorial University.
5. "The Extension Department," *Daily News*, 7 Oct. 1961.
6. Susan Sherk interview, 26 Oct. 2010; Sally LeMessurier interview, 5 Nov. 2010.
7. Julia Morgan to Raymond Gushue, 16 Feb. 1959; Gushue to Julia Morgan, 4 Mar. 1959, Extension – General, 1953–1960, President's Office Files, Memorial University.
8. "Extension Service Annual Report," Extension, General 1961–1962, President's Office Files, Memorial University.
9. Fred Earle fonds, Tony Williamson fonds, Archives and Manuscript Division, QEII Library.
10. George Lee interview, 20 Sept. 2010.
11. Ibid.
12. Susan Newhook, "The Godfathers of Fogo: Donald Snowden, Fred Earle and the Roots of the Fogo Island Films, 1964–1967," *Newfoundland and Labrador Studies* 24, no. 2 (Fall 2009): 171–98.
13. Edythe Goodridge interview, 24 Oct. 2010.
14. Library and Archives Canada, Snowden Papers, Personal D. Snowden 1961–1974, Snowden to MUN President, 10 Dec. 1974.
15. Arthur May interview, 7 Jan. 2011.

Students at the main entrance of the Parade Street Campus, 1952. (Photo from *Celebrate Memorial: A Pictorial History of Memorial University of Newfoundland*, originals held at Memorial University Library Archives and Special Collections.)

II

THE OLD PARADE
STREET CAMPUS

Memorial's first five presidents: Albert G. Hatcher (1933–52), Raymond
Gushue (1952–66), Stephen Taylor, Lord Taylor of Harlow (1966–73), Moses
Osbourne Morgan (1973–81) and Leslie Harris (1981–90). (Photos from
Celebrate Memorial: A Pictorial History of Memorial University of Newfoundland;
*Memorial Univeristy of Newfoundland, Official Opening of the New Campus,
1961*; and *Cap and Gown*, 1983–84)

The Creation of the Memorial University of Newfoundland

David G. Pitt

4

My brief visit home to Newfoundland in the summer of 1949 passed in more or less studious quietude — discounting the sporadic effervescence and bustle of a one-year-old child — and otherwise uneventfully. That is, until one fateful evening about mid-June when, quite out of character for me, I decided to attend a political rally being held in a nearby hall. My reason for doing so was not so much to hear the main speaker's message as it was, if possible, to find an opportunity after his performance to speak with him, perhaps to shake his hand and offer him my congratulations for pulling off the unlikely feat of coaxing the ancient colony (pardon: defunct Dominion) to become part of the Dominion of Canada. He was, of course, Joey Smallwood, recently elected Premier of the new province of Newfoundland, campaigning on behalf of the Liberal Party's candidate in the province's first foray into federal politics, Louis St. Laurent having called a general election for 27 June. Joe's task was a quite impossible one, something of which, I am sure, he was well aware: Bell Island and most of the District had voted strongly against Confederation, which meant against Joe Smallwood and the Liberal Party. But that, for him, merely enhanced the challenge: he loved the challenge of the impossible.

Being of the opposite persuasion from most Bell Islanders, I had no compunction about elbowing my way towards the front of the hall when the meeting ended. It was not an easy passage. Though most of his hearers would vote against his party, they could not resist the fascination and mesmerizing attraction the man himself evoked, whether one loved or hated him. Consequently, large numbers lingered behind to throng around him, if only to get a closer look at this unlikely *deus ex machina* of Newfoundland politics. Finally battling my way to where he stood, leaning calmly against the dais from which he had just spellbound his ambivalent audience, he was much the same as I remembered him from five years earlier: a slim, neatly groomed, and dapperly dressed little man. I seized his hand, shaking it while I congratulated him on his Herculean feat. He reciprocated my handshake with equal warmth and, looking me straight in the eye, asked with seeming genuine interest, "Do I know you?"

"Well," I replied, "we did meet a few times, back in the early forties, in the Common Room at Memorial College. You probably don't remember that. But I think you know my father, the United Church minister here, Reverend T.J. Pitt."

"Ah yes, I do. So your name is Pitt?"

I nodded agreement. He paused thoughtfully a moment, stroking his small chin. Then his face brightened and, laying a hand on my shoulder, he exclaimed, "Oh yes, I think I do remember you now! And what have you been up to since you were at the college?"

I told him, adding that I was now visiting my parents and planned to return to Toronto in September to complete my PhD in English.

He was silent a moment or two, his brow slightly furrowed, as if rapidly yet carefully processing what I had said. Then he spoke, very quietly, almost conspiratorially: "I wouldn't do that if I were you!" I could see him studying my face for some reaction.

"Oh? Why not?"

"Well, if you do that, you'll probably take some university job upalong and we'll never see hide nor hair of you again."

"True," I said. "But what would I do with my degrees in English back here? Memorial College is hardly . . ."

He interrupted me with a subtle smirk on his lips. "Ah, but Memorial College will soon be no more. We're going to have our own, full-fledged University of Newfoundland. The legislation to raise the college to university status is already being prepared, and will be passed in a few weeks' time. We're going to need new teaching staff right away, and I want to see bright young Newfoundlanders like you come home to fill the ranks."[1]

Slightly dumbfounded for a moment or two by his quite unexpected announcement, I soon found words to thank him for the compliment he had paid me, and told him that I was delighted to hear that Newfoundland was to have its own university at last, that it was something I had hoped for long ago as a student at the college, but didn't expect to see in my lifetime. I knew that the notion had been bandied about in college and other circles for a decade or more, even that some desultory planning had been done. But inquiries I had made on the subject, while visiting Dr. A.C. Hunter at his summer retreat in July 1947, had elicited only the vaguest of unenthusiastic replies. Smallwood's words now seemed to leave no doubt that at last a Newfoundland university was about to become a reality.

Even so, I was not at all sure that quitting my doctoral program just yet to return to Newfoundland was necessarily a good idea. Besides, I asked him, what about salaries? Would a small local university be able to compete for top-notch faculty with the larger, long-established, well-heeled universities elsewhere, not to mention the many new ones just springing up in both Canada and the States?

"Oh, don't worry about that," he interposed with a dismissive gesture of his hand. "Money is no object. We know we'll have to compete to attract the qualified staff we'll need." He talked as if the university was his own, not only to create but to administer once created.

I told him of the offers I had had, but which, wanting to finish my doctorate first, I had turned down. He nodded benignly, but he was not prepared to give up on me. He went on, "But you'd be able to finish a dissertation in your spare time, and you'd have your summers off to work on it. Besides we'll provide for leaves of absence for scholarly purposes — with pay!"

He was tempting me sorely, and he saw that he was doing so. My mind was awhirl. Suddenly, something I had dreamed of long ago was about to be realized, and I was being offered a chance to be part of it from the very beginning. My thoughts tumbled one over the other. Hamlet's quandary was nothing compared with mine at that moment. I knew all too well that I should have to borrow heavily in order to spend another year at the University of Toronto, even with my teaching fellowship and whatever I might salvage from my summer stint at Mount Allison University — which was unlikely to be very much, if anything. Marion and I now had a child to provide for, and working mothers with small children were still virtually unheard-of in respectable circles, even in Toronto. The temptation loomed larger and larger every moment I contemplated it, while the Premier of Newfoundland and Father of Confederation waited on my answer with an expectant smile.

Sensing that I was coming round to his point of view, he was first to resume the dialogue. "Suppose you talk it over, Mr. Pitt, with your family. Then, if you are really interested, go in to St. John's and call on President Hatcher. Tell him I sent you, and that I want you to be appointed straight off to the faculty of the new university. And I'd like you to see me afterward to let me know how he took it. Could you do that?"

I started to remonstrate, but he quickly interposed. "No, I'm quite serious about this. I'm certain you're the kind of person we need to help us get a *real* university, a *great* university, started . . . *launched out into the deep.* That, you remember, was Professor Paton's motto. Now we're going to make it come properly true."

I attempted to resume my remonstrations, but he continued, first with some flatteringly cajoling words about my peculiar suitability for the post, my relative youth, my academic accomplishments ("You know, I never had a chance to get a university education myself"), my knowledge (as he assumed) of modern university practices and policies, and so on. He then proceeded to tell me, rather confidentially, that he sensed that the "old guard" at the college would not be very supportive of what he planned to do, not because they opposed a change in the college's status, but because the plan was *his*. He had the feeling that Hunter in particular would not be very enthusiastic. "I think that his politics won't let him be on my side." The expression on his face, which I still vividly recall, graphically bespoke his feelings on the matter.

Smallwood was probably right. Though in my many subsequent close dealings with Hunter, who had little choice but to fall in line once the deed was done, I recall his voicing no actual anti-Smallwood or anti-Confederate feelings, there were many times when I was to have unmistakable glimpses of the unspoken and suppressed distaste, if not hostility, beneath his patrician features. But I also felt that Hunter's initial lack of enthusiasm for the new university scheme was chiefly his diverse but treasured conception of what a true university ought to be. It was decidedly not that of the typical modern North American model, which was what Joe Smallwood's more pragmatic charter envisaged.

When finally I freed myself from Smallwood's spell, I headed for home in a mental and emotional state of mixed euphoria, disbelief, and trepidation. Our conversation had lasted no more than 10 or 15 minutes — actually quite long for one who, since binding himself to the whirligig of politics, usually measured his conversational interludes in seconds rather than minutes — but it had suddenly shaken the ground beneath me, the ground — plans, hopes, prospects, goals — on which I thought I had firmly stood. That I might return to try to carve a future for myself and my family on the old Rock, with all its past associations of poverty, ignorance, isolation, and hope long deferred, had not entered my mind since I had first escaped five years ago, in 1944. I was then firmly determined, except for family visitations, never to return to its shores. I had seen little hope for improvements, economic or any other (which, after all, ultimately depend on economic viability). That some cataclysmic change in its circumstances might occur in the foreseeable future never entered my mind. That fog-bound, hide-bound, brain-washed isolationist islanders would ever be persuaded to throw in their lot with the rest of North America was, I then believed, as unlikely as the notion that someday Newfoundlanders might stop singing "God Save the King" or flying the Union Jack. But then I had not counted on Joe Smallwood. The unlikely if not impossible had come to pass, and like many others that heady spring I now had genuine hope that the "tattered Cinderella," having finally surrendered her virginity, might at last blossom, if not quite like a rose, at least like "wholesome flowers" in "our sea-walled garden," to borrow words from Shakespeare (*Richard II*, 3.4). That Joe Smallwood could also, against equally uncertain odds — apathy, timidity, parsimony, academic inertia — bring to fruition the dream of a "great" if "small" university (his words) in Newfoundland I had no doubt, and in spite of my other sanguine prospects I now felt that I had a chance if not a duty to help him achieve that goal. Many uncertainties and obstacles still beset the road ahead, but at least I had been offered a lift, bumpy though it might prove to be.

Marion was not overjoyed at the possibility — still only a possibility, not yet even a probability — of our settling in Newfoundland. After all, her parents and siblings were all firmly rooted in Ontario, to which she herself had become quite attached since settling there in 1942, working, playing, teaching, making friends. My recapitulating for her what Smallwood had said did not suddenly suffuse her mind and imagination with "heavenly radiance unalloyed." I sensed how she felt, but she made no attempt to dissuade me from doing what I was already seriously considering: calling on "Bertie" Hatcher, as Smallwood had urged me, if only to investigate the grounds of his confident predictions about the future of the college. My parents, whom, naturally, I also consulted, were quite enthusiastic about the prospect of our "coming home to stay." Both my parents were good friends of Hatcher's, himself a minister's son and a staunch pillar of the United Church. They were certain he would be a wise and sympathetic counsellor.

Having mulled over the idea for a day or two, one sunny morning in late June I boarded the *Maneco* for Portugal Cove, and, taking a taxi to St. John's, called at the "president's residence," one half of a plain, clapboarded three-storey duplex on Newtown Road, donated to the college by its first president on his departure. I was greeted at the door by Hatcher's wife, Emma, dressed for what appeared to be a house-cleaning enterprise, in a smock and a head scarf, and flourishing a long-handled duster, which teetered in my direction like a sinister wand about to whisk me away. A half-smoked cigarette dangling from her lips, she queried my presence on her front porch. I told her it was urgent that I talk with her husband, whereupon she turned and shouted to "Bertie" that there was someone to see him at the front door.

Since I had seen him last (in 1944), he had aged beyond what one would have expected (he was still in his early sixties), and his hearing aid was all too obvious. But he recognized me at once and greeted me amicably, as was his wont, and invited me in and ushered me to a venerable armchair beside a small, smouldering fireplace. Seated opposite me, he inquired about my parents, and then about my own activities and plans, in particular about my academic progress and prospects, which subject neatly introduced the purpose of my visit. Carefully I recounted to him my conversation with the Premier. He listened attentively, but in total silence, a faint, slightly ironic smile flickering upon his lips. His wife, who had followed us in, busily continuing with her dusting and other domestic chores as if I were not there, contributed to my increasing sense that I was navigating uncertain waters, despite her husband's initial apparent warmth.

When I was finished he rose slowly from his chair and, averting his eyes from mine, said quietly but quite emphatically, "David, I'm afraid you have been misled. I know of no *immediate* plans for the college such as Mr. Smallwood has outlined to you. You can't believe all that Joey preaches, you know. He often talks through his hat." He emitted a faint, wry chuckle.

"But," I interposed, "he was most definite, quite positive about it, told me that the Act was already being written."

"Be that as it may," he replied, with a gently dismissive gesture of his hand. "You can take my word for it that there will be no change in the status of the college just yet. Oh yes, it is true that elevating it to a university has been discussed over the years — in the college, in the board, by the government — and it'll happen, no doubt. But you can go back to your studies satisfied that you've not missed out on anything here, for now." (Learning later something that Hatcher must have known, that the college board, strongly urged by its Chairman, Dr. V.P. Burke — an ardent Smallwood supporter and the probable instigator of the prompt action that his government was taking — had that spring requested the interim provincial government to grant the college a charter, I am inclined to think that Hatcher was, for whatever reason, in his quiet, disarming fashion, pulling the wool over my eyes.)

I did not argue with him, though I felt even then that he was somewhat out of touch with events in process outside his private world. I did, however, venture to ask about the possibility of an appointment, whether Smallwood's promise was fulfilled or not. He admitted that the college was indeed short-staffed, and had been for some time. Moreover, he assured me, Hunter had often mentioned me as a possible recruit for his Department of English *at some future date*. But this was hardly a solid plank to build on.

He was quite definite that the budget (about $80,000, I was later to learn), already decreed for the college by the now-defunct Commission of Government, would not, unfortunately, permit a new appointment now. Two replacements had been made, he said, for departing personnel, but an addition was out of the question. Somewhat taken aback by his negative response and generally dismissive attitude, I decided to leave and say no more, declining Mrs. Hatcher's proffered "tea and a bun" and merely nodding in response to his parting benediction of best wishes for my future.

Perplexed by his assumption of ignorance, I could not help wondering whether, perhaps, he was right: that Smallwood was, after all, "talking through his hat." I decided I would seek confirmation one way or the other by speaking, if possible, with Smallwood's Minister of Education, Sam Hefferton, whom I had met a few times in the early forties when he was at Bishop Feild College. After some searching for his office, I eventually found it, but was told by a receptionist-cum-stenographer that he could not be disturbed, being in conference with another minister. I informed her that I was on an urgent mission on behalf of Mr. Smallwood. The name was an instant "open sesame." I was immediately ushered into Hefferton's office, where I found him and Leslie Curtis, Minister of Justice, and two or three other people whom I did not know, in the very process of trying to piece together a University Act — mostly, it seemed to me, of excerpts from the enabling legislation of other provincial universities. Having had the confirmation I needed, I did not linger long. I had learned what I needed to know, and besides, the two busy ministers still had a major task to complete.

Smallwood having asked me to let him know how my meeting with Hatcher went, I made my way — on foot — to Circular Road and the large house that had formerly quartered the Canadian High Commissioner, where Joe was now installed. Luckily for me he was in, though about to take flight again, and could spare me a few minutes. But that was enough. He seemed genuinely surprised by what I had to report on my visit with Hatcher, reinforcing the feeling I had had that the President had not been entirely frank with me. But when I had finished a quick summary of my conversation with Hatcher, Smallwood thanked me, faintly smiled — a tight little contraction of the lips — and said with a cocky tilt of the head, "We shall see!" As I turned to leave, he said my name and the words, "Don't think you've heard the last of this. But goodbye for now and good luck!" He was right: I had by no means heard the last of it.

The immediate sequel to the small drama just described was that a few days later, totally dismissing it from my mind, I left by train, ferry, and train again for Sackville, New Brunswick, and my busy stint as acting head and Professor of English at Mount Allison. So it was that, in early August when my summer theatre was playing itself out nicely towards its denouement, I was not really surprised to receive from President Hatcher a compendious "night letter" (a telegram of up to 50 words transmitted on the cheap during the night when telegraph keys played larghetto) confirming what I had believed for a month: "DEAR DAVID YOU WERE RIGHT STOP ACT TO BE PASSED VERY SOON STOP." He went on to ask whether it was too late for me to consider an appointment, possibly a lectureship. If still interested, I should submit a formal application to him soon. A few additional words of his were not, however, so promising: "COULD YOU TEACH OTHER SUBJECTS VIZ HISTORY PHILOSOPHY ET AL STOP."

Next day I scrawled and posted him a note, conveying my thanks for his telegram, assuring him that it was not yet too late, inquiring whether a lectureship was the best he could offer, and telling him that I would be in touch again when I returned shortly. But I made no reference to his "et al." I also wrote at once to Marion, giving her the gist of Hatcher's communication. Thereafter, until I finished my work in Sackville — a mound of examination papers to mark, underlings' results to scrutinize, final standings to be recorded — and headed homeward, I gave the matter little further thought. But I was quite resolved that, much as I wished to see the infant university get a proper start in life, I had no intention of hiring myself out as a midwife-cum-footboy at a handyman's salary. I suspected that a new, raw recruit in the ranks might very well find himself at the mercy of the long-entrenched rights and privileges, not to mention whims and prejudices, of his superior officers. That I might be called on for much more than simply shouldering a normal load of English classes had already been implied by Joe Smallwood, a notion reinforced by Hatcher's night letter and its reference to "other subjects."

Arriving back in St. John's shortly before the University Act easily cleared the House of Assembly, wishing to talk over the proposition with Marion and my parents before committing myself to anything, I decided against calling on Hatcher in person, but telephoned him instead — probably not the best alternative, since he was rather hard of hearing. I told him, and he eventually got my message, that I was interested and that I would submit an "official" application shortly. I recall that I also questioned him regarding the nature of the post I might be offered and what financial and other prospects it might bring with it. He was, as I remember, somewhat rattled by this, as if he had not fully thought the matter through. After some hesitation he confided that his reference to a "lectureship" was simply an opening gambit and that with my qualifications I should probably be offered something better. In response to my query about salary he told me that the figures for each rank were fixed by the Board (still the old College Board of Governors), but the figure he surmised for a starting Assistant Professor ($2,700 per annum) was little more than my Teaching Fellowship at Toronto. He did explain, however, that financing for the new institution was still in a state of flux and that a somewhat larger amount would probably be forthcoming later, when matters were more settled. But he needed a proper application from me very soon, which I promised to send him within a few days. It was a reasonable request.

Accordingly, as Hatcher had requested, I wrote a brief "official application" and posted it forthwith. The day was 13 August 1949. As we learned that evening, the Memorial University of Newfoundland Act had that day been passed by the House of Assembly. While I was happy to know that the deed had been done, I was disappointed that the government had not seen fit to drop *Memorial* from the university's name. I had been anticipating its emergence as the University of Newfoundland, in the style of most provincial universities — University of New Brunswick, of Alberta, of Saskatchewan, and others. I have learned since that Smallwood himself favoured dropping the sombre term, but was strongly advised against it for political reasons: he would alienate the war veterans' vote.

I heard nothing whatsoever from Hatcher for 10 days or more, and had almost abandoned any hope of being the first new appointee to the new university, when a letter from him arrived on 24 August. I learned later that he had had a protracted disputation with Hunter, not so much about me and my appointment, as about even attempting to implement the University Act that year. To Hunter, it seems, the inadequacy of previous planning, the precipitant intervention of Premier Smallwood — for whom and his government Hunter had little affection — the shortness of notice, etcetera, made immediate changes impossible. (I was later to recognize that Hunter had been almost right.) But without any reference to his delay in replying, Hatcher wrote that he thought "most favourably" of my application and was hopeful that he could arrange a suitable appointment for me shortly.

A few days later, having sent him a generally favourable response, I received a handwritten letter (27 August), in which he wrote in part as follows:

> I am now definitely prepared to recommend you as Assoc. Prof. of English here from Sept. 1949. I have good reason to believe that my recommendation to the Board (that is the usual procedure) will be favourably received.

I see your position with regard to the Ph.D. and any
arrangement we may be able to make later on will be to the
mutual benefit of both, I expect. . . .

Yours truly,

A.G. Hatcher

P.S. Come to see me when you can. . . .

H

P.P.S. Your starting salary would not be less than
$3100.00.

It was not a princely sum, but at least as an "Assoc. Prof." I was being set near the top of the ladder, so that any future elevation of salary
"floors" would lift me a little higher than if I had gone in on a lower rung.
Such a rise, Hatcher had previously confided, would almost certainly
occur even if all the machinery and structures of a full-fledged university
were not immediately set up. (In fact, no Board of Regents, as provided
for in the Act, was appointed until the following spring — of which
more later — but the old Board, in its declining months, was able to
implement a small retroactive increase in salaries, so that mine for that
first academic year was actually $3,200. I remember that when the rise
came through in January, we laid on a modest celebration of our good
fortune.) Hatcher was also confident that Ottawa would before long
introduce federal funding for Canadian universities. He had, it seems,
accurately surmised that the recently created Massey Commission on
the Arts, Letters, and Sciences in Canada would urge federal support
for universities — as it did, and with practical results!

A few days later, a telephone call to Hatcher having assured me that
I had indeed been appointed, Marion and I travelled to St. John's in
quest of a suitable — and affordable — place to live. We did not expect
it to be an easy mission. Despite a small post-war building boom, spurred
now by the first fruits of Confederation, the continued presence of numerous well-paid American service personnel still sustained inflated
rates for quality rental housing. Fortunately, our search was not a long
one. Following a few days spent admiring attractive quarters we could
not afford and looking askance at affordable ones we would not house a
dog in, we found a modest flat that provided most of what we needed,
albeit in a multi-layered sandwich of row houses in a less than prime

residential location, but only yards from the campus (for more than another decade still the former college site on Parade Street), and at a rate we could, by dint of frugal practices, manage to pay for.

1949: Rolling Out a New University

Still operating on the timetable of the former college, Smallwoodian events having moved too quickly to make adjustments possible beforehand, the first session of the new university began on 22 September 1949, the day of the autumn equinox. But, summoned by President Hatcher, I had been on campus for a couple of weeks by then. Because of his poor health, he was soon to be largely replaced as de facto President by A.C. Hunter. But even before Hunter returned from his long summer sojourn at his beach house in Salmon Cove, the President had summoned me to his office to help him get started on the stupendous task of transforming the 25-year-old impecunious junior college into a viable modern university. I soon suspected that my being called in before Hunter returned was not fortuitous. It was clear to me that Hatcher knew what Joe Smallwood had confided to me in June, that he could not expect much, if any, enthusiastic co-operation from Hunter, who still looked with disfavour if not supercilious disdain at the prospect of creating what he feared its planners had in mind: a North American style "multiversity," which, in contrast to his conception of a true university, one closer to the "Oxbridge" model, was little more than a glorified technical school or trades college, where (I think I quote him verbatim) "they award baccalaureates in basket-weaving and such-like mindless pursuits." Hunter had, I was told by a senior colleague, already been openly critical of Smallwood's precipitous action in passing the Act straightaway. He might therefore conceivably try to show that it had been badly timed, by creating unnecessary obstacles to its implementation. I know for a fact, because he told me, that not long after his return Hunter sent a letter to Education Minister Hefferton requesting an official inquiry into the whole University Act affair. I think he hoped that it might be found that something underhanded had been perpetrated. So far as I know, nothing came of his request.

Knowing that I had been one of Hunter's top students, that I had often spoken highly of his gifts as a teacher, and that he had often spoken of me as a possible addition to the English Department, Hatcher, it seems, needed confirmation that in the matter of the new university's constitution and future I did not share Hunter's hang-ups. He needed, it seems, confirmation of what I think he already believed, something he may have surmised from my first meeting with him in June and that may have influenced his support for my appointment: that I was a strong advocate of the concept of a university like those I knew best, a Canadian-style institution (though not necessarily a "multiversity") such as the Act now, in fact, embodied, and that I was prepared to work towards bringing about its full and proper realization. Our conversation that afternoon seems to have satisfied him that I was firmly on side. To Hatcher's credit I must stress the fact that although he had initially pleaded ignorance of any plans afoot — which may have been a strategic masquerade — once the change of the college's status was a *fait accompli*, he was as strong a champion as Smallwood himself.

I do not recall all that passed between us that afternoon. But I remember much of what was of most significance. I was, in particular, quite astonished by how little, in practical terms, had actually been done to anticipate it, despite all the years of "hoping" and "planning" for a full-blown university. I told him this, to which he responded, quite plausibly, that while the idea had indeed long been mooted, the necessity argued, in both the college and the board as well as in the conclaves of the Commission of Government, the upshot of any such discussions had always been the conclusion that a full-blown university was "too rich for our blood," at least for the present. As a consequence, it appeared that only a modicum of practical planning or forethought had ever gone into what had come to be generally perceived as some "far-off divine event," to which, perhaps, in time our small "creation" might eventually move.[2] The exception was the college's Department of Education or Teacher Training, thanks to the foresight and initiative of George Hickman, soon to be named first Dean of Education, where considerable planning had indeed been done and some of the plans already implemented. The Faculty Council had also made fairly elaborate if tentative plans for a 20-course degree program only a year or so earlier. But all had been shelved and apparently forgotten, at least by Hatcher.

Hatcher's most immediate concern, that damp northeasterly afternoon as he quietly but anxiously acknowledged to me (whom he seemed to be coming to view as his personal confidant), was that already eager, prospective candidates were lining up (not many: some half-dozen or so) who hoped to constitute the new university's first graduating class in 1950. These were students who had completed two years at the college and a third year or equivalent elsewhere. This, they hoped, would enable them to complete degree programs at the new university with one further year's work. Clearly, there was no easy or simple solution. Without the necessary structures in place we had no politico-academic policies, rules, and regulations under which we might act. The institution still had no Board of Regents and no Senate (the body that normally establishes programs of study, certifies degrees, and the like), nor would it for another eight months. There was a Faculty Council, a holdover from the former dispensation, but its powers had never included granting degrees. We could have decided that in view of the unusual circumstances we simply could not grant any degrees for at least another year — 1951 at the earliest. But that would have meant dashing the hopes of a very eager and conscientious group of demonstrably bright students. Or we could have decided that, again in view of the extraordinary facts of the case, we would allow them to pick up, cafeteria-style without a set menu, whatever they wished and was offered, and at the end of the academic year rubber-stamp their records and grant the degrees. But that would have been both defeatist and shameful, and probably dishonest and fraudulent as well.

This was the dilemma that faced Bertie Hatcher and all of us on the faculty in September 1949. He was well aware of its gravity. But I have to affirm that had it not been for his insistence that no academic fraud be perpetrated, no corners cut, no shoddy workmanship be allowed to undermine our new foundation, all these sins of omission and commission might well have blotted the university's first page. As he was to put it succinctly in his first Address to Convocation on 3 June 1950: "To confer a baccalaureate degree is a weighty and solemn act, never to be undertaken inadvisedly."

I soon discovered that I, at least initially, was to be his chief accomplice, particularly in the matter of devising viable regulations and programs of study whereby we could, in good conscience and without sacrificing proper standards of achievement, confer bachelor's degrees at our first convocation in June 1950 on the several students in line for them.

Having discussed with me at length the general predicament we were in and some of the desiderata of our cause, he turned to me and in a half-whispered, quietly conspiratorial manner, rendered almost endearing by his characteristic slight lisp, said, "David, do you think you could in the next few days work up some nice degree regulations for these nice candidates?" By *nice* in the first instance, I took him to mean "adequate and proper, but not too tough," and in the second, "good, well-meaning people who deserve to be treated fairly." His reason for asking me, a raw recruit in the ranks, to undertake this serious task was, he told me, the very fact that I was *new*, that I had been most recently in close touch with the world of Canadian academe, both as a student and as a teacher. I suggested that perhaps a small committee might be a more appropriate venue, and he agreed to appoint one that would look properly representative. But he added that I, who would be the convenor, should immediately set to work framing the "nice" regulations he had in mind and consult the committee afterwards. Otherwise, the process might get bogged down in lengthy but fruitless debate. The old, but still canny, professor of marine navigation knew very well that a committee on a ship's bridge is no substitute for a captain. With all the cocksure presumption of a Triton among minnows, I accepted the presidential commission and went home that evening, sat down at the table in the basement kitchen of our flat on Livingstone Street (I had as yet no desk at home), and in half an hour drafted what Hatcher and I agreed, as well as the committee later, was as "nice" a set of General Degree regulations as any "nice" student could wish for. A synthesis mainly of what I felt were the best elements of the degree programs of Mount Allison and the University of Toronto, institutions I knew intimately, they were to serve with few modifications, mainly those necessitated by the advent of new fields of study, our undergraduate students, the nice and the unnice, for many years to come.

Framing the first degree regulations, I was, of course, greatly constrained by the paucity of advanced courses available or likely to be available for several years to come. In the Arts departments only English, with my being added that year, was able straightaway to lay on courses at the third- and fourth-year levels. Since the degree program I proposed in Arts required a six-course major and a four-course minor, in effect, students seeking degrees in Arts initially had no choice but to major in English. (A course then — typically fall and winter — was the equivalent of two single-semester courses today.) Even after other departments were able to provide the necessary advanced course for majors in other subjects, with Dean Hunter's concurrence — in fact, his whole-hearted support — the Arts program continued for some years to require a student to take either a minor or a major in English.

Hunter, despite his lack of enthusiasm for the North American-style, 20-course program, fortunately accepted the reality. (I think the central place of English in the program weighed heavily in changing his mind.) With a few suggested minor changes and the addition of Classics as a *theoretical* alternative to English as a major or minor subject, he took the proposal to the Faculty Council (of which only department heads were members), where it was shortly approved.

According to Cyril F. Poole's biography of Mose Morgan, Morgan was later, unjustly, to malign Hunter for persuading "the Faculty Council and the Senate ... to approve the [BA] degree programme where you either had to major or minor in English or Classics"[3] — as if this were somehow a bad thing. But while it is true, as I have said, that Hunter as Dean piloted the regulations through the Council, and the Senate when it was formed, I was the one who had embedded some English courses as a requirement in the program and who would argue for its retention in future debates, knowing the paucity of the literary and humanistic culture in the backgrounds of most of our students. My concept of educating the whole person included an "educated imagination" (to borrow an apt term from Northrop Frye), as well as a literate mind, pen, and tongue. Fortunately, this was a point on which Hunter and I were in almost total agreement. The addition of Classics *was*, as I have said, Hunter's idea, but mainly because initially it was the only other department that could immediately provide a minor of four courses, two in Latin and two in Greek.

Drafting a set of degree regulations was by no means the only commission I was to be handed during that first month of the infant university's life. A.C. Hunter, who as head of English (as well as French and Spanish) was my immediate superior, had meanwhile returned from Salmon Cove. Reconciled finally to the new dispensation, he was now, quite properly, attacking the urgent matter of new courses in English, particularly at the third- and fourth-year levels — all the more urgent in view of the necessity of our being able to provide a major program in at least one Arts subject. As Professor and head of Romance Languages, he had a similar task to undertake in that domain, and so was consequently content to turn the creation of new, advanced courses in English over to me and our only other colleague in the department, Allison O'Reilly (later Feder), who had been appointed to a lectureship in 1948. She, too, was a former first-class student of Hunter's and, like me, a graduate of the University of Toronto. Having known and liked each other as students in the early forties, we made a compatible pair as we set about putting our heads together in the hope that, like Minerva from the head of Jove, fully-formed, ready, and able, the requisite anatomies of learning, at least in English Literature, might spring from ours. Faculty office space being scarce, Allison and I shared — with two members of other departments — a corner office on the main floor of the college building, so that we were able to work conveniently together devising the new courses. Since we were to teach them, we understandably devised ones that, while providing properly rigorous, scholarly syllabi, we would enjoy teaching and feel competent doing so.

Of the new courses devised during that first year — necessarily few, since there were only Allison and I, and Hunter part-time, to teach them — my favourite, which I designed as my own preserve, was a course embodying a conception of literature I had come to develop during my graduate years at Toronto under the influence of A.S.P. Woodhouse and F.E.L. Priestley, Marshall McLuhan and Northrop Frye. This conception (a sound one, I still believe) was that literature constitutes an epitome of human culture, representing as it does a symbolic transformation through language of the whole complex and varied life of the mind, at once an artifact and an element, a medium and a message, embracing the whole intellectual, emotional, and imaginative life of human beings. If the physiology of DNA had been current then, I should probably have thought of literature and described it as the DNA of human culture. As a title for the course, which I designed as the final one in the English major program, the keystone to the arch, I necessarily had to settle for a simple and not-too-daunting one that would convey a reasonable notion of what prospective students might expect and yet not totally baffle and mystify them. And so I chose what was wordy enough indeed, yet as concise and simple as my broad, ambitious field of inquiry could be reduced to in a label: English 6. A History of English Literature against the Background of the History of Ideas and General Culture. The other new courses we devised were more conventional in nature, but still sufficiently representative and demanding for undergraduates: the English Novel, British and American Poetry, Shakespeare and Other Dramatists, and the like. Most of these courses remained unchanged until the mid-fifties when student numbers and teaching staff increased and the Honours program was launched.

1949–1950: First Academic Year: Commencement, Censorship, and Convocation

The first session of the new university — or was it the last session of the old college? (even the President seemed uncertain) — began on the day published as the college's starting date, 22 September. As had been the custom since the college first opened in 1924, the session began with a formal assemblage of all students and faculty in the Assembly Hall, the students seated before the faculty, who occupied the stage in their academic regalia. I no longer recall all the details of the proceedings, which, with Hatcher presiding, were probably little different from those of my first assembly as a student in 1940. As a new recruit to the faculty, I was duly introduced and required to stand and modestly bow to the desultory applause of the bemused audience. Hatcher gave a reasonably accurate sketch of my academic career and credentials to date, on the strength of which, he announced, to the surprise of the faculty (and, I learned later, the chagrin of certain members), that I had been appointed to the rank of Associate Professor. He remembered that I had married an "Old Memorial," but seemed uncertain about an offspring, observing, somewhat confusedly, that he believed there was "a little Pitt just around the corner," thus covering both possibilities, ante- and post-natal.

That first year, whether seen as the last year of the college's life or the first of the university's, was in many ways a strange one. To some of the older members of the family, who had cradled and nourished the junior college through horrendously difficult years of Depression and War, it was also an unhappy, even a painful one. For them, as I was often made aware, the college's jubilee year (1924-49) was a bizarre combination of wake and baptism. It also was the first year in the life of the new province, whose displacement of the "Old Colony" was for many an emotionally wrenching experience (even for some who had voted for change), which helped to accentuate the strangeness of the time and the sense of dislocation.

Some, both faculty and students, still did not want to see the old college become extinct, who curiously resented the change that Smallwood had thrust willy-nilly upon them, as he had just done to their beloved old Rock. And the feeling was shared by many influential people beyond the campus circle — as witness the often curious, sometimes ambivalent greetings and testimonials from local dignitaries published in the 1950 issue of *The Cap and Gown* — who still tried to drag out the life of the college, just as there were those who did not want to see the once (so-called) independent country die. To me, of course, the change was never a death, either of a country or of a place of learning. It was rather, in both cases, a natural development, a naturally predetermined metamorphosis of a living and developing organism realizing the fulfillment of a latent potential. Yet, the metamorphosis of the college having happened so quickly, virtually without warning, in spite of all the previous proposals, suggestions, and rumours of the past decade or more, its realization with the stroke of a pen came to many as a traumatic shock, from which it took some time to recover.

The women members of the faculty seemed to be most affected. I remember more than once overhearing, without deliberately eavesdropping, a group of them — Helen Lodge, for example, in Education; Monnie Mansfield, the Registrar; Sadie Organ, the Librarian — over cups of coffee in Room 13 (the multi-purpose "Faculty Room": common room, cafeteria, reading room, meeting room, council chamber), commiserating with one another, observing how different things were, how hurried, even frantic the pace of life seemed to be, compared with the easy-going, almost tranquil tenor of the "old days." (I fear that their perceptions reflected something of the state of quiescence if not somnolence that had settled over the college once the pressures and stresses of the immediate post-war years had passed.) I think I understood how they felt, although, as I have reiterated, my own feelings about the former college and the former colony were very different.

Inevitably the life of the junior college lingered on at least until the

spring of 1950, overlapping, blending, occasionally contending with the
burgeoning life of the infant university, which sometimes, like Hercules
in his cradle, was forced to wrestle with a number of would-be stranglers.
Hunter, for example, who, as the President's health continued to decline,
assumed more and more of the presidential role, tried his utmost to
perpetuate his well-known but long-outmoded view of the college, as
properly acting *in loco parentis*. He would have liked to reinstitute the
compulsory wearing of academic gowns by students as well as staff. The
war had made gowns hard to come by and the rule had been relaxed. He
now saw no reason not to reinstate it, but there was little enthusiasm
among current faculty members for requiring students not to go "academically nude" (a favourite phrase of his), though members were generally happy to wear their own graduate gowns in class. (I was to wear
my Toronto master's gown until it was little more than a "thing of shreds
and patches.") Hunter, still the British grammar-school master, continued his periodic reconnaissance of the common rooms and other areas
where students might loiter unacademically engaged. And he still favoured, but soon found he could do little about enforcing, the old rules
requiring students to be "in college" from 9:00 a.m. to at least 4:00 p.m.
and to be always "in residence" in St. John's during college terms, unless
given presidential permission to be absent. He eventually came round to
a more enlightened conception of a modern university, but it took him
several years to do so.

Sadie Organ, the Librarian, also continued to enforce certain of her
archaic rules. These, it may be recalled, included restricting students'
access to certain books considered (by Sadie) to be unfit for innocent
youth.[4] As a library prefect at the college in 1944 I had come upon the
locked cupboards — one of which had inadvertently been left unlocked
— where she secreted the forbidden books and discovered what, in fact,
she had been hiding from us: books by Lawrence, Joyce, Steinbeck,
Caldwell, Farrell, and many others. Taking for granted that any such
policy of censorship had been abolished now that we were grown up,
were now a university, I had asked the students in one of my advanced
courses to read books by several of these authors. To my astonishment I
was told that they were not allowed access to them. Learning this, I
hastened to Sadie's small cluttered office off the Main Reading Room to
remonstrate with her on the subject of academic freedom and censorship.

But I found the exercise to be a pointless one. A well-educated, highly intelligent woman, she had received her early education at a Catholic convent, where censorship of reading matter and much else was a primary and unalterable fact of life. Consequently, she had her arsenal of arguments at the ready, and was annoyed besides at the presumption of a former student questioning her management. After all, she had taught part of the mathematics course in my first year as a student, and she felt no qualms about levelling her armaments at the effrontery of a stripling newcomer to the faculty doubting her omniscience in matters of students' moral welfare. To impress upon me the validity of her stance and the authority under which she acted, she cited a clause of the University Act that forbade requiring any student to study certain matter deemed "bad" for them (I no longer have a copy of the original Act and have forgotten the exact wording of the ill-conceived clause), which, she said, had been inserted at the specific request of Roman Catholic Archbishop Roche.[5] This I doubted. Roche had been a virulent opponent of Confederation and had summoned all the arguments and wiles he could muster to have the proposition defeated. It is hardly likely that Smallwood or his cohorts, in drawing up the Act, would have taken any advice from such a source. Sadie Organ, nevertheless, insisted that Roche would not have young Catholics exposed to matter that might pervert their morals, and she was not about to go against his wishes.

I tried to argue the case on behalf of liberal education, academic freedom, and so on, pointing out furthermore that I was not in contravention of the Act, since I was not *requiring* my students to read Lawrence and Joyce et al., merely suggesting that they might wish to dip into them. But I soon realized that I was contending with a mindset immune to modification, and shortly quit the field. But I had not given up. A few weeks later, having allowed the contentious issue to subside, I asked to borrow the key to the cryptic closet, in order, I explained, to extract a volume for my personal use. I was granted my request, with some apparent reluctance, but not until I had promised to use the book only in the library and, when finished, to return it to its hiding place behind the locked door. I did not promise, however, not to remove a half-dozen others and shelve them in the open stacks — in their proper shelf-numbered places, of course. (Each book had been duly catalogued and call-numbered when received, most of them part of a bequest in the will of a generous, liberal-minded bibliophile by the name of Harry J.W. Milley. Sadie Organ would never herself have voluntarily acquired them for the library.) Accordingly, before I left that afternoon, taking no book with me, I had surreptitiously liberated to the open shelves Lawrence's *Sons and Lovers* and *Women in Love*, Joyce's *Portrait of the Artist* and *Ulysses*, J.T. Farrell's *Studs Lonigan* trilogy, and several other "salacious" classics.

How long they remained at liberty before their release was noticed I do not know. I was never approached on the subject or in any way reprimanded by Organ or anyone else. But, whether or not my remonstrances and subversive action had anything to do with the case, or whether it was rather the death in September 1950 of the censorious Archbishop or some other circumstance, within two years or so the restrictive rule was lifted and *all but two* of the hitherto sequestered volumes were shelved where they properly belonged. And there the episode ends, except for a small, interesting, and somewhat amusing footnote regarding the volumes left in solitary confinement: a substantial, attractively bound two-volume set entitled *Poetica Erotica: A Collection of Rare and Curious Amatory Verse* (T.R. Smith, ed., New York, 1927), also part of the Milley bequest. (It is interesting to note that the set when first published by Boni and Liveright was "for subscribers only." Harry J.W. Milley must have been an interesting man.) What happened was this: shortly after the general liberation occurred, I was summoned to Miss Organ's office. As I entered, I noticed the infamous volumes lying on her desk. She glanced at them and at me, a ghost of a wry smile on her lips, a slight blush on her cheeks. "David," she said, picking up the books and passing them to me, not a little irony in her tone, "I am making you a gift of these. They're much more in your line than in mine. Would you like to have them?" Flabbergasted, I was momentarily at a loss for words. Blushing — as much, I think, as she did — I took them from her, stuttering a few words of acceptance and thanks. It was the most unlikely gesture I would have expected from her, the middle-aged spinster, guardian of public morals, enforcer of rules. But I took the books, tucked them under my coat, and shambled out, feeling rather like a purveyor of pornography.

Having astonished me once, Sadie Organ was about to astonish me again, and most of her colleagues as well: resigning her post to get married — in her fifties — for the first time. Our earlier contretemps, it seems, did not result in her bearing me any ill-will — quite the contrary. When, about that time (autumn 1957), she declined nomination by the then President (Gushue) to sit on a national commission to advise the federal government on the establishment of a Canada Council, she suggested me in her stead. I accepted, and as a consequence not only helped to establish one of the most important cultural institutions in Canada, but was able to have interesting encounters with several celebrated Canadian cultural and academic icons.

The freeing of the books in the library lock-up did not, however, end the English Department's censorship woes in the years following. All of these, as I recall, stemmed from objections by the Roman Catholic hierarchy, or by a parent who had its backing, usually to a novel we had included in the first- or second-year English courses. We regularly defended ourselves with the traditional arguments for intellectual freedom, artistic merit, and the like. As I recall, our original selection stood in all but one case. This was brought against us by a parent who, besides being a prominent lay official of the Roman Catholic diocese, was also a member of the university community. He knew the University Act and the unfortunate clause referred to, and in his view our choice of Hemingway's *For Whom the Bell Tolls* as first-year reading clearly required invoking it. His 16-year-old daughter, just entering university, was not to be exposed to such filth. Apart from much else that he regarded as objectionable in the book, one chapter went so far as to describe a man and a woman in a sleeping bag together. Because English 100 was compulsory for all students, the Act should be invoked. We argued strenuously for the novel's retention, but when President Gushue advised us that doing so might antagonize the entire Catholic establishment, with serious consequences for the university, we reluctantly yielded and replaced it with Forster's *A Passage to India*, about which, oddly, there was no objection.

Apart from being hobbled by some arcane regulations, the library itself, in 1949, was another — and a major — impediment to the college's becoming a true university. Its total number of accessioned books was a mere 15,000 volumes, a smaller number than might be found in the libraries of most North American high schools. At that time such relatively small universities as Mount Allison and Acadia had collections of 100,000 or more. They were, of course, long-established institutions, but they were representative of those that Memorial would now have to compete with and be measured by. I remember making the point that we needed not only a vastly enlarged reservoir of books, but also at least a sprinkling of scholarly periodicals (or learned journals), of which the library then had almost none. Fortunately, once the new Board of Regents and Senate were in place, new policies formulated, and increased funding made available, a drive to help the library catch up as quickly as possible was launched. By the time the university moved to its new campus on Elizabeth Avenue in 1961, twelve years after its inauguration, the library's holdings had more than quintupled.

But in the first academic year of the university's existence, we had to make do with what we had. And this was true of many other components of the university's structure and operation besides the library. We still had no general regulations or residence requirements, no design for a bachelor's hood, no degree rankings or classifications, no university calendar, no policy on transfer of credits. Our pass-mark needed to be revised upward from the 40 per cent it had been for years to the Canadian standard of a least 50 per cent. Our entrance requirements, too, had not been revised since I had been a student and needed serious modification. All these matters and more, we — I and the former college faculty, which the university had inherited — had to tackle straightaway, though it was patently impossible to accomplish it all in one academic year. Despite the doubts and misgivings of some, it was generally in good spirits and with goodwill that we fell to the rather daunting task. But it meant months of continuous and demanding work before our few fourth-year students could be properly certified and invested as Bachelors of Arts of the new university in June 1950.

As I have said, a major obstacle to achieving this goal properly and legitimately was the absence, during most of the academic year, of the essential superstructure of a university government: a Senate and a Board of Regents. Whatever the reason — and I have heard several — the new provincial government for many months neglected to set in place the all-important keystone of the arch, the appointment of a governing board, without which no Senate could legally be formed and thus no degrees validly conferred. It seemed that, having legislated its creation, the government had become so absorbed with other pressing matters that it had forgotten the infant university's very existence. I was particularly anxious, especially since, having been one of its midwives, I had been enthusiastically backing the notion, and encouraging others who were skeptical, of staging our first convocation, as we had promised, in the spring of 1950. But as late as March, the date of the convocation looming not far ahead, we were still operating in an academic-political quagmire. The old Board of Governors, at the request of the Deputy Minister of Education, continued to meet from time to time, mainly to ensure that the fiscal responsibilities of the institution were met, it having no authority to exercise the powers bestowed by the University Act on a Board of Regents.

The university's first Board of Regents was named, with Sir Albert Walsh as Chairman. The reason for the long delay may well have been the difficulty of finding a suitable Roman Catholic willing to serve as Chairman. The President being Protestant, traditional practice dictated that the Chairman of the Board be a Catholic. But since most of such possible candidates had been anti-Confederates and therefore unsympathetic to anything sponsored by Smallwood or his government, they would have declined appointment. A logical and very acceptable choice would have been Dr. V.P. Burke, who had been Chairman of the Board of Governors and a committed Confederate to boot. But on Smallwood's recommendation he had just been appointed to the Canadian Senate. Walsh, a Catholic and a closet Confederate who had served briefly as the province's first Lieutenant-Governor before being appointed Chief Justice, made a highly suitable choice for Chairman.

Though all the mechanisms were in place and operative, so much had awaited them that it meant a rather hectic scramble to the finish line. We did not accomplish that year all that had to be done to fully transmute the college into the university we envisioned, but we did achieve enough to enable us to mount a proper convocation in 1950. It was held on Saturday, 3 June, in the University Annex so-called, the former American USO Building on the campus. The weather was good, so we were able to parade in our academic regalia from the main building to the Annex, led by the five baccalaureate candidates (bearing their newly fashioned hoods) and the dozen or so three-year-diploma Engineering students in their undergraduate gowns. There, with President and Vice-Chancellor Hatcher presiding, assisted by the three novice Deans — A.C. Hunter, George Hickman, and Stan Carew — the first Memorial University degrees were conferred. Ironically, the first degree was not conferred upon a

Newfoundlander but upon a young French woman, Mlle. Denise Bonnave, daughter of the French Consul in Newfoundland.

Notes

1. David Pitt kept detailed diaries or journals dating back at least to the 1950s. Most of the dialogue in his memoir was not recorded verbatim at the time, but was based on his notes and his still good memory. It might be described as "a dramatic recreation of the events, based on his first-hand experience" — not fiction, but not transcript either (Robert D. Pitt).

2. "One God, one law, one element,
   And one far-off divine event,
   To which the whole creation moves." (Tennyson, *In Memoriam*, Canto 131)

3. Cyril F. Poole, *Mose Morgan: A Life in Action* (St. John's: Harry Cuff Publications, 1998), 75.

4. It may be that she was also pressured by the objections raised by the President, faculty members, members of clergy, or parents. On one occasion President Hatcher asked Sadie Organ "to have her library committee consider tagging the *Magazine Digest* as unfit to circulate. She hid the offending issue immediately," and the committee decided to cancel Memorial's subscription. Malcolm MacLeod, *A Bridge Built Halfway: A History of Memorial University College, 1925–1950* (Montreal and Kingston: McGill-Queen's University Press, 1990), 140.

5. Organ is perhaps referring to Clause 62: "The University shall not ... cause or suffer to be done anything that would render it necessary or advisable, with a view to academic success or distinction, that any person should pursue the study of any materialistic or skeptical system of logic or mental or moral philosophy" (An Act Respecting the Memorial University of Newfoundland, 13 Aug. 1949, *Statutes of Newfoundland 1949*).

Laying the Foundations: The Years Immediately after Confederation

John Hewson

5

I arrived in St. John's in September 1953 to teach at what was then Bishop Feild College, one of the collegiate institutions in St. John's that in those days had programs leading to matriculation and university entrance. I had just completed a BA in Classics at University College London and a year's post-graduate work in Education, also in London. I taught French, English, and history, although my first degree had been in Classics (Latin and Greek). At the time there were some 2,600 teachers in the provincial system, and only 116 (4.5 per cent) of us had a university degree. The second half of the twentieth century was to see revolutionary developments in education in the province.

I soon became the secretary of the local branch of the Humanities Association of Canada, which met monthly at Memorial University, on the old Parade Street campus, and consequently got to know most of the faculty of the early and mid-fifties. I also met and married a young lady by the name of Irene O'Neill, who at that time was the Assistant to the Bursar, a member of the staff, and I consequently knew all the administrative staff as well: there were less than a dozen. I not only got to know Paul Winter, the Bursar, who kept a very tight control on the purse strings, but also Monnie Mansfield, the Registrar, who, like many young women after World War I (which had obliterated a whole generation of young men), had never married, but looked after all the young female students, especially those from the outports, as if they were her own children. Sadie Organ I remember as a very capable and active librarian, and Helen Carew had just started a long career as Executive Assistant to several successive presidents. In the early years it was like an extended family, everyone knew the names of most of the students, and the administration consisted of four people: the President (Dr. Raymond Gushue), the Vice-President who was also Dean of Arts and Science (Dr. A.C. Hunter), the Dean of Education (Dr. George Hickman), and the Dean of Engineering (Professor Stan Carew).

In 1956 I began doing the first school broadcasts in French on the provincial CBC network, under the direction of Paul O'Neill (St. John's renowned historian), who was then the newly appointed CBC Director of School Broadcasts. I went off in 1957 to Université Laval in Quebec to do graduate work in French, completed an MA, and then went on to do further graduate work in linguistics, returning in the summers to work on the school broadcasts for the following year. In 1960, my graduate work complete except for the writing of a PhD thesis, I was offered a post at Memorial by Moses Morgan (a Newfoundlander always referred to as "Mose"), a very capable administrator, who had become Vice-President and Dean of Arts and Science on the retirement of Dr. Hunter in 1958. I was to be Assistant Professor of French, a linguist attached to the Department of Modern Languages (as it then was), to teach French phonetics and to organize a language laboratory for the new buildings on Elizabeth Avenue (the west end of which was still, in those days, a dirt road that ran into the country). The buildings, with woods and scrub behind them where now Prince Philip Parkway runs, were almost complete. We occupied the buildings in September 1961: Arts and Administration, Henrietta Harvey (the library in those days), the Gymnasium, and the Science Building, which had only three sides: the north side was added a decade later.

The last year on Parade Street (1960–61) there were 1,200 students, but it was also a banner year; for the first time the number of graduates at the annual convocation ran into three figures: exactly 100. The convocation parade came out of the main buildings and flowed along Merrymeeting Road to the auditorium of St. Patrick's Hall School, which was later destroyed by fire, and the site, alongside Bonaventure Avenue, is now occupied by condominium buildings. We moved onto the new campus on Elizabeth Avenue in September 1961, with 1,900 students, and some 30–40 faculty. Faculty meetings on Parade Street had been held in an ordinary classroom and chaired by the President, Dr. Raymond Gushue, who insisted that it was proper for teachers not only to be formally clothed (jackets and ties, for example), but also to wear their academic gowns. A tattered, stained, or faded gown was a mark of prestige: it normally went with a considerable reputation. Dr. E.R. (Edgar Ronald) Seary, for example, head of English and author of *Family Names of the Island of Newfoundland* and *Place Names of the Avalon Peninsula of the Island of Newfoundland*, had an ancient gown that had developed, with age, a sort of green sheen that made it look a trifle mouldy. The long sleeves of the gowns were also used for cleaning the chalkboard when the eraser was missing.

Students in the Memorial College days (1925–49) had also worn the short student gowns, which were still worn at Oxford and Cambridge when I was an undergraduate at University College London, where only students in the Law Faculty wore the undergraduate gowns (known colloquially as bum-freezers because of their shortness). In my year on the old campus (1960–61) there was a move by some students to reinstate the student gown, which was resisted by the majority. I remember Harold Paddock, later to be one of my colleagues in the Linguistics Department, as part of his student protest against bringing back the gown, striding across campus wearing a blanket with a hole in the middle (for his head) as a mock gown.

The original building on the old campus had been extended out to the corner of Parade Street; it had an added wing with a small gymnasium in the basement, which pedestrians can still look into as they turn the corner from Merrymeeting Road into Parade Street. The university had also inherited the USO that had been built by the Americans as a downtown recreation centre for their troops at Pepperrell Air Force Base (now Pleasantville). It stood on the south corner of Bonaventure Avenue and Merrymeeting Road, now one of the parking lots for The Rooms. Part of it was used in the 1950s for chemistry laboratories, and in the upstairs the English Department had offices. One of my first pleasant duties was to stroll across campus to the USO (United Service Organizations) building on the far northeast corner and introduce myself, as the linguist appointed to the Department of French, to Bill Kirwin, who had been appointed three years before (1957) as a linguist in the Department of English; he was later to play a vital role in the production and editing of the *Dictionary of Newfoundland English*. The provincial Department of Adult Education also used some of the downstairs offices and classrooms for evening classes. And the USO building had a hall with a stage that could be used for dances and theatrical performances: I was on stage there myself in 1960–61 in a performance of Tennessee Williams's *Inherit the Wind*, produced by George Palmer, who had just been appointed as a member of the new Extension Service.

After university status came with Confederation in 1949, and the first five graduates at the 1950 convocation, rapid growth of numbers required new buildings. Some were permanent extensions, some temporary, with the result that the new university buildings eventually ran the length of Merrymeeting Road to Parade Street, and down Parade Street to Ayre's new innovative supermarket on the corner of Harvey Road.

In the space now occupied by the headquarters of the Royal Newfoundland Constabulary and its parking lot, there had been a soccer pitch, used for recreational purposes, and also for one of the school soccer leagues: I remember watching a game there between Holy Cross and Curtis Academy in 1954. With continuing growth of enrolments, two temporary corrugated iron buildings — popularly known as the "tin cans" — were built on this pitch to provide more office and classroom space in the final years on the old campus. They leaked badly; cataracts of water sometimes poured in, and the winter wind whistled through them. I shared an office in one of them with Dr. Bill Summers, newly appointed as head of Geography, replacing Harold Goodridge, who had taught geography from the Memorial University College days through Confederation to the tin-can years. He was a renowned local artist who painted the mural in the entrance hall of the Confederation Building; his paintings can be found all over the city.

As a newly appointed Assistant Professor of French, I taught first- and second-year French language courses and a beginners' course for those who did not have the matriculation requirement of a second language. This latter course also accommodated four graduate students in History, because Dr. Gordon Rothney, head of department, had insisted that they could not possibly become competent Canadian historians without a knowledge of French (their matriculation language had been Latin). This was a visionary attitude at the time: Maurice Duplessis had died the year before, and the Quiet Revolution in Quebec was just about to begin. Two other students in that class went into politics; one (John Courage) became the Speaker of the House of Assembly during the Smallwood years, and the other (John Lundrigan) was elected to the House of Commons and became notorious for angrily accusing Prime Minister Pierre Trudeau, in the Commons, of using "unparliamentary" language, at which Trudeau, with much amused delight, claimed that he had only said "Fuddle Duddle." (For the full story and a good chuckle, Google "Fuddle Duddle House of Commons.")

There was no semester system: courses ran from September to April, with a break at Christmas. Dr. John T. Stoker had replaced Dr. Hunter as head of French, Dr. Alan Wilshere was Associate Professor, Dr. David Smith and I were Assistant Professors, and there was a Lecturer (Mlle. Janette Hamard from Angers in France). At this point there were 300 students in the first-year French classes; we had 60 students each, three hours a week, either Monday, Wednesday, Friday; or Tuesday, Thursday, Saturday mornings (from 9 a.m. to 1 p.m.). Tuesday and Thursday afternoons were for science labs and other out-of-class concerns, and Saturday afternoons were for recreation.

My first- and second-year classes and the beginners' class were in the tin cans, also known as the Temps (temporary buildings). Of the 300 students, Dr. Stoker took the 60 with the best Grade 11 marks, Dr. Wilshere took the next 60, and so on. I gladly volunteered to take the "dregs," those with the lowest marks, which for many was 50 per cent, the borderline pass. I did this because I had two advantages: I was a trained language teacher (the post-graduate year at London University's renowned Institute of Education), and had since spent four years teaching French in the Newfoundland school system for which I had also done the first-ever French school broadcasts.

I had also taught English as a second language in my three years at Laval, during which my francophone students taught me a lot about the grammar of my mother tongue. I was the native speaker, but they had studied English as a second language and knew far more about the grammatical details than I did at that time. As linguists know, native speakers' knowledge of their language is subconscious. They do not need conscious knowledge of how it works in order to use their language; the same is true for driving a car. Linguists, on the other hand, are like mechanics; they like to know how languages work, and I was able to bring my linguistic knowledge of French to the teaching of the language.

In those early days the students, many of whom had been taught in one-room schools by teachers who had only Grade 11 themselves, had got to where they were by dint of their own hard work. They were so grateful to have a teacher who could answer their questions and show them what to do that it never entered their heads to skip class: they were there to take advantage of an educational opportunity that earlier generations had never had. I gave them enormous quantities of work, six

translations a week (which they did without complaint), and stream-
lined the classroom process by having two students fill the chalkboards
with their own versions of translations into French before class. When
I came in, I would correct the two translations on the chalkboards with
commentary, while the other 58 students corrected their own versions
and asked questions about their own mistakes. At the end of the year
that French 100 class in the tin cans ranked third out of the five groups,
a big move from fifth and last where they had started; and it was all the
deserved result of their own hard work.

The move to the new campus in September 1961 was a time of great
rejoicing: each faculty member had a separate office in the brand new
buildings with new furniture and filing cabinets. The scientists all had labs
alongside their offices, and there was a gym in a separate building that also
contained a swimming pool, squash courts, and a bowling alley (where
Brian Peckford, later Premier of the province, could often be found during
his student years). The gym itself was so large that it could be divided into
two by a moving partition, so that two classes could be held at the same
time. It also had a stage and a sound system, and was used for examinations and graduations, the first of which was held at the opening ceremonies of the campus in the Fall of 1961, with nine honorary doctorates,
including Eleanor Roosevelt, widow of US President Franklin Delano
Roosevelt; Prime Minister John Diefenbaker; Premier Joseph Smallwood;
and distinguished notables both local and from abroad.

Premier Smallwood, known to the populace as "Joey," also organized a huge marching parade of the children from the St. John's schools
with banners and bands. I sat in the stands on the roadside with Dr.
Alain Frecker (born in Saint-Pierre of American parents), who at the
time was Deputy Minister of Education and later served in the Smallwood cabinet (1964–71) and as Chancellor of the university (1972–79).
The university also put on a play to mark the opening of the Little Theatre; it was Shakespeare's *Macbeth*, again produced by George Palmer,
with Denys Ferry as Macbeth and Sheila McGrath (who was then a
student at Memorial) as Lady Macbeth. I was part of the cast, playing
King Duncan, who gets murdered in Act I and then sits around waiting
for the curtain at the end.

The land on which the new buildings were constructed had been
completely stripped of the brushwood and trees that had formerly covered

the site, and the landscaping was still in progress, grass appearing through the early fall on the newly laid topsoil. The four new buildings and the few residences that had been completed stood somewhat starkly on a barebones landscape. As the campus grew, the roads were paved, flower gardens created, and trees planted — a whole grove of trees between the gymnasium and the Queen Elizabeth II Library. The trees and the flowers have grown and flourished with the growth and flowering of the institution itself.

There was a Faculty Room above the main entrance to the new Arts and Administration Building, with a small cafeteria shared by all the faculty. Since all four academic buildings and the residences were connected by tunnels, the Faculty Room (now turned into offices) was a meeting place just as was the old Faculty Room on Parade Street, next door to the Bursar's Office.

The new language lab was on the second floor of the Arts and Administration Building, across the hall from the Faculty Room, and it occupied most of my time in the first year on the new campus. I had been responsible for its design and installation. It was one of the first language labs in the whole of Canada, and to get it working I wrote the texts for French 100 and 200, and recorded the master tapes with Janette (Mlle. Hamard, who was soon to marry Brian Reardon from the Classics Department and become Mrs. Reardon) in the soundproof recording studio we had built into the corner of the control room. The two texts, *French Pattern Practice* and *La Pratique du français*, were published by Gage in Toronto, a company that was later bought out by American publishers. The lab ran all day from 9:00 to 5:00, with the help of student assistants, some of whom went on to interesting careers of their own: John Ottenheimer became a lawyer and politician who served in the Williams cabinet from 2003 to 2007; Chris Brookes was a godsend because he had technical abilities and could look after the machinery as well as the students as they worked at their exercises. He later became a researcher and independent reporter who wrote and recorded many radio broadcasts for the local CBC.

I have one fond memory of those early years before we hired a professional administrator and language assistants: a tape was brought to me from one of the booths, and a puzzled student assistant asked "What on earth is this?" I could understand all of the languages that were being taught at the time, so we put it on a tape machine, and I listened intently to something quite strange, and then, after a minute or so replied, "Spanish, backwards!" Some student had let the tape run out, and then changed the reels, rewinding the tape backwards. The machines had been advertised as foolproof; they were not, however, student-proof.

I was there in the language lab on 22 November 1963 when Dr. Fred Aldrich, an American who was the new Dean of Graduate Studies, came in looking for me and said in shocked tones, "John, they've shot Kennedy." I also remember General Rick Hillier as a student in the lab; he was a charismatic character even then, as a new student lately arrived in St. John's from Lewisporte. After his retirement from the Armed Forces, he became the University Chancellor, in July 2008.

At the end of the first academic year in the new buildings (1961–62) I did a brief survey of the students in the first- and second-year French language courses (French 100 and 200) to get student reactions to the use of the new laboratory. One remarkable fact that emerged was that only 20 per cent of the first-year students, all of whom had matriculated in French in order to register at the university, had heard the language spoken before coming to Memorial. Even more remarkable was the fact that only 10 per cent of the second-year students had heard French spoken before they enrolled at Memorial. The language lab was a new step in the right direction but there was still a long way to go.

One important goal consequently became to make sure that all teachers of French in the Newfoundland school system were able to speak the language in the classroom. New methods required the use of a core vocabulary established by educators in France: *Le Français fondamental,* which had two levels, 1,300 words of very high frequency and 1,300 essential words of lower frequency, for a total core vocabulary of 2,600 words to be taught in preliminary courses, preferably in the first three years. A course for instructing teachers, established by the French government and used around the world (*Voix et Images de France*), was finally introduced in 1967 and is described briefly by Tony Chadwick in Chapter 23 of this volume. Regrettably, second-language teaching has gone backwards in recent decades; a course presently used in the schools, for example, has no vocabulary control whatever. In one grade there is a discussion of exotic African trees, for example, where I do not know the French words because no one in my family knows the English words either!

The beginner's task should always be to master the basic vocabulary of the language by constant repetition and usage. Introducing disorganized vocabulary and exotic words interrupts that process and results in what the psychologists call retroactive inhibition. Students sometimes go on for years taking courses without learning the language, and the fault is always that of the teachers and the designers of the curriculum. By the 1950s it had become established that with proper organization and presentation of the materials, the basics of a language can be taught in three years. But if there is no proper organization of the materials and reinforcement of the learning, the new learning simply erases the old: retroactive inhibition.

Enrolments grew so rapidly in the 1960s that new buildings were sprouting up in previously undeveloped areas of the campus. In 1966 the French Department was moved to the new Faculty of Education Building, which had been designed to provide space for some of the Arts departments, to relieve pressure on the original Arts and Administration Building: the student enrolments doubled and tripled with the arrival of the baby boom generation. A new language lab, designed by the architect of the building, was built on the third floor, three times bigger than the original lab in the Arts Building. That original lab was eventually taken over by the Department of Folklore, which was then in the planning stages under the aegis of Herbert Halpert, a distinguished folklorist who had been recruited into the English Department by Dr. Seary. The province was rich in folklore and folksong, which was a part of the life of the remote communities of rural Newfoundland, where in the 1950s and 1960s electricity was gradually being installed, and in many outports people still crowded around battery radios to listen to the "Doyle Bulletin" every evening. Television, however, had already made its first appearance in St. John's in the mid-1950s, with fuzzy, snowy, tiny screens that in downtown St. John's regularly had a "ghost" from the signal bouncing off the South Side Hills and interfering with the direct signal from the station.

In the discussions that led to the 1967 Harris Report on the expansion of the university I had supported Dr. Halpert in his move to found a Department of Folklore, and he in turn supported my proposal to found a Department of Linguistics. We even thought about having a joint department, but eventually decided that although they overlapped (use of recorders and fieldwork in the outports, for example), in many ways they were more different than alike. The Harris Report consequently proposed that two new departments, Folklore and Linguistics, would be opened in September 1968.

But before that happened there was a crisis in the French Department (described in this volume by Tony Chadwick), and I was invited to meet with Vice-President Morgan and Dean of Arts Dr. Leslie Harris in the Arts and Administration Building. Mose opened the conversation by pointing out that with Dr. Stoker in the sanatorium on Topsail Road with a flare-up of a dormant tuberculosis, I was now the senior member of a department that had grown from five to more than 20 — 30 in all if one included the personnel of the language lab; and that I was the obvious person to take over the responsibility of the headship, which he would like me to do. While I was pondering this, Les Harris joined in by saying "I'm not sure if John would want to do it." He was aware, of course, that in less than a year I would be head of the Department of Linguistics and would have a lot of work to do to get the new department properly organized. Mose replied, with a chuckle, before I could say a word, "I believe he has what the English call Hobson's choice" (a free choice in which only one option is offered). I knew he was right: the other members of the department were all recent appointments, all but one of them from outside the province. In this way I became, in my last year in the Department of French, its head (pro tem).

During the late sixties I began to share with George Story the task of Public Orator, presenting candidates for honorary degrees at convocation. I found it a difficult task. A lot of research had to be done on the candidate's career, including a hunt for anecdotes to create a bit of fun for the occasion, and a strict time limit meant compression of a lot of information. George had a wonderful witty style, and in my first couple of attempts I did a very poor job of trying to imitate him. It was John Stoker who suggested to me that I should do my own thing and not try to imitate George: a truly excellent piece of advice. My own style turned out to be reflective and insightful, a nice balance to George's elegant and witty orations.

I had a good relationship with John Stoker. We knew that he was a type 1 diabetic, and that when his sugar levels were off balance he could be testy and short-tempered, normal behaviour for type 1 diabetes but not always good for collegial relations. He was, however, a fun person with a good sense of humour. I remember early one morning in his office he made a sudden angry remark to me, and I had to chuckle at the unexpected change of personality. So I said to him, "Wow, what did *you* have for breakfast?" which made him laugh, and the anger was over. We agreed on most things, and he was very supportive of my work in the language lab and the work in phonetics that I did to improve the students' oral skills.

In fact, in the second year on the new campus we experimented with having all first-year French students take the second class of the week together, all 300 of them, in a phonetics class that I taught in the Little Theatre (what is now the Reid Theatre). As well as work on pronunciation and the relationship of sound to spelling in French, I used to get them singing rounds like *Frère Jacques* and *Orléans, Beaugency*. In one class while this was going on, the President, Dr. Raymond Gushue, came in and sat at the back for a few minutes to watch the goings-on. He told me later that he had heard the singing from the corridor (300 voices!) and was so intrigued that he came in and sat down to listen. It may well be the only time that a President of Memorial University has sat in a classroom as an observer! The experiment was not continued: the regular teachers found that the loss of the midweek class was too disruptive.

George Story at this time was just beginning the work on the *Dictionary of Newfoundland English* with Bill Kirwin and John Widdowson, who came from the East Riding of Yorkshire in England, where I had lived in my teens. In order to talk to the elders in the small village where my family had moved (before the days of radio the old folks had never had any exposure to standard English) I had to learn the local dialect, which was like a foreign language to me with its *thee* and *thou*, and all the Danish words from the Viking invasions a thousand years before: *steg* for "a gander," *stee* for "a ladder," *wop* for "throw," and so on. John also spoke this dialect fluently, and he and I would delight in carrying on conversations completely incomprehensible to anyone else — we even did a brief sketch on stage in the Little Theatre for a university audience.

John was an incredible fieldworker; every spare moment he would hop in his Volkswagen and go off with his tape recorder. My first field trip in rural Newfoundland was with him. We went to St. George's Bay, Stephenville, and the Port-au-Port Peninsula in the 1960s, where we recorded native speakers of Acadian French, who had come across from Cape Breton Island early in the nineteenth century. The Trans-Canada Highway had been paved by 1965, but most of the local roads in the St. George's Bay area were still gravel. At Cap St-Georges, the end of the road on the north side of the Bay, we recorded preschool children who typically spoke only French until they went to school, francophone Newfoundlanders whose school was a form of English immersion.

I later went off on my own or with graduate students, especially to Conne River in Bay d'Espoir. In the sixties only 30 of the 100 miles from the Trans-Canada Highway to Bay d'Espoir were paved, and the only way into the Mi'kmaw settlement at Conne River (now an official reserve) was by boat. The Conne, where it flows into Bay d'Espoir, is a quarter of a mile wide and tidal. To cross it one parked the car in a little parking lot at the end of the road on the north side, blew the horn a few times, and someone would row across (in the old days) or come by speed boat to pick up the waiting passengers.

This work was certainly influenced by the example set by Ron Seary, who taught us all that a university should relate to its hinterland. He indeed led the way with his work on Newfoundland family names and place names. With the development of the Department of Linguistics, I determined that we would direct our attention to the Indigenous languages of the province, Newfoundland Mi'kmaw (then known as Micmac), Labrador Innuaimun (then known as Montagnais), and Labrador Innuttut (a dialect of Inuktitut, then known as Eskimo). There was also important work to be done on the historical remnants of the Beothuk language: vocabularies scattered in museums, archives, and elsewhere, of a language that scholars had declared to be related to just about everything from Egyptian to Norwegian to Algonkian (often spelled Algonquian, a French spelling, to be pronounced -kian according to most dictionaries: cf. eighteenth-century *Esquimau* > modern *Eskimo*).

I began the work on the Beothuk manuscripts in the first year of the Linguistics Department and began the study of Mi'kmaw at the same time to gain a knowledge and understanding of the grammar and vocabulary of an Algonkian language. Later I taught graduate students a course in Cree, a central Algonkian language, using the written and recorded materials prepared by Doug Ellis of the Linguistics Department of McGill. This enabled me to be familiar with the language of the Innu of

Labrador, whose language is a sub-dialect of Cree. Eventually I collected the vocabularies or dictionaries of four Algonkian languages, which enabled me to reconstruct a vocabulary of Proto-Algonkian by the method of comparative reconstruction. A team of computer personnel and linguists managed to devise a set of computer programs to do this work: the first time ever that such work had been done by computerized methods. I was able to use this prehistoric vocabulary of over 4,000 words, published eventually (1993) by the National Museum of Canada (*A Computer-generated Dictionary of Proto-Algonquian*), to show that at least 60 items in the Beothuk vocabularies bear not only lexical resemblances to Algonkian words, but also distinctive grammatical resemblances.

The three basic sources of the 360 surviving words of Beothuk were (i) the vocabulary collected in the 1790s by the Rev. Dr. John Clinch, Anglican priest and medical doctor at Trinity, from a little girl called Oubee; (ii) a vocabulary by the Rev. John Leigh, Anglican missionary at Twillingate, collected in 1819 from Mary March, then living in the household of John Peyton Jr.; and (iii) vocabularies from England that were apparently copies of a vocabulary taken down by William Epps Cormack from Shanawdithit at St. John's in the year before her death in 1829. These three collections were assembled, compared, collated, reconstructed, and, with a brief history, published in 1978 by the Newfoundland Museum (*The Beothuk Vocabularies*), a work for which a new updated edition will probably appear in the present decade.

The Department of Linguistics was founded in 1968 with two teachers — myself and Larry Smith, both of whom taught some joint courses with other departments. By the end of the seventies the department had 10 faculty members and a full graduate program. The university, in the same period, had become a "multiversity," with an administration almost as big as the original faculty, and had spread to the North Campus with new Engineering and Earth Sciences buildings and an ambitious and very successful medical school. Large flourishing trees grow from very small seeds.

A New-Found Land: Experiences
of a Faculty Wife in the 1950s

Elizabeth (Herrmann) Willmott

My husband Donald and I arrived at Memorial University in the late summer of 1956. Donald was the first sociologist hired by the university, where he taught at the Parade Street campus until 1959. During these years he was the university's only sociologist. His position was a cross-appointment with the university and the provincial Department of Public Welfare.

Don and I spent May 1954 to August 1955 in Java, where he was doing research about the Chinese in Indonesia. Trade between Indonesia and the outside world had virtually stopped. There were almost no tourists, and few native speakers of English. We both loved the experience, but felt cut off from familiar things. When Don was offered a Senior Lectureship in Asian Studies at Canberra, he rejected it. Both of us felt we did not want to make our home outside of North America.

I am an American citizen. Don is a descendant of English settlers who arrived in the Milton, Ontario, area in 1815. But he grew up in Sichuan, China, where his parents were educational missionaries for the United Church of Canada. We met during our undergraduate years at Oberlin College in Ohio. Don's PhD was from Cornell University, where he met the doctoral requirements in two fields, sociology and Southeast Asia studies. The climate of McCarthyism was strong in the United States. A focus on China, even on the Chinese in Southeast Asia, was a particularly difficult specialty for academics with integrity. I recall Professor Knight Biggerstaff, a renowned China scholar, giving a public speech at Cornell and reading *only* from newspapers. He did not say a word of his own. I also recall someone I gave as a passport reference shouting gaily across the street to me, "the FBI was asking me about you last week." It was considered normal!

So we chose to live in Canada. Don developed such severe hay fever at Cornell that we decided we could not consider living in a similar environment. In Canada, that meant not living in Ontario. Newfoundland promised to be allergy-free, and so it was! In truth, the advertised position for a sociologist at Memorial University was the only one in Canada that year. There was a hint of one opening in Edmonton, but it was not yet in place at the time. Lack of choice did not mean that he took the Newfoundland position reluctantly, or that I had feelings against it.

Yet my first impression as we took the single-track train, the "Newfie Bullet," across the island was of dismay that all was in such apparent disorder: wood fences made with upright stakes of all sizes and heights casually put together, piles of stuff lying about in yards. But there was also beauty all around us. Peter and Sophie Gregg, who were Oberlin and Cornell grads, were among our best friends. They were living in Grand Falls. Peter worked for the Newfoundland Wildlife Service, doing research on the beaver populations. We got off the Newfie Bullet to stay with the Greggs on our way to St. John's. I have a strong visual memory of the Bullet passing a stone's throw from their house, a toy train in a magical woods. I also remember they had to fetch water from a stream, and being told they had to break the ice to scoop up the water in winter. Peter had grown up in the big cosmopolitan cities of the world. His aim was to get as far away from them as possible. He once walked across the interior of Newfoundland, and was quite astonished to find the press crowded around him when he reached the coast. We spent our first Newfoundland Christmas with them in St. John's.

The Greggs and my husband and I were among the "outsiders" brought to Newfoundland after Confederation to take on tasks related to expanding provincial interests and to legal obligations subsidized by federal funding. We met many of these people both in the expanding university and in St. John's. It was an exciting time.

With virtually no houses for rent in St. John's, the university put us, and some of the other recent faculty, in publicly owned houses with subsidized apartments for the poor across our street. Our address was 20 Hoyles Avenue. In one of my first letters to my husband's parents in Alberta I wrote:

> We are more or less settled in our house here now —
> no drapes up, no bookcases or desk so papers and books
> scattered everywhere. We were happy to find the house
> waiting for us. The louses — they let us worry to the last

minute, didn't notify us about the house at any of the four addresses we gave them. We arrived in St. John's having failed in our efforts to get a hotel reservation and worried by the complete lack of places to rent listed in the newspapers. Then, all smoothed over as we were told about the house. It is really too small for us, but we feel in no position to even think to complain. We have two bedrooms, living room, and kitchen, and all the rooms are smaller than in our Calgary house.[1] ... The other side had produced a host of little ones who make good playmates for Kenny. They are wonderfully concerned about the ones a little younger than themselves. I am constantly amazed at the care they take of Ken. But they are always eating sweets, and each mother feeds the whole gang in turn. By lunch time Ken is stuffed. I am really at a loss about it. Just this morning a boy about 6 was playing with Ken. He disappeared out the front door and returned with an ice cream stick for Ken.

We have had several wonderful picnics so far, though the weather really does leave much to be desired. Our first Sunday we had a lovely picnic on a rocky beach (they all are rocky — rocks the size of your fist) with the blue sea and high cliffs all around. The second Sunday we had a cold drizzly picnic with some faculty on the top of a "mountain" with a view of the sea ahead, and woods and "ponds" (lakes) behind. And the top was covered with luscious blueberries. The next Sunday it really poured, but it was Ken's birthday, so we had a picnic in our car sitting on a pier at the harbour. This past Saturday was lovely, and we went to a little fishing village called Portugal Cove to sit in a cow pasture with a bull rather aggressively eyeing us and Kenny stepping on rocks and what looked like a rock but *very* unfortunately wasn't. But there was a glorious view of the sea, with waves beating white on the rocks and a view of the cute little village.

After a few days of experiencing St. John's, I exclaimed to Don in a stunned way that Newfoundland was another colony like Java, importing manufactured goods and exporting resources. I had not expected that anywhere in Canada, but have since realized that much of Canada still resembles an "undeveloped" country in many ways. Fishing was the only real local industry, although Joey Smallwood did make an attempt to "industrialize." He helped establish a shoe factory.[2] With no surrounding skilled-worker industrial base, it floundered. The shoes were sold at a Water Street store that specialized in Newfoundland-made items. They were beautiful, and I attempted to own a pair. I could not, however, find two shoes that were enough alike to fit both feet. The same store sold gorgeous hand-woven items. Over half a century later, I still wear a red wool scarf purchased at that time.

We built a sandbox for our two-year old, and neighbourhood kids from across the street made a ring around it just to stand and watch. I don't think they had ever seen a sandbox. Behind the house was a completely wild field, with stones and plants of great beauty. Other faculty with young children lived in the same area. We mothers made a kind of parade together every day with our toddlers and baby carriages, ending with tea at someone's house. I especially remember a festive tea with the family silver service being put into use for our afternoon informality at Elinor Eaton's home. Her husband, Doug, was a Newfoundlander who taught physical education. Beautiful Elinor was from Ontario.

I planted tulip and daffodil bulbs and made a rock garden at our second home, on Bonaventure Avenue, which we bought from public housing through university influence and later passed on to the newly arrived biology professor, Dr. Glen Bartlett, and his glamorous Italian wife. We had a sturdy fence built and put large flower boxes on the porch. It was our home. It was near a small shopping area at Churchill Square, which was great. But I missed the large rocky field of wild plants behind the Hoyles Avenue house. Still, it was a fun place to live, a mostly deserted main road with celebrities occasionally driving down it parade style. The Queen passed by a few feet from the front sidewalk with only our neighbours clustered to watch and wave. Once as I looked out the bedroom window, Lester Pearson drove by in an open car. As I was the only person on his route, he waved at me!

Despite all its deficiencies in being "up to date," St. John's more than satisfied our need for a permanent home and to be near familiar things and people. My Washington, DC, parents could visit by air. I could order from the catalogue, something I yearned to do in Java. I could even buy rye bread from Montreal at the plaza near our home! Downtown, the warren of little rooms made into a bigger Bowring's store had a wonderful cafeteria with a big glass window on the harbour. We often took our family there. Our little boy loved to stand at the window and look and look.

At the Newfoundland Academy of Art, I studied sculpture with Hans Melis, a talented sculptor from Holland, who was a bit bemused at the then small arts community he found when he got to St. John's. I even got a second prize in the Newfoundland art competition one year (professionals were not allowed to compete, a rather strange rule). Hans was commissioned to make a bust of Joey Smallwood while we were still in St. John's. It was a wonderful opportunity for him, and he later did busts of past people of prominence. He had a stack of photographs of Smallwood, taken at all angles. He told me he could easily make a good sculpture from them, something I understand from making busts myself. You just have to keep working the clay as you move from one viewpoint to another, and it all comes out right. However, Smallwood wanted to sit for him, so Hans went along with it. A copy of that bust is now displayed in the Memorial University Student Centre. The busts of the founders of Memorial University, which are displayed in the entrance of the Arts and Administration Building, are also by Hans Melis.

I have an MA in psychology and was invited to visit the local mental hospital, where I was offered a full-time job if I wanted one. But I was into having kids at the time, and our daughter Carol was born in the middle of our first winter. I did try to teach night courses at both the US Army base and in the adult education program in St. John's. These fell through. But if we had stayed longer, I am sure I would have found an opportunity.

I have always said living in St. John's was like being on a punctuated holiday in an exotic spot. Whenever the weather was good, and Don had no classes, we packed our two children in our VW Beetle and took off for the many coves and beaches near St. John's. I particularly recall Middle Cove with its stony beach. Local "entrepreneurs" would gather the wet stones tumbling in the surf. Their use is obscure as we never saw them anywhere. But some of Newfoundland's beach stones are among the oldest rock in the world. They tumble naturally to a shine that persists when they are dry. The workers first backed a small horse-drawn wagon down to the water's edge. Then, between waves they would shovel like crazy. As the surf rolled in toward them again, they would simultaneously yell and push the horse to go forward. Amazingly, they always beat the crashing waves. Several teams of horses and workers would be side by side. It was exciting beyond belief with the surf, the rolling stones, the intense shovelling, the shouting, and the excited horses.

And the June icebergs!!! No one then talked of whales. But we saw the sealers go out and come in again. We even indulged in seal flippers, prepared especially to satisfy our curiosity, at the home of Sid and Sylvia Wilansky.

There were things that were funny to an outsider like me in the St. John's of that day. For example, in spite of asking around it took me ages to figure out how to buy a fresh cod. The supermarket had only Nova Scotia frozen fish. The fish store downtown had exotic things, but no simple cod. Someone finally clued me in that if you took a newspaper for wrapping to a certain spot on the harbour in the morning there would be a boat with fresh cod. If we drove outside the city a certain distance, we could buy a huge cod for a quarter. If we drove far enough, the fishermen looked at us as if we were crazy when we asked the price of the fish they were unloading. They simply handed us one! A fresh cod is absolutely delicious, stuffed, covered with bacon, and baked.

Memorial University was so small in those days that almost everyone was involved in some kind of a "chore." Don's office was in a very ugly "temporary" building. The long and wide linoleum-covered hallway floor outside his office was washed clean of mud every day. It quickly became a mess. The reason was that there was no mat at the door to wipe shoes. This made no sense to us rational souls. Don inquired about how to get a mat at the door. He was told that Norman Brown, Oxford grad and philosophy professor, was in charge of that, so Don went and requested one! The rug materialized. Philosophy is, after all, a rational affair. Dr. Brown eventually moved to Queen's University in Kingston.

The Portuguese fishing fleet was amazing. We had just returned from travelling and living on the other side of the world. So we were accustomed to seeing new customs and artifacts. What made the Portuguese fleet exotic was that it was in Canada. Sailors playing soccer in Portugal would be expected. Coming across Old World sailors playing soccer while on my daily rounds in St. John's was a surprise. Picturesque sailing ships from another century filled the harbour when the fleet came in to weather a storm. They had little one-person boats stacked on their decks. Students went down to them for adventure and to try to purchase Portuguese wine. The Portuguese had a modern processing and hospital ship, but their impact on fish stocks was within reasonable bounds. Not so for some of the ships that came into the harbour. I recall a Spanish trawler with a long tube coming out the side that looked like an extended elephant trunk. We were told that it vacuumed fish up into itself. That day we stood wondering how long the fish would last with such technology entering in an increasing way. Not everyone understood, at that time, that fish were a limited resource. I recall a remark a student once made to Don about the Newfoundland economy: "There will always be fish in the sea." It was the inshore fishermen of Newfoundland who warned the federal scientists that the cod stocks were dangerously declining. We live with the failure to heed them.

During the International Geophysical Year (1957–58) we even had a group of Russians from a Russian scientific ship walking around town, and as guests in our home. Don was in the main office at Memorial when Russian scientists went to the university. He was asked to show them around — thus we had a group for dinner. I produced a bottle of sherry for about eight of us. They looked completely stunned, and one of them finally said: "I guess Canadians don't drink much." Many people were afraid of them. One of our babysitters expressed a fear of being kidnapped by the Russians. The irony is that they told us they were afraid to come into the harbour because they had been turned away elsewhere, I think in the Azores. They were so overwhelmed at being welcomed that they opened their ship to everyone who wanted to board. It was quite a circus.

Having grown up in a big city, like our friend Peter Gregg, I do not get particularly excited over their lure. Washington, DC, museums were a big part of my growing into what I am, as were marble buildings. When travelling in Europe, for example, museums were not a first interest. Landscapes and creative people were. I found these in Newfoundland, and now in Owen Sound, Ontario, a Canadian "cultural capital." When Don retired from Glendon College at York University, we left Toronto for this wonderful place near to the size of St. John's at the time we lived there. That size allows you to meet people you know wherever you go.

St. John's was a cosmopolitan place. We met an amazing array of interesting people: Brits with theatre experience; a Korean aristocratic physicist and his Canadian-Japanese wife; Jews who escaped the Holocaust; local artists and art students, often from prominent families; another Asia expert like Don hired to teach history. Historian Gordon Rothney and his wife were particularly good friends. Gordon was a staunch member of the Gower Street United Church and a teetotaller. He ran for office under the banner of the CCF (Co-operative Commonwealth Federation), disappointing many outporters, he said, when he campaigned without the expected free booze in the trunk of his car. We kept in touch with many of these people. The Rothneys went to Winnipeg. Dr. Horace Rosenberg, a Newfoundlander, moved to Ottawa. Paddy Drysdale, first in theatre and then in the English Department, edited a Canadian dictionary out of Scarborough. Gordon Goundry was hired as a provincial economist. He lamented: "If only Joey Smallwood would let me see the contracts before he signs them instead of after!" And he left even before we did. Everyone had a different reason, but many people besides us left.

We stayed in Newfoundland only three years. This had nothing to do with anything personal. Nor was the rumour true that Don's having completed his Cornell University PhD thesis while in St. John's was the basis for looking for a better job. Don never "job-hopped" to improve his status. By the way, I never attempted to influence him to leave a job or go where I wanted to go. (The decision about Australia was ultimately his.) It also had nothing to do with his experience as a teacher at Memorial. Rather, his role in the provincial government's Department of Public Welfare frustrated his liberal or left-wing "Social Gospel" background. It was difficult for non-Newfoundlanders like Don and me to be full contributors to the society in which we then lived. The retired Dean, who had moved to St. John's in the late 1920s, was still spoken of as if he were a Brit. Don's opinions did not count at the Department of Public Welfare the way they would have if he had been a Newfoundlander. He wanted to be effective. We moved to Saskatchewan in 1959, a place where he thought his work would have more local impact. Once in Saskatchewan, we became even more aware of the influence of his outsider status in Newfoundland. We found that everyone "belonged" in Saskatchewan no matter how recently they had moved there. The "pioneer" was still everyone!

We moved away from Newfoundland the year that the Trans-Canada Highway was extended across the island. When I told a St. John's native that we were going to drive across the country, meaning Canada, she replied that she also was going to do so. She, however, meant that she would drive across Newfoundland itself. Most residents of the Avalon Peninsula voted against joining Canada.[3] For them, Newfoundland was still a country. The new road soon ended that identity. But that first year it was rough, and few attempted to cross the island on it. We had not just a spare tire, but an entire spare wheel! At places the road was just two tire tracks with large stones sticking up. In another place, where they were still blasting, a fine clay-like dust covered the surface. It even got into our closed suitcases and arrived in Saskatchewan with us. We drove mile after mile without seeing another car. The "hotel" room we stayed in the first night had walls made of wallpaper-covered vertical boards. Yet at another spot, we encountered a modern, people-filled restaurant. I believe that the new ferry must have been in place, as I would surely remember a repeat of a passage on the ancient vessel.

And so we were gone. Our daughter Carol returned once when the annual meeting of the Learned Societies was held there. She was greeted with special warmth, being a "native Newfoundlander." Photos she took reminded us that much of what we knew still remains today, and that much has changed as well. Don can still play some of the traditional Newfoundland songs on his guitar and sing some of the words.

Notes

1. For information about the modernization of St. John's, see John Phyne, "On a Hillside North of the Harbour: Changes in the Centre of St. John's, 1942–1987," *Newfoundland and Labrador Studies*, 29, no. 1 (Spring 2014): 5–46.

2. Dr. Egon Koch of Hanover set up a shoe factory, Koch Shoes, in Harbour Grace; half of the $1.5 million of the start-up cost was provided by a Newfoundland government loan (*Encyclopedia of Newfoundland and Labrador*, s.v. "New Industries," "Shoe and Boot Making," "Koch Shoes Limited"); Gerhard P. Bassler, *Escape Hatch: Newfoundland's Quest for German History and Immigration, 1950–1970* (St. John's: Flanker Press, 2017), 138–45.

3. J.K. Hiller, "The 1948 Referendums," Newfoundland and Labrador Heritage website, http://www.heritage.nf.ca/articles/politics/referendums-1948.

Philosophy, Music, and Public Broadcasting: My Life in Newfoundland

7

Norman J.P. Brown

If you had asked me during 1951 where I would expect to be in about a year's time, I would not have suggested Newfoundland. I knew nothing about the place, except how to pronounce it. Following the completion of my BPhil thesis on Aristotelean ethics at Oxford, I was teaching night courses in aesthetics and ethics at the University of London and later English and Latin full-time at a Jesuit boys' school in Wimbledon, looking for a permanent university job in philosophy. Dr. Douglas A. Darcy, a scientist working on cancer research at the Chester Beatty Institute in London, who had just returned from a visit to his Newfoundland family, told the Catholic chaplain at Oxford that Memorial University wanted someone to start a philosophy department there; I surprised myself by writing and offering my services. (This was not the only thing that my family owed to the brothers of the Darcy family. Dr. James M. Darcy became our family dentist, and Brother Joseph B. Darcy, Principal of St. Bon's College, became the headmaster of our son, Paul.)

Before doing this I naturally discussed it with my wife, Catherine. We noticed that Newfoundland had the same latitude as Paris, which sounded *marvellous*! We decided to try it out. (My wife had studied history, and I, philosophy; unfortunately no one tested us on climate or geography. We found all that out for ourselves when we arrived.)

Anyway, my offer was accepted. But the Board of Regents did not move at breakneck speed. Part of the reason for the initial delay was the Board's misunderstanding of my Oxford BPhil, which was equivalent to its DPhil, a degree based solely on a thesis, whereas the new BPhil involved course work and a shorter thesis, designed to prepare candidates for a university job teaching philosophy. They were going to call it a DPhil, but decided against two degrees with the same name. After this was clarified, I was asked by the Dean, Dr. Alfred Hunter, to write a proposal for his consideration, which I did. Nothing coherent by way of guidance was given by the authorities. I know that he was favourably impressed by my effort, and I presume that the Regents were, too! It might be relevant to mention that the government's original plan for the university did not mention philosophy at all; but that omission had to be rectified when it was realized that Dalhousie University, which was the main destination of Memorial's pre-med students, required philosophy for all intending medical students.

In the course of these rather lengthy discussions, Dr. Hunter remarked to me in a letter regarding the Regents: "We have some masters in procrastination to deal with!" As a result, to make sure that we did not lose *all* our income, my wife (who was teaching history in Croydon at a school run by nuns) kept her job for the fall term, affording me a beautiful sunny voyage on the RMS *Nova Scotia* in August of 1952, while she had a frightful journey the following January on the RMS *Newfoundland*, which arrived a day late, covered in ice.

After a night or two in a small hotel belonging to a Memorial couple (I believe it belonged to the Faceys, from the Math Department), I lived for the time being in a lodging house not far below the Basilica, run by a delightful elderly lady whose name, I'm afraid, escapes me. In due course, I found a small house on Military Road. (This made me the Lieutenant Governor's nearest neighbour, though he was not mine.) I don't remember when our furniture arrived, except that the idea brings snow into my mind. But then every idea in a Newfoundland winter involves snow.

My term at Memorial coincided exactly with Raymond Gushue's term as President. Two well-intentioned new boys! He certainly treated me very kindly.

My program development in the first year included an Introduction to Philosophy and Logic, Moral Philosophy, Modern Philosophy from the Renaissance to the 19th Century, Ancient Philosophy (Thales to Plato, and Aristotle to Augustine), Medieval Philosophy, Philosophies of the 20th Century, and Philosophy of Mind (Some Philosophical Discussions in Psychology), although not all of these were presented every year! A few joint lectures were offered with members of other departments beginning in 1956–57, such as on political philosophy with Mose Morgan (then Dean of Arts and Science), on the philosophy of religion with the Rev. S.L.S. Allen, and on the concept of science with W.F. Forbes, though I can't recollect our enrolments in these classes.

In 1961–62 I took a sabbatical year at Oxford to conduct research on the ethical theories of the Canadian Jesuit philosopher Bernard Lonergan, spending weekends in London with my wife and young family in my old home in Ealing, where my mother still lived.

I enjoyed teaching philosophy at Memorial, especially after I was granted a second member for the department — Douglas Odergard in 1963. But by then I was feeling the need to belong to a larger department, and I took advantage of the offer of a post at Queen's University at Kingston, to which I moved in 1965 and where I spent the rest of my career teaching medieval philosophy, logic, and ethics, and exploring the nature and classification of speech acts in current linguistic theory. However, in the meantime my life at Memorial was by no means without interest.

At the time I was there, Newfoundland was notable for the good choirs it enjoyed, though not yet for orchestral music except for occasional visitors from outside. It was a very pleasant surprise when we heard that we were to have Murray Schafer as a composer-in-residence (for two years, if I remember rightly). As I remember it, the chief public manifestation of his presence was in the splendid work he did with brass players from the Salvation Army, whom he had playing through the large corridors of the university's main building. This was an ideal place for the antiphonal settings of the Italian Renaissance style. We also enjoyed the presence of Phyllis Mailing, Murray's wife, a fine mezzo-soprano who gave recitals on the local CBC, one of which I was privileged to accompany on the piano.

On occasion I played for weekday requiem masses at the Basilica. This was something of a challenge. The fine main organ in the rear of the church was supported by a small two-manual instrument behind the high altar, which if I remember rightly could be played from either console — and was still in place when I visited the Basilica some 20 years ago. This instrument was used for daily requiems, which the organist not only played but sang. I myself sometimes played and sang two masses one after the other on weekday mornings when the organist was away.

Perhaps my second most enjoyable musical activity in St. John's was accompanying the choir run by Ignatius (Nish) Rumboldt for CJON TV, a station whose guiding force was Don Jamieson (later to become, perhaps surprisingly, Canada's Foreign Minister). This connection with

CJON left me with a certain ambiguity of allegiances. My personal broadcasting was always on CBC radio, where the Director of Talks, Fred Scott, had become a good friend for whom I gave many varied talks over the years on philosophy, music, and religion. As well, I took part in different CBC musical performances. Now CBC wanted to open an active TV station, which CJON was anxious to prevent. I was led to believe that it was a final letter I wrote to the *Telegram* in support of CBC that caused Joey Smallwood to say to Don Jamieson "enough is enough," or words to that effect, so CBC went ahead. I can assure you, some 60 years afterwards, that I have never, before or since, had any other effect of such importance and immediacy on a public political issue! All of my documents relating to this affair were deposited in the Queen's University Archives.

What was my first most enjoyable musical activity? Nish asked me to take over his job of directing the Glee Club at St. Patrick's School, which I did with much pleasure in my last two years in St. John's. That did something to prepare me for becoming Organist and Choir Director at St. Mary's Cathedral in Kingston from 1975 to 2008. No, I didn't abandon philosophy; I worked in both positions simultaneously, officially retiring from Queen's University in 1987, though I taught part-time until 1992.

I should like to say a word about my wife Catherine, who began at Memorial what turned out to be a very successful career in history. She started in our last two years at Memorial to act as a teaching assistant for some classes at the request of Dr. Ronald Seary, who was temporarily in charge of the History Department. When we moved to Queen's, she then went on to get her doctorate with a thesis on Jean Gerson, Chancellor of the University of Paris (*c.* 1395). The thesis was later published by Cambridge University Press under the title *Pastor and Laity in the Theology of Jean Gerson*. Catherine Brown also had a stellar career as a teacher (winning two teaching awards) and administrator. She died suddenly and prematurely in 1993 in her sixty-fifth year.

I must say that meeting and having dealings with nice people was one of the things that notably marked our life in Newfoundland. Apart from friendships that developed at the university, we were quickly made welcome by the Freckers, the husband later becoming the Minister of Education; the two Renouf families, one brother being Memorial's

Registrar and the other being a lawyer in St. John's; and Sadie Organ, mathematician and librarian. I even remember Rex Murphy as an under-graduate in one of my classes, before he became a Rhodes Scholar at Oxford!

As for me, I am still here at 91,[1] enlivened and kept going by Jennifer, my second wife. I read the Memorial newsletter with great interest and am quite impressed with the bursary program. Jennifer and I visited St. John's a few years ago, and saw, among other things, Memorial, CBC, and the Christopher Pratt exhibition at the new art gallery, The Rooms. I have always loved Pratt's work; his images of Newfoundland have stayed with me.

Memorial University's first philosopher, Norman J.P. Brown (seated), preparing to give a lecture on the St. John's station of the CBC. (Photographer unknown.)

8

The English Department at Parade Street

Sandra (Drodge) Djwa

The head of the English Department at Memorial was E.R. Seary, an Englishman who had obtained his PhD from Sheffield. He was a caricature of the absent-minded professor, wearing a mouldy and decrepit gown, much in need of repair. But on closer view Seary had a piercing gaze and governed the department with a firm hand. His specialty, although I did not know it at the time, was *onomastics,* the study of the origin, history, and use of proper names. The two Newfoundlanders in the department were D.G. Pitt, an Associate Professor, and George Story, an Assistant Professor. Pitt had an MA, was shortly to obtain his PhD from Toronto, and later became E.J. Pratt's biographer. Story had a DPhil from Oxford, and Alastair Macdonald, the other Assistant Professor, was a Scotsman on a two-year contract, in the process of obtaining his PhD from Manchester. To me the English Department seemed entirely British, in faculty as in subject: even Story, in tweeds, looked and sounded very English. But there were undercurrents towards Newfoundland Studies that I was then completely unaware of.

Composition was the first step in English studies. I was lucky to be placed in the classes of Mrs. Jean Pratt, listed in the calendar as an Adjunct Professor with a BA. She had married Maxwell Pratt, a relative of E.J. Pratt. Always well prepared, she had a good sense of humour and opened new worlds to me in the field of language. The assumption governing composition classes seems to have been that a first-year student, very likely the product of a one- or two-room school, would be unprepared for university English classes. Consequently, instructors began at the basics of language with classes on synonyms and homonyms and the derivation of words. We then wrote short compositions on specified subjects. Mrs. Pratt was not prepared to tolerate sloppy research: she wrote in a firm hand on one of my essays: "You have a style but no content." A few years later, when I was studying at UBC, she sent me copies of Pratt's poems, newly published by D.G. Pitt. Still later George Story sent some of his essays on Newfoundland writing, including "The New-foundlander Who Is Canada's Greatest Poet" and copies of *The Pratt Lectures* as they appeared. I am grateful to both, who helped direct the course of my future academic life.

Alastair Macdonald taught us poetry from Oscar Williams's *Immortal Poems of the English Language*. He was shy, an aesthete of sorts, and not accustomed to lecturing. Some of the class continued to talk quite audibly as he taught. Early in the term he gave a fine lecture on Henry Reed's "Naming of Parts":

> To-day we have *naming of parts*. Yesterday,
> We had daily cleaning. And tomorrow morning,
> We shall have what to do after firing. But to-day,
> To-day we have *naming of parts*. Japonica
> Glistens like coral in all of the neighboring gardens,
>   And to-day we have *naming of parts*.
>
> This is the lower sling swivel. And this
> Is the upper sling swivel, whose use you will see,
> When you are given your slings. And this is the piling swivel
> Which in your case you have not got. The branches
> Hold in the gardens their silent, eloquent gestures,
>   Which in our case we have not got.

Macdonald had done his stint of army service and was explaining Reed's distinction between the mechanical rifle drill required for the taking of life and the simultaneous beauty of late spring: "Japonica / Glistens like coral in all of the neighboring gardens" — which the soldiers also "have not got." Pulling the bolt on the rifle, Reed writes, is "easing the spring." Listening to the cadences of the verse, I suddenly understood the parallels.

I went up to the lectern to tell him how much I had appreciated the lecture but added (mindful of admonitions in my classes in the Faculty of Education) that he needed to get the class under control if anybody was going to learn anything. At the next session he spoke very loudly and firmly and the talking subsided. Slowly the class settled down to

George Barker's "Sonnet To My Mother," with its affirmation of war-time courage and defiance: "Sitting as huge as Asia, seismic with laughter, / Gin and chicken helpless in her Irish hand, / . . . She will not glance up at the bomber, or condescend / To drop her gin and scuttle to a cellar . . . ." On the basis of this interchange we developed a hesitant friendship, which meant that whenever we bumped into each other on the campus, we stopped to talk about the poem then under class discussion.

In early spring of 1957, the Dramatic Society held auditions for a play called *Rope* — by London playwright Patrick Hamilton — to be presented in late March. The faculty advisor was Patrick Drysdale, a former member of the London Theatre Company, but now teaching English. Scenes from the play were photographed for the Memorial Yearbook and there I find myself at 18 — a slim young woman with her hair up, wearing a cocktail dress and chatting with a young man who is passing canapés. In the foreground is a large trunk (*Cap and Gown 1957*, 76–78). I played Leila Arden in *Rope*, a decorative but silly young thing whose boyfriend has not turned up at a cocktail party. The plot explores the psychology of his two friends, Wyndham Brandon and Charles Granillo, played by Harold Stamp and William Westcott, who model their actions on notions of intellectual superiority gleaned from Nietzsche. They strangle the missing guest (he had arrived early) and stuff his body in a trunk. Their old tutor, Rupert Cadell, played by Alastair Macdonald, becomes suspicious and uncovers the murder.

Macdonald and I were typecast and recognized this with some amusement. After rehearsals we would sometimes walk and talk our way to the tea room at the Newfoundland Hotel. We talked about the difficulty in learning our parts for the play, but mostly we talked about poetry. He sometimes spoke of his family in Scotland and I sensed he worried about his mother; apparently she had a small greenhouse. Occasionally I would hold forth on my ambitions and he would listen, making encouraging "hmmms," but often inserting a question that pricked my juvenile assumptions. Conversation still unimpeded, we would arrive at the tea room where he would order chopped egg sandwiches and tea for us both, through which we would continue to talk, and after which we would depart by our separate routes. The following year, when I was teaching at Curtis Academy, he would sometimes invite me to faculty parties also attended by Jean Pratt. I really enjoyed the intellectual give-and-take of these sessions. In retrospect, I remember Alastair Macdonald as somewhat diffident but kind, perceptive and intellectually generous. He knew, long before I did, that I would become an academic and, by his attention to my interest in poetry, encouraged me to do so.

Years later, in the summer of 1982, when I was writing the "Poetry" column for the *University of Toronto Quarterly* annual review of books in Canada, I had occasion to review *A Different Lens*, his third book of poetry:

> The different lens is primarily the eye of the artist fascinated by detail just outside the immediate angle of vision. ... Like Alex Colville's portrait of a young woman with a telescope, Macdonald often stands at the large end of the lens looking backwards. ... Time and its tricks of perception, the mental readjustments of a mature narrator perceiving a younger one — these shades of distinction characterize Macdonald's best poetry. Particularly impressive is "The Greenhouse," destroyed as the poet puts it "(in the disclaiming, quieting phrase) / by an act of God" and with it the "focus for images / of those meaning most to me, so that / there's now a further reconstruction / for memory to make."

David G. Pitt. (Photo from *Cap and Gown*, 1959, courtesy of Memorial University Libraries.)

9

"Forth into the Deep": How I Became a Sociologist at Memorial University

Ralph Matthews

Becoming a Sociologist

As undergraduates, we often made fun of Memorial's motto, *Provehito in Altum*, which the university translated as "go forth into the deep." The wags among us with high school Latin contended that it could also be translated as "Go off the deep end" or even as "Reach for the Sky" — the latter version favoured by those raised on a cultural diet of 1950s westerns after TV arrived in St. John's in 1955. Even in its official translation, the motto is simultaneously both prophetic and daunting. I suppose it has a ring of relevance for a maritime people whose existence has long been associated with the ocean and her treacherous depths. It perhaps implies that Memorial might help equip one for the leap into the depths of life. But, when it comes right down to it, the motto largely is a warning. It forebodes that one ultimately has to take the plunge on one's own, to sink or swim as one can.

This chapter focuses on my earlier experience at Memorial as an undergraduate and in the subsequent period when, while still a graduate student at the University of Minnesota, with Noel Iverson I undertook a study of the Newfoundland Community Resettlement Program. The experiences of these years have shaped me as an individual in that they gave me the social and personal skills to "swim" even when confronting deep water. While I may have metaphorically leapt into the deep, the metaphor also takes on another meaning as these experiences also deeply shape the person I have become.

By profession I am a sociologist, a field that I didn't know existed before I entered Memorial. In that sense, Memorial made me who I am. But my awareness of things social and of cultural differences began in my childhood. I wasn't born in Canada but in the country of Newfoundland before Confederation. Throughout my early years, Newfoundland was a patron–client barter society based on fishing. Merchant elites in St. John's supplied regional merchants with provisions from England to trade for salted codfish in remote outports. As these merchants set the prices for both the supplies and the fish, rural residents saw credit and debt, but little actual money. The Great Depression and poor governance bankrupted Newfoundland when almost a third of the population lived on a near starvation "dole" of food rations.

But World War II brought dramatic changes. Newfoundland was strategically located as a potential advanced fortress should Germany attack America. Four US air and naval military bases were built in New-foundland — one (Fort Pepperell) a few kilometres from my parents' home in St. John's. These brought cash jobs and an escape from peasantry for thousands, as well as the brash presence of thousands of young American servicemen.

Even though I grew up in what was then a suburb of St. John's and now is part of the inner city, my earliest memories are of a more tradi-tional society — the henhouse under our back porch and the raucous sound of the rooster at daybreak; the songs of Johnny Burke; the ice-man with his tongs regularly walking down our drive with a sawdust-covered block for our icebox; the jingling bells on the horse and sleigh of Mr. Lawlor, the butcher who lived a short distance away. But, by my pre-teens, I was also listening to radio broadcasts of VOUS, the "Voice of the United States Armed Forces Overseas," broadcasting *Amos and Andy*, *The Shadow*, and *Jack Benny* from the nearby military base. In short, the transition of Newfoundland society from traditional depen-dency to modern cash economy and the changing culture associated with that was my lived experience. This accelerated after 1949 when Newfoundland joined Canada and was transformed into a social welfare state by modern public services and socio-economic benefits such as family allowances and old-age pensions. I also experienced the hubris and often subsequent despair associated with development and modernization.

But then the polio scare came. I never got it, but my life was affected by it. Dr. Jonas Salk had yet to invent his vaccine and every summer this deadly and debilitating disease attacked thousands of teenagers in North American cities. St. John's was no exception as it now was ex-posed to many migrants. The only possible way to try and avoid polio was to escape to places as remote as possible. I was sent away!

My maternal uncle, Earl Noble, was a regional merchant in Notre

Dame Bay and White Bay, many miles from the closest roads. He operated village stores and had a schooner travelling to even more remote
communities bringing supplies for the winter and collecting the dried
salt fish. He and my Aunt Elsie had two sons and a daughter, all younger
than I. From about age 14 to 15, I was sent to live with this family each
summer. These were exciting times for me. I was an only child, my home
was a formal environment, and my life in St. John's was essentially sub-
urban. In contrast, my summers were spent in the warm and easygoing
household of my relatives and also in close contact with the broader
society of rural people living economically and geographically on the
edge. My male cousins and I travelled on the fish collection schooner
through one of the most remote populated regions of North America. I
became conscious of social differences in a way that I never had before.
I also came to experience the strengths that can exist in a culture of
poverty and the warmth of a way of life in which people must care for
one another to survive. I saw first-hand that a lifetime of hard physical
work was little guarantee of well-being or healthy old age. For the first
time, I saw what a different culture was like.

Back in St. John's, I did well in high school but didn't excel in any
subject. There was a prize for coming first, second, and third in any year.
I finished fourth — 14 terms in a row (i.e., nearly five years). I didn't
excel in any subject and never won the coveted English, Maths, Physics,
or Chemistry prizes. I was incapable of athletic achievement and
couldn't draw in art class. However, I did win a televised city-wide high
school debating contest (perhaps due to the coaching of Professor
David Pitt). Words and rhetoric became my friends. High school education in Newfoundland then ended at Grade 11 and I was only 16
when I finished high school and entered nearby Memorial University.

I had little idea what I wanted "to become" and had few role models
to guide me. No one on either side of my family had gone to university
and few had completed high school. My father, Ralph Matthews Sr.,
had been forced to quit school during the Depression and had worked
as a "shareman" on a fishing boat before migrating to St. John's, where
he ultimately worked supervising the manufacturing of Coca-Cola. My
mother, Golda Lee Noble, had a high school education but she died
when I was 12. My father quickly remarried and my British stepmother,
Evelyn Millard, had an MSc in Mathematics from the University of

London. She had come to Newfoundland to head Bishop Spencer Girls' School. Shortly after she married my father she became an Assistant Professor of Mathematics at Memorial so I had exposure to some aspects of academic life before landing there myself. Evelyn was kind and supportive, but I was dismal at mathematics. My father wanted me to become an accountant based on his friendship with someone who handled "accounts" for a local building supply company. In his words and with the reasoning of one who survived the Depression, it was "a field in which you will never be out of work." I leaned towards being a lawyer. In Newfoundland, many lawyers were outspoken public political figures and I knew how to score points in debate, so it seemed an ideal profession to me. But bowing to my father's wishes I registered in the Bachelor of Commerce program. As my one elective course in first year, I enrolled in the introductory sociology course. I was forever changed by it.

Sociology opened a new world for me. I was previously unaware that there was a field of study that could analyze my experiences in a changing Newfoundland. I devoured it. However, it was not just the subject matter that captured me. It was sociology's intellectual stance. When people in later years have asked me why I became a sociologist, I often answer that it was "because I can think in grey." By this I refer to the fact that much of social science reasoning is relativistic rather than reductionist. We do not deal in facts but in contextualized interpretations — for the meaning of facts is always subject to those frames of reference that we bring to them. My intellectual strength, I have come to realize over the years, is that I can intuit "stories" in empirical data that other people may have trouble seeing. Sociology doesn't make things up, but it does provide interpretative understandings.

When I entered Memorial University in 1960 it had approximately 1,450 students, about four times the size of my high school. The joint Department of Sociology and Anthropology had two tenure-stream professors, a British anthropologist (Ian Whitaker) and a young American sociologist (Roger Krohn), who was joined by another (Noel Iverson) a year later. Iverson was probably the first truly cosmopolitan thinker I ever got to know well. In anthropology, I was exposed to Whitaker's analysis of the Sami people in Scandinavia; Evans-Prichard's studies of the Nuer of (now) South Sudan; and Malinowski's, Ruth Benedict's, and Margaret Mead's studies in the South Pacific. Beyond introductory sociology, my knowledge of that field was esoteric by the standards of what others would see as its central approach. For example, in the sociology of work and organizations, instead of learning about American work and economic, educational, and health organizations, I studied Marc Bloch's *Feudal Society* (1962)[1] as an exemplar of social organization. My course on urban sociology did not cover modern cities but the historical rise of them as depicted in such works as Fustel de Coulanges, *The Ancient City: A Study on the Religion, Laws, and Institutions of Greece and Rome* (1874)[2] and Henri Pirenne's *Medieval Cities* (1944).[3] However, it was Roger Krohn's social theory and social psychology courses from which I derived both my love of conceptual thinking and an approach within sociology that focused on role behaviour more than social structure. From then to now, my approach to sociology has been actor-centred and action-focused.

Yet, my most formative experiences during my university years occurred not in university but as a summer welfare officer. When Newfoundland entered Canada, many of its social workers had only high school education. In the post-Confederation period, summer upgrading courses were put on for them in St. John's while university students (often from Sociology) were hired to temporarily replace them in their districts. For two summers I was sent to ever-more remote areas, first Bell Island (the site of a recent mine closure) where I was trained in a three-person office, and then on my own to Western Bay, Tors Cove, and Red Bay, Labrador. In that role I was responsible for the administration of able-bodied food relief for many indigent families, child welfare support, travel of unmarried pregnant girls to birthing facilities, and basic "relief" for the multiple maladies that affect the poor, the feeble, the old, and those without social support. Unlike my "polio summers" when I was an onlooker, now I was partly responsible for the survival of the most vulnerable. There also were crisis events.

When the departing welfare officer from Western Bay brought me to my boarding house on a warm summer evening, the glow in the western sky was not from the setting sun. The whole interior of the peninsula was ablaze and a threat to some 30 communities. When the wind changed, all those on one side of the Trinity–Conception Peninsula were evacuated to the other side. The entire population of the coast was in danger and I was responsible for their emergency food and housing relief. The departing officer handed me keys to every church, church hall, and service club lodge along the coast in case emergency shelters were needed. His more chilling gift was the radio contact signals for three vessels waiting offshore in case inhabitants of some communities were driven into the sea. I now had command of a flotilla! I was 18 years old.

The following year Red Bay, Labrador, provided even more stark responsibility. I travelled there in mid-May on the *Northern Ranger*, the first coastal boat out of St. John's in the spring. We quickly encountered heavy pack ice and for nearly two weeks moved cautiously only by day. In Bonavista, Twillingate, and other communities, "floater fishermen" came aboard, headed to Labrador to fish there during the summer. They had no money for bunks and slept body to body on the floor. I had grown up hearing how my great-grandfather and grandfather had similarly "gone to the Labrador" as young men. Indeed, my great-grandfather died of a heart attack at age 46 en route to Labrador. The boat's other crew members could not turn and bring him home as that would end their fishing season and threaten the very survival of their families through the coming winter. Instead, they put his body in a barrel and covered it with the salt used for curing fish. His mummified remains were returned to his unsuspecting widow when the boat returned in the autumn. On this voyage I came face to face with the privation that was my heritage.

In contrast, I had a private cabin right under that of the wireless operator. One night I heard much shouting in the wireless officer's room. In the morning I learned that our sister ship, which we had passed only hours earlier on its return journey, had been crushed by the ice and sunk during the night. The awareness that this could happen to us became poignantly real when the captain announced that he would go no farther than St. Anthony, which we reached that afternoon.

Soon after debarking, Cal Reynolds, the regional welfare director in St. Anthony, had me flown on the Grenfell Hospital emergency float plane over to Red Bay, Labrador. There, for nearly three months, I travelled by open boat and pickup truck to the other communities in my district. I quickly became aware that life on coastal Labrador in the early 1960s was often harsh and short. The week after I arrived, the small son of the local merchant (in whose house I was boarding) died from severe burns. No medical assistance could reach the community due to intense fog and crushing ice. A few weeks later, in another community, a married couple drowned while out at sea, leaving five children orphaned. I was the responsible government agent for the future well-being of those children. I interviewed the various extended families and learned that the uncles and aunts of those children wished to raise them with their own children but, given their own meagre incomes, needed welfare assistance to do so. However, the long-resident local priest wished to send them to Mount Cashel Orphanage in St. John's for better educational opportunities. To my surprise, my plea for welfare assistance to allow them to stay with their loving relatives was supported by the Director of Child Welfare in a public wireless announcement and over the volatile and public outbursts of the priest — an astonishing decision at that time to override powerful Church authority.

These responsibilities and decisions were mine — at age 19. I couldn't anticipate that they would provide background and confidence that have been fundamental assets for much of my later life. They also provided the social interaction skills that have been of much use in my research, enabling me to build trusting relationships with resource workers, First Nation members in British Columbia, and rural community leaders.

Back at Memorial in my final year, for my honours thesis I wrote a paper called "Summer Suburbia" that documented the clique formations of the St. John's upper-middle class (of which I was a part) around the yacht club where they had summer cottages. My professors were intrigued by this window on a closed society they had difficulty entering. In response, I became intensely committed to becoming a sociologist. The two sociologists who were my mentors (Krohn and Iverson) had both completed their doctoral theses under the supervision of Don Martindale at the University of Minnesota. I was overwhelmed with gratitude and anticipation when I was accepted for graduate study in the Department of Sociology at Minnesota. I was 20 years old.

A Returning Interlude: The Study of Resettlement in Newfoundland

In the spring of my second year at Minnesota, I received a telephone call from Noel Iverson (who had by then moved to the University of New

Brunswick). He invited me to join him in the summer of 1966 as a co-investigator for a study of the Newfoundland Resettlement Program. Agreeing to do so gave me a primary focus for my research and writing for the next decade.[4]

In the early 1960s, the government of Newfoundland undertook a program known as "centralization." Its declared aim was the elimination of isolated communities by moving their inhabitants to other locations that were said to have more opportunities, services, and jobs, as well as better education for children. A similar perspective dominated the newly created federal Department of Regional Economic Expansion (DREE). Whereas the provincial interest was largely with saving costs and possibly providing better opportunities for rural residents, the federal focus had conceptual underpinnings. It incorporated a theory that economic development occurs at "growth points" where geography and economy coincide to produce economic opportunities and an available workforce. From such a perspective, Newfoundland's dispersed population was seen as an impediment to economic development and the two levels of government combined to create the Newfoundland Resettlement Program with the declared aim of closing up to 700 communities and moving their populations to identified growth centres. Even at the time, the underlying assumptions seemed problematic in the Newfoundland context. The Resettlement Program was based on the assumption that building larger centres of unemployed people would be a significant attraction for industry. This was unlikely given the distance of Newfoundland from any major market and the lack of advanced education and skills that industry needed. The result was that thousands were moved from areas where they were engaged in meaningful part-time work in fishing, into larger communities where they remained unemployed. To monitor this program, the Newfoundland government provided funding to Memorial University's new Institute for Social and Economic Research (ISER). Iverson and I were the recipients chosen to carry out the study.

Our 1966 report, *Communities in Decline*, was published by ISER Books in 1968 and, after multiple editions, is still in print.[5] In our report we were able to speak not only *about* rural residents, but *for* them. Our report argued that lack of adequate information combined with the spread of rumour contributed to mob characteristics of collective behaviour.

Those who had moved almost universally informed us that they didn't want to move but felt forced to do so "because everyone else was going."

Thus began a heady period for me. Over the next two years, the Iverson-Matthews report became the subject of countless Newfoundland news editorials and political commentaries. In many respects I was living a double life. Back at the University of Minnesota I was struggling to complete my master's degree, given the time I had devoted to the resettlement study and its aftermath, and was facing the threat of being dropped from the program because of my slow progress. In Newfoundland I was a feted keynote speaker at a conference on our report and at another entitled "Changing Tides." An hour-long interview with me taken during the latter conference can still be found on YouTube, a medium that didn't exist for decades after I actually gave the interview. If there is one professional accomplishment in my life of which I remain most proud, it is that my work and my words played a noteworthy role in bringing an end to "resettlement" as a deliberate government strategy.

Notes

1.   Marc Bloch, *Feudal Society* (Chicago: University of Chicago Press, 1962).
2.   Numa Denis Fustel de Coulanges, *The Ancient City: A Study on the Religion, Laws, and Institutions of Greece and Rome* (Garden City, NY: Doubleday, 1956 [1874]).
3.   Henri Pirenne, *Medieval Cities: Their Origin and the Revival of Trade* (Princeton, NJ: Princeton University Press, 1952).
4.   For example, Ralph Matthews, *There's No Better Place Than Here: Social Change in Three Newfoundland Communities* (Toronto: Peter Martin Associates PMA Books, 1976).
5.   Noel Iverson and Ralph Matthews, *Communities in Decline: An Examination of Household Resettlement in Rural Newfoundland* (St. John's: ISER Books, 1968).

First Steps Bound for the Smiling Land; Planning the New Campus

Chung-Won Cho

Introduction

One day in June 1958, I saw Lucjan Krause in the physics laboratory at the McLennan Building in the University of Toronto. I was working there as a post-doctoral research assistant to my former doctoral supervisor, Harry Welsh.

"How are you, Lucjan? How are you and your family enjoying Newfoundland?"

"I am leaving Newfoundland and on my way to Windsor to take up a new position at Assumption College, Chung-Won," Lucjan replied, to my surprise. He was one of those very few friends in Canada who remembered my first name correctly and used it often.

He was carrying hand luggage with a tag indicating the destination of "Sydney." My immediate question to him was: "Have you been to Australia this year?"

He said: "No, it's Sydney, Nova Scotia. There is a city named Sydney in Nova Scotia, you should know."

That was the extent of my knowledge of Atlantic Canada.

It was not Lucjan's first visit back to the University of Toronto's Physics Department since he left in 1955. I still remembered reading an advertisement, in the spring of 1955, which was posted all over the department for a faculty position at Memorial University of Newfoundland specified as "Associate Professor of Physics." Along with my fellow students in the research labs there, I was wondering how a fresh PhD could be appointed to a senior faculty position. Subsequently, Lucjan applied for the position when he had finished his PhD thesis and got the job. I learned later that Memorial's faculty salaries were so low in 1955 that a fresh PhD in certain academic areas had to be appointed as an Associate Professor in order to be competitive.

During my early days at the University of Toronto, Lucjan Krause and I were graduate students together under the same supervisor, along

with more than a dozen others. He had been a Polish freedom fighter
during World War II, ended up in England, finished university there,
and got married. He was a PhD student when I arrived in Canada on
Christmas Eve 1953. His wife, Margaret, typed the final copies of my
MA thesis in 1955.

When I saw Lucjan in 1958, he was stopping by Toronto for a while
to work on a research paper with Welsh. He was on his way to Windsor
to take up a new position as head of Physics at Assumption College.

Lucjan was quick to find out that I planned to stay in North America a little longer to get further training in physics research. He decided
to persuade me to go to Newfoundland and take the job that he left
vacant. There was a remote possibility of a research job for me in western Canada, which Welsh was trying to secure for me. Lucjan told me
that he was able to get a research grant and had planned to start a spectroscopy project at Memorial before he decided to move on. Since I was
in a similar field of research as his, he thought I could fit in nicely.

I asked around to find out what kind of place Newfoundland was,
particularly the city of St. John's. To my utter disappointment nobody in
my research group knew anything about the place. To my research supervisor, who was a well-established Canadian of many generations,
Newfoundland was known only as a fishing centre. He thought that a
person had to like the smell of fish if he lived there for a long time. I
learned later that there was one physics graduate student from Newfoundland, David Wood, in the low temperature physics research group
at the University of Toronto.

Even before I gave Lucjan any positive response to his suggestion,
he wrote a letter to Syd Breckon, then head of Physics at Memorial
University. Almost immediately, Syd came all the way to Toronto to
look me over and to persuade me to join Memorial in a couple of
months.

Soon after his return to St. John's, I received a telegram from Syd
with an offer for a position of Assistant Professor of Physics, a two-year
provisional appointment, effective 1 September 1958. I knew the going
salary for a new PhD in Physics. The best deal I heard at that time was
the salary of a fellow graduate of the University of Toronto who received
an offer of an industry position from General Dynamics in the US. He
was offered $10,000 (US) per annum. It was a fabulous salary for a new

PhD. My faculty supervisor, Harry Welsh, told us that it was more than his own salary then. The average starting salary in Canadian university teaching positions was considerably lower. The salary offer I received at Memorial was certainly competitive.

When I received the written offer, I decided to accept it. Although my original plan in North America was to continue my research training until I gained reasonable competence for independent research before returning to Korea, I debated in my mind that I could gain deeper understanding of physics through teaching basic topics for two years, and at the same time I could improve my fluency in English through lecturing. It was indeed a challenge I did not want to miss. After all, it was only for two years.

Shortly after I received the telegram offer, I replied my acceptance of the offer by wire. It was an early July day in 1958. It meant that I had to be in St. John's to take up my job in two months.

I was staying then at a rooming house near my lab and taking meals at a student co-op residence. No furniture or appreciable household goods had to be moved to the new address in St. John's. Not even many books had accumulated during my stay in Toronto. The only piece of furniture I was renting, with special permission from my German landlord, was an upright piano that I used occasionally. Surely, I did not need as long as two months to prepare my move.

That's what I first thought. Life did not turn out that simple.

In the early 1950s only a small fraction of the students at the University of Toronto were foreign students from the Far East. I was the first graduate student from Korea in the Physics Department. Shortly afterwards, the first-ever Japanese foreign student in geophysics arrived. Common ties of language, culture, and academic interests quickly led us to closer friendship. There was also a small but close-knit Japanese-Canadian community of about 10,000 around the city. In the absence of any Korean community, it was only natural that my Japanese friend and I soon became regular social visitors to their homes and their community gatherings.

One thing led to another, and at the time of the proposed move to Newfoundland I had been dating for some time a Japanese-Canadian friend, Joyce (Etsuko Shimano). All available information about Newfoundland pointed to a place that was geographically as well as culturally very distant from now-familiar Toronto-centred Canada. Joyce and I had to have serious discussions. It did not take too long to reach the decision that we should get married before my departure for Newfoundland and start a life together in the new land. Our sudden surprise plan meant much trouble for Joyce's parents. But Joyce was successful in convincing her parents to approve our plan. Now the maddening rush started.

Honeymoon Flight

Our wedding day was 30 August, which meant that my arrival date in St. John's had to be later than 1 September, the beginning date of my appointment. I had to let Syd Breckon, head of Physics at Memorial, know about the delay of my arrival. Syd did not seem to mind, but he was surprised to learn that I would be coming with my new wife. For shipment of our personal effects, including wedding gifts, Joyce's father packed everything, using many blankets given us by friends who believed Newfoundland was a very cold place. All were shipped by CN.

In those days of propeller-driven turbo-jet planes, Viscounts and Vanguards, a flying trip had to include many stops. From Toronto, there was no direct flight to St. John's or Halifax. We decided to have a leisurely flying trip with stopovers at notable landmark cities, such as Montreal, Quebec City, and Halifax. It was thus a special "honeymoon flight" for us. On the island of Newfoundland, our plane stopped first at Stephenville. Our next stop was Gander. As we flew over the interior of the island, we looked eagerly down to get the first glimpse of the land where we were about to settle. Joyce exclaimed, "Look at those lakes! They are like water puddles after a rainstorm!"

We were met at the airport by Syd in his Austin mini and taken to the Newfoundland Hotel. We were told we could stay there for up to a week at the university's expense, and soon moved into a bachelor apartment in Churchill Square.

Thus my brand new job as an Assistant Professor of physics at Memorial University started in earnest. The three-man Physics Department as well as some 90 members of the university faculty soon became my extended family. The student population of 1,000, including those in graduate programs, kept the faculty and a very small number of administrative staff busy.

Initiation at Parade Street

When I was a child, I heard so often from many grownups who talked about changes they witnessed in their lifetime. Their stories were usually about innovations in society, as well as their way of life in general. The stories always sounded exaggerated. However, as I began to reflect about my life at Memorial, I could not help thinking that it has turned out to be the most bizarre story of all.

For me, it was a huge cultural plunge when I made the decision to stay in Canada and have a family. I always had my own idealized fantasy about traditional academic life. I certainly expected many challenges. But had I ever realized how rapidly the whole world was changing then and what all this involved? During my stay in Toronto, I paid very little attention to what was happening in the world outside the Physics Department save sporadic news stories about Korea that were filtered through the North American media. I had followed developments in physics fairly well, but I was totally uninitiated in everything else.

When my wife and I arrived in St. John's, I found myself in the middle of the real world, utterly unfamiliar. Suddenly life became full of challenges. I was constantly seeking advice from newly acquainted friends, particularly Syd Breckon and Corb Noel, then the second faculty member in the department. He was from an old Newfoundland family and a good friend of Mose Morgan, then Dean of Arts and Sciences. He was, in fact, the first member of the Physics Department, appointed even before Syd Breckon.

It was the time when the baby-boom generation was about to knock at the doors of universities. Signs of the sudden expansion of existing universities throughout North America were everywhere, and the explosive creation of new universities in Canada had started. At the same time, spectacular developments in science and technology started to control our lives at amazing speed. And I had to learn all about Canadian political realities vis-à-vis Newfoundland.

When I joined Memorial, I found that there had never been a single member of the faculty who was of non-European descent. I became somewhat self-conscious. In the following year, however, the first East Indian member joined the Biology Department. It did not take too long to transform the university faculty multi-racially, closely following demographic changes in the Canadian population.

Memorial University's main building, two storeys high with a basement, was located on Parade Street. The office of the head of Physics was situated at the west end of the second floor, and Corb Noel's office was nearby, off the first-year general physics lab. My office was not in the main building but at the lower level of an annex to the United Service Organizations (USO) building, the smaller of two buildings situated to the east of the main building: my office was attached to the second-year physics lab. These USO buildings were temporary wooden buildings built by the United States armed forces during World War II, which were then inherited by Memorial University. Some members of the English Department, including George Story, occupied the upper-level offices of the building.

The Physics Department had a part-time secretary, working in the head's office two or three afternoons a week, who provided typing and filing services. Lab instruction manuals and test and exam papers had to be typed by her and mimeographed. No technical assistant was available for the repairs or the construction of lab equipment. Needless to say, many official letters were handwritten. Even purchase orders issued by the university's Bursar for external purposes were handwritten. Since Syd, head of Physics, had some sort of hang-up about using a typewriter, I was able to keep the department's only portable typewriter in my office for my own use.

I still remember seeing one secretary shared by Ray Gushue, President of the university, and Mose Morgan, Dean of Arts and Science. Their offices were adjacent to each other. Their doors opened to their common secretary's office, occupied by Helen Carew.

I was quickly introduced by the head of Physics to the daily routines of being a faculty member at Memorial, as well as detailed departmental priorities. Since membership on the university Senate was limited to deans and heads, Syd Breckon became a direct and reliable source of information regarding all decisions affecting academic policies of the university. My almost-daily sessions with him touched on many topics. And, of course, I heard a lot about Mose Morgan, the hard-working Newfoundlander who became the most important man in the university.

In my first year I taught one second-year course with a lab and a third-year course in theoretical mechanics. I was asked to develop a senior lab course from scratch, and to initiate an experimental research project that was to become a basis for our graduate program, yet to be introduced. If my memory serves me right, I taught eight new physics courses during my first three years of teaching. In addition, I was told that one-third of my time had to be used to serve on various committees, faculty-wide as well as university-wide.

One of the unexpected challenges I faced in teaching the second-year course was that the students had not yet been exposed to calculus. In order to help students understand basic physical terms and concepts with the necessary precision, which were often "contaminated" by the adaptation of popular terms, I had to rapidly improve my communication skills in English and deepen my understanding of their ordinary daily experiences.

I am sure that senior members of the administration must have had some complaints from students at the beginning. Fortunately, nobody told me about them. Much later, Mose Morgan told me about a student who came to the Dean to complain about his inability to understand certain lectures. He knew that student was taking one of my courses. He automatically assumed it was my course. To his surprise, the lecturer in question was not me, but a well-known native Newfoundlander who spoke with a touch of a British accent. It was not a physics course. Apparently, the student had no complaint about me.

We had to rely heavily on internal funding for research. The granting committees of the National Research Council in Ottawa, with minuscule budgets, always had their priorities mismatched against us, favouring better-established universities in Ontario and Quebec. There were no industrial partners, and no private funding of significance.

Fortunately for science departments, we had a Dean who was genuinely interested in building up strong science research bases at Memorial. There was, however, one important factor I had to consider. The university was about to make a considerable financial investment to establish a reasonably sophisticated experimental facility for a particular research area of mine. Under such circumstances, I thought, I had to ensure that the use of the facility would not be terminated through the sudden departure of the researcher. I therefore recommended to Syd that we should seek a second spectroscopist for our faculty before the department took any definitive action to set up a research facility for "high pressure infrared absorption spectroscopy." I was successful in convincing Syd in this regard.

Thus in 1959 we saw an enlarged Physics faculty, adding my former fellow student Jim Hunt, a second spectroscopist from the University of Toronto. That year, Corb Noel decided to take a leave to study at Cambridge University. His *locum tenens*, David Rendell, then a PhD student at the University of British Columbia, also temporarily joined the faculty.

Initiation Process Continues

My professional life unfolded under ever-increasing pressure to bring Memorial to a par with other growing Canadian universities. As I look back at Joyce's and my involvement in the local community during this initial period, I cannot help but think that we arrived in St. John's at the most opportune time. It was indeed our fortune to have received the full benefits of the famous "Newfoundland hospitality."

Soon after our arrival in St. John's, the Chancellor, Lord Rothermere, hosted a fall faculty reception at an off-campus location. All members of the Board of Regents, faculty and their spouses, plus invited guests including members of the cabinet of the Smallwood government, were invited for the occasion. It was one of the most important social events in town. In view of the importance of the occasion, Joyce decided to wear a Korean dress for the reception. Coincidentally, a Korean dress ensemble, which was specially made and sent to her as a wedding gift from my aunt in Korea, had arrived shortly before the reception. It was a rather elegantly conservative, medium-weight silk dress with a black base colour and light flower patterns on it. It was the first time Joyce had ever worn Korean attire. A press photographer who was there took a picture as she shook hands with the host. A large photograph appeared in the newspaper the next day.

At the reception, as I recall, the wife of one of the cabinet ministers approached Joyce gingerly. Fully expecting Joyce to have difficulties with the English language, she spoke slowly and introduced herself: "My name is Mrs. Lewis, L-E-W-I-S. Do you understand what I am saying?" She then decided to quietly move away without carrying on a conversation.

I also remember the office party hosted by President Ray Gushue.

Soon after December mid-term exams were over in 1958, we all gathered one afternoon in a small room on the second floor of the main building. No alcoholic drinks were allowed anywhere on campus then, but the strict rule was relaxed at this special party. There was even a guitar lying on the floor to be used for carol singing. Before we started carols, there was a call for a volunteer to perform. I am not sure exactly what prompted me, but I decided to sing a Korean song using the guitar. It was indeed a very pleasant party.

Doug Eaton, Professor of Physical Education, with the help of his wife Elinor, played an important role in making many new faculty members feel at home. The Eatons actively sought out newcomers and tried to identify existing members of the faculty who might share common interests with them. Shortly after our arrival, Joyce and I joined a small bowling group, which Elinor and Doug organized. We met regularly one evening every week. After a game, we went to the home of one of the members for refreshments. It was indeed a great way to get to know each other. Joyce and I still remember many pleasant home visits, tasting many of Newfoundland's delicacies for the first time.

At the university I heard many faculty members speaking with various European accents and thought that Memorial's faculty was quite multicultural. Of course, there was no other member of non-European origin at Memorial besides me, but it was the same situation in most of the other Canadian universities of the day. Despite the general multicultural atmosphere, there were some members whose views on the future of the institution were stiflingly parochial and provincial. Such views may have reflected the prevailing outlook of the people in general, as we detected quite often from ordinary citizens. Nine years of being Canadians did not seem to heal the strong resentment by some citizens against Confederation with Canada.

Throughout her life, Joyce had been a member of the United Church of Canada, regularly attending Sunday services before we were married. As soon as we got settled in town, one of Joyce's priorities was to decide on her home church. We tried a different church every Sunday. This junket continued for several weeks. During this period, Joyce met Pat, a newcomer from Ontario who was also in search of her permanent home church. Her husband, Blake Hyatt, was a newly appointed pathologist at the General Hospital. Sometime later, Pat and Joyce decided to join a newly organized congregation in the northeast area of the city, St. James United Church. The congregation was then temporarily meeting in the McPherson Academy auditorium on Newtown Road. Don Brown, the minister of the church, knew I personally had no intention of joining the church as a full member. But both Joyce and I were immediately welcomed into the church community. We soon joined the church choir and so did the Hyatts. One thing led to another, and I eventually had to stand in as a choir director. In spite of my lack of experience, as well as my ignorance of church music and service liturgy, the church gave me complete freedom, not interfering with my choice of anthems and special service music.

Science as World Culture?

All faculty members then regularly visited a common coffee room on the Parade Street campus. One spring morning in the last week of lectures for the year 1958–59, I went to the coffee room for a break at about 11:00 o'clock. It was almost empty except for two or three faculty members. Among them I spotted Cater Andrews, head of Biology. When I joined him with my cup of coffee, he said: "Phew! I am glad it is over!"

"What happened?" I asked.

"Today was the time to discuss Darwin's theory of evolution in my first-year course. I knew some students were very nervous sitting in the lecture when I discussed that topic. I always feel so awkward talking about evolution to my first-year students. As usual, before I started the lecture, I told them: 'I am going to discuss the theory of evolution today. If you would rather not stay and listen, you are free to leave.' Nobody left the room this time. Anyway, I am glad this lecture is over for this year."

I looked at him dumbfounded. I did not know biology professors felt so awkward lecturing on evolution. I was well aware of historical conflicts between Christian churches and scientists who contradicted religious dogmas concerning natural occurrences. Looking back, at the time of my arrival in North America I was surprised by the general public's attitude towards science. At best, science was considered as trade skills useful in supplementing and expanding the standard of living of the human physical being, but not an intellectually significant human activity. For a young man full of idealistic enthusiasm who came and expected the land of limitless scholastic stimulation for scientific growth, these local realities were disappointing. I thought then — after all, the science of today was forged out of a European cultural base and people must be proud of that fact. It was puzzling. Why did so many of them seem to distance themselves from scientific constructs of realities or remain outright hostile to science? From my perspective, this contradiction was extraordinary.

Not long ago, Koreans, Japanese, and others in East Asia decided to open their doors to the West and copy European ways of life. Japanese were particularly overwhelmed by the results of industrialization in Europe and accepted and absorbed their intellectual basis at face value. Much of Asia's own traditional culture yielded to the new. Any traditional belief that contradicted the natural laws of science was automatically branded as superstition or exaggerated tales of fantasy, for example, the existence of ghosts and the afterlife, as well as the belief that regular exchanges between human and animal lives were possible at certain times. Newly established schools even downgraded our traditional culture and replaced it with new European-based arts and music. For us, then, literature, philosophy, science as well as arts and music — all from the Western world — became the new culture we embraced. It is therefore not surprising that many of us were so thoroughly converted to the culture of science. We were all dazzled by the fruits of technology that followed.

Life in the Physics Department

In terms of undergraduate degree programs, things are usually straightforward as long as reference points for academic standards are clear. By and large, the department enjoyed autonomy in this respect. The situation was, however, quite different when the possible graduate degree programs and faculty research were to be considered. These choices were highly sensitive to local conditions and momentary expediencies within the workings of the institution. Since the cost involved in such initiatives in globally competitive areas of research in physics of the day was usually substantial, one cannot easily avoid possible conflicts of interest among decision-makers in the university.

Since we considered that the ultimate quality of undergraduate teaching was closely linked to faculty research activities, it goes without saying that the development of an academic department had to go hand in hand with quality research carried out by members of the faculty. The building of a research facility infrastructure thus became the fundamental issue to us.

There was one troubling aspect of our departmental research plan. Syd Breckon was a nuclear physicist trained at McGill, where Lord Rutherford once worked and discovered that alpha particles are helium nuclei. Syd was closely associated with the construction and operation of its proton-synchro-cyclotron. I am sure that he had a certain plan in mind with regard to his future research activities when he joined Memorial University. The Memorial of 1953, however, was not in a position to encourage him to develop research in his own field, which was then considered the most expensive to set up.

From our departmental perspective, it had another important implication. Nuclear physics in general had become the cutting-edge topic since the atomic bomb blasts of 1945 and the subsequent atomic energy developments. In order to develop our own honours BSc program, which compared well with those in other Canadian universities, we could not leave out courses related to nuclear physics. To teach such courses competently, we needed specialists in the field. In turn, active specialists require some research facilities on the spot to keep up with the developments in the field. Even purely theoretical research requires proximity and accessibility to an active group, usually including experimental components.

Earlier, I presented the circumstances that led me to accept the position at Memorial University. I subsequently made the request to the university that led to the appointment of Jim Hunt, my former student colleague at Toronto. My predecessor, Lucjan Krause, had planned to initiate research in molecular spectroscopy at Memorial as early as 1956. He received the first National Research Council (NRC) grant in the department. His research, however, was still in a preparatory planning stage when he left St. John's to assume a new position as head of Physics at Assumption College, which later became the University of Windsor.

My appointment to the department in 1958 therefore provided an impetus for the continued planning of research in experimental molecular spectroscopy at Memorial, albeit in a different direction. The field of experimental molecular spectroscopy has been a focus area of research in Canada for some time; the University of Toronto, University of Saskatchewan, and the Research Council of Canada in Ottawa were historically important centres at the time, having gained considerable reputation worldwide. Above all, the research instrumentation cost for a project, including support facilities, was not considered overly expensive to set up in comparison to other competitive projects, such as nuclear physics research.

As we planned to set up an experimental research facility, it became obvious that we had to build up in-house technical support capabilities, such as a machine shop and an electronics shop. Such support facilities also became essential for the maintenance of our senior-level undergraduate laboratories as we developed more complete sets of experiments.

In addition to support facilities, we also required supplies of unusual substances such as liquefied and solidified gases. Only a small supply of dry ice was available locally before the Physics Department installed local production facilities for liquid air, liquid nitrogen, and liquid helium, manned by specially trained technicians. Other science departments as well as the Faculty of Medicine gradually became heavy users of these cryogenic liquids. The Physics Department had to take the initiative in these developments, which are now considered essential components in so many areas of research and routine laboratory procedures.

Unlike some universities located near highly industrialized centres, we had to prepare for the in-house supply of these essential materials. The implication was that, to ensure research activities in physics and related subjects were reasonably current, Memorial University had to be the sole provider for the start-up costs for the facilities and equipment, as well as the personnel for in-house maintenance. Funds to purchase commercially available ready-made research instruments were usually met by individual research grants distributed annually by the National Research Council in Ottawa.

Research initiatives at the Physics Department thus led to taking steps to establish the basic research support infrastructure at Memorial, which eventually developed into university-wide facilities related to many scientific research projects undertaken by all departments: machine shops, electronics workshops, high-capacity cryogenic facilities including liquid helium production, etc.

The first step in the initiation of support systems took place in 1960 with the appointment of Bill Gordon, a machinist/technician, as well as the installation of a simple machine shop facility within the Department of Physics. A small attic room in the main building at the Parade Street campus became our first machine shop. We also tried to assess university-wide demand for liquid air/nitrogen supplies for research purposes. As the plan for the new university campus on Elizabeth Avenue became finalized, we proposed a small liquid air production machine to be installed in the basement of the proposed Science/Engineering Building, where we planned to have three research laboratories. We were already working in the new Science Building on the Elizabeth Avenue campus about one year before the official move of the university took place.

The use of computational techniques is central to many physics-related teaching and research activities. At Memorial, we regularly taught how to use logarithm and slide rules in our elementary courses. Then hand-held calculators appeared, followed by desktop computers and centrally provided computer systems. These developments have been extremely rapid, with increasing consumer pressure exerted on every one of us.

When I grew up in Korea, we depended on the abacus for elementary calculations. The abacus in common use in Japan and Korea in those days was somewhat different from the ancient Chinese type with large and heavy beads; two round beads at the top and five beads below a divider, forming a vertical column. Our abacus was typically about 16 inches wide, about 2 inches high with more than 30 columns of small sharp-edged beads; in each column, there was one bead above and five beads below a divider. It was light enough to be easily held by a child.

The use of the abacus for additions, subtractions, multiplications, and divisions was considered then as one of the essential skills to be acquired at elementary schools in Korea and Japan. Every school child had to learn the skill for two to three years as an academic subject, involving long and many numerical figures at high operating speeds. Speed competitions were held regularly between expert abacus users.

Then, there was the news story of the invention of electronic computers in the Western world, which could perform computations at high speed. It was therefore not surprising that the news media in Korea started to discuss possible speed competitions between electronic computers and abacus experts during the early days of computer development.

In the late 1940s, I even remember reading a story in a local newspaper that an abacus expert was faster in complex calculations than early versions of electronic devices. While Koreans and some others stuck to the abacus for computations, technology marched on.

The first electronic computer, a second-hand Ferranti machine, was installed in the Physics Department at the University of Toronto around 1955. As far as I know, it was the first computer in any Canadian university. The new device fascinated everybody in the department. It was still vacuum tube technology with a punch-card system, installed in two specially air-conditioned rooms in the department. Transistors were yet to be developed out of known physical properties of solids. No integrated circuits, no hand-held calculators were even contemplated. Computer technology was still in its infancy. Yet, I learned Fortran Format programming language using that Toronto machine, and used it to calculate some parts of my PhD thesis research.

No small university like Memorial could ever think of having an electronic computer even as late as 1959. The best labour-saving computing device available for an average university faculty member, other than a slide rule, was an electric calculator, which was in fact an age-old handle-operated mechanical calculator adapted for electrically motorized movements.

In 1959–60, the Physics Department decided that we should have an electric calculator of our own. A statistics course offered at Memorial already had an array of these calculators in its lab. As a budget item, Syd Breckon allocated $1,000 for the electric calculator. Three models were available: Marchant, Monroe, and Frieden. Companies sent their salesmen to demonstrate. In view of the relatively large sum of money involved, the department spent half a year of trial and discussion before we finalized the purchase of a Monroe machine.

As with the development of a technical support system at Memorial, the need to install a computer also arose from our research activities in the Physics Department. It was therefore not surprising that, initially, a faculty member in our department was closely associated with that development. David Rendell completed his PhD thesis on a topic in theoretical nuclear physics at the University of British Columbia in 1961 and joined the department as a regular member of the faculty in that year. When the time came to consider a possible installation of an electronic computer at Memorial soon after we moved to the new campus, David took a leading role since his doctoral work involved some use of a computer.

The first computer installed at Memorial was an IBM model 1620. Soon David's contemporary, Dr. M. Lal, a PhD in nuclear physics from UBC, joined the Department of Mathematics with the specific responsibility of looking after the computer, as the use of the computer was becoming widespread throughout the university.

In late 1961, soon after our move to the new campus on Elizabeth Avenue, Mose Morgan decided to ask the NRC's advice for future plans in research and graduate programs in science. A committee headed by the then President of the NRC, the late E.W.R. Steacie, himself a chemist, came to visit Memorial. The visiting committee consisted of one chemist in addition to Steacie, a biologist, and a geophysicist. We, the members of the Physics Department, were somewhat disappointed by the fact that the NRC included a geophysicist, Tuzo Wilson, to represent the whole discipline of physics. Their justification might have been that Wilson was then a member of the Physics Department at the University of Toronto, although his section of geophysics was more or less an independent sub-discipline of physics housed in a separate building on the campus.

The NRC committee's report became a blueprint for research activities in science departments at Memorial. For the Department of Physics, as we more or less expected, the report strongly recommended that we should consider initiating research and degree programs in geophysics. Ernie Deutsch was appointed in the department in 1963 to initiate undergraduate as well as graduate degree programs and research in geophysics.

Initially, I resented the hint by policy-makers in the central academic community of Canada that universally competitive physics research could not be developed in a new and geographically remote area of the country like Newfoundland, and that locally relevant applied research was quite suitable for us. I was too young and too much of an academic idealist to agree with such a view. Some researchers, including me, developed a strong dislike of the Ottawa mandarins who controlled Canadian science, because they failed to help small and remote universities engage in basic research of international significance. Be that as it may, even we come from aways get acclimatized sooner or later. Departmental research interests gradually gravitated towards more locally relevant projects within our individual specialties. We then shifted our criticism of Ottawa mandarins. They were ignorant of our needs in this newfound land.

The establishment of teaching and research programs in geophysics in 1963 in the Department of Physics — born out of the NRC's urging — was a major event during the early stage of developments at Memorial. In addition, attempts were made to set up research projects in physical oceanography as early as 1961. But the conditions for the plunge were not quite right for the initiation of such projects until around the second half of the 1970s. The first physical oceanographer joined the department in 1977.

There was one environmental project within the Department of Physics, which I was able to participate in as early as the 1960s. The moratorium on the atmospheric testing of nuclear devices by the superpowers was in force by 1961, although the international treaty was signed about two years later. Radioactive fallout from the materials created in the troposphere was almost immediate following a nuclear test. The continuous fallout from the accumulation of minute-sized radioactive waste materials, originally trapped in the stratospheric region, created considerable public concern. Relatively long-lived radioactive nuclides such as strontium-90 in atmospheric fallout were of particular interest, even after a long period of cessation of the tests. Strontium-90 was a new man-made radioactive isotope, a product of the fission of uranium-235. The half-life of the nuclide is about 28 years, comparable to a human generation. Because strontium is chemically similar to calcium, strontium-90 in atmospheric fallout can be accumulated in human bones, posing potential radioactive hazards for the human body from within.

We also became aware that in St. John's we could have a larger than average fallout rate because of the city's geographical latitude of 47 degrees north. In terms of atmospheric structure we are located directly under the "tropopause gap," where atmospheric mixing takes place between the stratosphere and the troposphere relatively easier than at other locations on earth.

The radioactive wastes driven into the stratosphere as a result of atmospheric tests, conducted to develop increasingly powerful nuclear weapons, first stayed within the stratosphere. They eventually fell down to the troposphere through the gap in the tropopause. The radioactive wastes that entered the troposphere eventually reached the surface of the earth as fallout. Because of the location of the tropopause gap, there was a general concern that St. John's might receive larger than average fallout, and we thought that the actual amount of fallout had to be monitored.

As expected, some preliminary published data by the federal government monitoring group indicated a trend of a higher than average fallout rate in St. John's. We decided therefore to set up a lab to analyze the radioactive fallout in rainwater and air samples as well as in locally produced food such as milk.

The university assisted us in providing a fund to purchase a sensitive radioactivity counter especially designed for low-level beta-counting. Just before we moved to the new campus, we were able to set up a research lab in the basement of the new Science Building and hire a graduate student to work on the project. Although it was outside my own specialty, I decided to supervise a graduate student on the project at the MSc level.

Now, the real story starts. . . .

A Misunderstanding

One day I received a telephone call from Dean Mose Morgan. He requested that I write a non-technical report on the fallout research project. President Ray Gushue wanted it, I was told. I was delighted to receive such a request. After all, it was not every day that a university president with a non-science specialty showed such interest in what a physicist was doing. I tried to write the report as fast as I could and made sure that it reached the President within a couple of days via Mose.

A few days after I passed the report to the Dean, I happened to be in my office between lectures. I heard a knock on my office door. When I opened the door, I was surprised to see President Gushue standing there! Unannounced! I was so startled. After all, I was still a green and junior member of the faculty. He said that he came to apologize for the mix-up he had caused. He was sorry that this misunderstanding caused me to write an unnecessary report. Then he told me what really happened.

One day, in the early 1960s, he had become alarmed by the reported high dropout rates in Newfoundland's high schools. It was indeed an important media story at the time. He asked Mose if any studies had been done on the subject in the university. He admitted that he might have said "fallout" instead of "dropout" to Mose. Mose told Ray Gushue that I was doing the research. He was indeed surprised. Mose told him that he would ask me to prepare a report.

The President was not aware that he had wrongly used the word "fallout" instead of "dropout" until he read my hastily written report. He realized that Mose misunderstood his query, and decided to come directly to me to explain the mistake. He said he felt so bad about creating extra work for me that he had come to apologize.

I was flabbergasted. I was somewhat disappointed by the fact that the request did not come from his genuine interest in our physics project. I was, however, overwhelmed by this gesture, which showed his sensitivity and thoughtfulness in dealing with a member of his faculty. This particular incident is deeply etched in my mind whenever I think about my early life at Memorial University.

My direct contacts with Ray Gushue were not frequent, particularly after we moved to the new campus. I must say, though, that it was indeed my privilege to have known him. He was a straight-talking but extraordinarily warm person. I have fond memories of him, which I still value.

Planning the New Campus, 1958–59

It was quite obvious to me when I arrived at Memorial University in 1958 to teach in the Physics Department that there was a sizable group of visionaries among faculty members, who possessed the necessary determination, energy, and ability to build Memorial as an institution of high calibre. It did not take long for me to identify such individuals, though I found some of them quite parochial in outlook, at least in the eyes of an overly idealistic young person who had just joined the academic life and who believed in the global nature of a university. Still, I found that many things remained to be done.

Ongoing planning had already been undertaken by many academic departments and others for the eventual construction of new campus buildings. I was told that the building plans had been ready for more than a year. Syd Breckon, head of the Physics Department, a professional

engineer, was keenly interested in designing the space for his department in the new Science Building. He spent a great deal of time making
innovative suggestions, including AC and DC electric power for physics experiments and other utility specifications. The building plan for
the departmental layouts looked good when it was shown to me shortly
after my arrival. But when the university celebrated the tenth anniversary of its establishment as a degree-granting institution in 1959, we still
did not know when the new campus would actually be built.

There were repeated requests to the provincial government for the
initiation of the construction of the new campus in view of the rapidly
increasing student enrolment. In the period of 10 years since the inception of Memorial University, student enrolment had increased from 307
in 1949 to 1,146 in 1959, according to the student newspaper *The Muse*
(9 February 1959).

I was told that operating funds for the university were covered by
the per capita post-secondary education grant coming directly from the
federal government.[1] Memorial was then the sole institution in the
province entitled to the federal grant. The situation changed in early
1959. The real cause of this change was actually related to a political
change that had taken place in Ottawa while I was still in Toronto. I
remember it well, as it was my first experience of governmental change
in Canada. It was the first time since I arrived in Canada that the Lib-
erals lost a federal election. In the morning after Conservative John
Diefenbaker claimed a victory, a young Hungarian graduate student, a
former "freedom fighter," told me how impressed he was to watch
government change hands so peacefully without bloodshed.

Unfortunately, Newfoundland's Premier Joey Smallwood could not
get along with the new Progressive Conservative government in Ottawa.
The situation boiled over in the early part of 1959. Smallwood accused
Diefenbaker of violating Term 29 of the Terms of Union, which guaran-
teed sufficient financial assistance to bring the province's social service
standards up to a par with that of Canada.[2] The Premier declared 27
March 1959 as a Day of Mourning to mark a betrayal of the federal
government against the interests of Newfoundland.

Students from Memorial University responded strongly in support
of the Premier, organizing a mock funeral procession, complete with
motorized hearse, followed by students in black gowns and black arm

and head bands. They travelled from the Parade Street campus to the Colonial Building.[3] On the steps of the building, Smallwood gave a fiery speech. At the end, a student shouted: "You don't have enough money now. The death of Terms of Union means no new campus?" The Premier shouted back: "No, you will get your university!"[4]

The Premier was definitely moved by the strong support of the students. Their demonstration was also a resounding success in making the provincial government yield to the university's wish for a new campus. It was the first firm public commitment by Smallwood to promise the start of the construction of the new campus. *The Cap and Gown* of 1959 quoted the Premier: "We're going to start construction of all the buildings together! We're going to start construction this spring! You'll get your university!" After several years of foot-dragging, at last, he gave the university the go-ahead to finalize building plans and work out the details of moving. The Premier turned the sod at the site for the new campus buildings on 23 May of the same year.[5]

Notes

1. Education was a provincial responsibility. "During the 1950s the university received its money from three main sources: the annual operating grant from the province, student tuition fees, and, after 1952, the federal government. Beginning in 1952 the federal government made annual grants available to universities based on a per capita population basis." Melvin Baker and Jean Graham, *Celebrate Memorial!* (St. John's: Memorial University of Newfoundland, 1999), 20. Also K. Brian Johnston, "Government and University: The Transition of Memorial University of Newfoundland from a College to a University" (PhD thesis, University of Toronto, 1990), Table 8.1. Dissertation Abstracts International DAI — A52/11.

2. The conflict between Smallwood and Diefenbaker over Term 29 is described by Richard Gwyn in *Smallwood: The Unlikely Revolutionary* (Toronto: McClelland and Stewart 1999), 217–38; the text of Term 29, "Provision for Financial Review," is on p. 224. See also Joseph R. Smallwood, *I Chose Canada* (Toronto: Macmillan of Canada, 1973), 414ff.

3. *Cap and Gown* (1959), 15, with a four-page spread of photographs of the "'Term 29' Demonstration," 162–65: students carry anti-Diefenbaker placards, such as: "DIEFENBAKER / THIEF N' / FAKER."

4. The reporter of the *Evening Telegram*, 28 Mar. 1959, had a slightly different

version: "One student asked the premier if Ottawa's decision on Term 29 would mean the cancellation of plans for the construction of a new university. 'No!' shouted back Premier Smallwood, 'it makes no difference . . . . You'll get your university . . . and construction will start this year.'"

5.   Photos *Cap and Gown* (1959), 12–13, 17; Baker and Graham, *Celebrate Memorial!*, 29, 31.

Dr. Cho (left) and unidentified colleague using an infrared spectrometer. (*Photo from Memorial University of Newfoundland and its Environs: A Guide to Life and Work at the University in St. John's,* courtesy of Memorial University Libraries.)

III

NEW DEVELOPMENTS

The Science and Engineering building. (Photo from *Memorial University of Newfoundland and its Environs: A Guide to Life and Work at the University in St. John's*, courtesy of Memorial University Libraries.)

The Grand Opening of the Chemistry-Physics Building, 1968

11

Howard Clase

That, at least, is what it says on the plaque on the side of a pillar in the lobby of the building, but I was there, and it isn't entirely correct.

I had joined the Chemistry Department as a junior faculty member in September 1968 as part of the wave of new appointments that occurred when this new building allowed the expansion of the Faculty of Science. Until the previous year all of its departments had been crammed into the original building, which is now occupied by parts of the Biology, Biochemistry, Psychology, and two or three small Arts departments. When I arrived, the Chemistry-Physics Building was starting its first year of full operation and a new building in possession of a full complement of faculty and students must be in want of an official opening.

At the appointed time anyone who wasn't engaged in teaching was expected to be there as part of their duties, but this didn't seem to apply to really important personages: the Honourable Premier was nowhere to be seen.

Whether he was indisposed, had another appointment he considered more important, or just didn't want to attend an outdoor event in pouring rain was never explained, but he sent along a junior cabinet minister to fill in for him. This young man — he was scarcely older than I was — was popularly known as "Young Billy Rowe" to distinguish him from his father, Senator William Rowe.

The problem of the rain was easily dealt with. The ceremony was moved from the exposed front steps to a small landing at the back of the lobby that overlooked what, in those days, really was a breezeway — an open space under a side wing of the building supported by a row of huge concrete pillars, one of which stood just in front of the landing. Here the 30 or 40 members of the dragooned audience stood around protected from the rain if not the breeze, waiting to be addressed by the eminent personage, or at least his substitute.

I well remember Mr. Rowe's opening remarks, which went something like this. "Good afternoon Ladies and Gentlemen," then staring at the pillar in front of him, "I think this is the first time I've been invited to address a post," and after a dramatic pause, "but now come to think of it it's rather like being at a cabinet meeting." After which, no doubt, he went on to praise the provincial government's forward-looking education policy and stress the importance of investment in the sciences for the future of the great province of Newfoundland and Labrador, or words to that effect, but for some reason I cannot remember any other actual details.

Folklore at Memorial, or How I Came to Newfoundland

12

Neil V. Rosenberg

M emorial University's Department of Folklore exists because of Herbert Halpert. Coming to Memorial in 1962, he joined a group of regional literature, language, and folklore specialists in the Department of English, including George Story, E.R. Seary, William Kirwin, and John D.A. Widdowson. They and their students helped pioneer Newfoundland Studies at Memorial. In 1968, when the Department of Folklore was created, Halpert became its first head. I joined him in the fall of 1968, as the department's second full-time member.

In many ways the department still bears his stamp. In this article I give a brief account of Halpert's training, experiences, and accomplishments at Memorial. I also describe how he brought me to Memorial. This is not the first time I have written about Herbert.[1] I count myself lucky to have known this outstanding scholar who was both teacher and colleague.

New Yorker

Herbert Halpert was born in New York City in 1911. His parents were Hungarian immigrants, secular Jews. His father was a schoolteacher. In his teens he became interested in folksong. He learned to sing sea chanties, and eventually owned a mandolin and a five-string banjo. He later said he was "one of the early 'city-billies'," singing folksongs at parties during his undergraduate years at New York University.

There in 1934 he took a folklore course with Mary Elizabeth Barnicle, a charismatic English professor and folklorist who is today best remembered for the recordings she and her husband Tillman Cadle made of "Lead Belly," the great African-American singer and guitarist Huddie Ledbetter. Barnicle encouraged Halpert's intellectual interest in folklore and introduced him to its New York scene. Through her he met the young Alan Lomax, newly famous as a folksong collector. He also met

Charles and Ruth Seeger, composer-scholar parents of performers Pete, Mike, and Peggy.

In 1936 he decided he wanted to study folklore and began work on an MA in Anthropology at Columbia. His advisor was Ruth Benedict, whose book *The Patterns of Culture* was standard reading in American university anthropology courses. His thesis topic was children's singing games in New York City.[2]

In 1937 Herbert got a job with the Works Progress Administration (WPA), a federal agency created during the Depression years to help create jobs for cultural workers, joining their Federal Theatre Project as an advisor on folksong in the theatre. That and scholarships from Columbia kept him afloat as a grad student during a period when the Great Depression was still a fact of life.

Columbia's anthropology program, headed by Franz Boas, pioneered techniques of ethnographic field research, a topic that fascinated Herbert. Another of his teachers was pioneer ethnomusicologist George Herzog. Herzog and Benedict encouraged him to try his hand at field recording folksingers.

Field recording during the 1930s was not easy. The equipment consisted of heavy battery-powered turntables that used large acetate or aluminum discs. They worked like record players, except that the needle cut a groove — the recording — into the record. The discs — record blanks — were heavy and easily damaged.

In addition to toting and operating this gear, the field recordist had to know how to use the microphone. Halpert was hunting for old songs; hence he took his equipment to remote sites in the Catskill and Pocono mountains in New York and Pennsylvania and to the Pines region in New Jersey. The roads were rough, often unpaved; the people he recorded typically lived in modest homes without electricity. They were usually older and had never before met someone who wanted to record their songs.

Herbert turned out to have a knack for field recording. Not only did he learn how to find informants willing to sing, but he also developed a productive personal style of interviewing, a fascinating combination of curt and friendly at the same time. Subsequently he wrote interestingly about his research work and that of others in a series of WPA publications. Recognized for his skills as a researcher, he gained further experience as an ethnographer in 1939 by collecting songs in the southeastern United

States for the Library of Congress and the WPA. Today the field recordings he made during the 1930s are available in digital form from the
Library of Congress.

At Indiana University, World War II

By 1940, when he finished his MA coursework at Columbia, Halpert
had become interested in folktales. That year he began working on a
doctorate in folklore in the Department of English at Indiana University
(IU), studying with one of the world's leading folktale scholars, Stith
Thompson.

An avid lifelong bibliophile, Halpert bought and sold books to his
students, colleagues, and the libraries of the institutions at which he
worked, beginning with IU. Along the way he amassed a splendid personal library, which is now a separate collection at Memorial's Queen
Elizabeth II Library.[3]

As a teaching assistant in IU's compulsory English composition
courses he had his students do weekly essay assignments that involved
collecting and writing about folklore. This was a teaching technique he
would develop and refine during his career, one that enabled him to
collect and teach folklore in a systematic way within the context of the
English courses he often taught.

Teaching brought him in contact with young people of limited means
and rural backgrounds who were often the first in their families to venture into a college education. His training at Columbia had imbued him
with Benedict's idea of "cultural relativism." Collecting folklore from
one's own experience or from friends and relatives was, as Halpert explained in class, a way of showing each student how they belonged to a
culture with history as deep and meaningful as that of any other culture.

This approach succeeded in engaging the interests of students from
rural Indiana, where he started, to outport Newfoundland, decades later.
Coming to terms with folklore from a personal perspective was, for him,
part and parcel of learning how to write.

At Indiana he founded a lively regional quarterly journal, *Hoosier
Folklore Bulletin*. By then the war had begun. He continued to edit it
after 1943 when he was inducted into the US Army Air Corps. He spent
three years in the Air Transport Command, much of it as an Information

and Education officer. During his travels he collected folktales, some of which he published in folklore journals.

It was at this point, in 1945, that Halpert first visited Newfoundland. After duty and in pursuit of folklore in Gander, he met pig farmer, former Barrelman, and future Premier J.R. Smallwood. Herbert recalled, "he told me that there was no point in my collecting folktales because he had already collected them himself."⁴ Of course, Halpert did look further and in later years enjoyed telling this tale about his first meeting with Newfoundland's Father of Confederation.

That same year, back in Indiana on leave, he married fellow folklore grad student Violetta Maloney, who was also on leave (from the Navy) at this time. Out of the Army early in 1946, he received a fellowship from the Rockefeller Foundation that enabled him to finish his Columbia MA thesis.

That fall Violetta, known to all as Letty, took a job teaching English at a liberal arts college in Ohio. Herbert spent the year finishing his doctoral dissertation, a study of folktales he'd collected in 1940, "Folktales and Legends from the New Jersey Pines: A Collection and a Study."

Academic Career

In 1948, as a new doctorate in English with wartime educational administrative experience and a strong publishing record, Halpert was an attractive candidate on the burgeoning academic market. He began his career as Professor and Chairman of the English Department at a small college in rural Kentucky, where he was also head of the Division of Languages and Literature. By 1962 when he came to Memorial, he'd been Dean at another small college, and visiting lecturer at large universities in California, Arkansas, Indiana, and New York.

During these years he established himself as one of the leading American folklorists, publishing extensively on a variety of topics. His graduate training in anthropology and literature, along with natural aptitude for and experience in ethnography and bibliographical acumen, combined in Halpert to produce what was then considered the ideal mix of skills for folklore, a scholarly pursuit just beginning to perceive itself as separate from rather than an adjunct of other disciplines. Recognized for his theoretical writings, he was voted President of the

American Folklore Society in the mid-1950s.

In these years of extensive activity he worked intermittently with the help of Letty and others to revise his doctoral dissertation into a book. This lifelong project received diminishing attention after they came to Newfoundland. John D.A. Widdowson, Herbert's disciple, finally completed it in 2010, 10 years after Herbert's death at the age of 89, one year after Letty's death at the age of 90.[5]

I learned about Halpert soon after starting graduate work at IU's Folklore Institute in 1961. Like Herbert in the 1920s, I'd been a young folk music fan and performer in the 1950s. Again like him, I decided I wanted to study the stuff. Early in my apprenticeship at IU I heard about him: he was a famous folklorist. His dissertation, which sat on the shelves of the Folklore Seminar Room in the library, was often pointed to as a model study, and his notes to the Ozarks autodidact folklorist Vance Randolph's four volumes of folktales were commended to us as the best in folktale annotation.

I also discovered his field recordings when I began working as a graduate assistant in IU's Archives of Folk and Primitive Music (later renamed the Archives of Traditional Music). This magnificent collection of sound recordings had come to IU in 1948 when Halpert's old teacher, George Herzog, moved there. Included were copies of Herbert's New Jersey and New York recordings.

When Archives Director George List put together a demonstration tape with examples of the interview techniques of master folklore fieldwork recordists, the exemplars were Alan Lomax, IU Folklore Institute Director Richard M. Dorson, and Herbert Halpert. All of this piqued my curiosity about the famous scholar, but I heard little about him until 1967.

Return to Newfoundland

In 1962 Halpert, then 51 years old, joined Memorial's Department of English as Associate Professor. He soon introduced folklore into the curriculum and encouraged an interest in aspects of the subject by junior colleagues on the Memorial faculty, particularly John D.A. Widdowson, trained in England as a linguist.

Herbert spent his summers in the mid-1960s travelling the outports with a tape recorder, working with Widdowson and others to collect the old folktales they would eventually publish in *The Folktales of Newfoundland*. They also recorded songs, mummer's plays, life histories, and much else.

During this time of rapid change — road building, resettlement, Canadianization — he was responding to widespread local feelings about the importance of documenting the old ways of life that were disappearing. But even before joining Canada, folklore was highly valued in Newfoundland's intellectual and political circles. On 26 May 1947, at the convention debating Confederation, Smallwood spoke of his vision of Memorial, then a two-year college, becoming a four-year institution that would advance the study of Newfoundland topics, citing folklore as an example.[6]

Halpert's research was welcomed at Memorial. In 1967 the Faculty Council (there was just one then) approved the creation of a Department of Folklore offering a range of degrees. He believed that the recordings and student papers he'd been collecting since his arrival in Newfoundland constituted an archive. The administration considered it a valuable teaching and research asset. But how was he to organize it? To answer this question he embarked on a visit to established folklore archives in the United States. This is when we met.

In April 1967 I was an IU Folklore Institute staff member. Part of my job entailed co-ordinating two archives: the Archives of Traditional Music and the Folklore Archives. Consequently, I was delegated to show Halpert the shop. I was pleased to spend time with this scholar of whom I'd heard so much, and enjoyed talking with him about the nuts and bolts of archives.

After our tour, he recorded an interview with me about archival systems: accessioning, cataloguing, storage, and so forth. He needed to store his tapes properly, saw wooden cabinets we'd had built for that purpose, and asked for plans. I promised to draw them up and deliver them to him at the American Folklore Society meeting in Toronto that fall.

There Herbert spoke at a panel on the politics and strategies of establishing the discipline more firmly in universities. Others on the panel told tales of wheedling department heads, deans, presidents, and regents to insert folklore into the curriculum and folklorists onto the faculty. Halpert painted a very different picture. He said that as of 1 April 1968 he was being given a department. Memorial University had created it for him, along with three levels of degrees in folklore — BA, MA, and PhD.

He explained that the official understanding behind this academic largess was that, because he was the only member of the new department, its graduate degrees would be based on new research in the field and on the research materials he'd collected since coming to Newfoundland in 1962. Teaching would be limited to a few courses taught by him and specialists from other departments, particularly the Department of English. One such specialist was Richard E. Buehler, who had been a fellow folklore graduate student with me at IU.

I gave Herbert the plans I'd drawn up and he told me something of the work on the archive he was assembling since we last spoke. Buehler filled me in on his life in Newfoundland, which he found both weird and exciting. I had no idea that in less than a year I would be joining him.

Joining Halpert

The following summer (1968) my job at IU ended. I was teaching summer school at the University of Texas when Halpert contacted me. A young English professor who'd been teaching a course in folk music at Memorial had unexpectedly left. When Herbert heard I was free, he went to the Dean (there was just one Dean then, Leslie Harris) and talked him into creating a position in the new department — Lecturer-Archivist. I was offered the job. Flattered to be asked, I was happy to have a chance to leave the strife-ridden US with its assassinations and riots to work with this great scholar at a new department in peaceful Canada. I accepted. I was 29 and had never been to Newfoundland.

I returned to Indiana briefly to pick up my family, who'd stayed there while I was in Texas. While loading the car, my wife Ann and I got into a conversation with a neighbour who asked us where we were going. "To Canada," we said. "I'm from Nova Scotia, where are you headed?" "New-FOUND-land," we told her. She corrected us: "It's NEW-f'n'-land."

A first step past the unknown! At least we now knew how to pronounce the name of our new home. Wondering where we would live in St. John's, I phoned Dick Buehler, the only person I knew there besides Halpert. I asked his advice about finding a house. He said the house next door to theirs might be available.

Several years before, Memorial had built a bunch of houses in several east end St. John's subdivisions for rental to faculty members. The idea behind this scheme was to give new faculty members time to find permanent homes. The Buehlers were in one of these university houses, on Fox Avenue, a new street north of campus. Memorial leased these homes on a strict yearly basis. Dick told me his neighbour was ready to move into a new house but couldn't break Memorial's lease. Would we be interested in taking it over for the remainder of the term?

I expressed interest, so a second call was arranged for me to talk with the neighbour, geologist Michael G. Rochester. He described the house to me — a three-bedroom split-level with ample front and back yards. I asked "How about the location?"

"Well," he said, "it's on a paved road." That took me aback — I had assumed that a house in a large city would be on a paved road. What was I getting into?

Working at Memorial

On 10 September 1968 I arrived to begin working in the Department of Folklore. I started teaching at once. The university put us up at the Battery Hotel until our furniture arrived. In an upstairs suite the four of us (our daughters Teya and Lisa were five and three), the dog (a husky), a cat, and my instruments made for a crowded room. While mom, kids, and dog went out to pick blueberries on the Battery, I stayed in with the cat and unwound after class by picking the banjo at full tilt.

In a room across the hall from us was a popular band from Vancouver, the Irish Rovers. They were in town for a series of sold-out concerts. Their new single "Liverpool Lou" was on the radio frequently. One morning during breakfast at the coffee shop counter, a diminutive man sat down a couple of stools from me, pulled out a tin whistle, and began playing a tune. This was Will Millar of the Irish Rovers. We soon fell into conversation. He said they'd heard banjo sounds coming from my room and wanted me to join them for a jam session. I obliged, and that was my first experience with live music in Newfoundland, or anywhere in Canada.

After a couple of weeks we moved to Fox Avenue, which was indeed paved. Higgins Line, the main road leading from the subdivision down to the university on which I drove to work, was not.

My job had two parts. The first was as Archivist in the Folklore Department's new archive. The entire department was housed on the third floor of the Arts and Administration Building, across the hall from the Arts Café, in a large room originally designed as a linguistics lab.

Glassed-in walls divided it into three parts. In the middle was a large space containing Herbert's library and most of the archive files. Letty, who had been on the university library staff, now kept a desk here, her de facto office. She was working for the archive to create a subject file system. There were some other desks for student assistants. On the west side was Herbert's office, which he shared with the department secretary. On the east side was a space devoted to recording equipment with a tiny room at the back meant to be a recording booth. That became my office as Archivist.

The archive didn't get its present name until a month or so after I arrived: George Story, Herbert, and I were huddled outside the east door of the Folklore Department, near the men's room. We'd just finished meeting to discuss a Canada Council grant application that would enable us to hire tape transcribers for the archive. We needed a formal name to fill a blank on the application.

George and Herbert had recently completed work on *Christmas Mumming in Newfoundland*. The archive was filled with research documents — tapes, manuscripts, cards, and questionnaires — related to this amazing folk calendar custom. Now George was using some of this material as he led work on the *Dictionary of Newfoundland English*. He and Herbert, agreeing that the archive's name should reflect this duality, settled on "The Memorial University of Newfoundland Folklore and Language Archives." Then George wondered aloud — "Why archives? It's just a single institution. Let's call it 'The Memorial University of Newfoundland Folklore and Language Archive.'" It was a bold change — linguistic history is on the side of "Archives" — by a man schooled in the thinking of Samuel Johnson and the great language scholars who followed him. In his naming of the institution, Story's logic trumped tradition.[7]

The other half of my job at the Department of Folklore was to teach a yearly course (semesters came several years later), "Introduction to Folksong." For this I shared an office with Dick Buehler and his editorial assistant across the hall from the department, next door to the Arts Café. Its two windows looked south over the main drive in front of the building to Elizabeth Avenue and beyond toward the South Side Hills — a wonderful panorama.

Buehler brought to Memorial the editorship of the American Folk-lore Society's quarterly journal, *Abstracts of Folklore Studies*. Halpert, who although he did no editorial work was listed on the masthead next to Buehler, proudly described *Abstracts* as the first international journal to be edited at Memorial.

From the moment I arrived Herbert taught me informally about local culture as he was experiencing it. He was always doing fieldwork. In 1971 he went into a St. John's hospital for a small operation. He shared his post-op recuperation room with a man from central New-foundland. By the end of their first day together Herbert had learned that his roommate had worked in the woods and knew at least one old logger's ballad. Through Letty, whom I saw daily at the Folklore and Language Archive (MUNFLA), he passed me a message: bring me a tape recorder. I did, and we recorded the ballad and an interview (MUNFLA accession 71-051).

Herbert's graduate students were mainly from rural outport New-foundland, small but important places in the fish business like Elliston, Conche, Moreton's Harbour, and Harbour Buffett. If you think of this large island (world's 16th, just ahead of Luzon, just behind Cuba) as a tiny continent, then St. John's was its Manila, its Havana, its New York or London. Herbert's "townie" (St. John's) students, following the pre-dominant stereotype that associated folklore with outports ("around the bay," "baymen"), said they had no folklore. Herbert told them that "St. John's is the biggest outport."

Nevertheless, like most folklorists at that time, he focused on the hinterlands where the oldest and most interesting folklore seemed to persist. Today we're grateful for this emphasis on finding and recording the outport old-timers who preserved the old ways, for ultimately it led to the great collection of folktales, to mention just one example.

But in spite of trips to the outports, our lives unfolded in St. John's. Its largest business was Memorial, which at the end of the sixties had grown by 300 per cent in three years and was polyglot — not only with people from every corner of the island, but many young new faculty members from all over North America, Europe, and beyond.

This was a time of intense cultural education for all involved — for me particularly with regard to music. As I began teaching the folksong course, I consulted with Herbert about local traditions. I've mentioned that he owned a banjo and a mandolin. However, I never saw him play them. His days as a folk music enthusiast were long gone, even though he taught well about it and could, when opportunities appeared as in that hospital room, collect and study it.

I quickly learned from him and my students that in rural Newfoundland, instruments (usually accordions) were associated with dance music. Singing was usually unaccompanied — old ballads from the British Isles or new compositions like them. The only exception was country music with its guitars, generally viewed as an unwelcome incursion from international popular culture and therefore rarely collected or studied. Rock and roll was dismissed as kid stuff.

From a professor's point of view, the older songs were easier to teach about, particularly because they often had cognates in hinterland musical traditions elsewhere. But I was not just interested in studying the history of texts. I wanted to learn how things worked in their cultural context, as musical systems.[8]

Like Herbert, I owned a banjo and a mandolin. I had been following folk music since my early teens, and by the time I came to IU was deeply involved with bluegrass, a form of country music with folk music connections. Elsewhere I have written in some detail about my dual experiences as an apprentice scholar at IU and an apprentice country musician at Grand Ole Opry star Bill Monroe's country music jamboree park in Bean Blossom, Indiana. My activities as a musician, unlike Halpert's, grew and continued.[9]

Herbert and Letty, knowing I was an active musician, introduced me to their son Nicholas. A guitar-playing teenager, he was deeply involved in the local folk music scene. Letty told me how he and two other young folksingers from St. John's had, the year before, represented Newfoundland in song at Expo in Montreal. Nick was a big fan of singer-songwriter Fred Neill, and was already composing award-winning songs.

He introduced me to his musical friends. Acoustic folk rock was their popular music, and they could be heard performing it at several local coffee houses as well as on campus. Just before I came to St. John's I'd been in a folk rock band led by fellow IU folklore graduate student Peter Aceves (Narváez), playing mandolin with his new compositions. This was an exciting new direction for my music. When I arrived in St. John's, I found it fit in with the folk rock music scene. It was rewarding to perform and jam with new friends among the local coffee house performers.

Although I'd played bluegrass professionally in Indiana, I set this aside for the time. Both bluegrass and folk rock were genres in which voices and instruments combined; there wasn't a lot of difference between them in some ways. I kept in practice with bluegrass banjo playing, got to know bluegrass musicians in the Maritimes, and began publishing articles and album notes about bluegrass history.

In 1971 Ann and I, along with folklore grad student Shelley Posen and local singer Mary McKim, started Sneed Hearn and the Smiling Liberators, a band that played a mix of bluegrass and folk rock. We played downtown bars, university lunch hour concerts, and other local events like Memorial University Extension's Kite Festival.

In 1972 I met Ted Rowe, who'd just returned to Memorial after graduate studies on the mainland to join the faculty of the Department of Psychology. Ted had grown up listening to and playing country music on the guitar in Heart's Content, Trinity Bay, and was starting to play bluegrass. In 1973 we decided to form a band. Ted suggested the name, the title of an old fiddle tune known everywhere in Canada and particularly popular in the Far North: "Crooked Stovepipe." At first the band included Shelley and Ann from Sneed Hearn. Since then, several generations of musicians have played with us. In 2013 Ted and I celebrated our 40th year with a retrospective album (our fifth) launched at the LSPU Hall in downtown St. John's.

One of our goals in starting this band was to include in our repertoire bluegrass versions of popular Newfoundland songs and tunes. In that time of what Sandra Gwyn called "Newfcult" we wanted to make a statement about local culture in our own musical voice that combined singing and instruments. Over the years we often played at the annual Newfoundland and Labrador Folk Festivals at Bannerman Park in downtown St. John's.

Throughout my teaching career I studied and taught classes about issues of musical tradition. Halpert encouraged me to give papers on Newfoundland topics, and his example as a fieldworker motivated me to conduct extensive research during the 1970s in the Maritimes on the relationships between folk and country music. Musical experience informed my scholarship. I also continued to write about bluegrass, from a new perspective created by new research and distance from the scene

I'd been immersed in at Bean Blossom, Indiana. Today my 1985 book *Bluegrass: A History* is still in print and often described as the definitive work on the subject.[10] In 1997, I received a Grammy Award for my brochure accompanying the Smithsonian/Folkways reissue of Harry Smith's recording, *Anthology of American Folk Music*.

Writing is one thing, teaching another; throughout my career I taught a wide variety of courses, and this eclecticism was reflected in the broad range of essays in a book dedicated to me by former students and friends, both scholars and musicians, in 2005. Edited by my colleagues in the Department of Folklore, Martin Lovelace, Peter Narváez (who came to Memorial in 1974), and Diane Tye, this substantial book — *Bean Blossom to Bannerman, Odyssey of a Folklorist* — was a surprise presentation at my retirement party.[11]

Among those at the retirement party when this wonderful gift was given were Letty and Nick Halpert. Their presence reminded me that day of how deeply Herbert's work affected my career.

Accomplishments

Mine was the second festschrift published by the department; the first was *Folklore Studies in Honour of Herbert Halpert* (1980), which I edited with Kenneth S. Goldstein.[12] Its collection of essays, which the volume's dedication called "a small step towards honouring one of North America's leading folklorists," reflected the diverse group of academic friends and students he'd known over a career that connected him with scholars in Canada, the US, and the British Isles.

Herbert's office door was always open for students, friends, and colleagues. He enjoyed being consulted by all and sundry about research in progress. In his early years the Institute for Social and Economic Research was located in the same building as the English Department, and he'd gotten to know the young anthropology post-docs, who discussed with him their research in small communities in rural Newfoundland. Mumming emerged as a common theme. A symposium was suggested, ultimately resulting in *Christmas Mumming in Newfoundland* (1969), the first book to emerge from Halpert's work at Memorial.[13] It was a collaborative affair assembled with George Story's elegant editorial guidance, containing essays on the topic by anthropologists and folklorists.

It received many favourable reviews and helped to make mummers and mummering cultural icons in Newfoundland.

Others have chronicled the growth of the department and his research.[14] Here I touch only a few high points. In 1973 Herbert left the headship to become Henrietta Harvey Professor of Folklore. By the time of his retirement in 1980, he'd been involved in the creation of the Folklore Studies Association of Canada and seen Memorial's graduate program with its growing faculty attract students from across Canada and elsewhere. Folklore degrees are given by a relatively small number of universities and colleges; the combination of this fact with Herbert's renown began drawing students to Memorial from all over North America, Europe, and beyond. Today Memorial graduates play a prominent role in the international folklore scene.

Halpert continued to work in his book-filled office on campus after retirement. His magnum opus, published in 1996, was a joint work with Widdowson, *The Folktales of Newfoundland: The Resilience of the Oral Tradition*.[15] It embodied the meticulous research techniques he'd developed and practised over a lifetime, with field-recorded texts, informant biographies, linguistic analysis, and exhaustive annotations tracing and explaining the history and meaning of each tale.

Although the study of folklore emerged in the European romantic nationalist movements of the late eighteenth century, in his work Halpert strove to move beyond local, regional, and national politics to develop and teach ways of documenting traditions of everyday life in a precise and scientific manner. His experience in dealing with the politics of culture began early in his career. By the time he'd arrived in Newfoundland he was able to focus on his research and avoid enthusiasts, revivalists, and popularizers, for all of whom he had little patience.

He did have patience for interested students, and trained many who followed in his footsteps. From his youthful start at the forefront of his generation of folklorists, he knew the value of encouraging budding scholars. His publications, still widely cited, set examples for many. In his later years these and his other professional accomplishments were recognized with honorary degrees from Memorial and the University of Sheffield, and in membership in the Order of Canada. Ultimately his greatest honour rests in the continuing existence and growth of folklore studies in Canada through Memorial's Department of Folklore.

In my 37 years of working and teaching in the department I met many bright young students and got to know stimulating faculty members. I am sustained still by what I learned from, with, and for them. I'm particularly proud of contributions to public life in Newfoundland that grew out of my courses.

The "Music and Culture" course, begun in the 1970s, led incrementally to the creation of today's graduate degrees in ethnomusicology, supported by the Memorial's Centre for Music, Media and Place, a research facility with public outreach programs that include a diverse range of academic forums and musical performances.

I spoke earlier of Herbert's lack of patience with enthusiasts, revivalists, and popularizers. My perspective as an archivist led me in a different direction. I believed that MUNFLA should not just be a resource for scholars-in-training but also an accessible public repository. Enthusiasm, revival, and popularity are inevitable cultural responses to the valorization of local culture; it's our responsibility to provide stewardship for the public use of our research data. In the 1980s I began teaching a graduate seminar, "Public Sector Folklore," that dealt with such issues. It helped pave the way for the creation of the post of Intangible Cultural Heritage (ICH) Development Officer for the province of Newfoundland and Labrador, the only such office in Canada.

It's gratifying to know that Newfoundland's cultural traditions are better understood and celebrated today through these public-oriented institutions that grew out of the work at the Department of Folklore.

Notes

1. See Neil V. Rosenberg, "Herbert Halpert: A Biographical Sketch" and "The Works of Herbert Halpert: A Classified Bibliography," in Kenneth S. Goldstein and Neil V. Rosenberg, eds., *Folklore Studies in Honour of Herbert Halpert: A Festschrift* (St. John's: Memorial University of Newfoundland, 1980), 1–13, 15–30; Rosenberg, "Herbert Halpert 1911–2000," *Folk Music Journal* 8, 2 (2002): 256–58.

2. For Halpert's personal account of his interest in studying folklore and his early fieldwork, see Herbert Halpert, "Coming into Folklore More Than Fifty Years Ago," *Journal of American Folklore* 105 (1992): 442–57.

3. "The Herbert Halpert Folklore Collection," Memorial University, Queen Elizabeth II Library. At: http://www.library.mun.ca/qeii/cns/special/

Halpert.php.

4. Herbert Halpert, "Preface," in Gerald Thomas and J.D.A. Widdowson, eds., *Studies in Newfoundland Folklore: Community and Process* (St. John's: Breakwater, 1991), xiii.

5. Herbert Halpert, *Folk Tales, Tall Tales, Trickster Tales, and Legends of the Supernatural from the Pinelands of New Jersey*, ed. J.D.A. Widdowson (Lewiston, NY: Edwin Mellen Press, 2010).

6. J.K. Hiller and M.F. Harrington, eds., *The Newfoundland National Convention, 1946–1948. Debates, Papers and Reports*, vol. 1 (Montreal and Kingston: McGill-Queen's University Press, 1995), 580–81.

7. See Herbert Halpert and Neil V. Rosenberg, "MUNFLA: The Development of a Folklore and Language Archive at Memorial University," *Laurentian University Review* 8, 2 (1976): 107–14; and Halpert and Rosenberg, "Folklore Work at Memorial University," *Canadian Forum* (Mar. 1974): 31–32.

8. Neil V. Rosenberg, "Introduction to Folksong," in Bruce Jackson, ed., *Teaching Folklore* (Buffalo, NY: Publications of the American Folklore Society, New Series, 1984), 139–49.

9. Neil V. Rosenberg, "Picking Myself Apart: A Hoosier Memoir," *Journal of American Folklore* 108 (1995): 277–86.

10. Neil V. Rosenberg, *Bluegrass: A History* (Urbana: University of Illinois Press, 1985).

11. Martin Lovelace, Peter Narváez, and Diane Tye, eds., *Bean Blossom to Bannerman, Odyssey of a Folklorist: A Festschrift for Neil V. Rosenberg* (St. John's: Memorial University of Newfoundland, 2005).

12. Kenneth S. Goldstein and Neil V. Rosenberg, eds., *Folklore Studies in Honour of Herbert Halpert: A Festschrift* (St. John's: Memorial University of Newfoundland, 1980).

13. Herbert Halpert and G.M. Story, eds., *Christmas Mumming in Newfoundland: Essays in Anthropology, Folklore, and History* (Toronto: University of Toronto Press, 1969).

14. Martin J. Lovelace, Paul Smith, and J.D.A. Widdowson, "Introduction," in Lovelace, Smith, and Widdowson, eds., *Folklore: An Emerging Discipline. Selected Essays of Herbert Halpert* (St. John's: Department of Folklore, Memorial University of Newfoundland, 2002), ix–xxi; Jeff A. Webb, *Observing the Outports: Describing Newfoundland Culture 1950–1980* (Toronto: University of Toronto Press, 2016), 145–98.

15. Herbert Halpert and J.D.A. Widdowson, *The Folktales of Newfoundland: The Resilience of the Oral Tradition* (New York: Garland, 1996).

Philosophy Down to Earth at Memorial

F.L. (Lin) Jackson

13

I grew up on Newtown Road, a half block from the old Memorial College, but it was not until I was 25 in 1953, having worked for some years as a meteorologist and air radio operator, that I signed in at the college as a first-year Arts student. I had somehow come to feel a pressing "need to know"— to know *what* I had no idea. I took first-year English, history, physics, French, and Greek and even "went to London to see the Queen" as a Canadian Navy officer cadet. I even met my wife to be, Marion: a lovely, exciting year indeed. But though fully enjoying the whole first-year academic experience, I knew it wasn't enough. I wanted to know . . . *everything*!

In 1955, married, and my employer, Air Canada (TCA), having moved me to Halifax as a flight dispatcher, I immediately signed up at Dalhousie with the notion that maybe psychology would satisfy this uncertain urge (isn't *it* about "everything"?). It didn't. But on attending elective seminars in philosophy under James Doull and George Grant, I finally found myself totally smitten. Philosophy! This was it!

Yet, for practical reasons, I felt obliged to soldier on to graduate degrees in experimental and clinical psychology, did a Dutch "doctorandus" at Utrecht, and for a time thereafter practised as a clinician. But my heart was not in it. So finally, to save my soul, I signed up with the philosophers for a second graduate degree at Dal, then transferred to the University of Toronto to do the PhD, planning a thesis on nineteenth-century philosophy under the tutorship of a distinguished Hegelian, Emil Fackenheim.

And then, who should knock on the instructors' room door at Toronto one day but Norman Brown, for some years Memorial's lone philosopher. He had received an offer from Queen's in 1965 that gave him freedom to devote himself entirely to his special scholarly interests, and was seeking to replace himself (if that were even possible!) and a colleague, Douglas Odergard, who had joined him only in 1963. Enrolment at Memorial was burgeoning, department heads given free rein to enlarge their staffs and programs. So Norman had been given the go-ahead to hire three philosophers to re-staff the Philosophy Department. I of course jumped at the chance.

For the headship he had already sought out an English Thomist, J.G. Dawson, who, for some reason he refused to make clear, was known to all as "Peter" (*Petrus illegitimus*, we would teasingly call him). A man of excellent reputation, he had been a visitor at Memorial a couple of years before. He also met another (now thankfully defunct) Memorial cultural criterion.

Denominationalism still ruled the roost in Newfoundland education, no less at the Memorial College than in the public school system, where educational policies were subject to vetting by a council of three Department of Education gentlemen representing the three main local Christian denominations. The Rhodes Scholarship, for example, was awarded to an Anglican student one year, a Catholic the next, and then to a "Protestant: Other" the next. The selection of faculty, too, was subject to the same principle with the aim of maintaining a rough three-way denominational balance in professorial hirings. When it was proposed to add a philosopher to Memorial's faculty, it was insisted this person be Catholic since that would ensure familiarity with the standpoint of St. Thomas Aquinas, the thirteenth-century thinker whose works the Roman church had officialized as having set a theological limit to the scope of philosophy itself.

As unduly censorious as that practice might seem today, the administration could not have made a more excellent choice in selecting Norman Brown as Memorial's first philosopher. Though specialized in the work of St. Thomas Aquinas, he was broadly read in the Greeks and the Moderns and became well known and admired on campus as a true intellectual: broad-minded, eclectic, popular, patron of the fine arts. He was to have considerable influence upon developments in the Arts and Sciences as Memorial moved to become a full degree-granting university. On moving to Queen's, he would become internationally known as an authority on Thomistic philosophy.

So given the go-ahead in 1965 to re-staff the Philosophy Department and having already lined up Peter Dawson, Norman had flown to Toronto to offer me a position as number two. I have no idea of the why or whence of my being recommended, but I suspect the novelty of my being a *Newfoundland* philosopher (then a rather rare species) may have had some influence. The next couple of years saw Peter and me sharing the initiative of extending the philosophy program and finding new faculty. Space was very limited on the new campus. We were at first settled four to a room in the gymnasium, then for a few years crammed in the Arts building while awaiting more generous quarters in the temporary buildings. We then occupied Building 10, along with faculty from Classics and Religious Studies, until the early nineties when the Arts Annex was finally completed.

In what follows I would like to identify two general factors requiring our consideration as Peter Dawson and I sat down to come up with a relevant, down-to-earth program in philosophy appropriate to the situation at Memorial. The first question was how to deal with certain significant debates going on within philosophy itself at the time. The second was how we could co-ordinate our offerings with those of other departments in the Arts faculty, especially the social sciences, though this latter attempt brought into play my own views on certain local cultural issues.

At Toronto I had become vividly aware of the extent to which certain radical counter-philosophical arguments, originating in the nineteenth century and casting doubt on the very legitimacy of speculative thought, had achieved predominance on the menu of universities worldwide. By the twentieth century these arguments had morphed into distinct schools, generally distinguishable into positivist and nihilist, roughly reflecting the reactionary/revolutionary wars that paralyzed the century. "Positivism" denies the validity of any and all conceptions that do not refer strictly to "positive" fact, i.e., empirical data. "Nihilism," on the contrary, denies the validity of *all* pretense to objectivity due to the sheer, impassable limit imposed by the ineluctable subjectivity of the existential "I."

Both agreed that any speculative inquiry seeking to discover and disclose intellectual or ethical principles underlying human experience must be regarded, not just as nonsense, but *absolute* nonsense, i.e., nonsense in principle. But, we philosophers might object, the claim that empirical knowledge is alone valid cannot itself be established *empirically*; nor is the existential claim that an objective knowledge is impossible one that is *subjectively* obvious. In short, any and all such anti-philosophical doctrines are *themselves* philosophical.

As these schools of thought became predominant in universities through the century, it became a burning and divisive question among academic philosophers as to whether, or at least how, their subject should henceforth be taught. If philosophy is about ideas, and ideas are only unscientific trash in our heads, why continue teaching the Greek greats who started it all (*philo-sophia* — "the craving for knowledge"), or the later Enlightenment thinkers who invented modernity and its principles of ethical freedom, scientific certainty, and the rights of individuality? Should we join the "postmodern" revolution and teach how philosophy has shown itself to be nothing more than existential nonsense or else based on a clear misuse of language? Nietzsche, after all, had announced that God is dead and so likewise is Truth, while across the Channel, Bertrand Russell, A.J. Ayer, and others had declared all philosophical propositions invalid that could not survive the empiricist "verification principle." Or as Louis Macneice saucily described their position:

> Good-bye now, Plato and Hegel,
> The shop is closing down;
> They don't want any philosopher-kings in England,
> There ain't no universals in this man's town. *(Autumn Journal*, Canto XIII)

This issue of the relevance or meaningfulness of philosophy preoccupied the professoriate everywhere, dividing departments and confusing curricula. Academic philosophers found themselves obliged to keep up with the authors of these contradictory and destructive critiques, even while paying grudging respect to the historical greats like Aristotle, Spinoza, Locke, or Kant. According to the new dogma, if the teaching of traditional philosophy is worthwhile at all in a postmodern world it is, as Derrida put it, only as writing its own obituary, clearing away the rubble of its own ruined foundations, and speculating as to what it must mean now to live and think in a post-philosophical world.

Peter and I were of one mind, however. We had no wish to see this intra-philosophical squabble come to dominate our plans for an extended philosophy program. With Newfoundland youth finally having free access to their own full-range university education, we felt it our first obligation to emphasize the broadly humanistic-universal, ethical-intellectual outlook that it had always been the traditional interest of the teaching of philosophy to provide.

The second issue in regard to redesigning our department's program had to do with the changing status of philosophy within the Arts faculty. Traditionally it was a required subject, introducing students to the basic logical, epistemological, metaphysical, and ethical elements and presumptions implicit in all human inquiry as such. But this had all changed. Over the course of the twentieth century a succession of strictly empiricist sciences of things human — psychology, sociology, anthropology, etc. — appeared on the scene. These new "human sciences" were seen as wholly superseding the older philosophical approach to such matters, the latter seen as no more than so much meaningless speculation. As a consequence, philosophy lost its privileged role as the "science of science" to become a mere optional choice for those who, for some reason, still found "meaningless speculation" interesting!

Of these new human sciences, the one with which we philosophers became somewhat involved at Memorial was anthropology. Early on we shared a group of offices in the Arts Building with members of the then young Department of Anthropology and so got to attend the introductory seminars of new appointees, shared speakers, debates, etc. My own office lay across the hall and it seemed that every time I looked up I would catch well-known anthropologist Raoul Andersen staring back at me. My mistake. It was just a habit of his to stare into space when pounding out his fascinating articles about Newfoundland on a noisy typewriter (remember typewriters?). Moreover, Peter Dawson and the new head of Anthropology (Robert Paine) had become friends, the latter spending a good deal of time visiting our digs, sitting in on our seminars, ever trying to wise us up to the new reality that philosophy's days were over.

It was clear the special mission of Memorial's anthropologists was to initiate and promote the extensive study of "Newfoundland Culture," characterized as unique even though there was little idea locally that there even was such a thing! I never quite knew how to react to this idea; half of me respected scholarly work in principle, welcomed new ideas, and shared an interest in Newfoundlanders' history and manners. My non-academic half, however, as a colonial boy born under Responsible

Government and having lived and worked all over the island, was somewhat skeptical regarding what those who had "come from away" might
wish to tell us as to who we really were and what our past and present
life was all about.

The idea that life in the Newfoundland outports gave evidence of a
highly unique culture soon caught the public's attention and aroused a
healthy renewal of interest in our history and manners, a new pride of
place and peoplehood. The local youth in St. John's were happy to act
out the role social scientists were to script for them: dressing like fisherfolk, uttering exaggerated versions of the outport lingo, and, at local bars,
offering honorary citizenship to tourists with nerve enough to kiss a raw
cod. *Evening Telegram* columnist Ray Guy coined the term "Newfcult"
to describe the English-murdering, cod-kissing delights of the Duckworth Street rubber-booters. A lovely word![1]

But of course it reeked of ambiguity. Representations of Newfoundland manners and traditions on the part of some social scientists either
did not ring true to a native eye, ear, or memory or were simply false.
One visiting anthropologist, for example, described "mummering" as
the symbolic dissolution of people's past year's identities so that fishing
captains might freely pick next year's crews without prejudice; another
described a "scoff" (a hearty social fun-feast) as an act of rebellion
against the local merchant involving raiding his field of turnips. Nonsense. We cringed at such ridiculous caricatures of outport life that
ignored what we locals vividly knew to be integral to it, e.g., a simple
sense of civility, a deeply religious perception of life, the attachment to
"old country" manners, customs, and speech. The new mythology would
instead make Newfoundland's fisherfolk over into pristine nature people or unlikely revolutionaries who, were it not for evil governors, etc.,
would surely have built Jerusalem in this not so green and pleasant land.

A related vignette: during the halcyon days of the local anthropological gold rush, my wife and I were invited to a large gathering of
visiting anthropologists, concluding a major conference on Newfoundland's "cultural heritage." We noticed that we and another H-dropping
neighbour had been the only Newfoundlanders invited and the only
ones sitting on chairs! As the evening progressed we realized the real
reason for our presence was not as friends or academic colleagues, but as
specimens: as live cultural data! This realization evoked giddy reflections

on our part as to just who was observing whom. In any case, we speci-mens spent the rest of the evening observing the curious traits of *homo anthropologicus*: their floor-sitting habits, pseudo-nativist garb, etc. But this raises an epistemological question: is it really possible to divide humanity into culture-bound specimens and culture-free observers? What if the specimens should become observers, or the observers specimens? Does being a specimen preclude objectivity? Is theoretic detachment a prejudice? Is "social science" itself a cultural phenomenon? From a phi-losopher's viewpoint such questions are not at all trivial!

A book I wrote later toyed with the image of a stream of enthusias-tic social scientists having headed for the outports in their Land Rovers encountering a parade of young outporters heading into town in second-hand pickups.[2] What I meant to convey was the contrast between the Newf-cultic account of local history and culture and a realistic sense of who Newfoundlanders actually were and where they were headed. We were not "noble savages"; our history was the history of the British Empire; our government, customs, slang, and religious life reflected that of the "old country," i.e., England and Ireland. Our education (at least in the towns) was based on the model and texts of the English school sys-tem. Newfoundlanders knew their island as a historical and present link — technological, cultural, and commercial — between Europe and the Americas, and this, too, was a factor in our cultural self-consciousness and pride of place.

Ever a modest people, Newfoundlanders aspired to civility. The focus of the educated was always on the larger world beyond the peasant-like situation that somewhat still obtained in the smaller outports. In the absence of advanced educational institutions, those who would pursue a higher education or a profession were forced to leave the country, to the detriment of the society they left behind. Given this situation, the open-ing of Newfoundland's very own degree-granting university was to have an enormous impact. A new spiritual dimension had been added to an otherwise truncated culture, and this, we thought, imposed a special obligation on those intellectuals who would now propose to provide it.

I emphasize that my own public views on the Newfcult issue were always presented as those of a concerned Newfoundlander, not an aca-demic philosopher. But our debates with the anthropologists did help convince us that the likelihood of philosophy electives ever turning up in social science programs was very slim; the prejudice that philosophy was so much outdated, unscientific nonsense was just too general in that quarter. So we turned our attention in a different direction. In addition to a traditional program of first-order philosophy courses in logic, metaphysics, ethics, history of philosophy, etc., we would offer a series of second-year "contemporary ethics" courses of practical interest to students in the various professional schools. This worked very well; the schools bought right into the idea. Peter had introduced himself to those in charge of their respective curricula, suggesting the addition of a second-year philosophy course specifically addressed to the logical and ethical issues peculiar to their chosen fields. He was most successful in this and eventually on our syllabus appeared a list of second-year ethics courses tailored to the interests of the various professions: medicine, engineering, education, nursing, social work.

Resolved not to encourage current philosophical biases to take root, we deliberately sought out people varied in their interests and not dogmatically attached to some contemporary school. Among Peter's first choices were Floy Andrews Doull (logic, Descartes), a former Louisiana Dominican sister who had "jumped the wall" to specialize in philosophy and whose popular course in formal logic was the first video version to be presented at Memorial. Then August Wiedman (aesthetics), a patriated German artist versed in the philosophical greats. Then Vance Maxwell, a Spinozist out of Nova Scotia, and Michael Langford, an English Anglican priest out of Cambridge. Later came Les Mulholland, a resolute Kantian; David Thompson, a graduate of Louvain; and Tyrone Lai from Hong Kong, interested in the philosophy of science.

At peak enrolment in the seventies we were able to hire several two-year visitors, one of whom, Peter Harris out of Cambridge, stayed on permanently to represent our interests at Corner Brook, later joining us on the main campus as my successor as head. Two former Newfoundland students, John Scott (the Greek greats) and Toni Stafford (German idealism, Kierkegaard, et al.), both bearing degrees from Edinburgh, would return to join the staff. John was to take on the headship after Peter Harris; and Toni, the first woman graduate of the department to receive a doctorate, would be in charge of our graduate program well into the next century.

Our degree program in Philosophy itself was accordingly so structured at both the undergraduate and graduate levels as to take advantage of our staff's widely differing interests. It was divided into three streams — the philosophical greats (hello again, Plato and Hegel!); philosophy of science; and ethics — which gave each faculty member plenty of opportunity to hold forth on her or his favourite theme. Each of us would contribute to the teaching of our popular interdisciplinary courses while ensuring ample opportunity to develop our own particular specialties in junior, senior, and graduate classes and seminars. Accordingly, unity and rapport reigned in the department, not only on the job but socially. Some were known for their extracurricular talents: August Wiedman, a sculptor himself, would give illustrated public lectures in the fine arts; Leslie Mulholland, an actor on the local stage, was an Aikido expert, as was Michael Langford, who was also a part-time priest.

Floy Andrews, who on arrival fell in love with rustic Newfoundland, bought a house and meadow in Clarke's Beach where she grew potatoes and raised chickens and cows. She married my beloved mentor, philosopher James A. Doull, former chair of Classics at Dalhousie, and earned herself the title "The Goat Lady" on the CBC TV program *Land and Sea*. Summertime, we would all come down to her farm to grill burgers and "make hay" (in the fall, literally!). She and James rank first among Marion's and my very best lifelong friends.

The atmosphere of co-operation and mutual respect that obtained among members of the department in those days was, in my view, unusual. There was little sign of competitive animosity, noisy or quiet, among the scholars on our faculty, as is typical, or at least not uncommon, in many academic institutions. All seemed, on the contrary, to affirm one another. This meant a lot of social goings-on. Peter Dawson early set the scene with frequent all-invited get-togethers at his home up until his retirement after five years as head. He was an exceptional host, not only in the memorable feasts he served up at his home, but in how he could make you feel you were part of a worthy enterprise. He had a way of instilling in everyone a sense of intellectual camaraderie, which was unusual but necessary to the type of program we taught.

By 1990, the countercultural heyday and the Cold War were over. The universities were on tight budgets everywhere and hiring cut short. "Downsizing" had become a troublesome issue at Memorial and the question whether cutbacks might be necessary, especially in the Arts, was for a while worrisome. But I had retired happily in 1993 to winter snobbishly in Mexico and to return full time to my own primary scholarly interest, which had long been the philosophy of G.W.F. Hegel and the nineteenth- and twentieth-century reaction thereto. I was able to publish a number of papers on that topic for various philosophy journals, including the journal *Animus*, which Floy and I had founded. Any acquaintance with, or involvement in, philosophical goings-on at Memorial since has been at best second-hand. At the time I joined the staff of the new university in 1965, the question whether indeed philosophy could any longer legitimately be regarded, or regard itself, as either science or art was very much in the air, even among contemporary philosophers themselves. My former colleagues and I, however, had taken some satisfaction in the conviction we had answered this question positively, not just by providing for more or less traditional BA and MA degree programs in Philosophy itself, but by offering a wide range of logical, epistemological, and ethical courses specifically aimed at bringing "the science of everything" down to earth for Memorial's professional students.

Notes

1. Ray Guy describes himself as "a child of the Newfcult Renaissance" in "On the Newfoundland Renaissance," *Evening Telegram*, 24 Apr. 1976, reprinted in *Ray Guy: The Revolutionary Years* (Portugal Cove-St. Philips, NL: Boulder Publications, 2011), 366. Guy is responding to Sandra Gwyn's "The Newfoundland Renaissance," *Saturday Night* 91, 2 (Apr. 1976): 34–48.
2. F.L. Jackson, *Surviving Confederation: A Revised and Extended Version of "Newfoundland in Canada"* (St. John's: Harry Cuff Publications, 1986).

Sowing the Seeds of Memorial University Botanical Garden

Howard and Leila Clase

It was in the fall of 1968 that Howard first visited Oxen Pond. He had recently arrived in St. John's to take up a faculty position in the Chemistry Department at Memorial University and a colleague, Allan Stein, offered to introduce him to the Newfoundland outdoors by taking him fishing. At that time, it was possible to drive down to the head of the pond from Mount Scio Road along a rough track. They unloaded his canoe from the roof of his car and spent a fruitless hour or so out on the water. This turned out to be the only time Howard has ever been fishing on a Newfoundland pond, but far from the last time he visited this particular pond, which became part of our lives. In those days, his main hobby was birdwatching and, recognizing the potential of the area as a convenient, nearby site for birding, he soon became a regular visitor.

The track down which we had driven had once given access to a lawyer's summer home[1] from the 1920s, the foundations of which were still visible at the top of a steep rise just beyond the head of the pond to the left of the main track. After that, it continued straight up the hillside to a small, sheltered level area beneath the rocky outcrop, which also had foundations, but of more modest dwellings. There were other signs, such as rusty bedsprings! These had been from the country cabins of some St. John's families that were destroyed in the fire of 1962. A narrow valley containing a small stream that led down to this tiny plateau from the northeast had been dammed in the early days of the Botanical Garden to create a small, deep reservoir, which could act as a source of water in case of a fire. This reservoir remains although it is rather overgrown. The larger house had a small stream running nearby that never seems to dry up, which we presume was their water supply.

There was still one inhabited building along the track within the present area of the Botanical Garden. On the descent from Mount Scio Road to Oxen Pond, a spring in the bank on the right-hand side near the bottom now flows into a rock-lined basin. This spring was the water supply for an elderly couple who lived year-round in a one-room shack opposite the spring. Howard occasionally met one of them carrying a bucket of water across the track when he passed down it. This dwelling had been abandoned by the time the Botanical Park was established. Unfortunately, a quiet track in the woods just outside the city attracted not only naturalists and fishermen but also those with garbage and old furnishings for whom the city dump was inconvenient. The woods, particularly on the lower side of the track, were full of rubbish.

The middle section of this track, from the present Cottage Garden to the lawyer's house foundations, remains. If you look carefully you can still see the route it formerly took among the trees at either end.

At about this time the provincial government was considering setting up an "Oxen Pond Biological Reserve" in this area and was in the process of acquiring land. It handed this project over to the university for implementation. As a first step, a 2.5-acre site to the southwest of this track was taken over by the Biology Department in 1968. After a short-lived biology research project on part of the site[2] it was decided to set up the area as a Botanical Park.

By this time, we had moved from our rented university house on Meighen Street to a bungalow on Gleneyre Street in what was then the independent community of Wedgewood Park. We had been told of this house by our new neighbour, Bernard S. Jackson, who was already a natural history friend. His first career had been as a gamekeeper in the UK, but his interests were far wider than what were needed for that job. He was an all-round naturalist with a special love for butterflies; a photographer; and a keen gardener, with a particular interest in alpine plants. Most of this was self-taught. He had first come to Newfoundland in 1958 and had had several contractual jobs related to wildlife, one with the Hudson's Bay Company and others with the provincial government. A trail in Butterpot Park was named "Jackson's Walk" after him — we don't know whether it still exists. He returned to the UK for a short while to work with the Royal Society for the Protection of Birds and to marry Olive, one of the daughters of the Edinburgh family who had fostered him after his childhood in Lancashire. Then he returned to Newfoundland to serve on the "Newfoundland Land Use Survey." This job involved his becoming familiar with many remote areas, both on the island and in Labrador. However, in the early 1970s his contract was at an end, and the Jacksons had bought their tickets to return to the UK.

Only a few weeks before his departure, someone in the university administration had put two and two together and offered him the job of developing the Oxen Pond site as a "Botanical Park." This botanical garden and nature reserve would have a particular emphasis on indigenous plants. As neighbours and friends of the Jacksons we were aware of the general drift but were not personally involved in these early stages, much of which we learned about only later.

The first job was to clear up the land. Right from the start Bernard had an unconventional approach to any sort of construction work. Instead of using heavy machinery he persuaded the university administration to buy a large, strong horse, Charlie, who did far less damage to the environment in dragging out the garbage from among the trees and grubbing up stumps to clear paths than any yellow-painted machine would have done. Board and lodging were found for Charlie with Aly O'Brien, whose family farm was just down the road. At this stage Bernard was assisted by Gerry Yetman, who had worked there as a summer student in 1971 and joined as a permanent employee responsible for outdoor construction and management in 1974. Another inspiration was to involve local people as much as he could. As well as Aly, he hired two young men from nearby on Mount Scio Road as labourers. By getting local people involved in this way he hoped he would have the community on his side and suffer less from vandalism, a hope that was largely realized. Once Bernard had moved onto the site he was responsible for security and used to patrol the wilder parts of the park with his large black dog (first, a Doberman and then a black Labrador) at odd hours, sometimes to the consternation of berry pickers and courting couples, who had unknowingly strayed within the boundaries where they were not well marked. On one occasion, though, when he came across a group of teenagers, their protestation that they didn't know they weren't supposed to be there wasn't very convincing as they had just climbed over a six-foot, chain-link fence!

Once the area was cleaned up, cunningly winding trails were constructed throughout the wooded area in such a way that they seemed a lot longer than the distance actually covered and passed through as wide a variety of habitats as possible. Regrown boreal forest areas were regenerating after a fire in 1962 that had burned over about half of the hillside.

While there was no real bog, a fen (more fertile than a true bog) was fairly extensive, into which the provincial flower, the pitcher plant, had to be introduced as it did not occur naturally anywhere in the park. Two breakwaters of dumped fill, covered with enough soil to enable indigenous plants to grow, were created in the pond: a short one from the southeast side to protect the head of the pond where the ducks now gather and a larger, curved one from the northwest side, creating a large sheltered lagoon in which water plants like cattails could be grown. The larger one soon became home to a colony of the introduced but widespread green frog. Eventually, a small number of pinioned ornamental ducks were brought to the pond for a few years, but these days the resident population is free-flying and feral if not fully wild, including from time to time some interesting wild ducks that are attracted to the pond.

Over the years, signs of human occupation have slowly disappeared. One that had already disappeared was a small sawmill on the western side of the pond, which Aly told them about when they were planting some poplars and native hazels and discovered a deep layer of sawdust. A few garden stragglers hung on around the lawyer's house for many years. Howard remembers seeing clumps of Canterbury bells and daffodils until relatively recently, but now only a patch of that most tenacious of plants, rugosa rose, still flowers in the area. These original trails have been improved and slightly modified over time, but the basic plan is as it was laid out in those first few years.

Meanwhile, work was also going on up nearer to Mount Scio Road. The original house was renovated as the manager's house and Bernard and his family moved in there. A greenhouse was constructed adjoining the house at the back and the foundations of a rock garden for Bernard's beloved alpines were laid alongside it. This arrangement meant that the electricity meter on the end of the house could only be approached by climbing up over the rocks. Bernard frequently related how one day he went out to find the meter reader carefully treading on his precious plants. In response to the burst of invective that Bernard was capable of in such circumstances the man replied, "I'm sorry sir! But I knows it was the rock garden and I didn't want to damage the rocks!" Eventually the house's foundations were found to be wanting and it was removed, although the greenhouse and a much-extended rock garden are still there. The replacement director's house, which was built closer to the

Field Centre, now serves as additional office space and as a base and lunchroom for the outside workers.

As the horticultural aspects developed, further professional help was required. A young horticulturist, Dianne McLeod, became the third full-time employee. Even before the greenhouse, a number of cold frames and a pit house were constructed in an area down below the house, where the "Wild Life Friendly Garden" is now. The pit house, a kind of underground greenhouse, was dug back into the slope so that while the door was at ground level, the bulk of it was underground, giving the plants within some protection from the frost. The roof of the pit house and those parts of the sides above ground were of greenhouse glass.

Bernard was a master of making maximum use of meagre resources; the headquarters building was largely built by his own staff without involving "Planning and Works." We are not sure how he managed to avoid this red tape, but it almost certainly saved a lot of time and money. He also decided to tap into the enthusiasm and spare time of interested volunteers, even at that time known as "Friends of the Garden." When the park was opened to the public, initially at weekends only, volunteers helped staff the desk and walked the trails to provide some security. Leila was part of a trio that also included Alice Park, who lived nearby on Mount Scio Road, and Sylvia Cullum, a well-known art restorer living in St. Phillips. They helped Dianne with potting up seedlings, planting out annuals, and weeding the rock garden. Guided nature walks were scheduled, and Howard was asked to lead a Sunday morning bird walk. Since birds begin their activities as soon as it gets light and are most active just after dawn, we wanted to start as early as possible and decided that 7:00 a.m. would be a good compromise between what birds and people thought was a good time to get up on a Sunday morning. However, when very few people showed up, we soon changed the time to 8:00 a.m. After a few years, we switched to the fortnightly schedule that continues to this day, now in partnership with other birding "Friends." In those early days, Dr. Peter Scott led a few Wednesday evening wildflower walks, too. These became part of the now extensive interpretation program that the Botanical Garden offers, which had begun even before the park officially opened when Bernard started taking groups of schoolchildren from the Catholic School Board around the area.

Initially, then, the "Friends" were a group of volunteers with no formal structure. Organization came later when it was realized that an incorporated body could raise funds independently and tap into sources that the Garden itself, as part of the university, could not access. What had been a "Botanical Park" with a manager and a staff of two has become a fully fledged "Botanical Garden" with two directors — Research and Public Engagement — about a dozen full-time employees, a host of student assistants during the summer, more land, two large greenhouses, a tractor, and a much larger area of cultivation. But the seeds for all of this were sown in the early 1970s when Bernard Jackson was persuaded to cash in his tickets back to England and make his career here in St. John's.

Thanks to Leila, my late wife, for contributing her own memories and for jogging mine; she spent more time up there in the early days than I did. She was a helpfully critical editor and proofreader. Also, my appreciation to Bernard Jackson, Gerry Yetman, Anne-Marie Madden, and Tim Walsh for filling in a few gaps and correcting some vague memories. I apologize if any of the latter still remain. HJC

Notes

1. David Rendell, retired Professor of Physics at MUN, informed us that this belonged to Stephen Rendell, one of his distant cousins.
2. "Report of the Committee of Enquiry into the Oxen Pond Project," Chairman Fabian O'Dea, MUN, 1971.

Business @ Memorial: Reminiscences of Progress and People

Robert W. Sexty and James G. Barnes

The Progress

Although commerce courses were first taught within the Faculty of Arts and Science at Memorial in the early 1950s, during that decade and into the early 1960s the curriculum consisted primarily of courses in accounting and economics. Then President Raymond Gushue sought the input of local chartered accountants, including J.C. Newland of Peat Marwick Mitchell, in establishing the first courses in accounting in 1954. President Gushue also solicited input later that year from corporate and public-sector leaders across Canada in the design of a program of courses leading to the degree of Bachelor of Commerce. Individuals contacted included the presidents of Canadian National Railways, Dominion Steel and Coal, Bowater's, Imperial Oil, and the Anglo-Newfoundland Development Company, as well as the St. John's Board of Trade. Feedback from these organizations was comprehensive, dealing largely with the need for deeper coverage of areas within accountancy, including taxation, as well as recommending the inclusion of a course dealing with "labour problems and employee relations."[1] Even then, a number of enlightened business leaders advised the university to place emphasis on the inclusion of a broader selection of courses. Donald Gordon of CNR, for example, advocated the inclusion of a course in communications, to contribute to "the development of an ability to present concise and lucid written and oral reports."[2]

The university issued a press release on 1 April 1955 announcing the establishment of a course of study leading to the degree of Bachelor of Commerce. This four-year program was designed to "give the students the necessary background in accounting, economics, and business, without sacrificing the broad educational foundation of the standard degree in Arts."[3] In February 1956, J.C. Newland, who had played an important advisory role in the creation of the program, was appointed a visiting lecturer in accounting.[4]

The first two Bachelor of Commerce degrees were awarded in 1957 to Harold Wareham and Clarence Keeping. In 1957, Peter J. Gardiner, a chartered accountant holding an MA from Oxford, became the first full-time faculty member in the Department of Commerce. Part-time instructors during these formative years included the Executive Manager of the Newfoundland Board of Trade (later, University Registrar), Harry Renouf; local chartered accountant James Conway; and lawyer (later Judge) P. Lloyd Soper.[5]

Peter Gardiner continued as the only full-time faculty member in the Department of Commerce until 1963. The faculty complement experienced a significant increase in 1968 when six new faculty members joined, bringing the full-time number to eight. By 1990, there were 40 full-time faculty members in Business Administration.[6] The number of degrees awarded increased to 189 undergraduate and 26 graduate degrees in 1990.[7] The Department of Commerce continued to operate as a department within Arts and Science until 1973 when the program became the School of Business Administration and Commerce, coincident with the establishment of the co-operative program. In 1981, the Faculty of Business Administration was created, with Dr. Barnes as the first Dean, as, by then, the first graduate program in Business had been established.[8]

The Commerce program was housed in the Arts and Administration Building until 1974 in close proximity to neighbouring departments, Philosophy and Religious Studies. The influence of these departments on the Business faculty, or vice versa, cannot be ascertained. A different type of religious influence came into play in 1974 when the school moved to Queen's College, the Anglican theological college. In 1976, the growing school moved to space in a wing of the new Engineering Building.[9]

The year 1979 was memorable because the school moved into its own two-storey building on the North Campus. The faculty quickly outgrew this building and two floors were added in 1987.[10] In addition to increasing numbers of students and faculty, and an expansion of physical facilities, there were many academic achievements during the 1970s and 1980s. Co-operative education was introduced in 1973, following the lead of Engineering and with the assistance and advice of A.S. (Bert) Barber of the University of Waterloo. Memorial's Business School became the first in Canada to establish a mandatory co-op business program.[11]

Planning for a graduate degree in Business was begun in the mid-1970s under Robert Sexty's leadership as Associate Director and the first students were admitted into the MBA program in 1978. Memorial's MBA has always served a majority of part-time students, allowing individuals to complete their degrees while in full-time employment. In 1984, a part-time undergraduate program was introduced to cater to the needs of increasing numbers of part-time students. The first distance education business course was offered in 1980.[12]

Research grants obtained by faculty increased from one for $2,000 in 1976 to five totalling $134,290 in 1990.[13] Course innovations were introduced throughout the 1970s and 1980s to include Business Communications (1971), Business Ethics (1976), Small Business (1979), International Business (1981), Women in Management (1986), and Management and Technology (1987). Program development, research activities, and curriculum innovations led to the recognition of Memorial's Business program across Canada.[14]

During the late 1970s and into the 1980s, the school/faculty grew rapidly in terms of student numbers with a commensurate increase in faculty members. The school continued its innovative approach to business education and to outreach initiatives in particular. With the establishment of the P.J. Gardiner Institute for Small Business Studies in 1978, we became the first Canadian university to create a centre dedicated to the study of small business and entrepreneurship. The Centre for Management Development was established in 1980 to deliver non-credit courses and programs to the local management community.[15] The Advisory Board also was established in 1980, comprised of local and national business leaders whose role was to support and foster the goals and objectives of the school. The Advisory Board played an immediate role in supporting the move to faculty status in 1981. Later, led by Advisory Board members Vic Young and Rex Anthony, efforts to persuade Premier Brian Peckford to support expansion of the faculty were successful, and plans were put in place leading to a doubling of the size of the Business building in 1987.[16]

The Associates Program was established in 1985 to encourage provincial and national businesses to establish closer links to the faculty and to provide a source of ongoing external funding.[17] In 1988, business programs were offered for the first time at Memorial's Harlow Campus.

Starting in 1984, students began participating in national case competitions and were very successful.[18] In that year, an Entrepreneur of the Year award was established.[19] In 1988, following an initiative led by Chancellor Paul Desmarais, the faculty welcomed its first students from China, sponsored by the China International Trust and Investment Corporation.

The People

Throughout the years, many surprising, humorous, and fond memories can be recalled relating to various stakeholders, including colleagues, staff, and administrators.

Because we were close neighbours in the 1960s with philosophers and theologians, Business faculty made friends with these faculty members and some have remained colleagues. One faculty member in Philosophy was an enthusiastic investor and eagerly scanned the department's tickertape stock reports daily.

In the 1960s and 1970s, the department's secretary practised fortune-telling on a Ouija board. The personal fortunes and misfortunes of faculty and staff were predicted. There is no record of how many were accurate.

While we were located at Queen's College, Canon George Earle was Provost. He was born on Change Islands and attended school there and on Fogo Island. In addition to being a well-known Anglican clergyman, he had a reputation as a storyteller. The cafeteria was staffed by women connected with Canon Earle's Fogo roots and experiences. Thus, the cafeteria staff was referred to as Canon Earle's "Fogo women." Canon Earle's stories and the Fogo women's cooking resulted in a sense of camaraderie and good times at coffee and lunch breaks.

Many books have been written by faculty over the years. A colleague claimed for years that he was writing a book on "love." No one had the courage to ask how the topic related to business or management, and the book never surfaced.

Competing for our share of the university annual budget was not always easy. As no significant investment in capital equipment was needed to run the faculty, our cost per student was always at or near the lowest in the university (along with Religious Studies and Philosophy).

The cost-efficiency of the faculty proved a less-than-hoped-for factor in persuading successive administrations to provide additional funding to allow for growth.

Our competition for resources and recognition was made no easier by the attitude of one President who offered the view that he was "not sure there is a place for business studies in the modern university." However, we were exceedingly fortunate in the early years to have the unfailing support of Vice-President and, later, President M.O. Morgan and of a series of vice-presidents (Professional Schools), Angus Bruneau, Ian Rusted, and Al Cox, who never doubted the rightful place of the faculty within Memorial and supported our growth through the 1970s and 1980s. The period of greatest growth in the faculty and in its academic and out-reach programs coincided with the term as Chancellor of Paul Desmarais, who demonstrated interest in and support for the work of the faculty.

No discussion of people is complete without mentioning students who must be given special recognition. Many students who graduated from Memorial's undergraduate and graduate programs in Business between 1957 and 1990 went on to occupy leadership positions in business and management as executives or entrepreneurs, in public administration, in professions such as law and accounting, and in the non-profit sector. They are heads of numerous national and international corporations, public utilities, telecommunications providers, airlines, marketing, and financial services firms, to mention only a few. Others became judges, leaders in community organizations, ambassadors, and even politicians.

Overview

The period between the early 1950s and 1990 was one of impressive growth for what became the Faculty of Business Administration. From the first stirrings of business studies, with its emphasis on the teaching of accounting and economics, to a full-fledged faculty offering a full range of undergraduate and graduate degrees in Business Administration, business studies had truly come of age by 1990. The university had sought input from corporate and public-sector leaders in the establishment of the program and had allowed it to grow and evolve over the years. The emphasis on accounting gradually gave way to a more balanced approach to management education with the inclusion of courses in all other areas of management. Looking to prominent Canadian and international universities as role models, Memorial's Business School set out to become an innovative, community-oriented, outward-looking organization, producing graduates who would go on to leadership roles at home and around the world, contributing to the growth of local businesses and the provincial economy, and carrying out leading management research. By 1990, that goal had been largely reached.

Notes

1. Letter from Donald Gordon, Chairman and President, Canadian National Railways, to President Raymond Gushue, 22 Dec. 1954.
2. Ibid.
3. Press release, Memorial University of Newfoundland, 1 Apr. 1955.
4. Memorandum from the President to the Secretary, Board of Regents, 16 Feb. 1956.
5. Memorandum from the President to the Secretary, Board of Regents, 29 Oct. 1956.
6. Robert W. Sexty and Gina Pecore, "Tracking History and Strategy at Memorial's Faculty of Business," in Barbara Austin, ed., *Capitalizing Knowledge: Essays on the History of Business Education in Canada* (Toronto: University of Toronto Press, 2000), 257–58.
7. Ibid., 257–59.
8. Ibid., 255–56.
9. Ibid., 254–56.
10. Ibid.
11. Ibid., 255–56.
12. Ibid.
13. Ibid., 260.
14. Ibid., 257.
15. Ibid., 256.
16. Ibid., 258–59.
17. Ibid.
18. Ibid.
19. Ibid., 260.

The Division of Junior Studies

Michael Collins

16

The Beginning

My arrival at Memorial in 1969 was, you could say, the result of a chance illness. When I was studying to become a teacher in the UK, the head of the department told us that we shouldn't stay in our first teaching position for more than two years so as not to give future employers the impression that we were stuck in a rut. How times have changed! Having completed my teacher training I accepted a position at a boys' grammar school in Sussex, teaching botany, zoology, and general science. Although I was enjoying my teaching position and wished to remain at that school for the foreseeable future, well through my second year I was mindful of what that department head had suggested. I started to look through the pages of the *Times Educational Supplement* (*TES*) for a temporary position elsewhere for a year or two. I decided that if I was indeed going to take a break from teaching then perhaps I should take the opportunity of working abroad, as a number of my friends had done. I eventually narrowed my choices to three, namely, volunteer teaching in Uganda (as this was in the time of Idi Amin it is probably just as well I didn't take a job there), pursuing a doctorate at a New Zealand university, and Memorial, which had posted a job advertisement in the *TES*. I decided that I would take the first position I was offered.

I had not really considered Memorial as a definite option at that time. When I wrote to get more information about the position, I was notified that Professor John Griffiths, then the director of the new Division of Junior Studies, would be visiting London in the near future to interview interested applicants. The day of his visit was a regular school day and I was loath to ask for a day off to attend a job interview as I didn't want the school to know I was actively seeking a position elsewhere. I put the Memorial letter aside and waited for a response from the other places where I had applied. As it happened, fate intervened. A month or two later I came down with a throat infection and my doctor told me that I should not be in contact with school-age children and should take a week's break from teaching. I decided to spend my week's convalescence at my parents' house some distance from the school. It was while I was there that I suddenly remembered the letter from Memorial that I had earlier set aside. I reread it and found that Professor Griffiths's visit to London happened to be on the last day of my convalescence. I could travel up to London to see him and then take another train back to the town where I taught, ready to start teaching again the next day, and nobody would be any the wiser. As it turned out, the interview was a brief one and when I saw the starting salary being offered, which was significantly more than I was making as a teacher in the UK, I agreed to take the position at Memorial for two years. The next day I informed the school that I would be taking a two-year break from teaching in the UK — a two-year position that, as for many of us, became a 40-year university career. Strange how a throat infection could change one's life so drastically! And the rest, as they say, is history.

The New Division

When I arrived at Memorial in the fall of 1969, it was as a Lecturer in the Division of Junior Studies (a.k.a. Junior Division), a new division set up the previous year as the result of a Senate Committee's investigation into high first-year course failure rates.[1] (Senior Division was the term applied to the regular courses above the first year.) The new Junior Division employed experienced high school and college teachers, many of whom came from the Newfoundland high school system or from the UK. Classes were relatively small, usually around 36 (24 or so for Foundation courses). As a 1982 publication explained:

> The Division of Junior Studies provides an introduction to the different learning environment of university and, as such, its first concern is to ease the difficult transition between high school and university education. This problem is confronted in a number of ways, for example, by providing an opportunity for students to catch up in areas they may have missed in high school, by ensuring limited class size, and by the provision of instructors especially interested in teaching first-year students.[2]

The 1970–71 Junior Division calendar lists some 69 full-time instructors in subjects including biology, chemistry, English, French, German, history, mathematics, physics, and science. In addition to these full-time instructors there were part-time and sessional instructors, as well as a number of Senior Division faculty, who also continued to teach first-year courses. The director of the division when I came to Memorial was Professor John Griffiths (Department of Chemistry), and he was followed the next year by Dr. Arthur Sullivan (Psychology), who later left to become the first Principal of the new Sir Wilfred Grenfell College in Corner Brook. He was succeeded by Dr. Keith Winter (Chemistry).

The division was responsible for the Foundation Program as well as the First-year General Studies program. Grade 12 was introduced in the Newfoundland high school curriculum only in the mid-1980s. Not all students were prepared to begin the study of courses in each discipline, either, because they had not attained a sufficiently high level of achievement in the high school course to succeed in the regular university course, or had not taken that subject in high school. For example, at that time, not all students had the opportunity of taking subjects such as chemistry or physics in their schools and, thus, did not have the necessary background to start a regular university course in that discipline. For such students special preparatory courses were offered in biology, chemistry, English, mathematics, and physics. These were one-semester courses that did not carry university credit.

Later, Intermediate (or "fat") credit courses were introduced for those students who were not quite ready to undertake regular courses but who were better prepared than students taking Foundation courses. These Intermediate courses (or 1200 courses) included background material in addition to the content of the regular first-year courses. They required additional class periods each week, but allowed students to complete the entire course within the one semester. Another important aspect of the division was the attention paid to faculty advising:

> Equally important, Junior Studies carries out a comprehensive programme of student advising, aimed at introducing students to university life. Advisors are available to help students adjust to the new spirit of teaching, learning and study,

and to offer assistance to those who may have problems with career decisions or of a more personal nature.[3]

Each instructor also acted as a faculty advisor to around 20 students in his or her classes, meeting with their advisees five times a semester. Since the student advisees were also members of the advisor's own classes, meetings were relatively easy to schedule and the connection between advisor and advisee was a strong one.

I remember Junior Division as a unit that fostered innovation in teaching and learning practices. New approaches such as the Personalized System of Instruction (PSI) and Computer-assisted Learning (CAL) were strongly encouraged. PSI generally consists of self-paced learning materials divided into modules, each of which must be mastered before going on to the next one. It is also characterized by a lack of lectures and by printed materials as the main form of communication. In CAL the computer is used as a teaching device, and individual students learn material, which is then tested, and feedback is given before new material is presented.

The division was unique in that faculty members from different disciplines were in constant interaction with one another so that the sharing of ideas was not restricted to one's own subject area. This interaction was facilitated, in part, by the close proximity of the faculty members from different disciplines since the division was originally housed in temporary buildings on the site now occupied by the Queen Elizabeth II Library. Coffee breaks in nearby cafeterias further facilitated communication between faculty and staff, as did the monthly faculty meetings since the division had its own faculty council. The division was also noted for its frequent social activities, usually planned by the division's administration. All of these activities and events served to further integrate newcomers into the university community, and into the local community, as many of us were from outside the province and the country.

High School Interviewing

The division also became responsible for the spring high school interviewing program in which (primarily) first-year instructors visited every school on the island to talk with Grade 11 students who had expressed an interest in attending Memorial. These interviewing trips gave us, particularly those from outside the province, the opportunity to meet our prospective students and become familiar with their schools and teachers as well as their communities. It also gave us the opportunity of visiting parts of the province that we might never otherwise have seen. I always looked forward to those school visits, particularly the out-of-town ones. These trips were often accompanied by various unforeseen happenings, such as flat tires in the middle of nowhere; late snowstorms causing school cancellations and forcing us to revise our itineraries constantly; broken-down ferries; and, sometimes, less than ideal accommodations. In fact, spring interviewing was so eventful that it deserves a separate article.

Dissolution of Junior Division and General Studies

In 1984 the Board of Regents approved the Senate's recommendation regarding the restructuring of the Junior Division and the establishment of the School of General Studies.[4] As a result, the Junior Division, as such, was phased out and Junior Division faculty and staff became members of the regular (Senior Division) departments. The administrative aspects of the division were taken over by the School (later Division) of General Studies, which looked after academic regulations pertaining to first-year students, information visits to high schools, and the spring interviewing program. Finally, in January 1994, the Senate voted to abolish the Division of General Studies and most of its remaining functions were taken over by the Registrar's Office.

So ended a unique experiment in Canadian university education. Nowadays, Junior Studies is just a memory as nearly all of those who came to Memorial as appointees to the division and stayed here have retired, and new faculty are not at all acquainted with this distant and distinct phase of Memorial's history.

Notes

1. Arthur M. Sullivan et al., "Report of the Senate Committee on the Feasibility and Desirability of Junior Colleges in Newfoundland," 1966.
2. *Guide to First-year Courses* (St. John's: Memorial University of Newfoundland, 1982), 1.

3. Ibid.
4. "Digest of Senate Decrees and Resolutions, September 1969–May 1992," Office of the Secretary of Senate, Memorial University of Newfoundland, Oct. 1992.

The Queen Elizabeth II Library at dusk. (Photo from *Celebrate Memorial: A Pictorial History of Memorial University of Newfoundland*, originals held at Memorial University Library Archives and Special Collections.)

Bill Pruitt and the Establishment
of the Bonne Bay Marine Station

Don Steele

I n 1957 the world woke up one morning to hear with astonishment that the Russian satellite Sputnik was now circling the globe. Since this was at the height of the Cold War, Western countries, the United States in particular, became rather hysterical with the thought that they lagged behind the Russians in rocketry and in science generally. Thus began the so-called Space Race and, at the same time, a great increase in spending on science. We entered the era of Big Science and money became available for grandiose projects. For example, in addition to the Space Race, there was a proposal, called Project Mohole, to drill to the Mohorovičić Discontinuity, the boundary between the earth's crust and the mantle.

Not to be outdone, biology came up with the idea of the International Biological Program (IBP), in which a major study would be to compare the production and productivity of comparable ecosystems at different latitudes. The expectation was that this would yield an understanding of the biological processes involved. Marine systems were to be included and the Gulf of St. Lawrence was selected as a study site. A ship was chartered to cruise around the Gulf collecting samples. In addition, it was decided that a shore station on the Gulf should be set up so that samples could be collected daily. Probably because of Marshall Laird, who was the head of the Department of Biology at Memorial and also a member of the National Research Council, the shore station was to be established on the west coast of Newfoundland. The next step was to choose a location on the west coast. Accordingly, W.O. Pruitt Jr. and I, in the Department of Biology, were recruited to travel to the west coast to find a suitable site for the field station. We were to accompany the head of Biology from McGill, who was in charge of the Gulf of St. Lawrence study.

Thus, Bill Pruitt and I flew to Deer Lake where we met the head and hired a car. The next two days were spent driving around the west coast between Western Brook and Lark Harbour. At times I felt like I was in an episode of the television series *Twilight Zone* or an Ingmar

Bergman movie. We inspected several houses where the roofs were collapsing, and in Lark Harbour we were shown an idle fish plant that had last been used as a movie theatre. The 16-mm projector sat there, covered in dust, with the film just as it had been left after the last showing. When touched, it disintegrated into small pieces and fell like the leaves of a gingko tree. We finally settled on a house across from the ferry wharf in Norris Point and this is where the Biological Station — now the Bonne Bay Marine Station — is today.

When it came time to find accommodation for the night, Bill Pruitt announced that the Holiday Inn and Glynmill Inn were too grand and that we should find a simpler and less expensive place to stay. This we did. Since the head of Biology at McGill insisted on having his own room, Bill and I shared another.

Bill Pruitt (1922–2009) was a likable and interesting character. He was a mammalogist, who was happiest working in the field in primitive conditions. This is why I believe he insisted on staying in a simple, cheap hotel. Personally I didn't care one way or the other. He was of medium height and stocky. He had deep-set hooded eyes that had spent a lifetime looking for mammals on snow and ice. While at Memorial he had a beard and what remained of his hair was worn very long.

In the morning I was surprised to find that my arms had a number of red welts. I thought no more about it until a large flea crawled out from under my sweater when I was sitting in the back of the car. This I collected and put in a small vial. On my return to St. John's I sent the vial with a letter to the Board of Health, but I never received an acknowledgement. Bill thought the episode quite hilarious, especially as he had no insect bites.

Bill and I drove back to Deer Lake where we caught the plane for St. John's. However, we got only as far as Gander because of the weather in St. John's. All the passengers were bundled into a yellow school bus for the 330-km ride to St. John's. By now it was raining heavily. Halfway to St. John's the windshield wiper gave out. Ever resourceful, the driver and some passengers tied pieces of string to the wiper, which then was pulled from side to side by passengers on either side of the bus.

Meanwhile, the passenger in the seat behind Bill had been consuming a bottle of rum. After a while he became happy and started patting Bill's long hair, which was hanging over his shoulder, and started making comments about how nice it was. Bill was quiet for a while but then exploded, telling the offender to stop or he would put his lights out, or words to that effect. The man was suitably cowed and made only whimpering sounds for the rest of the trip.

We eventually reached St. John's. It was three o'clock in the morning when I arrived at my front door. The house was quiet, and I wasn't sure what I should do since I was afraid I might be transporting more fleas in my clothing. Finally, I decided that in order to enter the house without waking up my wife, I would go in through the basement door. I would also undress and leave my clothes outside. By now the rain had stopped and it was chilly, so I thought this might finish off any residual fleas that I was carrying. Naked, I climbed the basement stairs, only to be met at the top by my wife Vladis, armed with our son's baseball bat. Hearing the peculiar noise, she thought the house had been invaded by a burglar.

Bill Pruitt had come to Memorial after being fired from the University of Alaska.[1] He was one of the academics at the University of Alaska who had studied the area where thermonuclear devices were to be used to construct a harbour on the coast of Alaska. This effort came at the time when the proponents of the peaceful uses of nuclear energy, such as Edward Teller (father of the hydrogen bomb), were desperately trying to find peaceful ways to employ nuclear devices. The program was called Project Plowshare after the widely known prophecy in the Book of Isaiah 2:4, "They will beat their swords into plowshares and their spears into pruning hooks. Nation will not take up sword against nation, nor will they train for war anymore."[2] One big idea was to excavate a new Panama Canal at sea level using nuclear devices. The new canal would be larger and would not have locks. Since there were concerns about the stability of thermonuclear excavations in coastal sites, it was decided that the method should be tested before the canal was excavated. Alaska was sparsely populated and had a long coast line, so attention was focused there. The recently granted US statehood meant that there should be no international complications, although Russia was not far away.

However, the site selected for Project Chariot, as it was called, is only 60 miles from Point Hope, a flat spit projecting into the Chukchi Sea. As such, it intersects the migration route of various sea mammals and has been the site of an Inupiat settlement for thousands of years. Although their existence depended on the sea, the people also harvested caribou. Caribou eat lichens and, since lichens have no roots but are dependent on the atmosphere, they accumulate radioactive ions, which enter the food chain when they are eaten by caribou. Although Project Chariot was supported by the state of Alaska and the University of Alaska administration, the residents of Point Hope together with some academics prevented the project from going ahead. Bill Pruitt and several others lost their positions at the university, and were effectively blacklisted from obtaining US positions.[3] Thus Bill came to Memorial, where he stayed for four years. This is one instance in which Memorial did the right thing. Subsequently, in 1993, the University of Alaska awarded honorary degrees to all those still alive who had been involved in the protest[4] and Memorial followed suit some time later, in 2001.

Thanks to Cheryl Pruitt and Joan Scott for information on W.O. Pruitt.

Notes

1.   Dan O'Neill, *The Firecracker Boys* (New York: St. Martin's Griffin, 1994), 195, 258–59.

2.   Ibid., 25. Holy Bible, New International Version®, NIV® Copyright ©1973, 1978, 1984, 2011 by Biblica, Inc.® Used by permission. All rights reserved worldwide.

3.   O'Neill, *The Firecracker Boys*, 258–61.

4.   Ibid., 265–66; "Delayed Accolades for Alaskan Scientists," *Science* 260, no. 5111 (21 May 1993): 1070, at: http://science.sciencemag.org/content/260/5111/1070.1.

Fire, Floods, and Rumours of a Ghost: Recollections of a Librarian

18

Dorothy Milne

The Henrietta Harvey Library

In 1980, the St. John's campus library of Memorial University was called the Henrietta Harvey Library. It occupied the building that faces onto the original campus quadrangle and still bears the name of this benefactor. As it is not a large building, by the time I arrived in 1980 it was horribly overcrowded. There were stacks with some of the most heavily used books in the basement and a few more stacks on the second storey, but the main level was occupied by staff and service points such as the circulation desk, the reserve room, and the card catalogue. In this pre-computer age, there were banks of wooden catalogue cabinets with drawers full of 3" by 5" cards, which had been carefully typed on manual typewriters by women in the staff area nearby. In one of these rooms, staff (almost all women) sat in rows of desks typing out order forms, accounting forms, book receipt forms, and so forth.

The reference librarians were crammed into an area on the main floor. The ceiling in this area was two storeys high, the architect having decided to grace the building with an atrium. Like all atria in libraries, the empty space above the reference department wasted floor space much needed for bookshelves or student seating, and allowed the noise of ringing phones, staff conversations, and student queries at the front desk to travel with booming clarity into the study areas on the second floor. There were perhaps a hundred workspaces for patrons in the entire building at a time when the campus community numbered more than 12,000.

To house the journals, a two-storey temporary building was built next to the east side of the Henrietta Harvey building and linked to it by a connecting hallway. Most of the library's collection could not fit into the main building or the temporary building. Most of the books and journals were held in a storage facility on O'Leary Avenue. Messengers were sent there several times a day to retrieve items requested by patrons. Along with the inconvenience of having to apply for items and then wait for their delivery, browsing was not possible. This situation was far from ideal. As a result, there was pressure for a new, larger library to be built. Remarkably, the Students' Union (MUNSU) offered to pay a large share of the construction costs from the funds it had accumulated with the original purpose of building a better student centre. In 1978, construction on the new Queen Elizabeth II Library began.

When the Henrietta Harvey building entered its last days as a library, it was showing some signs of age. Aside from normal wear and tear, however, there were two troubling signs. One was the appearance of char marks on bulletin boards. Librarians arriving in the morning would often find little piles of ashes on the floor of the tunnels where someone had lit a small fire. The fire-lighting fad had gone on for months, and now someone was setting fire to flyers tacked to the bulletin boards inside the library. The flames burned the paper away and charred the bulletin board when they reached the thumbtack. This was not a comforting observation in an old building full of brittle paper. The other unsettling aspect was the appearance of critters after dark. Like most libraries at that time, the Henrietta Harvey had a "no food" policy. Patrons were expected to go out to eat. The theory was this: if people ate in the library, food scraps would attract vermin, and then the vermin would attack the books. Whether or not food scraps were the cause, the Henrietta Harvey building had a large population of resident silverfish. As I worked in my office on the basement level in the evening I would see them scurrying across the floor. And if I walked very quietly over to the display case that housed a large historic tome, I could see rows of silverfish nibbling on the margins of its pages.

The Queen Elizabeth II Library

At some time in the 1970s, the Newfoundland government informed the Queen that a new library was being planned for Memorial University and requested permission to name the new library in her honour. The new library was to be five times bigger than the Henrietta Harvey. It took several rounds of discussions with Buckingham Palace before the Queen agreed. The sticking point was whether or not the Newfoundland government could guarantee that it would provide sufficient funds to get the library built to the size and standard proposed. After those conditions were met, the Queen came in 1978 and performed the sod-turning for the new library. Also present was the architect, Charles Cullum. Though Cullum was British-born, he designed many buildings in Newfoundland, as well as elsewhere in Canada and abroad. Another of his noted buildings is the Johnson GEO Centre.[1]

In designing the new library, Cullum consulted with Louis Viagnos, University Librarian at Dalhousie University. Aidan Kiernan served as the government representative on the planning team and later, as a university employee, supervised its construction. Peter Clinton, the head of the Information Services Division, was effectively seconded to the planning process, where he was responsible for a great deal of the detail work.[2]

The QE II Library's ski-slope shape attracted much discussion and spawned a city-wide myth, often repeated by cabbies, that it was built backwards due to some oversight by contractors.[3] To the uninitiated, it seemed logical that the reading room should face south, not north. In fact, the building was designed (as all good libraries should be) to shield books from sunlight damage on the south side, and to let in as much natural light as possible for reading on the north side. Thus, the south side of the building is five stories high and has a long, low horizontal window on each of the above-ground levels. On these floors, strong southern light reaches only two or three metres inside; the stacks are set back by that distance so the direct sunlight does not reach the books. On the north side of the building, each of the top four floors extends further than the one below, providing eight half levels of seating for readers in one large, open room. The windows are as large as possible to maximize the amount of northern light (the best light for reading) available during daylight hours. It is possible to stand on the highest level and look down the full length of the reading room. One unintended consequence of this design is that it quite possibly provides the best paper airplane testing site in St. John's, as students have proven over the years. One intended consequence is that the reading room has floors too weak to hold book stacks. This design was purposeful: to prevent the Library's administration from ever reducing the amount of patron seating in order to accommodate an expanding book collection, as had happened at the Henrietta Harvey Library. Over the next 30 years, the collection grew rapidly and books were once again stored in a warehouse, but not one patron seat has been displaced.

The Move

The library was moved from the Henrietta Harvey building into the QE II Library building in December 1981. Shelving had previously been installed in the empty floors of the new building, but staff furniture, cabinets, etc., and books still had to be moved. The aim was to move these to the new library over the two weeks of Christmas break to be ready for the beginning of the new term in January. An enormous number of books had to be moved in a short time in an organized way so that any title could be located quickly upon request.

It was far from a simple move because two sequences of books and journals — those at the Henrietta Harvey Library and those stored in the warehouse — had to be merged into a single new order in the QE II Library. Under the supervision of Florence Attwood, the head of the Circulation Division and unsung heroine of this task, library staff measured thousands of feet of shelving in the two locations. They measured and recorded the shelf space that would be needed for the books in each small subject sub-specialty in both locations. These measurements were then mapped onto the shelving available in the QE II Library so the two sequences could be merged. The planning was done so accurately that once underway, the move went without a hitch. At every moment, library staff knew exactly where to put their hands on each item that might be requested.

The task of moving the books and journals was assigned to Household Movers. The company had never moved an entire library before. To facilitate the task of moving the books without disturbing their sequence, they designed and built a type of cart that had a frame that allowed the library shelves to be moved without disturbing the books. Six shelves of books could be unhooked from the stacks in one library, hung on the cart, wheeled to the new library, and then detached and hung on the shelving in the new location. Using this method, almost all the books from the Henrietta Harvey building and from the warehouse were moved into the new building by the beginning of the new term.[4]

Some time after the move was complete, the librarians learned that the university administration was impressed that it had gone so smoothly. Apparently, they had expected weeks of confusion into the winter term.

The librarians found this amusing. What is key to librarianship more than specialized training in organization?

Post-move Blues

For several years after the move, the QE II Library was plagued by frequent, unexpected fire alarms. It became clear that this was an unexpected consequence of having a sprinkler system. The fire alarms were set off by sudden reductions in water pressure caused by construction in other campus buildings or repairs to city mains nearby. The reason this happened was that the triggering mechanism for the fire alarm system interpreted any drop in water pressure as a sign there was a fire in the building. Whenever the fire alarm sounded, the librarians and staff first cleared the building of patrons and then left themselves. They had to wait outside for 20 or 30 minutes until the fire engines came, the firemen searched all five floors exhaustively, and finally sounded the all-clear and permitted people to re-enter the building. At first, this was a bit of a novelty and a slight cause for worry, but with time the alarms became part of the routine. They were greeted with a shrug, followed by departure to the Thomson Student Centre for an extended coffee break. No one seriously thought the building was burning up in their absence.

Over the years, the fire alarms did signal the possibility of a real fire in the building only two or three times. Usually, the cause was smoke from a malfunctioning motor in the heating or ventilation system.

While the sprinklers never went off as a result of a fire, they were, ironically, the cause of much water damage to the books and journals. Some fault in their design or manufacture resulted in some of the sprinkler heads going off without warning from time to time, for no apparent reason. The water sprayed from the sprinklers caused a huge amount of damage. Since wet books get ruined by mould very quickly, each sprinkler accident required an emergency response. It was all hands on deck if the accident happened when the library was fully staffed; a telephone tree was set up to summon rescuers to the scene if the accident occurred in the evening or on the weekend. At times there were as many as 15 people working in the library when it was closed, hurriedly locating all the damp books and transferring them from shelves onto carts. The damp books were rushed to a commercial deep freezer facility in town where they stayed for many weeks or months as they dried from the frozen state.

Spend the Money Fast!

In the late 1970s and early 1980s, the library had to build its collection of books and journals from one adequate for a college to one suitable for a university. To build depth in specific subject areas quickly, whole collections of books were bought as job lots on the second-hand book market or from other university libraries. Some of the surprising items in those job lots are still on the library's shelves. Much of the job lot purchasing was over by 1980, but in the early 1980s the library still received large unexpected amounts of money to be spent on books at the end of the budget year. The amount was unpredictable. The President would send a portion of whatever funds had not been spent in other lines of the university budget. A mad scramble ensued to spend the windfall money during the last few weeks of the year. Spending $40,000 one $20 item at a time within two or three weeks was a challenge. Interesting stratagems involving currency exchange and invoice pre-payments were devised. The library's administration had it down to an art. By the mid-eighties, however, the days of year-end windfalls and of buying just about what any faculty members wanted were over.

Cuts, Cuts, Cuts

By the late 1980s, the days of easy purchasing of books and journals were over. A period of increasing austerity set in, continuing through the 1990s and 2000s as the number and costs of journals skyrocketed. The era of journal cuts began, and with it, more difficult relations between librarians and faculty members.

Technological Change

The years between 1980 and 2010 were a period of intense technological change as all aspects of library work were computerized. Over the years, library workers' writing tools progressed from pens, to manual typewriters, to electric typewriters, to desktop computers and laptops, and for calculations, from pocket calculators to spreadsheets. New software upgrades came fast and often. For library users, the card catalogue was slowly replaced, first by microfilm readers and later by computer terminals. It is hard to say who hated the microfilm catalogue more — faculty or librarians. The complaints were many and vociferous. Everyone was glad when microfilm was replaced by the online catalogue.

Coffee Breaks/Fish and Chips/Celebrations

In the 1980s, people working in the library took an hour for lunch and 15-minute coffee breaks in the morning and the afternoon. They enjoyed good food, coffee, and company (and for some, cigarettes) at the cafeteria in the Arts and Administration Building, or the Education Building, or the Thomson Student Centre. Over time, people stopped taking these breaks, working through them at their desks instead. Work in the earlier days seemed to be both more focused (between breaks) and more relaxed socially.

Birthdays, engagements, baby showers, and other events often were celebrated in the divisional office areas, with the women in one staff office providing coffee and treats for staff in other offices. These were occasions for the women to display their remarkable baking and cooking skills, though more so in the 1980s than in recent years. The food in those home-cooked days was delicious.

Larger staff celebrations, such as goodbye parties, were held in the large staff room on level one. At these events, a row of tables the length of the room was set up and filled with dozens of potluck dishes and plates of baked goods. There was enough to feed 100 people or more. Library retirees, family members of the celebrant, and other guests were invited to these events. For many years, the annual Christmas party was held in this room as well. This was a sit-down event and the turkey dinner was catered. The staff room was reduced to half its size during renovations in the early 2000s, putting an end to larger-scale celebrations in the building.

Charity

The staff room was used to stage the library's annual charity sale in November of each year. Along with staff-produced crafts and baked goods and potted plants, there was a jumble sale of clothes, books, and miscellaneous items, some more unusual than others. The proceeds of this sale went to the library's charity, Iris Kirby House, which shelters women and their children experiencing relationship abuse. The divisions competed to see which could raise the most money for this charity each year, with the winners being announced at the Christmas party.

The divisions also competed in fundraising for Kirby House by putting together attractive Christmas baskets full of food and drink and various small ornaments or gift items. Tickets were sold on the baskets.

One unusual source of income for the charity was the collection of dropped coins. Coins found on the floor were put into a jar. By the end of the year, about $80 would have been collected for the cause. In the 1980s, the coins were mostly pennies, but as the 1990s rolled on, it appeared that people now often made no effort to pick up the nickles as well.

The Ghost in the Library

The QE II Library has a ghost. Possibly two. Some people who work in the building after hours firmly believe this. Some security guards who walked through the building at the end of each day have reported sighting it on several occasions. Some of the late-night cleaning staff were most reluctant to work in the library in the wee hours, especially if they were working alone. Undeniably, when the lights were turned off on the upper floors, walking among the stacks could be an unnerving experience.

Some librarians and library administrators were in the habit of working late into the evening. They were sometimes the only people left in the building after the lights had been turned off. Dim back-up lights provided just enough light to move around. On one occasion in the late evening when the library was closed, I rounded the end of the reference stacks on the main floor and suddenly came face to face with a security guard coming in the opposite direction. In surprise, neither of us said anything for a moment. When I finally said "hello," the security guard looked greatly relieved and said, "Thank goodness, I thought you might be a ghost."

Notes

1. Joan Sullivan, "Charles Cullum 86: Architect Changes Newfoundland's Cityscape," *Globe and Mail*, 25 Mar. 2013. A photograph of the Queen "turning the ceremonial sod" is in Melvin Baker and Jean Graham, *Celebrate Memorial! A Pictorial History of Memorial University of Newfoundland* (St. John's: Memorial University of Newfoundland, 1999), 63.
2. Richard Ellis, personal communication, 25 May 2017. Ellis was a Division Head in the library at the time of the events described. He served as University Librarian in the QE II Library, 1982–2007.
3. "MUNsolved Mysteries: Ever Wonder if the Queen Elizabeth II Library Was Built Backwards?" *MUN Gazette*, 28 Nov. 1996.
4. Richard Ellis, e-mail, 30 June 2017.

Queen Elizabeth II turning the ceremonial sod for the new library. (Photo from *Celebrate Memorial: A Pictorial History of Memorial University of Newfoundland*, originals held at Memorial University Library Archives and Special Collections.)

Arts and Administration Building. (Photo from *Memorial University of Newfoundland and its Environs: A Guide to Life and Work at the University in St. John's*, courtesy of Memorial University Libraries.)

IV

NEW ADVENTURES: ARRIVING

The Little Theatre. (Photo from *Memorial University of Newfoundland and its Environs: A Guide to Life and Work at the University in St. John's,* courtesy of Memorial University Libraries.)

Newfoundland's Pull

Raoul Andersen

19

In late August 1966, my wife Irene, our two little children, and I said our goodbyes to friends in Grand Forks, North Dakota, climbed into our 1964 Ford Custom station wagon and began the long drive east to Newfoundland. We crossed the bridge over the Red River into Minnesota, then drove and tented across the state and northern Michigan and on through New England to Bar Harbor, Maine. From there we took the ferry to Yarmouth, Nova Scotia, where a Customs and Immigration official interviewed us. I told him that we were bound for St. John's, Newfoundland, where I was to join the Memorial University faculty for two years and undertake research.

We were surprised when the officer told us we needed some papers to enter and remain in Canada as we planned. (A letter of appointment and our passports weren't enough.) Over the previous three years we had entered Canada many times without being asked about papers. And we had even remained there for several summer months in 1964 and 1965 when I did fieldwork and taught at the University of Alberta. No one at Memorial had informed us about such matters. I don't know why but the officer allowed us to enter on the understanding that we would report to Immigration in St. John's upon arrival there. Crossing the border was much less problematic then.

We continued our drive up Nova Scotia's eastern shore en route to Cape Breton Island and North Sydney to reach the ferry to Newfoundland. I had a lot on my mind, especially fisheries, as we travelled northeast. I had dropped a research opportunity focused on the Great Lakes and looked forward to one in Newfoundland. During correspondence leading up to our departure, social anthropologist Robert Paine, then Director of Memorial's Institute of Social and Economic Research (ISER), had suggested I consider doing a study of either Newfoundland's offshore trawler ground fishery or its whaling industry during my two-year stay at Memorial University.

Whichever I chose would be my first marine fisheries research experience, and I anxiously pursued every opportunity to learn about eastern Canada's fisheries as we made our way. On 3 September I logged the following in my notebook:

> Arrived in area of Blandford, N.S., this day in search of "Norwegian" whaling operation said to be located nearby. While in Bar Harbor several days earlier, met a retired stationary engineer returning from vacation in N.S. He advised me that the N.S. whalers there were taking about 21 whales/month as of June '66.

Going Whalin'

Once on the eastern shore road we had no trouble locating the coastal whaling operation I wanted to investigate. When we reached the village of Blandford I drove down to the open-air slipway and factory at nearby New Harbour, where several large fin whales (the large baleen whale, *Balaenoptera physalis)* were being processed. I found my way to Karl Karlsen, the operation's owner. After some discussion during which he alerted me to the environmental and political sensitivity of the whale hunt there, he gave me permission to join the *Chester*, his whale catcher, early the next morning.

With much of our remaining cash, I lodged Irene and our children in a small nearby motel. My notes record that at 4 a.m. on the next morning, 5 September:

> Arrived at New Harbour whaling station in rain. Squally. Station was bright with large lights used for night processing. One whale carcass was in process. This fin whale was brought in last night at about 9 p.m. by one of the smaller catcher boats. Seas were moderately heavy in the harbour area. The large whale catcher *Chester* does not come all the way into the station with its catch.

At about 5 a.m., two hardy Nova Scotian seamen and I boarded a power dory that took us out to the *Chester*. It stood offshore in the dark with its lights ablaze. Once alongside, we heaved on board the crew's mail, provisions, and several repaired (straightened) harpoon shafts recovered from earlier kills. Then I climbed aboard and began my first real sea experience. We quickly steamed out to the hunting grounds on Green Bank at the tail end of a hurricane. It was a wild ride through the night. Near noon the next day the sea had calmed and the fog had lifted. Soon we had taken three fin whales. They were secured to the *Chester* and we returned to port to land the whales for processing. Upon arrival in the wee hours of 7 September, I went ashore for a while and watched the flensers at work as they stripped the blubber and flesh from the whales.[1]

It was near dawn when I left and drove our car back to the motel where I found Irene and our little children huddled together in bed. Late on our first night out I had used the ship-to-shore radio to call and tell her that the hurricane would probably delay our return for another day. Irene told me how, during my absence, hurricane-force winds and heavy rain had buffeted and rocked the little motel and worried her. The sea-wise motel keeper reassured her that our boat probably had to ride out the storm for a while before getting back. His wife later helpfully observed, "Oh, they just have to ride with the storm a while and then he'll get back." But then she added how she understood Irene's worry because she had recently lost several close relatives in a similar storm.

The prospect of losing a loved one at sea and its impact on a family became a personal and unavoidable part of Irene's and my understanding, especially a year later when I began my research among Newfoundland's offshore fishers. We shared it with them. During my short whale-hunting trip I had met the legendary torment of seasickness common to many seafarers. But I'd gotten over it. The rest of the trip was exhilarating and I regretted leaving the *Chester* and her crew. In those moments I felt ready for whatever the Newfoundland fisheries might demand. Surely the *mal de mer* wouldn't torment me like that again. 'Tis wonderful shockin' how naive one can be. But that's another story.

Later that morning we left Mahone Bay and resumed our journey. We reached North Sydney that evening, boarded the ferry *William Carson* by about 9:00 p.m., found our two-berth cabin, and bedded down with our children — two-year-old Randy and four-month-old Cindy — for a night's sleep. I slept hard that night.

I was eager to reach St. John's and Memorial University. Yet my thoughts were a swarm of ideas and uncertainties. I still knew little about Newfoundland and what Irene and I would face here. And I didn't know how Robert Paine would react when I told him I hadn't completed my PhD thesis. In teaching full-time at the University of North Dakota I had worked hard to do so. It was based on fieldwork with an Alberta First Nation community and it was quite unrelated to what I expected to do in Newfoundland. Once in Newfoundland it took another two years to complete while I also divided my time between teaching courses and researching the fisheries.

What Pulled Me to Newfoundland?

While I was a doctoral student earlier at the University of Missouri, Irene and I were both employed. I taught half-time as an instructor (of sociology) in the joint Sociology and Anthropology Department, and Irene had a clerical job at the state cancer hospital. We rented a small apartment, got by on about $15 for groceries per week, and saved S&H Green Stamps for Melmac tableware.

One day in 1962 a flyer about Memorial University of Newfoundland's ISER pre-doctoral fellowship program caught my attention. Memorial's location and ISER's fellowship program resonated well with my interests in modern North Atlantic fisheries and those who live from the sea. It also fit well with my parents' Norwegian origins. (My father's parents died when he was only about seven or eight years old, but after living on a west coast island near Kristiansund N. [north] with about eight of his siblings, all except the youngest gradually immigrated to the United States and settled in Chicago. He later spent some time seafaring on the Great Lakes aboard coal-fired freighters and tugboats. My mother, also from Norway, was under five years old when she arrived in the US with her mother, father, and an older sister. They, too, settled in Chicago.) I was aware that anthropological studies of modern fishery industries and communities were few at the time. But the advertisement for ISER's program offered a mere $3,600 stipend per year and I felt that, short of a more substantial grant or fellowship, I needed a full-time teaching job and salary to enable my research.

By 1963, I had completed mandatory coursework at the University of Missouri and had a full-time position at the University of North

Dakota. In 1964, a small grant from the National Museum in Ottawa supported a summer of field research in Alberta. Around late 1965 Robert Paine offered me a two-year teaching and research fellowship. Despite a salary reduction it gave me a full year's time for research. I accepted it in the spring of 1966.

I still knew little about Newfoundland and Labrador, Canada's newest province. However, while visiting the University of New Brunswick in early 1965 I met Louis Chiaramonte, one of ISER's research fellows, who was visiting friends at UNB. What he told me about ISER's program was encouraging. On another occasion back in Grand Forks, I happened to tell one of the University of North Dakota's MA candidates in Sociology, Tom Garland, that I was about to leave for Newfoundland. He responded that he was from a fish merchant family in Gaultois, on Newfoundland's south coast. We didn't have time to talk after that so it didn't add much. About two years later I visited Gaultois and, indeed, Garland's was its major merchant. The ISER fellowship fit my interests and Chiaramonte's encouragement helped to pull me to Newfoundland. Chiaramonte and I later became friends and long-time colleagues.

Port aux Basques

It was a calm crossing. Just before dawn the next morning, the loudspeaker on the *William Carson* announced we were nearing Port aux Basques. I went to the main deck's public area, where the atmosphere was a mix of familiar odours: fuel oil, tobacco, coffee and toast, beer, and salt air. I joined the yawning and dishevelled travellers meandering about, many with pillows or blankets under their arms. Others sat or lay about in various rumpled states. Some still slept on the deck, even under tables, or were just crawling out from under blankets here and there. The most bleary-eyed souls had either sat up all night in the lounge where alcohol — mainly beer — was served, or they had made futile attempts to doze on the large reclining chairs misnamed "sleepers." I was glad we had booked a cabin for the crossing. But we were lucky to get one. On later crossings we were sometimes among the sleepless and unkempt.

Now very close to Port aux Basques, I went to the open deck outside. The ship's lights hardly penetrated the fog and mist beyond a few yards. Neither the coast nor harbour was visible until we nosed past the navigation lights leading into the channel towards the ferry slip. Ashore, large lights illuminated a landing zone flanked by rugged, sheer stone cliffs in grey, green, and darker colours. It seemed a very harsh and forbidding coastal environment compared to the Lake Michigan I had known in my youth. What lay ahead seemed more mysterious.

We disembarked and began the long drive to St. John's. As dawn illuminated the landscape, fascinating new sights kept our attention as we drove and camped along the way: the Long Range Mountains, forest areas — some recently burned over — unfamiliar river and sea coastlines, and signatures of glacial scouring in sparsely forested hills and valleys littered with rock and countless small bodies of water, streams, and bogs. When we reached the Avalon Peninsula, glacial after-effects were especially evident in the bare forest stretches strewn with granite boulders.

The post-glacial landscape seemed one of nature's battlefields. We learned later that the little lakes we saw were "ponds" in Newfoundland parlance. Berry pickers went about their business here and there along the way. The landscape's striking beauty compensated for the rough sections of the single-lane Trans-Canada Highway still under construction. We noticed the many small white signs along the highway between Port aux Basques and St. John's: "Thank you, Mr. Pearson." Thanks for what? we wondered. Was it our introduction to a paternalistic federal–provincial order?[2]

St. John's

Before departing North Dakota we had learned that Memorial had acquired several houses in St. John's for rental to its new faculty. I had arranged to book one by phone and expected it to be ready upon our arrival in early September. However, when we arrived it wasn't finished and the university put us up in the new Holiday Inn motel. We moved into a single room: two adults and two lively little kids. Two-year-old Randy enjoyed racing up and down the hotel corridors on his little wooden, four-wheeled Tyke Bike, a red and yellow toy we hadn't shipped with movers.

Living rent-free in a new motel was a kind of boon, yet also problematic. With little cash to live on and no credit cards, we continued our camping ways. Irene and I usually ate breakfast and sandwich lunches in our room — peanut butter and jelly were basics — and we had light dinners in the smaller of the motel's two restaurants. While I was at the university during the day, Irene remained at the motel with the children. There being no laundry around, she used the motel's bar soap to wash our clothes — mainly socks and underwear — and dried them in our room. Washing diapers commanded more attention, however, and soon she was using the motel's washing machine, although it seems we still dried our clothes in the room.

We scrimped along until one day I felt compelled to ask the university Bursar for a salary advance. He told me "We don't do that." So we ran tight some more until my first paycheque arrived. We resided at the motel for about a month while the few furnishings and other household effects we had shipped from North Dakota remained in storage in St. John's. During our stay we enjoyed a close friendship with another newly arrived couple, Sam and Rusty Tibbo, and their two children. They, too, were awaiting access to accommodations in town. Sam was originally from Grand Bank, one of Newfoundland's major groundfish trawler ports. The RCMP had just reassigned him to St. John's after assignment in Prince Edward Island, Rusty's home province. After Irene and I left the motel, we remained close friends of the Tibbos. And when visiting Burin Peninsula communities I sometimes stayed with Sam's widowed mother, who lived alone in Grand Bank. She taught me much about life in her community. It had been a major centre during Newfoundland's offshore banks schooner fishing era from about the last quarter of the nineteenth century until the 1940s, when it became a groundfish trawler fleet and frozen fish processing centre.

Meanwhile, I made daily trips to my new department's offices in Memorial's Arts and Administration Building in advance of the teaching term to meet new colleagues and prepare for fall classes. I was relieved when Robert Paine, ISER's Director, who was also the senior member of the Sociology and Anthropology Department, accepted my arrival without a finished PhD as a common uncertainty in advanced research. I had thought its completion doable. But the unexpected delay seemed reasonable due to Irene's serious medical problems after our daughter's birth. And we had to change housing shortly before leaving North Dakota. Optimism seems essential to moving on.

In any event, at Memorial I was to teach during the fall terms of

1966 and 1967, and conduct field research and writing during each suc-
ceeding spring–summer period. In the spring of 1967 I'd select either
Newfoundland's whale fishery or its deep-sea trawler fishery for study.
Both seemed fascinating. I expected to have enough spare time to finish
my thesis during the fall session. But it was impossible to work in our
close living quarters during those first weeks. And during evenings and
weekends I helped Irene manage our two small children's needs. That's
exhausting work. I had to wonder how single parents manage without
help. My disillusionment escalated when fall term teaching began. My
unfinished academic business distracted my attention from our new
setting's living challenges.

Almost daily, I checked the progress on our rented house on the
city's east end until Miller Ewing, the university's housing chief, informed me that it was available. We eagerly departed the motel the next
morning and drove the short distance to the house at 44 Slattery Road.
I recall how signs seen somewhere advertised it as an "Award Winning
Carter Home," one of several new, one-storey, unattached, single-family
homes developed by the then recent MHA Walter Carter, who later
became an MP in Ottawa.

Other new Memorial faculty renters were scattered here and there
among non-university families. From outside, ours seemed a comfortable three-bedroom house. Upon quick inspection inside, we were met
with a light, oak-floored dining area and a garish colour medley of hallway and bedroom carpeting. Its rooms were all freshly painted. The hot
and cold water ran, the fridge and stove were installed in the kitchen,
and the brick fireplace in the living room had been completed (sort of).
We knew the basement was unfinished. Otherwise, it appeared ready to
live in. So we began to move in with our camping gear. But when I entered the bathroom there was a hole in the floor where the toilet should
have been! We immediately stopped moving in, returned to the Holiday
Inn, and I informed the university housing office, which, as one would
expect, claimed ignorance of the oversight.

I also phoned the university Bursar and told him that we'd be at the
motel for at least another night. My news didn't seem to bother him. I
must have mentioned then that living in the motel had about exhausted
our funds. Hearing this, he told me that we could charge our meals at
the motel. In fact, we could have done so from the start. Wow! No one

had told us that before. I never expected such generosity from the university. What a shock! We had unnecessarily wasted our resources all that month. Well, we made it a point to enjoy our first and last free meals in the motel's main dining room that day and the next morning.

Our "bad" fortune seemed a little less painful when we checked out soon after and moved into the house — three bedrooms with a tub, shower, and a toilet. But it smarted later when we learned how other incoming faculty in similar family situations had been provided with two rooms during their motel stays at university expense. This disappointment eased when Irene told me that by not having paid rent for a month, we had saved enough money to buy our own washing machine. Great news! No more worry about scrub boards.

We're East-enders

We had settled into a new rented house in an area of St. John's known locally as the "East End." Irene remembers it as like "living in the country." Some streets were still unpaved and the homes were under construction. As we settled into the community we knew we had much to learn about the province's history, Memorial University, our new neighbours, the denominational educational system, living on an island, and much more. For example, food stores nearby had mostly canned goods and frozen foods. Fresh fruit and vegetables were limited. Likewise, bakeries were few. Most Newfoundland families baked their own. In our area of town, local "fresh" milk was sometimes sour and cottage cheese had often been frozen. Humorous little experiences were enlightening. Once when I ordered a banana split off the menu at a nearby fast-food shop, I was served three scoops of ice cream covered in whipped cream. No banana. Another time I ordered a cheeseburger and received a slice of cheese in a bun. No burger. I felt foolish both times.

We soon learned that one's family history, community of origin, occupation, education, schools attended, location of one's home in the city, and English dialect all were important matters in Newfoundland. And we realized that we were part of a fast-changing, welcoming local community where the university figured prominently. The university was rapidly expanding since its move from Parade Street in 1961 to its present location. This meant many new faculty arrivals. We were often termed "come from aways" or just "CFAs." To accommodate new faculty, Memorial had purchased a number of newly built single-family houses in the area. (When private developers protested and claimed the university action was unfair competition, the university soon sold the homes, many to its new faculty.)

In our east-side area, some Newfoundlanders didn't initially seem keen about having so many "professors" for neighbours. There were three houses on our small, south-side stretch of Slattery Road between Tobin Crescent and Ennis Avenue. Each was occupied by a university family (Andersen, Bishara, and Gogan; American, Egyptian, and Irish, respectively). All had young children. Other faculty families were directly across the street to the north, several more around the corner west of us, and another right behind us. Irene remembers the time a lady called at our home. She lived only a few houses east on Slattery Road and was collecting for a charity. When Irene opened the door and chatted with her, the lady asked what kind of work I was in. Irene said, "Oh, he's out on a fishing boat." At that news, she thought I was a fisherman, and told Irene how nice it was to meet her because she didn't like having to speak with university people.

Our move to Newfoundland took Irene, with two small children, far from the support of her family and good friends. But she bravely put up with this sacrifice of security. As strangers to our neighbours, there were times when she had to deal with family crises alone, especially when I was away, sometimes at sea. For example, one day when I was at sea she slipped and fell on the basement stairs while doing laundry and broke her ribs. She managed to get a neighbour to care for our daughter while she went to hospital, but couldn't find anyone to take our boy. We knew of no early child-care centres in the city. In the event, she drove herself to and from hospital by having little Randy shift the car gears while she steered. He quietly waited while Irene was examined and bandaged. She never told me about this until I returned to St. John's. She took a lot on her shoulders.

Irene gradually developed friendships with our non-university neighbours as she took our children for walks in our area. But it wasn't always easy, and not just due to our unfamiliarity with Newfoundland dialects. Many of us newcomers were certainly "different" in that we were from "upalong" — usually meaning Toronto or elsewhere on the mainland. An English accent usually signalled England, the mother country. That familiar accent meant less to fear.

It was easy to assume that we would conform to the values and attitudes of our countries of origin. During the 1960s, news media, especially television, bombarded Canadians every day with disturbing news about American domestic and foreign events. Shortly before we left North Dakota, "Camelot" had fallen with JFK's assassination and there was news of the US government's role in the suppression of democracy in Chile. By the mid-1960s the American nation seemed in a turmoil of racial conflict (such as the destructive Watts race riots in Los Angeles in 1965) and mired in an increasingly unpopular war in Vietnam that fuelled a growing anti-war movement in the United States and internationally. Despite President Lyndon Johnson's "Great Society" reform agenda, distrust of government was widespread and a growing counterculture movement even seemed to spill over into Canada.

Neither my wife nor I supported the war. We didn't even like our children having toy guns. But some of our new neighbours, including other CFAs, may have wondered if we were of a stereotypical violent "ugly American" sort. Would we teach our Newfoundland students values contrary to those of their parents? Some might have felt it best not to get too cozy with our sort. And some locals, including Memorial faculty, saw us CFAs as invasive colonizers in a land, *their* land, only recently added to the Canadian Confederation. So we'd unfairly taken jobs from Newfoundlanders and other Canadians. If our geographic mobility wasn't a mere temporary professional move, it meant far more to Newfoundlanders. In some ways we were having a "first-generation immigrant experience."

Our Midwestern American dialect was an easy cue to our alien origins. When speaking with many locals for the first time, people would often observe, "You're from away, aren't you?" And when discussing the identity of other people in the area, we might be told, "Oh. They're one of the So-and-Sos of St. John's," i.e., a prominent family. Hearing this on one occasion, Irene jokingly responded: "Oh? Well, we're the Andersens of Chicago." "Oh, really?" declared a neighbour seriously. We met a strong sense of class hierarchy in St. John's.

While I was busy with teaching and the research that led us here, Irene managed daily activities involving our home and children. They, in turn, met, played, and became known to other local children. This helped to gradually diminish our strangeness and negotiate our integration into the area. We had adjusting to do. For example, the local habit of leaving infants parked in buggies outside one's home for fresh air while a parent did household chores inside challenged our common mainland security concerns. Irene and I both hesitated to do the same lest our children might be kidnapped.

I remember the Christmas of 1968, when our son Randy went astray in Bowring's large Water Street store. Loudspeakers were alerting everyone to hunt for him when an older man entered. Hearing the speaker and seeing the stir, he approached a clerk and told him there was a little boy in a red cap and blue jacket sitting in the store window, sucking his thumb and watching the little moving elves of its Christmas display. Maybe he had found the elves' secret way into the display area. The older fellow said that he had seven children of his own and reassured Irene that nobody kidnaps children in Newfoundland.

Religion and Education

Since we planned to be in Newfoundland for only two years, we didn't expect our children to attend school here. Off and on, we watched Vanier Elementary School being constructed on Ennis Avenue and around the corner from our house. It looked like a very nice school when finished. However, since our arrival we had noticed how every school-day morning we saw many parents drive their children here or there in town to get them to the "right" school. Likewise, in the afternoon they scooted about town to bring them home again. This routine made little sense to us, perhaps because we were both products of non-denominational, public elementary and high school systems, where children went to schools within walking distance of their homes.

Cynically, I wondered at first if this regime existed to benefit gas stations and oil companies. But its roots soon became clear when we understood the important historical role of denominations in Newfoundland and Labrador schooling. Issues around this system came to us later when our first child entered school. Luckily, our son was admitted to the United Church-affiliated Vanier Elementary School down the hill from our house. By chance alone, he had been baptized in the right denomination. Popular thinking was changing about the province's denominational control of schooling, partly due to the arrival of many newcomers from away. For example, when one Pentecostal Memorial faculty member and his family had no auto to get to the "right" school across town, they tried to have their little girl enrolled in the United Church's Vanier Elementary School. But Vanier initially denied her admission due to a different religious affiliation. In reaction, her parents — accompanied by their child — created a local media *cause célèbre*. They picketed Vanier until it relented and admitted her. Another university professor and his family in our area claimed no religious affiliation. As a result, their daughter was also denied admission to Vanier. A month after the school term began she was admitted to the Pius the Xth Roman Catholic Elementary School. But a year later Vanier admitted her. It was much closer to her home.

A Challenging Academic Department

At Memorial my new colleagues in Sociology and Anthropology, and in other departments, were always a changing international mix of young scholars. Anthropologists I knew best during my first two or three years included Tom Nemec, R. Geoffrey Stiles, Louis Chiaramonte, C. Alexander Goodlad (a fisheries geographer), and Cato Wadel and Ottar Brox (the latter two from Norway). Each arrived with their special fisheries interests. Geoffrey Stiles, Cato Wadel, and I collaborated in editing several volumes on fisheries research.[3]

Robert Paine was always open to discussing our individual research ideas. He was a positive catalyst for seminars and workshops. Robert was never "directive" about my approach, whether theoretical or ethnographic. But he was always willing to share ideas, and always thinking about how ISER might contribute more to understanding Newfoundland and Labrador society and culture and its place in the North Atlantic. Among other work produced from varying ethnographic and theoretical perspectives, this was the kind of research undertaken by the early ISER anthropologists: James C. Faris, *Cat Harbour: A Newfoundland Fishery Settlement* (1966); Melvin Firestone, *Brothers and Rivals: Patrilocality in Savage Cove* (1967); Tom Philbrook, *Fishermen, Logger, Merchant, Miner: Social Change and Industrialism in Three Newfoundland Communities* (1966).

We were there to add to our understanding of the province. Before I arrived at Memorial I probably expected my research to be part of a single highly organized ISER project. I soon realized it wasn't. Each of us worked very much on our own. The freedom of being funded for the research and the challenge of that time were energizing. Especially after the previous three years as the sole anthropologist at the University of North Dakota.

I settled into full-time teaching introductory anthropology during the 1966 fall term under the department's two-semester regime. It departed from the nearly impossible regime of delivering a four-field program (physical anthropology, archaeology, linguistics, and cultural anthropology) all in one term, which was common in the States. It was a refreshing change for me.

I often heard some instructors remark that their students had an "inferiority complex." When asked to give evidence, they often said it was the students' reluctance to speak in class. This psychological labelling seemed simplistic and self-serving. I wondered if the instructors had difficulty engaging their students. If students were more reserved, it might be for several reasons: No doubt some felt academically unsophisticated because of their origins in small outports and schools "around the bay." Or their early schooling might have been so formal, authoritarian, and reliant upon rote memory that they shunned speaking in class. And, likely, self-consciousness about their different regional dialects versus those of their instructors made them uneasy. Many faculty members from away had different English dialects.

Being new faculty we probably knew little about the Newfoundland of our students. On the other hand, many of our students were already experienced in or actively supporting themselves in seasonal fisheries, forestry, and mining industries, as well as the subsistence production activities basic to their family and community lives. They *knew* about the land and sea and its economic challenges to their lives. In these respects I felt many of our students were quite mature and individually able and eager to learn and make their futures. I realize now that the Newfoundland I met in the late 1960s was rapidly changing. And it's now two generations away from the strangeness that Newfoundland and Memorial held for so many of us at the time.

During the winter months of 1967 I worked on my thesis. That spring I rented a Volkswagen "bug" and drove down the gravel, pothole-ridden Burin Peninsula road to survey its fishing communities. That road had a well-earned reputation for ravaging cars and trucks. I visited Marystown, where a new fish plant was being built to receive ground-fish from its new fleet of stern trawlers. Then on to Little St. Lawrence and its remnants of a whaling station dating to about 1905–10. I had chats there with an old fellow who had worked for the station back then. He explained that it processed only a few whales and was soon abandoned.

I went on to the peninsula's offshore trawler fishing ports at Burin, Fortune, and Grand Bank. At Grand Bank I became familiar with its history as a banks schooner fishing centre that had become the base of a modern groundfish trawler fleet and fish-processing plant. I walked into the past when I stepped into the shop of its last traditional marine blacksmith, Wilson Osborne. He freely shared his rich knowledge of the passage of time there. Walking about the community it seemed two rich worlds of experience and meaning pervaded the lives of those living here: what it had been and what it was now becoming. By this time I was confident that Newfoundland's modern offshore groundfish trawler fishery would be my research focus.

Before that trip, I felt that Newfoundland's whale fishery was near its end. I had visited the still active whaling station at South Dildo, Trinity Bay, where I met whaler captains Johan Borgen and his son, Arne Borgen. The elder captain was retired but he had hunted whales in Newfoundland waters from a Hawke's Harbour base for some years. His son, Arne, presently skippered the large whale catcher tied up at the plant dock. About a year or two later he moved it to British Columbia, presumably to continue whaling there. Both men have since passed away. The South Dildo station was Newfoundland's last active coastal commercial whaling station by then. (In 1972 the Canadian government declared a moratorium on all commercial whaling in Canada.[4])

Late in the spring of 1967, I made my first trip to the Grand Banks aboard a new groundfish stern trawler. It was the *Grand Prince* (Captain Freeman Hatch), owned by the Bonavista Cold Storage Company. It was based at Grand Bank and supplied its fish-processing plant there. In contemporary economic terms, it was a "vertically integrated" industrial operation. On that trip, sea sickness challenged me again, this time for days, and the roar of high-speed diesel engines and the screech of winches on deck were deafening. And that background noise often complicated my efforts to hear what members of the crew said when we talked together. And, of course, when I could hear them, different Newfoundland dialects often baffled me. I wondered if I could accomplish anything at this point. But I persisted, chatting up the skipper and his mate in the quieter wheelhouse; and Captain Tom Bartlett, the fleet shore skipper, below the rear deck where fish is sorted for retention and icing or returned to the sea. Captain Tom was aboard this time to familiarize himself with this new trawler. It was my only trip to sea that year.

By then I knew it was terribly inefficient and difficult to switch back and forth between writing up my First Nation research[5] and going out on trawlers. So I postponed further trips at sea until the spring of 1968. But during those months I often went down to St. John's harbour to explore the marine life there. There were informal chats with fishermen and sealers in shops and other hangouts near the harbour. With what the sealers had told me in mind, I climbed aboard the old steel-hulled sealing vessel, *Algerine*, to explore it. And, of course, there were the Portuguese White Fleet vessels, their crews and stacked dories that fascinated the community. The harbour was always a refreshing attraction.

In the 1970s I became editor of and contributor to another volume on fishing communities, this time in the North Atlantic area, for the World Anthropology Series.[6] It interrupted my most interesting project, however: a biographical account of one of the most skilful and experienced Grand Banks captains, Captain Arch Thornhill, based on interviews with him.[7] Captain Thornhill's career encompassed the changes in fishing on Newfoundland's Grand Banks, from dories operating from schooner mother ships in the early twentieth century to the transition to groundfish trawlers by the late 1940s.

The sea, how we humans use it and its resources, will always remain a challenge to our understanding. What was the pull of Newfoundland? It was the pull of the sea.

Notes

1.   Raoul Andersen, "Hvalblas," *North Dakota Quarterly* 57, 4 (1989): 48–56. "Hvalblas" is the Norwegian equivalent of "Whale ho!" for when a whale is sighted.

2. The federal government agreed to pay 90 per cent of the cost of all new construction of the Trans-Canada Highway in 1963, and the slogan was adopted: "We'll finish the Drive in '65 — thanks to Mr. Pearson" (*Encyclopedia of Newfoundland and Labrador*, s.v. "Highways").

3. Raoul Andersen and Geoffrey Stiles, eds., *Man and the Sea: Human Factors in Marine Environments* (New York: Simon & Schuster, 1971); Raoul Andersen and Cato Wadel, eds., *North Atlantic Fishermen: Anthropological Essays on Modern Fishing* (St. John's: ISER Books, 1972).

4. For an account of shore-station whaling in Newfoundland and Labrador, see Anthony Dickinson and Chesley W. Sanger, *Twentieth-Century Shore-Station Whaling in Newfoundland and Labrador* (Montreal and Kingston: McGill-Queen's University Press, 2005).

5. Raoul Andersen, "Alberta Stoney (Assiniboin) Origins and Adaptations," *Ethnohistory* 17, 1 and 2 (1970): 49–61; Raoul Andersen, "Agricultural Development of the Alexis Stoney," *Alberta Historical Review* (1972): 16–20.

6. Raoul Andersen, ed., *North Atlantic Maritime Cultures: Anthropological Essays on Changing Adaptations* (The Hague: Mouton Press, World Anthropology Series, 1979).

7. Raoul Andersen, *Voyage to the Grand Banks: The Saga of Captain Arch Thornhill* (St John's: Creative Books, 1998).

Queen's College, home of the Departments of Sociology and Anthropology from the mid-1970s to the early 1990s. (Photograph by Stephen Harold Riggins.)

20

From Bowling Green to St. John's, and Early Years in the Medical School

Sharon Buehler

The Call

In 1967 my husband Dick Buehler and I were living in Bowling Green, Ohio, when he came home one day to announce that he had been on the phone with a person in Canada who wanted him to accept a position as lecturer in Folklore and English. It was an unexpected response to a whimsical moment of letter-writing to Newfoundland and Queensland. In June of 1964 we had received our degrees from Indiana University — Dick an MA in Folklore, and I an AM in Zoology — and welcomed our first child, Kelly. In August we moved to a small college in Vermont where Dick taught English and, in our second year there, I taught biology. Our first salaries were $6,000 each; we were ecstatic. Two years later we moved to Bowling Green, Ohio. I worked as a research assistant in Drosophila genetics and taught some night classes with the university extension program. Dick was working on his doctorate in Folklore and doing some editing.

After that phone call, I remember sitting in the Drosophila lab, looking at a wall map of North America and thinking we were going to the ends of the earth. Certainly very far away from our Midwestern roots and a grandmother who had not had much time with her first grandchild while we were in Vermont and who had told us with absolute certainty that she would never get on a plane.

When Dick brought the word that he had decided to take the job, I was eight months pregnant with our second child, Michael. I didn't want to go. A move to Newfoundland, for however brief a time, would mean resettling thousands of miles away from either of our families in a totally strange place (in those days Memorial often didn't fly people in for a series of interviews and a look around). We would be the first in seven generations to move away from central Illinois. I think it was the only major decision in our married life that we didn't discuss at length, but Dick was unhappy with the program in Ohio and really wanted to move. And, of course, it is always nice to be needed. Still, my mother would miss much of the early years of her grandchildren; we were just too far away to travel to Illinois more than once a year and although she eventually conquered her fear of flying it was too expensive for her to come often.

Dick had to take summer school exams before he could go to Newfoundland. So I elected to go back to Illinois to my mother's for the last month of pregnancy (prenatal advice of the day) and we drove across Ohio and Indiana and into Jacksonville, Illinois, my home town, stopping every hour to let me walk around the Volkswagen bus (as prescribed by my Ohio doctor) and let Kelly (nearly three) and our border collie, Gadhar, stretch their legs. Dick hurried back to classes and Kelly and I lived in the home I'd left when I married almost 10 years earlier. Ah me, in retrospect it went well but I was soon, in many respects, my mother's daughter. I escaped full-day, every day, exposure to the mother–daughter dialogue through my mother's nursing shifts and my volunteer work putting together surgical kits and autoclave packs. Michael arrived the day Dick's exams finished. Dick broke all the speed limits from Ohio, held his newborn son smuggled in from the hospital nursery at midnight, and then headed northeast to Newfoundland with our border collie the next morning. He was to start work at Memorial the next week.

We Arrive

The three of us followed in six weeks, to the day — the first day when a new baby was allowed to fly in those days. We met Dick on a blustery October evening at the then quite small St. John's airport. We arrived on Fox Avenue to a newly built house sited on a dirt road with no sidewalks, no curbs, and no trees. Two other new arrivals to the English Department, waiting for accommodation, had just vacated their rooms in our house. I remember that the house echoed with bareness and everything seemed so unfamiliar. But the overwhelming emotion was comfort — we were finally all there together. Thus began our "two years" in Newfoundland.

My introduction to the physical presence of the university was that night with a trip to Dick's office to call back to Illinois to tell my mother that I had arrived safely in Newfoundland with Kelly and Michael; the telephone had not yet been hooked up at 40 Fox Avenue. On that snowy, drizzly October night after 12 hours en route, I remember pulling in to the loading bay at the back of the Arts and Administration Building and going up to Dick's third-floor office and calling back to a mother who had seen one daughter off to Washington State and another to a place that was, as far as she was concerned, somewhere in the Arctic. Being thousands of miles from "home" and set adrift in a windy, barren, muddy expanse of new houses, I cried (and laughed) a lot that first week or two. But, being back with Dick and, thankfully, after a few sunny days and sleep, things began to look better.

Fox Avenue

Gradually I met the neighbours, nearly all university faculty who were settled in the two blocks of new university houses from Ridge Road down to Higgins Line. In our block were the Royces, Leytons, Puxleys, Rochesters, Hammers, Gorsts, Ralphs, and Gregorys. Within the next couple of years the Foltzs, Hertzbergs, and Rosenbergs had moved in. Don and Florence Johnson next door to us were Newfoundlanders. We always felt some sympathy for them, surrounded as they were by "university types." Down the next block were the Englishes, Rehners, Pastores, and Mongars.

The first neighbour I met was Judy Ralph; Earl was a new hire in Chemistry. Her two-year-old had just stepped in mud up to his high-tops and she came over to wash it off with our outside tap. (They didn't yet have a workable tap; lots of things were not workable yet.) The Gregorys and the Gorsts were from England; the Leytons, Puxleys, and Rochesters from mainland Canada; the Royces, Ralphs, and us from the US. In fact, in one of the first of those strange Newfoundland coincidences, the Royces had moved from my hometown in Illinois where Gerald had been teaching at a small liberal arts college. We neighbours learned a lot from each other: language ("taps" not "faucets," "in hospital" not "in the hospital," "chesterfields" versus "couches"), kettles with plugs instead of stove top, long telephone conversations versus short ones conditioned by paying for local calls. I was invited over by my next door neighbour, a Canadian, to see "my new chesterfield" and, thank goodness, she pointed. I was expecting a coat.

Dick basically worked nine to five, as most faculty in the Department of English did in those days. I don't remember any flexible scheduling or working from home (except for marking papers and devising exams, of course). I spent days at home in the new university house we had been assigned to. Workmen came nearly every day to finish this or that bit of the house. I rarely understood what they were asking; most of the workers were from the southern shore with a thick accent and lightning-fast delivery. Taking Michael out in the buggy with Kelly alongside was difficult most days with rain, drizzle, snow, and unfinished road underfoot. So unless I took Dick to work to get the car for grocery shopping or other errands, I was mostly in the house during a very bleak and dark fall and early winter. That Christmas, the first away from any family, was difficult but, shared with an equally isolated couple from Britain, turned out to be quite memorable. The greatest frustration that day was trying to get through to the States by phone to wish our families a merry Christmas (and my mother a happy birthday). Long-distance calls on holidays were quite a challenge in those days. I remember February that year, 1968, very well; it was reported that we had had a record 13 hours of sunshine for the month. When the weather (and our road) improved and people started moving outside I met more neighbours, like us, new faculty from the UK and US, and we developed our "stoop-sitting" coffee breaks with our children playing around us. There were 30 children under three years in our two blocks of Fox Avenue, the offspring of faculty from History, Anthropology, Chemistry, Economics, Physics, and Political Science. Some became very good friends. Most eventually moved away but many stayed in touch.

The Memorial Connection: Extension Service, the Children's Centre, and the Open Group

The influx of new faculty and staff in the late 1960s brought many women with small children who had not yet returned to work and had some time to spare. The Extension Service, which provided a diversity of expertise to the rural areas of NL, an extremely important part of the outreach of the university, also offered a number of art classes held on the fourth floor of the Education Building. Many of us signed up for classes with Don Wright, Frank Lapointe, David Blackwood, and Peter Walker.

In an early meeting of new faculty wives in 1968 there was concern that there weren't adequate educational opportunities for our preschool children. So five of us began the Children's Centre — June Mongar, whose husband was in Political Science; Felicity O'Brien, who later worked in Geology; Kay Matthews, a trained midwife and wife of a historian; and Pat Wright, a trained early childhood educator and wife of Don in Extension. Surprisingly, despite ups and downs of funding and many moves of site, the Children's Centre still survives.

The Open Group was an amateur theatre group that grew out of a gathering of faculty members and people from the community. Over the years, the group produced plays and workshopped a number of the plays of Mike Cook, faculty member and playwright.

I think of these days of the university in the late sixties and early seventies with its significant expansion of faculty as an explosion of initiatives. I was just so very lucky to be part of them.

Early Days in Academia

Meanwhile, Dick was coping with the culture shock. Having made it through undergraduate and graduate school in jeans and fatigues and L.L. Bean shirts, he was now required to wear a white shirt, dress pants, and an academic robe. Finding a master's degree robe was not easy but Dick persuaded the keeper of the robes to let him have one marked for discarding. It had a few tears and unravellings, but it suited both Dick and the requirement. I had never anticipated ironing white shirts for a week of classes. I can't remember when that requirement was dropped — probably about the same time women could wear slacks as well as skirts — but we celebrated.

He also discovered underground transport — the tunnels from the Arts to the Physical Education, Chemistry, Education buildings, the library, and the Breezeway. However, being pretty much claustrophobic he mainly travelled over ground. Almost everything was on the main campus except the residences "across the road" and the brand new Arts and Culture Centre on the outer edge. The current library site was filled with "temporary" buildings, which in our time housed a number of departments including Philosophy and the new Medical School. The student centre in its early form was a small building between the temporary buildings and the back of the Arts asnd Administration Building. The "student" CIBC branch was there, a barber shop, a travel office, and, if I remember correctly, student health. And of course, the Breezeway, a big noisy pub, was a gathering place for students and faculty for serious and silly discussions. The library was just across from the Arts and Administration Building and housed the main collection as well as the archival material and the expanding computer facility/services.

Oral thesis examinations were held in the boardroom of the Arts and Administration Building. The candidate sat at one end of the long table with examiners, internal and external, and the supervisor along the sides. All robed. There was usually a prologue to the examination by the Dean of Graduate Studies. In those early days, this was Fred Aldrich, who usually found some kind of reference, regardless of the dissertation discipline, to the giant squid, his area of study. Years later, when I had my PhD defence, my external examiner, a graduate of Oxford, was astonished by the formality. Convocation, for as long as I can remember, was in the Arts and Culture Centre — in full academic dress with carefully researched and finely written orations to introduce those receiving honorary degrees. It was and still is a wonderful spectacle and very impressive to non-academics; my mother loved it.

Academia was very social in those days — sherry parties in the apartments/homes of department colleagues; department gatherings on campus; rounds of parties at Christmas with hardly a weekend evening unbooked. These were almost always "dress-up," with both alcohol and food provided by the hosts and substantial food not served until midnight — a hard schedule for young parents with children rising early. Bring-Your-Own Booze (BYOB) and potlucks came much later. In a much smaller faculty we made many friends at these social occasions and through connections with Extension, the Children's Centre, and the Open Group. And, again, as with neighbours, quite a number are still here, much to their surprise, I think. Many of us in those early conversations, frustrated with weather, availability of goods and services, and the difficulties and cost of travel, gave it two years and then it was back to more familiar settings. But strangely, in retrospect, many of us stayed and enjoyed the freedom and opportunity of being an academic in a small place within a network of people from all sectors of the community. For a large number of that late 1960s, early 1970s influx of faculty from mostly the UK and the US, coming to Newfoundland was an adventure. Once through the inoculation phase, it was an adventure that "took."

The Temporary Buildings and the Beginning of the Medical School

The so-called "temporary buildings" were a collection of unattractive, low, beige buildings sprawling in the space where the Queen Elizabeth II Library now stands. When I first started to work at the Medical School, it was the summer of 1969. Ian Rusted had been appointed Dean and occupied an office beside the main corridor along with increasing numbers of new faculty housed initially in T7. At the end of our "Medical School hall" was the office of the Associate Dean, Ken Roberts, part of a "T" addition to the end of the hall. It housed not only the Dean's office but the animal care facilities on one side and the small medical library on the other. Various labs and offices lined the corridors, which included equipment rooms with autoclaves and ovens, fridges, and a constant-temperature microscope room. There was one big room for seminars. I especially remember the seminar room because those of us working as research assistants were rarely in that room except on special occasions when prominent outside speakers came. Then we were often fished out of our labs to be bodies in seats. Often there was much unfamiliar jargon about subjects I knew little about, but being in the presence of researchers well known in medicine was always a perk.

I first worked with Ken Roberts in immunology. We had three lab rooms to work on immune responses in white blood cells. These were primarily tissue culture labs, so much depended on the prevention of contamination — use of hoods and sterile equipment. When we got our first PhD student, Richard Warrington arriving with a brand new medical degree from the Royal London Hospital, UK, I was transferred to his lab. Yves Legal was the second doctoral student; he was probably best known as a black belt judo teacher and coach. Richard went on to Winnipeg as a clinician and researcher in immunology. The other people in Ken's lab were Deborah and Philip Hyam, who came to Newfoundland as newlyweds and exceptionally well-trained techs from the London Hospital. Phil became the mainstay of all things microscopic, and for many years was the head of the electron microscopy lab. They eventually moved to Toronto, where Phil was the pathology lab manager at Toronto Hospital and primary representative for Leica microscopes and Deborah worked at the Ontario Cancer Institute in one of the first stem cell labs. The other big immunology lab was Bill Marshall's, across the hall. Bill had been Ken's doctoral student. I find it interesting in recalling those early days that the initial emphasis was on basic science and bench research (research with non-human subjects). Nowadays, among those working on curriculum from the three divisions of the Medical School — Clinical Science, Basic Science, and Community Health and Humanities — there are constant discussions among those working on curriculum about how much basic science a medical student needs; clinical science always had priority, with basic science and community health trailing behind.

I remember much of that first summer of work as moving through a corridor filled with boxes. Microscopes and other equipment were coming in to be set up for the first students, due to arrive in the fall of 1969. There were 16 in the inaugural class. Most were from Newfoundland but several were from outside — New York, Montreal, Toronto. Now 50 years later a number are senior practising specialists and family practitioners in key medical positions across the country.

Friendships from Early University Days

The Medical School was the centre of my work both pre- and post-PhD. So many of my friends came from days in the temporary building, and then the half-finished and finally finished Health Sciences Centre. Bodil Larsen, Penny Hansen, Phil and Deborah Hyam, Sheila Drover, Verna Skanes, Bill Marshall, John Barnard, Heather Dove: all worked in immunology at one time or another over their careers. We were graduate students or research assistants, post-docs or lab and administration staff when we worked together. Ken Roberts was a key figure in the research lives of many of us and, unfortunately, after retirement he left for Nova Scotia, and finally England. We missed him. His influence on many of us, both as mentor and friend, remains. Two of his British students, Bill Marshall and Jim Barrowman, were recruited to the Medical School in the early days. As a graduate student I worked with Jim, who headed up Graduate Studies, and as a research assistant with Bill and

Ken. I was amused that they conducted research meetings in the same way. There was always a notebook or a pad of paper where notes were taken throughout the discussion, and ultimately crowded with small sketches or outlines to guide the next experiment or step in the study. Immunology was part of the Basic Sciences division of the Medical School.

Outside immunology were a number of other persons coming originally from Britain (ties between Newfoundland and Britain in the recruitment of early faculty were quite close) or the US. Brian Payton not only ran what we called the audiovisual services for the Medical School but, as a physiologist, regaled us with delightful stories of medicinal leeches. He threw wonderful office Christmas parties; with carefully composed, hilarious slide and video shows and, like Bill Marshall and Penny Allderdice, developed entertainingly instructive demonstrations of their fields for medical students. Penny was one of many Americans recruited to the Medical School. She came to beef up our genetics program, built on the remarkable opportunities provided in Newfoundland where decades of isolation and large families, and the wonderful commitment of those families to take part in research that might benefit others, made work on familial conditions so much easier. However much Penny may be remembered for discoveries that ended up in the genetics bible, she is remembered by many as the person who picked up people who had fallen between the cracks — a casual chat in the cafeteria with someone in for chemotherapy or waiting on a chair outside a clinic totally alone and frightened by the whole institutional surround — and took them home for supper.

Of those early research assistants in the Medical School, three of us — Penny Hansen, Sheila Drover, and I — went on to complete our doctorates and eventually end up on the Medical School faculty. Penny was a key researcher in medical education and was on the executive of the International Union of Physiological Sciences. Sheila, the youngest of us, born in Fleur-de-Lys, is a well-funded researcher in histocompatibility (HLA) contributions to breast cancer and immunological disease. The others from early Medical School days also remained friends in retirement — John Barnard from England who ran the very busy clinical and research immunology lab and Heather Dove who was first senior secretary in immunology and then in graduate studies in medicine.

Deborah and Phil retired to Nova Scotia but keep in touch. Bodil came to the Medical School from Norway as a post-doc working with HLA but also over the years has made a significant contribution to the development of Memorial's Botanical Garden. Verna, who grew up in Lumsden, arrived as a graduate student, became Associate Dean of Research and Grad Studies (Medicine), and in early retirement chaired the national boards of Canadian Blood Services and subsequently the Canadian Stem Cell Network Corporation.

And those early neighbours — the Gregorys, Ralphs, Rosenbergs, and Children's Centre and theatre colleagues — Pat Wright, Kay Matthews, Elke Molgaard, Jean Guthrie — have remained part of my retirement life. It has been long days since the late 1960s and 1970s and our coming together through the university, but the friendships endured.

21

The Biophysics of Excitable Tissue: Teaching in the Medical School

Brian Payton

My Journey to Memorial University

I was born in East Ham, in the Greater London area. When the war came in 1939 I was first evacuated to Suffolk. Then during the "blitz" I was evacuated to South Wales and lived with a family that was active in the St. John's Ambulance Brigade. I too became interested in first aid and joined the Ambulance Cadets. I became interested in pursuing a career in medicine, and when, at age 18, I was obliged to register for national service, I was accepted by the Royal Army Medical Corps (RAMC) and was trained as a pathology laboratory technician in the Hamburg laboratory of the British Army on the Rhine. I did my medical degree at the University of London Charing Cross Hospital Medical School, and PhD at St. Bartholomew's Hospital Medical School. My research involved looking at the action of drugs on a chemically mediated synapse, the frog neuromuscular junction.

I immigrated to New York to do research at Columbia University and at the Albert Einstein Medical School of Yeshiva University. During the Vietnam War, as a "resident alien" in 1964 I had to sign up with the draft board. Fortunately I was "of an age [34] no longer fit for military service." I was offered a position as Assistant Professor of anatomy at the Albert Einstein, but I was concerned about the violence and racism I encountered in the US. It was the time when Martin Luther King Jr. was assassinated and I did not want my two young boys to grow up in that environment. There are some really wonderful things in the US: the national parks, the Smithsonian Museum, many other museums and art galleries, the Library of Congress (available to all) and other good public libraries, the Lincoln Centre, the National Institute of Health, and fine research institutes throughout the country. But I felt the United States was really not my country.

Then I saw a poster announcing that a new Medical School was to be opened in Newfoundland. The poster described it as being beside a tree-lined lake. Like most people I knew little about Newfoundland, but it seemed a very interesting opportunity. I had always been interested in teaching. Helping to found a Medical School from scratch sounded like a great challenge. The Canadian scene was also attractive. These were the "Trudeau Years" — refreshing after the US.

I sent a letter expressing interest in 1968 and was interviewed in late May 1969. I awoke to see snow falling outside my window. Having taken a number of snapshots during my visit, my wife wanted to know on my return to New York why all the children were wearing parkas! Indeed, the weather when I arrived was not the greatest. But not only had I found the people I met in the university friendly and enthusiastic, I found the people in the province to be equally friendly. Despite the weather I was enthralled with the idea of coming to Newfoundland and was able to talk my wife into agreeing that I should accept the position that I had been offered as an Associate Professor of physiology.

At my interview I met Dr. Ken Roberts, the Associate Dean of medicine and a Professor of physiology. Ken was a medical graduate from King's College in London and had also graduated with an honours degree in physiology and a DPhil in pathology from Oxford University. The plans I was shown and the ideas regarding the curriculum were very interesting indeed.

At that time only a handful of faculty had been appointed. The first class of students were going to enter in the fall of 1969. All the people that I met were very enthusiastic and were prepared to consider ways of doing things differently from the old traditional ways. Part of the plan was to avoid having a rigid departmental system but rather to have an organization whereby basic science disciplines such as anatomy, physiology, pharmacology, and biochemistry would be more integrated, both from a teaching and research point of view. In addition, there was also a definite plan to expose students to health-care programs and clinical material very early in the teaching sessions and, when appropriate, to combine that exposure with the basic medical sciences.

There were only five members in the faculty: Ken Roberts; Nigel Rusted, the Dean; Bill Marshall, Professor of immunology and also the Director of the post-graduate program that was to be developed; and Charles (Chick) Campbell, the Project Manager. During my interviews I was sent to see Chick Campbell. I believe any potential candidate was sent to see him as he had already been recognized as a person who could spot an idiot or a misfit.

I came to St. John's in August 1969 after driving up with the family from New York in my eight-year-old Ford Falcon. On arrival my wife and I and our two sons, aged eight and six, were put up at the Kenmount Motel for a week. Our accommodation involved all four of us occupying a rather small room. After that we found an unfurnished house to rent on Allandale Road, just opposite the Arts and Culture Centre. The furniture from our apartment in Fort Lee, New Jersey, was not due to arrive for a week or so. Staff in the Medical School worked wonders to make sure we not only had something to sleep on but also had a table, some chairs, pots and pans, and cutlery enough to see us through. The Medical School at that time had this type of help available for incoming faculty. It was not done by the university but by the kindness of other faculty, staff members, and their spouses.

The medical students were not due to arrive until September. I had only been able to take up my appointment in late August, and there was a frantic period of getting some of my teaching organized before the students arrived. In the early years of the Medical School we were located in temporary buildings on campus, on a site where the Queen Elizabeth Library now stands.

I found those early years at Memorial to be among the most rewarding years in my career. Our first class had only eight students (five men and three women); the class size grew to 24 in the subsequent year when 16 more students were added. By the time I retired, the class size had increased to 56. One of Memorial's big advantages was the small class size. It has now grown to 80. No longer will there be the same close relationships between students and professors. As well as getting our teaching commitments under control, we were also busy planning and attempting to incorporate collaboration of different disciplines in new teaching programs. In addition, much time was spent participating with architects and others regarding the design for our own needs and the teaching laboratories. All of which affected time for research. For basic scientists whose career advancement depends on research, this was very demanding of our time.

After a year or so, when the Medical School was looking for somebody to head and organize the media services, and as my research output was suffering, I thought that would be an interesting additional challenge. I had long been interested in photography and graphics, and also had some video experience before I came to Memorial. A significant amount of space was allocated for such services. The media service was also to be responsible for classroom support. It involved equipping the photographic and video services with good cameras, lighting and recording equipment, as well as dark room and processing facilities, so it was expensive to set up. Fortunately, federal support provided an adequate budget. In addition to my physiology appointment, my position as the Director of Medical Audiovisual Services made me responsible for this task.

Looking back, not only did we start full of enthusiasm, but so too did the students. I have no regrets about the move.

"Outrageous" Teaching Demonstration

I had always thought that teachers should enjoy teaching and students should enjoy learning and that a little humour included along with lectures and demonstrations is worthwhile. One of my early teaching responsibilities was in a course for first-year students titled "The Biophysics of Excitable Tissue," which looked at the detailed electrical and chemical properties of nerve and muscle cells. The course included mathematical formulas describing membrane properties — an approach not popular with some medical students. No doubt in a vain attempt to make students see that what they would be hearing about in the course was relevant to understanding the nervous system, it seemed appropriate to start by outlining for them a very simple reflex they were already aware of, the knee jerk — the reflex shortening of the quadriceps muscle that follows stretching the patellar tendon by hitting it with a reflex hammer. To start I demonstrated on a subject how this could be exaggerated or diminished in certain situations. The biophysics course would be looking at the responses of individual nerves and their effects on muscle cells in detail. Also, we would be considering the structure of both nerve and muscle cells and the sensory mechanisms within muscles that detect changes in length. However, I pointed out that other reflex responses could be quite complex and unexpected. The following demonstration illustrated this.

After drawing the students' attention to another well-known reflex, that when presented with a sudden bright flash of light the eyes blink by a reflex response, I went on to question whether there are any other responses that occur in association with that stimulus, any other muscular events in the face? Does it involve any effects on the heart? The first step in science involves making reliable observations of events and recording them. As to the facial musculature we can observe changes in them directly. In order that all the students would be able to view this response closely I had technicians from our unit set up a video camera on a subject's face. I also had the output from the camera displayed on monitors and fed into a video recorder so that we could look at any response again. I had connected our seated subject (Gareth Gauthier, the supervisor in Medical Audiovisual Services) to an electrocardiogram machine that would, among other things, record the electrical activity accompanying each heartbeat and the heart rate. Again, we would be able to look at any response afterwards in detail. A bright light was to be made by a photographic flash unit.

To ensure that they were all looking at the video monitors at exactly the time the flash was due to be triggered in front of the subject, I informed them that I would do this by reciting a countdown: five . . . four . . . three, and before zero I fired a starting pistol with blanks that had been concealed on the lectern. As expected, the extremely loud noise in the rather small classroom caused all the students to turn their heads towards it. There they saw a mad professor holding a pistol in his hand that was pointing at the subject. At the sound of the gunshot the subject had suddenly brought one of his hands to that part of his head at which the gun had been pointing. Within his hand the subject had been hiding a small rubber teat filled with blood, which now seemed to be distributed all over him and his white singlet. Almost instantaneously their gaze also took in the blood-spattered subject. Following a couple of shrieks, a few "aahs," and a couple of "Jesus's" there was dead silence. Fortunately, every time I have carried out this demonstration, no brave burly male student has ever leapt to his feet and, at the risk to his life, attempted to disarm the mad professor.

When order was restored we were able to consider the wide variety of motor responses that were brought about, including responses in some of the organs innervated by the autonomic nervous system! This was 1969, before Americans and for that matter a Canadian had taken up entering school or university classrooms and shooting students. Of course, it would now be impossible to carry out this demonstration.

Most of my professional life has been in Newfoundland. I became a Canadian citizen many years ago. I know I shall never be considered here as a Newfoundlander and will always be a CFA. But I must admit that Blake's "Jerusalem" still echoes more in my heart than "O Canada" or the "Ode to Newfoundland."

My Introduction to the School of Nursing

22

Pearl Herbert

In 1978 I was collecting data at the Grace Maternity Hospital in Halifax for my MSc degree at Dalhousie University. One day, when I had nearly finished collecting data, the nursing supervisor who was my liaison person said that she had just returned from attending a workshop in St. John's where she had spoken to Hope Toumishey, a faculty member at the Memorial University of Newfoundland School of Nursing. An outpost nursing program was starting at Memorial — a two-year diploma in community and primary health care and nurse-midwifery — and they were looking for somebody to teach midwifery in the second year. I submitted an application. I soon heard back and was invited to attend an interview. I flew to St. John's and met members of the School of Nursing. Miss Margaret McLean, the Director, was in the General Hospital at the Health Sciences Centre with a back problem. I was taken to her room where she was lying flat in bed. This was a strange situation as I felt torn between helping her to get comfortable and realizing that she was interviewing me for a job.

At Dalhousie University I had asked about the starting salary for an Assistant Professor. At the interview in St. John's, when I inquired about the pay scale, I was told that there were no salary scales and that one was paid what the Director and a committee considered appropriate. I was asked what I thought I should be paid and I gave my answer, a starting salary of $20,000 a year. Later, I discovered that new faculty could receive a salary similar to those who had been employed for several years. Without the university having a union there was no guarantee that years of teaching would be recognized.

This was a time of fiscal restraint, when Pierre Trudeau's government had frozen all financial grants. Although I went to a few other interviews, the answers were always the same: they were unable to hire me at the present time. I obtained my degree but had no employment and little money; and, having been a student for the previous two years,

I did not qualify for unemployment insurance. I did manage to obtain a temporary nursing job that I did not enjoy. Then some months later Miss McLean telephoned to ask if I still wanted the position teaching midwifery. That was my first choice and so I was happy to arrange to move to St. John's. Within a day or two I also heard from other locations where I had been interviewed, and one where I had not applied, offering me positions, but I had already agreed to join the faculty at Memorial University on 1 September 1979.

As I was eager to move to St. John's, I was told that I could apply to the Nursing Director at the Salvation Army Grace General Hospital in St. John's for a temporary nursing position in the case room. I applied for this position and for registration with the Association of Registered Nurses in Newfoundland (ARNN — the "L" was added a few years later). I gave my resignation at the Halifax Infirmary Hospital to finish at the end of May. At the beginning of June I moved — 75 per cent of the expenses were paid by the university. The movers were surprised by the small number of my possessions as I was living in furnished accommodation. Previously, I had to pack my own trunks and arrange for them to be moved. Now I felt that things were improving. But my first impressions of St. John's made me wonder about this!

In St. John's I was met at the airport by some faculty members who took me out to supper and then to a movie. It was an awful movie about people being tortured. It turned out that they had taken me to the wrong movie!

I was taken to the home where I was going to housesit for the summer until I found my own accommodation. It was very sparsely furnished: no stove, no fridge, a hot ring on which to boil water, and very little cutlery and china as the owner had packed most things and moved them to be stored at the house of another faculty member. Consequently, I had my main meal at the hospital. But there were mice at home. A neighbour's cat enjoyed a toasted mouse that had become stuck in the toaster!

In those days there were not many apartments for rent in St. John's. It took a few weeks before locating an apartment that happened to be near the university. In Halifax I had been told by the bank that my account would be transferred electronically. Fortunately, I did get a bank slip showing the amount in my account. In St. John's I went to a bank close to the SA Grace General Hospital to open an account, and found that in this province they did not use computers for transferring accounts. Since I needed money to buy some furniture, I was told to go and get what I required and then my account would be adjusted when the information arrived from Halifax. That took about three attempts, as the wrong information kept being sent through Canada Post. In the end it worked to my advantage. By the time my account was sorted out I was able to accumulate some money and ended up having sufficient funds to cover the cost of my purchases.

I arrived in St. John's to find that nurses were on strike. When I went to the hospital to sign the necessary employment forms, I asked the nurses on the picket line why they were striking but nobody could really tell me all the details. Increase in pay was one reason, working conditions another, but there were also several other reasons. So I went to work. I had a temporary nursing licence as my records, requested by mail, had not arrived. Working in the case room at the SA Grace General Hospital gave me an opportunity, prior to taking students into the unit, to meet the various nurses and physicians (obstetricians and family doctors) who provided obstetric care.

I started at the Memorial University of Newfoundland School of Nursing in September, with an office in the temporary building that gave easy access to the south campus where much of the university activity was located, including the faculty dining room at Gushue Hall. The Queen Elizabeth II Library was being built and the student centre was in the Thomson Building. One advantage of being in the temporary building is that I could just walk into the building and be at the door of my office — and the windows opened. The disadvantages were that the School of Nursing's administration offices were on the other side of Prince Philip Drive in the Health Sciences Building and so was the Health Sciences Library. The traffic lights had just been installed at the corner of Westerland Road and Prince Philip Drive following a fatal road accident involving a student. The building of the Columbus Drive overpass over Kenmount Road was commencing and when completed the flow of traffic increased, resulting in the death of another student and the building of two walkways over Prince Philip Drive.

I remember attending an orientation at the School of Nursing for the four of us new faculty who started that September. None of us had a doctoral degree. I may have been the only one with a master's degree (very different from today's expected qualifications). I understood that I was hired because I had a skill that was required.

One of the first things I was asked to do was to go to the gymnasium in the Thomson Student Centre and help with the registration of nursing students. All the students registered in person including those attending St. John's College, where Roman Catholic male students lived. Some of these students were preparing to enter the priesthood and they did not look comfortable wearing their stiff white collars, perhaps for the first time. To sign up for courses the students had to go to the table where members of their faculty were seated. I discovered that students often paid their fees in cash as not everybody in this province had a bank account.

The outpost nursing program was to prepare registered nurses to practise in remote areas in the country. At a meeting in June 1977, held in Corner Brook to review northern medicine,[1] it had been announced that the Dalhousie outpost nursing program would no longer be using the northern Newfoundland and Labrador sites. A request was made by the International Grenfell Association, which in 1981 became the Grenfell Regional Health Service, that Memorial provide the program and include nurse-midwifery.

In the beginning I shared the teaching of midwifery courses with Hope Toumishey. After two years Hope went on sabbatical leave and I became co-ordinator of the 10-month midwifery program. When I first started I taught the midwifery clinical sessions and spent six months based in St. Anthony. This arrangement had disadvantages as it took me a while to get to know people. When I returned to St. John's six months later some had left and there were new people with whom to become acquainted. When I became co-ordinator of the program, another faculty member was hired as the clinical person. Other faculty at Memorial University taught two out of three semesters: the third semester was their research semester. However, we were hired to teach for three semesters annually; there was no non-teaching semester. When students were on a break, we might be requested to visit instructors in other locations. Even with a tenure-track position, there was little time for any research except in circumstances where a faculty member could be asked to study a particular issue. One was able to update knowledge and skills, however, as in August 1980 I was able to observe and attend lectures at the

Neonatal Intensive Care Unit of the University College Hospital, London, England. In February 1982 (arriving the day of the *Ocean Ranger* disaster) I also attended the three-week intensive course at the Montreal Diet Dispensary. These opportunities provided me with useful information for the midwifery program. The midwifery program was stopped in 1986 because classes were small due to limited clinical placements; and the diploma programs were gradually being phased out, as nurses in this province are required to have a Bachelor of Nursing degree.

There were three other diploma programs for registered nurses in addition to the midwifery program (community and primary health care, mental health nursing, community health nursing), and in the winter semester when the midwifery students were in clinical placements I would teach some of these courses for mature students. The generic undergraduate nursing program consisted of five credit courses that included classroom teaching, clinical laboratory sessions, and clinical time in the hospital. Halfway through the semester there would be the extended clinical of a week of eight-hour days, where faculty members took students into the hospital every day. In the spring semester, I was expected to take these beginning students into the case room for their clinical experience. When the midwifery program was cancelled, I found that I was teaching in the generic undergraduate program.

In the 1980s the School of Nursing had fewer faculty members than now. Another milestone was that the master's degree nursing program was just starting. There were no nursing classes on Fridays and in the morning there was a faculty meeting in the Health Sciences Centre. In those days I said little but observed the dynamics of the various personalities. As I got to know the different members of the faculty, I found them to be friendly and helpful. There were also social events at faculty members' homes, often the Director's home: first at Margaret McLean's log house in St. Philips and then at her home in St. John's; later at the home of the next Director, Caroline White. These were good times where we got to know each other outside of our professional positions.

This was the beginning of nearly 17 years at Memorial that ended when the "package" retirement incentive was offered in 1996. Many changes have occurred since I arrived at Memorial, and not only in the classroom where 34 years ago faculty used reel-to-reel films and overhead transparencies, now replaced by advanced multimedia equipment.

Faculty are now expected to engage in research and publish, and the Memorial University of Newfoundland Faculty Association (MUNFA) union ensures that time is allowed for this. Paper communications are now often replaced by electronic mail. In St. John's faculty members were all based on campus, but now they may be in an office in a different location in the city. Back then faculty members knew the students in their classes; with distance education now, students may never come to St. John's or even to Canada. Currently a cohesive class of past students returns for reunions, to meet their former professors and to share memories and the latest news. In the future reunions may become obsolete. Is there is a reason for graduates to come to meet people they have never previously met? Life was different 30 years ago and there were both good times with faculty and with students, and times when things could have been better.

Note

1.   International Grenfell Association and Memorial University of New-foundland, *Proceedings, Conference on Northern Medicine and Health, June 23–25, 1977* (Corner Brook, NL: Memorial University of Newfoundland, 1977).

23

Falling on My Feet
Tony Chadwick

In early April 1967 I was suddenly faced with looking for a teaching position. I had been teaching since October the previous year at the École des Mines, in Nancy, France, and had been counting on continuing in that position for a second year. Departmental politics, however, provoked an upheaval and all who were not tenured, including *lecteurs* like myself, were informed that contracts would not be renewed. I rushed out to buy a copy of the *Times Educational Supplement* and the *Times Higher Education Supplement,* and after a long search found an advertisement for six tenure-track positions in the Department of Modern Languages, as it was then styled, at Memorial University of Newfoundland. So I decided to immigrate to Canada.

What little I knew of the province was restricted to the stamps I had collected as a child, growing up in Stoke-on-Trent in England: a seal on one, and a banking schooner on the other. And the stories told to me by a colleague in Nancy who had just completed a two-year contract in that department. One of our duties was to record the scripts for a new English-language program being developed by the tenure-track professors of English, and each week, while the technician was setting up the recording studio, he would regale me with stories of life in St. John's. They were no doubt embellished in the telling, but many were hilarious — snow-clearing mishaps (a truck loaded with snow backed into the harbour, the driver got out, shook off the excess water, and decided that was enough for the day); vintage port being sold off for a dollar a bottle because it was old; the antiquated liquor licensing laws (purchases were rationed to one bottle of liquor, or a bottle of wine, or 24 beers per day) — and some were not so funny: the lack of fresh vegetables and good cheese; the inability to leave the island because of fog; poor air service.

After calling my wife-to-be to confirm that she was agreeable to such a leap into the dark, I submitted a simple letter of application, listing the three referees who had supplied references for me the previous year, and waited for a reply. And waited. Finally, I called Dr. Stoker, the head of the department, to find out where my application stood, and found out that I had been appointed and a letter sent! When I pointed out that I had not received it, he promised to get a telegram sent out, which I received the next day: "Appointed. Salary $6000. Regards, M. Morgan." I had no idea who M. Morgan was, but on the strength of the telegram, I set about applying to emigrate ... and to get married.

Further correspondence with Dr. Stoker revealed what my teaching duties would be, and an indication that teaching summer school was a possibility, starting on 23 June. Since I would not receive my first salary cheque until the end of September, I jumped at the chance to earn some money to tide us over from the end of June.

Formalities completed, I arrived in St. John's, via Gander, to be met by the acting head, John Hewson, who knew nothing about the promise of summer school teaching; all those positions had been allocated. My wife and I spent a week in the Kenmount Motel (then on Elizabeth Avenue) while we found accommodation (a basement apartment on Johnson Crescent), arranged a loan with the Bank of Montreal ("You have a position at Memorial? No problem!"), bought a cheap car, and set about familiarizing ourselves with St. John's.

The Department of Modern Languages (French, German, Spanish, Italian) was in the process of moving into the newly constructed Arts and Education Building, the language laboratory equipment was being installed, and, since I had no teaching duties, I signed up for a training course in the audiovisual program that I would be using in September, "Voix et Images de France." Some of my new colleagues were also registered — Daphne Collins (wife of a future editor of *The Telegram*), who taught French and Italian; Roger Ozon, who was originally from St. Pierre; and Michael and Frances Wilkshire are the ones I remember — so besides learning the technicalities of film-strip projection and a new-to-me tape recorder that rewound to the beginning of the current sentence for easy manipulation, and the preferred techniques for class repetition of the phrases to be learned, I became acquainted, through a high school teacher who was also taking the course, with what I could expect from my students in September. He explained that, like many other teachers of French in the school system, he had majored in mathematics! Being the most junior teacher in his first school, he was "persuaded" by the principal to teach "some" French in his first year, on the strength of his having completed one year of French studies at Memorial. The "some" turned out to be "all," and since he could not find a position teaching his preferred subject he had accepted his fate and was trying to improve his oral skills by taking this course (conducted entirely in French).

Towards the end of August, other new appointees arrived. At that time, with year-long courses, students who had failed an exam in April were allowed to re-sit in August. Dr. Stoker asked the new appointees to mark these supplementary exams as a way of preparing them for the standard of work they might expect. I agreed to take on an extra evening class (an audiovisual class of six hours) on top of my regular 12 hours of day-time teaching, six hours of evening class (another audiovisual course), and two hours of language lab supervision. Twenty-six hours.

While the audiovisual classes drained a lot of my time, I needed little preparation and there was no marking. I was given the advanced audiovisual class, which was a real treat since only four students were qualified to take it. Their French was already excellent. So instead of following the rather pedestrian content set out in the textbook, we spent most of the time discussing subjects that were of interest to them. My two first-year classes were quite different. In the very first class, having ascertained that the marks awarded in the Grade 11 exam bore little relation to the student's level of ability, I set about revising/teaching the present tense of *donner*. I wrote the six forms on the board (students had not yet had the chance to purchase textbooks) and pronounced each carefully, getting the class of 30 students to repeat. However, when I got to *ils donnent*, a student put up his hand and said I had pronounced it incorrectly, and proceeded to show me the correct way, as taught to him by his high school teacher: "eels donent," each consonant clearly and deliberately sounded. I was somewhat taken aback by this, and pointed out that I had studied French for a considerable period of time and had just spent the best part of a year in France. The student was not impressed by my experience, continued to mutter about my incompetence, and did not return for the second meeting of the class.

As the third week of classes began, I was settling into a fairly hectic routine. My wife had not learned to drive, so if she needed to go anywhere I would drive the short distance to our apartment, deliver her to where she needed to go, then return to campus for my next class. Then came the next bombshell. With my salary cheque at the end of September I received a letter stating that British subjects would be deducted income tax at the regular rate, but would have it rebated at the end of their probationary two-year contract. Great news. But it applied only to British subjects . . . the four French nationals, hired like me in September, were outraged.

I finally got to meet "M. Morgan" at the first meeting of the Arts and Science Faculty Council. He was the Dean! During the summer, when I was appointed, he had been the Acting President, and so had been responsible for confirming new hires. It was an impressive sight as over 200 faculty members crammed into the Arts and Education Building lecture theatre. The business of the meeting was quickly dispatched, as Dr. Morgan dealt efficiently with the various committee reports. I was slowly accustoming myself to the structure of university governance with the myriad committees feeding their work from the departmental level, to faculty council, and then to Senate. This introduction was facilitated by Peter Royle, with whom I shared an office.

When the Education Building was first opened (and for many years afterwards) it was called "Arts and Education" since a large portion of the building was occupied by Modern Languages, and many of the classrooms were used by departments still housed in Arts and Administration. I think it was when Modern Languages (by then French and Spanish, German and Russian) moved to the Science Building, around 1972, that the "Arts and" was dropped.

While the Arts and Education Building was new, it was not large enough to afford individual offices to all tenure-track faculty members. In addition, the Modern Languages Department, which had had special difficulty in retaining professors, had been given a dispensation allowing it to hire husband-and-wife couples, but . . . they were not allowed to share an office. So Peter's wife, Elizabeth, and Michael Wilkshire's wife, Frances, shared.

Lack of space was not the only inconvenience in the new building (which had its "twin" in the new Chemistry-Physics Building). The heating/cooling system was, we were told, very sophisticated, yet in those few weeks of the training course in July, when the sun was warm, the heating was on. Rumour also had it that Honeywell, which had designed and installed the system, had not yet trained their local technicians, something they failed to do for a number of years. So on the Victoria Day and Labour Day weekends, Honeywell sent a technician from Chicago to make adjustments.

Social life in that first year in St. John's was an eye-opener for me. Until then, I had lived as a student, enjoying simple pleasures that involved drinking and dancing. As a faculty member, even though still probationary, I had moved up one class from working-class to middle-class, but without any prior training in the required social mores. Imagine my surprise, then, when Peter and Elizabeth Royle invited my wife and me to a dinner party just two weeks after we arrived. The occasion was to say goodbye to Brian Reardon, a Classics professor, and his wife, Janette (who taught in Modern Languages). He was leaving to take up a professorship at the University of California, a very prestigious move for a man in his forties. The fourth couple was Patrick and Frankie O'Flaherty. Patrick was one of the young stars in the English Department, a Newfoundlander who had excelled at the undergraduate level and then completed a PhD at the University of London in two years. His wife was equally dynamic, and so we got our first taste of social and intellectual life at a very high level. Pre-dinner conversation was brisk, fuelled by copious servings of alcohol, and debate continued fast and furious throughout the seven-course meal, Peter producing wine after fabulous wine (where had he got his supply?), and Elizabeth course after elegant course. I realized that I would have to revise any plans I may have had for entertaining in St. John's.

Social occasions at that pitch were not uncommon in my first term at Memorial, but one other event deserves mention. Our new President, Lord Taylor of Harlow, arrived in the fall of 1967, and to welcome him, and the large number of new faculty members, the university decided to hold a reception in the main dining room of Gushue Hall. Memorial had for years found it expedient to look for new professors in the United Kingdom, since attempts to attract Canadians had largely failed. And, because of the Vietnam War, many US academics had been attracted to Memorial. However, few from either source elected to stay for more than the initial two-year contract. The Modern Languages Department reckoned on a 40 to 50 per cent turnover every year, so among the 800 or so professors milling about in Gushue Hall, nearly 200 of them were new hires. I wandered around, frequently replenishing my glass while making the acquaintance of new and old hands. Eventually, Dr. Morgan managed to subdue the noise enough to introduce Lord Taylor. I can't recall anything memorable from what he said, but I do remember his imposing presence, a tall, heavy-set man with strong facial features and a shock of white hair. He had been granted a life peerage on the strength of his service as Minister of Health in the coalition government in Britain (and subsequently in Clement Attlee's cabinet), in which position he had steered through Parliament the bill establishing the National Health Service. I'm not sure why Joey Smallwood chose him to be Memorial's President, but it was an inspired decision. In spite of Taylor's occasional gaffes, he pushed for the establishment of the Medical School and encouraged faculty members to strive to put Memorial on the academic map.

As the academic year progressed, so did the preparations for a major initiative in the structuring of academic life for students. While the number of first-year students was growing each year, so was the number of students leaving after one year, or even one term, the so-called "Christmas Graduates." The latter group, often from small fishing villages, would return to teach in the schools they had recently left and eventually complete their degrees via summer school. It made it easier for them to finance their university education, and filled gaps in the teaching ranks of the school system. The final details for the start of Junior Division were made, and some hiring had already taken place. Class sizes for most subjects were to be limited to 30 in first year, with particular focus on English and mathematics, the smaller classes making it possible to require more writing (and marking) in English and more personal attention in maths. That restructuring, of course, required many more classrooms, and so were created the "temporary" modules that were to be a feature of Memorial's campus for many years to come. Some are still there, some 45 years later. Slowly, Memorial's retention rate improved, thereby justifying that bold experiment.

And so Memorial was on an expansion path that followed similar developments elsewhere in Canada, prompting Lord Taylor to quip that Canadian universities formed an empire on which the concrete never sets.

Another enterprise, of a non-academic nature, was the creation of a theatre group. In the late fall of 1968, Dick Buehler (English and Folklore) and I met at a party (I think in connection with the Children's

Centre, an independent school that our families participated in) and after a few beers (a leitmotif of Open Group activities) began to talk about Dick's passion: theatre. I had heard that he had been involved with a summer Repertory Company (the capital letters indicate the awe in which I held such an institution) before coming to Newfoundland, and he was miffed that he could not break into the St. John's theatre scene. He had, he told me, auditioned on a number of occasions for the St. John's Players (SJP) and for Sylvia Wigh's Freelance Players, and had proposed directing a play for the SJP, but had been shut out, a situation that I no doubt wrongly attributed to their prejudice against come from aways, wrongly because the leading lights in the SJP and Sylvia Wigh had all arrived in St. John's as adults and so could not themselves claim to be Newfoundland-born and raised.

As our conversation developed, it became clear that Dick wanted to form a theatre group that would stage classic plays that the other two groups did not want to tackle, especially from the European and American traditions. He had the experience to take on anything, and his enthusiasm convinced me that it was worth making the attempt. I had had some acting experience in high school and university, and had recently been in two SJP productions: *Love Rides the Rails, or Will the Mail Train Run Tonight*, a 1944 reproduction of a late nineteenth-century melodrama in which I played the villain; and *Tom Jones*, in which I had a bit part as the Irish officer who engages in a fencing duel with Tom over a woman. Dick knew a couple of Newfoundlanders at the university who were interested in forming a new group, so an initial meeting was arranged to take place in a classroom shortly after that party, in November 1968. I can't remember if the meeting was advertised in the *Evening Telegram* or if we relied solely on word-of-mouth, but 10 or so people showed up. I can recall the following being present: Dick, myself, John and Muriel Roddis (John was an instructor at the College of Fisheries — now the Marine Institute), Dr. Bill Marshall (Faculty of Medicine), Ann Alexander (wife of David Alexander, History), Pat Byrne (English), Norman and Pam Kipnis (Norman was with the Department of Mines), and Michael Cook, an animateur with Extension and subsequently a member of the Department of English. In short order we agreed that we would indeed form a theatre group, an executive committee was chosen (no such thing as a formal election on that occasion), and the first production selected: Cocteau's *The Mad Woman of Chaillot*. Dick proposed the play so it was automatic that he would direct it. The details of financing the first production escape me, but we probably all chipped in a nominal amount to cover advertising auditions, with the rest coming from the box office.[1] Suppliers of materials must have been very trusting to have given an untried group credit!

The question of a name for the group naturally took up some of the time of that first meeting. Most of those present had had experiences similar to Dick's: they felt shut out of an established group, with little prospect of breaking in. So when Bill Marshall proposed the eminently simple and direct name of "The Open Group," it was immediately adopted without further discussion. This is how the initial group was subsequently described in an "information sheet, undated, presently in the possession of Professor R. Buehler."[2]

> ... university professors, students, filling station attendants, provincial civil servants, vocational and public school teachers, shopkeepers and clerks, doctors and housewives.

Up to this point none of us had worked through the experience of producing a play in St. John's. Some of us had performed on the Arts and Culture stage, but we were not aware of how its technical facilities were operated or managed. We knew of the existence of the Little Theatre on the campus of the university, but nothing about its rather antiquated lighting system, its limited stage area, wings, and dressing rooms, or even about whom to approach to make a booking. But we were launched!

The activities of the Open Group continued to occupy a lot of my spare time from the beginning until about 1974, at which point many of the founding members were drawn away to other matters. But the group was instrumental in integrating many members of the Memorial community into the life of St. John's and in keeping them beyond their initial two-year contract.

Notes

1. In fact, correspondence in the Buehler archive indicates that Memorial University of Newfoundland contributed seed money in the form of a

grant of $500 and a loan for the same amount. Later correspondence between Dick Buehler and the university's Comptroller indicates that the loan was, according to the university's books, $365. The loan was repaid. Michael Cook, who was employed as an animateur for theatre by MUN's Extension Service at the time, was probably instrumental in securing this funding.

2. As reported in an undated proposal for a conference paper, "The Open Group and Michael Cook's Real Openings."

Come From Away at Memorial, 1964

Roberta Buchanan

24

I Leave England

It was 1964, the year of Shakespeare's quatercentenary. Here I was at the prestigious Shakespeare Institute, Birmingham University, where I had gone to do my PhD. After two years my fellowship ran out, and I still hadn't finished my thesis. I was hired as a research assistant, then promoted to research associate at a stipend of 50 pounds a month. I was employed in the menial but necessary tasks of checking quotations and bibliographical references, proofreading the Institute's publications, doing research for the Director, Professor T.J.B. Spencer, even, in one case, rewriting an article for *Shakespeare Survey*. When the librarian suddenly left, I was also asked to fill in her position, on a temporary basis. At the weekly seminars, I made the tea and handed around the biscuits.

At Birmingham University, the social and academic hierarchy was rigidly maintained. I found myself in a kind of grey area. I was neither student nor faculty. I was not entitled to eat in the plush Faculty Club; my place was in the cafeteria with the staff, for my status was somewhat lower than that of a faculty member. There seemed no prospect of advancement. Young male graduate students were "mentored," as we say now, given some teaching experience; women students weren't. In 1964, the term "glass ceiling" had not yet been invented. It was more like a concrete ceiling. Glass at least suggests that if persistent you could smash your way through it.

Birmingham seemed to me a dismal, dirty, and depressing place. I rented a room in a dreary brick terrace house on the Bourn Brook, a polluted trickle garnished with rusty bicycles, old paint cans, and other urban trash, which always seemed to be shrouded in industrial smog. I had to get away — but how? Desperation gave me courage.

I opened *The World of Learning*, a huge compendium of all academic institutions in the universe, and began at A. I sent a letter to the University of Alaska — the farthest possible spot from Birmingham — asking them if they had any openings in their English Department and enclosing my CV. I got a polite but negative response: "Thank you for your interest in the University of Alaska . . . ." I scrutinized the weekly job ads in the *Times Literary Supplement*: universities in Ghana, the Gold Coast, Khartoum, and Malta were looking for lecturers in English literature. I was interviewed for Malta, but the other candidate, a handsome young man from Oxford, got the job. Another ad: Memorial University of Newfoundland, in Canada; sent off application and CV. One day a telegram arrived at the Stygian gloom of the dark-panelled Shakespeare Institute — immediate reply demanded, prepaid — offering me a job as Lecturer in the English Department at the princely salary of $6,500 per annum, $500 above the minimum rate for Lecturer. I was ecstatic and accepted immediately. "You're just the kind of person we need in Canada," the young man interviewing me at Canada House for my immigration papers said.

I sailed on the *Empress of England* from Greenock (my parents lived in Scotland) to Montreal, with my immigrant's suitcase — a heavy affair with a wooden frame and a tray inside. Five days later I arrived in Canada. We went through immigration in Quebec City, and then disembarked at Montreal, where I was to get the CN train for the long journey to the east coast. On the train I had my own luxurious "roomette," and after a good night's sleep woke up in my new country. How clean and spacious it looked after crowded and filthy Birmingham!

I Arrive in Newfoundland

At last I arrived in Newfoundland, my new home, via the ferry to Port aux Basques, and then a bumpy two-day railway journey on the "Newfie Bullet." On the 21st of August 1964, my new boss, Dr. Seary, head of the English Department, and his wife Gwen, met me at the station and drove me to the Kenmount Motel. I found them "very English, considering they've been here 11 years," I recorded in my journal. The hotel seemed to me the height of luxury. I marvelled at the huge "treble" bed, all for me, and lovingly catalogued in my journal the features of my "super room": two wooden walls and a wooden ceiling, "very modern"; my own private bathroom and toilet in one corner; towels, soap, matches, Kleenex, stationery, and even a pen provided on the house; wall-to-wall carpeting, air conditioning, tourist information on Newfoundland, a picture of the landscape, and television.

I went downstairs to the dining-room and had an expensive dinner of an enormous piece of fried salmon with "French fries," which I carefully noted were chips. The waitresses were very funny-looking, dressed in white uniforms with white shoes, like nurses, except that they had little yellow aprons. I overheard one of the tourists saying, "The first time I went tuna-fishing I was six." There was an air of unreality. Was it all a dream?

I was brought down to earth with a bump by — cash. I had a hundred Canadian dollars, which seemed to me a large sum, and was dismayed to read posted on the door of my motel room that it cost $9 a night plus 5 per cent tax. It took no mathematical genius to calculate that if I spent 10 nights, with even minimal eating, I would be broke. And my first paycheque was at the end of September.

I was 26 years old. I was in a strange country where I knew no one. I had no teaching experience. I was scared. In honour of my new country, I had bought a large bottle of Canadian Club, a 40-ouncer, at the duty-free shop on board ship. I had a pack of cards. I sat on the floor of my room, played patience, watched tear-jerkers on television, and drank rye and ginger ale.

So began my new life in Canada.

First Impressions of St. John's

The next day was Sunday. The hotel room began to get on my nerves. I saw a notice in the lobby about church services. I hadn't gone to a church in years — but what else could one do on a Sunday? I took the bus to the Anglican Cathedral. The people in hats, the asking forgiveness for their sins "for there is no health in me" did not cheer me up. After the service I walked down to Water Street, where some men whistled and shouted unintelligible remarks as I passed. A shop grandly called THE LONDON NEW YORK AND PARIS had the oddest models in the window dressed in strange outdated fortyish clothes and hairstyles. There was a chill wind, laced with a whiff of fish; not many people about except a few lonely-looking sailors. I caught the bus back to the Kenmount Motel and sought the artificial comfort of my whisky bottle.

"The MUN"

On Monday, I went to the Bursar's Office to get a loan to tide me over until payday; they refused. (In England when you get a new job you can always get an advance on your salary.) Here was a dilemma! How was I to manage? I must move out of the expensive Kenmount Motel at once. Most of the faculty were away for the summer, but fortunately I met a colleague in the English Department, Dr. Jim Francis, a tall red-bearded man (also English). He drove me round town and up Signal Hill in his red sports car, and told me I must *never* call New-fin-land New-*found*-land. Then he cooked me lunch in his apartment and "gave a long disquisition on the irrationality of women." I summed up his character in my journal: "He is very dogmatic, in that he does not expect dissent from his opinions. I argue a little, but not much as it (argument) seems ultimately futile — altho' he thinks it changes all minds but women" (22 August).

Despite his odd opinions of women, Dr. Francis was kind and helpful. He found a widow who took in a respectable female boarder at a very reasonable price, breakfast and dinner included — more for the company, she told me, for she had been married to an American GI and had a generous pension. She showed me a room filled with an enormous double bed covered with a bright pink satin spread, and just enough space to cram in a large dressing-table with mirror. I paid my "astronomical" bill of "over twenty-seven dollars" at the motel, and moved in immediately. (Afterwards I found out that Memorial would pay for my hotel as part of my moving expenses.)

Dr. Francis showed me round the university — "the MUN, as they call it here" — which seemed very small compared to Birmingham University. It was built on an exposed position on top of a hill — "winds wuthered outside — very clean and pleasant inside hw. — marble floors and all." I moved into my office on the third floor, with a view of a ridgy hill covered with trees (Pippy Park), and laid out my textbooks on the empty bookshelves. Every day I took two buses to the university. It was very cold in my office, the wind howled and moaned in the roof, and the rain beat against the windows. I sat at my desk staring at Lily's *Campaspe* in *Five Elizabethan Comedies*. I was to teach three different courses: Elizabethan drama, English 200 (starting with Aristotle's *Poetics*), and

Bibliography and Research. Soon getting sick of *Campaspe*, I went over to the library (tiny, compared to the huge edifice of Birmingham University Library) and started looking at all the bibliographies of English literature in the reference section. At 11 o'clock I went for coffee in the coffee room. Here, everybody — faculty, staff (even the janitors) — and, later, students — had their coffee in the same place! The coffee room closed at 11:30. At 12 the reference section was locked, as if mad thieves might take off with its heavy tomes in the lunch hour. At noon everybody drove home and everything closed down until two — the reference section, the offices, even the switchboard. There was nowhere on campus to get lunch. I walked down to Churchill Square where I could get coffee and a sandwich in Ayre's Supermarket. Then back to the office to try and make notes on the now detested *Campaspe*. At five I took the bus back to my boarding house, where a huge meal awaited me — a large halibut steak with potatoes, turnips, and peas, jello and tinned (canned) fruit for dessert, and tea. I ate alone, for my landlady did not eat with me. Then I went to my room and went to bed, since there was nothing else to do.

After a few days of sitting alone in my office, having lunch alone in the supermarket, and dinner alone in the boarding house, I became very depressed. Time was passing. I didn't seem to be making much progress with *Five Elizabethan Comedies*. I sat in my office in rising panic and thought of all the books I hadn't read. Soon the students would return and term would begin. How would I manage? One evening at dinner I could no longer suppress my anxiety and started to cry. My motherly landlady packed me off to bed.

My long-time dream was to have a place of my very own instead of living in a room in someone else's house, as I had done in England. Dr. Francis took me to see an apartment (I learned not to call it a "flat") on Queen's Road. On the third floor, it had a large sitting-room with a fireplace, a bedroom, kitchen with fridge and stove, and bathroom; hardwood floors. Best of all was the large window with a stunning view of the harbour, Signal Hill, and the Narrows. All this for a hundred dollars a month, including heat. I could watch the sun rising over Signal Hill, shining on the sea, the ships sailing into the harbour through the Narrows. From that moment I fell in love with St. John's.

I found out that it was easy to get a bank loan in Canada, and borrowed $100 against pay day. I bought an iron bedstead from a friend of my landlady for $20. At a second-hand furniture store I bought a table, some chairs, and a chest of drawers for a very modest sum. (When they were delivered, I grandly gave the men a dollar tip.) My crate of books and pictures arrived. I was delighted. The living room had not only the view of the Narrows but also of Prescott Street, which plunged steeply down to the harbour, and I could look down into the tall row houses and see people washing their dishes in their kitchens. The bedroom had a view of the Basilica with its clock, Queen's Road, and Rawlins Cross with its two drugstores and Murphy's superette, which sold everything from plastic buckets to rabbits (in season), from coal to carrots. On Prescott Street there was a small basement laundry where I could take my sheets.

My spirits rose. I had a good job — university Lecturer — with generous pay of $400 per month (I immediately put down $100 on a record player, to be paid in instalments). I had an apartment of my own. Best of all, I had escaped from grimy old England with its wretched cold bedsitters and dank bathrooms with wet towels, Birmingham with its polluted air, rows of grey dismal houses, and snobby university. Here wooden houses were gaily painted in different colours. The sun shone and sparkled on the sea. I had finally "arrived."

I Begin Teaching

Teaching was just talking about literature, wasn't it? How difficult could it be? After all, I loved literature. I bought a second-hand tape recorder and attempted to practise a typical lecture — say, on *The Duchess of Malfi*, one of the four tragedies I would be teaching in English 200. Alas, after a few sentences and ers and ums I dried up. I couldn't think of anything to say. I made several discoveries: I would have to write out all my lectures and read them. And: it took me an hour to compose one page of lecture notes, not counting the preliminary reading. It took six typewritten pages (single-spaced) for one lecture. That was six hours of writing.

My office mate, Dr. Elisabeth Orsten, arrived back from Oxford. She smoked a pipe, much to the horror of the President, Dr. Gushue, who told her that it tarnished the image of the university. There were other young women faculty. Olga Broomfield, a Newfoundlander, kindly gave me her notes on the Bibliography course, which she had taken as a student from Dr. Story (famous as one of the compilers of the *Dictionary of Newfoundland English*). An Albertan, Diane Schlanker, of Ukrainian ancestry — one of the few "Canadians" (i.e., mainlanders) in the English Department — lived a few doors down from me on Queen's Road, and we soon became friends.

I grew more and more anxious as the beginning of semester approached. The students would soon find out the gaps in my knowledge, and I would be ignominiously fired! I couldn't sleep, my stomach was in a constant knot. I went to Dr. Kennedy, just a few blocks down on Queen's Road, and asked him for some tranquilizers. He said he didn't prescribe tranquilizers. I was distraught — perhaps I cried. Anyway, he relented and wrote me a prescription. Thus fortified, I went to my first class — Bibliography and Research. All I had to do was explain to the students what the course was about and give them a reading list. These were all honours students, the crème de la crème. To my horror, my tongue felt thick, my speech was slurred, and I found it difficult to think. Tranquilizers were not the answer.

What a semester that was! I've never worked so hard or been under such pressure. It was worse than Finals. I had a nine o'clock class on Tuesday, Thursday, and Saturday (English 200, 50 students); an evening class, Tuesday and Thursday (Elizabethan drama); and my bibliography class Monday and Wednesday. I cut one hour of the bibliography class so that the students could go to the library and look at the bibliographies assigned for that week and report back on them to the class. That still meant eight hours of lectures to prepare. After my nine o'clock class I rushed home to write the lecture for my evening class. This class had several highly intelligent teachers in it, and I was always crippled with nervous diarrhea before it. Luckily, as soon as I started my lecture it disappeared. On Sundays, I had to research and write the bibliography lecture on the History of the Book. And how I wrestled with Aristotle's *Poetics* — a difficult text I could hardly understand myself and that was hell to explain to the second-year students. No sooner was one lecture prepared and delivered than it was on to the next one. I was always in terror that some student would ask a question I couldn't answer, for a professor should know everything about her subject, I thought. I read as much as I could.

I knew what kind of professor I *didn't* want to be. I didn't want to be like Dr. H., at Keele, who looked over the students' heads at the wall behind us as if we were contemptible. I didn't want to be sarcastic and put students down. I would treat them with respect, always. I would never, ever say, like Dr. K., that Jane Austen was a great writer because she had a "masculine mind." And I was not going to treat Newfoundland with disdain, as some of my colleagues did, as the intellectual and social boondocks. After all, I was a colonial myself who had been born in South Africa. In fact, I encouraged my bibliography students to choose a Newfoundland writer as the subject for their annotated bibliography, if they wished to do so. That was the smartest move I ever made, for it was in this way that I came to know something about Newfoundland literature.

My nemesis was teaching poetry on Saturday mornings to the second-year students. My method was from I.A. Richards, *Practical Criticism*, one of our textbooks: go through the poem line by line. Explication. Our poetry anthology gave two critics' different interpretations of each poem. This confused the students, who thought there was only one interpretation — the teacher's — for every poem had a "hidden meaning," and it was your job to tell them what it was so they could write it on the exam. Since I was very bad at remembering names, and more so when I was nervous, I had the whole class sit in alphabetical order, so that I could call on them in turn and knew exactly where they sat. They hated this, as it separated friend from friend. Saturday mornings were poetry torture. I called on each student in turn to give their interpretation of the line or stanza. I didn't realize that some students were so shy that they never spoke in class. I was traumatizing them by calling out their names and insisting that they answer. In the other classes — Aristotle's *Poetics*, followed by four tragedies — I gave lectures. But it seemed to me that poetry was different and needed to be discussed.

Things came to a head with Wordsworth's "Ode on the Intimations of Immortality." Several Saturdays had been spent in trying to get through this long poem, line by line. On the third Saturday the students' patience snapped. I found written in large letters on the board: "NO MORE IMITATIONS OF IMMORTALITY."

Poor students! How they suffered at the hands of an inexperienced teacher who was obliged to learn by her mistakes. I tried to arouse their interest. I remember asking the question: Why should we be interested in a play — Webster's *The Duchess of Malfi* — written four centuries ago? Does it have anything to say to us today? And then trying to convince them that it did. It was a damned difficult play, too. At that time, the courses lasted a whole academic year, two semesters. So we were together for a long time. The students were very forgiving. At the last class, much to my surprise, they clapped. Apparently that was the custom at the time: that the students would show their appreciation in the last class. A very nice custom, for a new teacher.

I had made it to the end of term. Gwen Seary told me that Ron Seary thought highly of me. In spite of all my fears, doubts, and anxieties, it seems that I had passed the test with flying colours.[1]

Note

1. A longer version of this was published in Don F. Mulcahy, ed., *Coming Here, Being Here: A Canadian Migration Anthology* (Oakville, ON: Guernica Editions, 2016).

Edgar Ronald Seary. (Photo from *Cap and Gown*, 1959, courtesy of Memorial University Libraries

25 On Being Head of the Math Department

Bruce Shawyer

In 1984, in order to celebrate the sixtieth birthday of my PhD supervisor, David Borwein, I helped to organize a surprise conference at the University of Western Ontario (UWO) with the participation of his former students and close collaborators. We tried, in collaboration with his wife, Bessie, to keep it a surprise for David.

One of his former students is Bruce Watson, who was at Memorial University. My wife Jo was teaching the Geography of Canada at Brescia College, an affiliate of UWO. She had by then set foot in every province of Canada except Newfoundland (as our province was then known: now Newfoundland and Labrador). She saw an opportunity here, and suggested to me that I ask Bruce Watson to get me invited to give a colloquium talk at Memorial. This Bruce was kind enough to do so, and I visited Memorial in the fall of 1984.

We arranged to stay over the weekend and do a little sightseeing. This included a visit to Signal Hill, where the wind was so strong that we were not able to get out of the car. We also went for a drive "around the bay," in particular to visit Harbour Grace. We stopped just before entering the town, because suddenly the rental car was making a funny noise. I got out and looked down to find a flat tire on the driver's front side. We managed to limp along to a service station at the entrance to the town and got help to put on the spare tire. The mechanic noted the round hole on the side of the tire he had removed, and commented, "That looks like a bullet hole." Later we discovered that this was the first day of hunting season. Was this just a misaimed shot? Or was it a message? Well, with the spare safely on, we did get safely back to St. John's.

Soon thereafter, I saw the advert for a new head of the Department of Mathematics and Statistics at Memorial University. Since we had enjoyed what we had seen of Newfoundland and its people, I threw my hat into the ring, and was pleased when I received an invitation to be interviewed.

I was asked to arrive on Tuesday 13 November 1984, and to depart on Saturday 17 November — for a three-day interview! Since my wife had already experienced a visit, it was decided that I should take our elder children with me — ages 15 and 14 — so that they could find out something about the place they might be forced to move to.

On day one I was interviewed, in turn, by the Dean of Science, the Vice-President (Academic), the Dean of Education, the Dean of Arts, the Dean of Business Administration, and a representative from Sir Wilfred Grenfell College in Corner Brook. I met with various members of the department and gave a colloquium talk. The day ended with a wine-and-cheese party with members of the department.

On day two I met, in turn, with the Statistics Group, the Applied Mathematics Group, the Analysis Group, and the Algebra and Topology Group, and was also interviewed by the Assistant Dean of Part-time Graduate Studies. The day ended with myself and my children being taken out to dinner by the Dean of Science and his wife. More on that later.

On day three, I was interviewed, in turn, by the Headship Search Committee, the Director of General Studies, the Dean of Medicine, the Dean of Engineering, the Dean of Graduate Studies, and the Director of Extension Services, and met the heads of science departments informally over coffee. My final formal interview was with the Dean of Science. The day ended with myself and my children being treated to a dinner with members of the Mathematics and Statistics Department.

In the meantime, the two children had explored St. John's and visited some schools, where they felt they had been made very welcome.

The dinner with the Dean of Science and his wife was held at the Kenmount (Chinese) Restaurant. It started with the Dean offering the children each a glass of wine. Now, they were aged 14 and 15 and on their best behaviour. They looked at me, and I gave them a quiet nod. The Dean poured each a small glass and then also for me, his wife, and himself. He showed them how to make a wine glass sing, using a dampened finger to run around the rim! Later, when the bottle was empty, he showed them how to make the bottle sing by blowing across the top. Later, back in Ontario, the children told me that they thought the Dean of Science was "a neat guy!"

At the final dinner with the members of the department, my children were made to feel very welcome, and this helped them to enjoy their first visit to St. John's.

I must not end without telling you about the final interview with the Dean of Science. His last question was to ask me what salary I would expect if I were to be offered the job. I stated the amount of the salary that I would receive the next year if I were to remain at UWO. The Dean's reply was one word — "extortionist." I knew then that, if offered the job at Memorial, I would not come for less than that figure.

Well, sometime later, I did get the job offer, and despite being shot at during my first interview, I did accept it. I'll say no more, except that years later, in talking with a person I will not name, he told me that the Dean of Science had consulted him about the extortionist, and that he had told the Dean "If you want someone, you have to pay what that person is worth."

I thoroughly enjoyed my six years as head of Mathematics and Statistics, and the subsequent 11 years in the department as well.

That is how I came to be at Memorial University.

So there I was in August 1985, the head of the Department of Mathematics and Statistics, newly arrived in St. John's, having driven with my family — my wife and the four children — all the way from Ontario. We had bought a house on Cochrane Street, but it (and our furniture) would not be ready until about five days after our arrival. We stayed in the Hotel Newfoundland (as it was called then) quite close by.

I took the Metrobus up to campus — quite a circuitous route — and announced myself in the department main office. They were not quite ready for me, but found me a temporary office near the main office, where I could park a few belongings and wait for the head's office to be vacated. I was made welcome by the head's secretary and the departmental administrator. I had made a visit in mid-April, when I bought the Cochrane Street house, and had a few informal meetings with some of the faculty, who were then quite anxious to meet me.

It took a couple of days to get the names right (never my best point) and to begin to learn the way Memorial worked — who was important where, etc. But I must say that the majority of people were kind and welcoming, and this made a nice starting impression. I will say that I found the people in the department a great group of people to work for and only had a couple of unpleasant incidents in the six years I worked for them.

There was, in fact, very little to do, because the retiring head had organized everything long before I came: such as who was teaching what, and who was serving on what committee. He told me that he wished me well, and that he would not interfere in anything I did unless he felt it was not for the good of the department. And he kept his word. I think we got along well.

I am by nature a democrat, and like things to be well discussed and group decisions taken. This was strange to some members of the department, who expected a more autocratic rule. At that time, the faculty was not unionized, and had been used to a head being a decision-maker on his own. Well, they would have to get used to me and my ways.

I spent a lot of time visiting faculty members in their offices, having discussions on what they considered important for their own careers and for the department itself. And I made a point of being a regular attendee at coffee breaks (even though I had been instructed by my doctor in Ontario to cut down on the amount of coffee I drank, to help keep my blood pressure under control). And there was lunch. At that time, there was a Faculty Club in what is now the Junior Common Room, where many faculty had lunch, and here was a chance to meet people from around the university.

Now, my wife wanted the spouses of my colleagues in the department to meet this CFA who had been brought in. So we decided to hold dinner parties in our Cochrane Street home. Since the total departmental complement (faculty and staff) was about 50, we could not have everyone together, so we had several parties. Our children were marvellous at welcoming people and ensuring that they were well taken care of. We are told that these events were a great success in many ways.

Another thing happened to me in my first semester here. First, I was "inspected" by the President Emeritus, Dr. Moses Morgan, commonly known as Mose. My secretary announced that Dr. Mose Morgan was here to see me, and I had no idea who this person was. However, I welcomed him into my office, and soon discovered that he was just trying to find out what sort of person I was. He was still interested in the well-being of Memorial. We had a very pleasant chat for about an hour, and then he departed.

A little later, I was "inspected" by Dr. Doug Eaton. Doug was then the Director of Alumni Affairs, having previously been Director of

Physical Education. Again, this was someone trying to find out what sort of person I was, for he was also very interested in the well-being of Memorial. We did become good friends, and I miss him sorely. He is also well remembered as the first president of the Friends of Pippy Park. Many people do not realize that the university campus is in fact located in Pippy Park, which was established many years ago as a land for institutional building. The original plan for Memorial University was to be located around Long Pond, but that did not happen, perhaps a good thing for the ecology of Long Pond.

In the middle of my six years as department head we had a new Dean of Science. My only problem with him was that I could not get enough funding for all the good projects of the people in the department. As a result, it was necessary to say "no" to some people more often than I liked, and, in one case, I began to wonder if he thought it was me being against him (which was not the case). And, when my second three-year term as head was coming to a close, the Dean tried to persuade me to extend the term. He said that the department was well run. But I had had enough of being the bearer of bad news and wanted to spend more time on mathematics and less on administration. So I politely and firmly declined his request. Shortly thereafter, the department had a new head, and I tried to follow my predecessor's rule of not interfering unless I felt strongly that something was not good for the department. This is not to say that I agreed with everything, but I tried to keep my mouth shut, not an easy thing for me. As a result, I was able to return to my first love in mathematics, geometry.

Being able to teach geometry was a delight, but there was one real difficulty — I could not find a suitable text. As a result, I started to write out course notes that were initially just handed to students. A couple of years later, when I had them in what I considered to be reasonable good shape, they were printed in advance and sold to the students as a textbook. There was no money for me in this, and any profits went to the department. Some colleagues actually used these notes as a course text, both at Memorial University and elsewhere. So, several years later, when I received a request to submit a possible text to a publisher, I sent these notes in together with the solutions manual for all the problems that I had set for the students (but which was never printed out except for colleagues). Almost by return, the publisher told me that a combination of these two manuscripts was the basis for a book, and encouraged me to proceed. This I did, and so came into being *Explorations in Geometry*, published by World Scientific in Singapore.

When I turned 65, Memorial still got rid of people summarily at one second after midnight on 1 August following one's sixty-fifth birthday. This, of course, is not the present practice. However, having taught for 40 years in three different universities, I felt that I had done my stint and was happy to retire. Now, Memorial has given me the official title of "old and useless," but in Latin. The word "emeritus" was originally given to Roman soldiers who were no longer of any use to the Roman army, hence "old and useless." Not many people can be pleased to be officially "old and useless," but, in this case, I am.

Computer in action. (Photo from *Memorial University of Newfoundland and its Environs: A Guide to Life and Work at the University in St. John's*, courtesy of Memorial University Libraries.)

26

Coming to Memorial: The Wife's Tale

Jo Shawyer

I'm the wife.

Of the man who came to Memorial. So I came too.

He came for a position at the university. I came with the children. It was 1985.

Most of my career has been in the era before the institution of maternity leave, registered daycare, and spousal appointments. Thus, in Ontario, in 1970, I parked my PhD and academic career until the children were older and in school.

However, for 10 years or so, while the children were young, I continued as an independent scholar, tucking my research activities in and among my children's schedules and needs. I taught sessionally at several institutions in London, Ontario — Western University, Brescia College, and Fanshawe College — where I taught travel agents their geography! I was especially happy to serve on a committee for a master plan for Fanshawe Pioneer Village. I researched and curated several photographic exhibits, one for a rural township, the other for an urban neighbourhood. I wrote a community history by taking my toddlers along with me to interview the older residents. They delighted in feeding the children cookies (and the children did not complain!) while I wrote down their stories. Through these many activities I came to know and enjoy the collegiality of neighbours, bureaucrats, archivists, and academics who enjoyed historical and geographical research.

But then we came to Memorial.

We were delighted to come to Newfoundland and Labrador in general and pleased about my husband's appointment as head of Mathematics and Statistics at Memorial University in particular. But I left behind in Ontario my early research for a second book and my fascinating master plan committee. And all my archival colleagues and contacts. And peaches, field-grown tomatoes, and corn.

I had to begin again. How to transition my interests and research from a landscape anchored in nineteenth-century pioneers, my own ancestors among them, to a fishery? What did I know about the fishery? The sea? Boats?

However, this was Newfoundland and Labrador, a welcoming place, I had heard.

Immediately upon arrival in St John's I was offered and accepted a sessional position (a contract for each term) in the Department of Geography at Memorial. But, being an independent scholar, I explored beyond the university and into the town. On a stroll down Water Street I chanced to notice a sign on a door: "Museum Association of Newfoundland and Labrador." I went in and introduced myself. Within a week I had become the secretary of MANL's provincial executive.

That was the beginning of 20 years of volunteer work to help develop community museums across the province. What a steep learning curve it was: flakes and root cellars and Orange Lodges and denominational schools. And, everywhere, the fishery. It was a remarkable exposure to an evocative cultural landscape.

An inquiry at the Agricultural Research Station on Brookfield Road led to my curating the first provincial exhibit of the history of agriculture in Newfoundland and Labrador: a whirlwind investigation of archives and photographic collections and interviews. This project was a real pleasure for me. I learned about the performance of agriculture in this province, which was in many ways different from the farm where I had grown up in southern Ontario. And I was welcomed into the Agricultural History Society of Newfoundland and Labrador, whose mandate is to research the role agriculture has played in the history of this province.

Curiosity took me to City Hall to meet the urban planners. They contracted me to create a heritage inventory of the commercial premises on Duckworth Street. Through this research, I expanded my circle of archival acquaintances and enjoyed lecture-lunches with the St. John's branch of the Atlantic Planners Association.

The sessional position became a contract position (a contract from September to April).

To develop a field area conveniently near for teaching purposes, I began to document the history of the Memorial University campus, which is located within the C.A. Pippy Park. In fact, Premier Smallwood created the park in 1966 to be a landscaped setting for his clutch of new provincial buildings: Confederation Building, Trades College, Arts and Culture Centre, and Memorial University. I researched and published an article about the C.A. Pippy Park as a policy landscape. With a quick dash to England I extended my master's research, undertaken at the University of Nottingham and its associated School of Agriculture. To a 1943 landscape of farm structure provided by wartime food records and my 1963 field study of the same area, I added another survey to create a longitudinal study across 45 years. I continued my interests in London, Ontario, by keeping an eye on the development of Fanshawe Pioneer Museum. And I helped my Ontario neighbours document the creation of a student ghetto in their midst and trace its origins to new and controversial changes in provincial residential legislation. But my half-researched book — a rural landscape study in Ontario — was too difficult to pursue during my short visits there. Remember, this period was pre-Internet.

I secured a tenure-track position.

At this time I was invited to join a three-year SSHRC-funded team to study agricultural policy and landscape in Cape Breton. This position extended my knowledge of Atlantic Canada by connecting me with the Nova Scotia Agricultural College at Truro. Our SSHRC team — a philosopher (Dr. Mora Campbell), a plant scientist (Dr. Norman Goodyear), two folklorists (Dr. James Moreira and Dr. Richard MacKinnon), and a geographer (me) — gained insight into how Cape Breton farmers navigated their farms through the web of legal, safety, market, and environmental policy and regulations that governed them.

A new teaching experience was broadcasting long-distance education to Burin and Labrador City through Memorial's Telemedicine system. For this, I was required to write the course manuals. The teaching was done in a studio in front of a faceless monitor. I could not see the students and they could not see me. But I was able to jot notes and draw diagrams of wind systems and prairie survey systems on my monitor in three different colours! One perk, which appealed to me as a geographer, was obligatory associated travel to Labrador and the Burin. But — the trips were in February.

Three years later — tenure. Associate Professor. Age 57.

I was drawn into my colleague Chris Sharpe's research about the policy and landscape history of Churchill Park. Who lived there before the St John's Housing Corporation expropriated the area in 1944? And how to explain the origins of the slum area (site of City Hall) that was intended to be partially relieved by the creation of Churchill Park? Chris and I also shared authorship for a chapter in Steven High's *Occupied St John's*. This was a study of the wartime landscape in St John's.[1]

Then it was time to retire. Compulsory. Age 65.

After a long academic gestation that led to a brief university career, I am an independent scholar again.

The research transition from Ontario to Newfoundland and Labrador is virtually complete. My personal volumes of the *Encyclopedia of Newfoundland and Labrador* are worn through use. The *Dictionary of Newfoundland English* is well-thumbed. Flakes, root cellars, and the Commission of Government hold no fears for me. Chris and I have recently written a book, *Sweat Equity*, about a Newfoundland co-operative housing policy, a post-Confederation (1949!) initiative of the provincial government together with the federal Central Mortgage and Housing Corporation.[2] And we are working on a book proposal for our extensive research into Churchill Park and the downtown slum.

This wife survived coming to Memorial. Indeed, I have thrived in this beguiling landscape. I have travelled the province and found a place among new friends, colleagues, landscapes, and archives. It's been a fascinating and a satisfying run. Lobster, blueberries, and moose have been delicious replacements for peaches, tomatoes, and corn.

But that rural landscape study in London, Ontario, half-researched, still calls me. Unfinished business. That is my only academic regret of my coming to Memorial.

Notes

1. Christopher A. Sharpe and A.J. Shawyer, "Building a Wartime Landscape," in Steven High, ed., *Occupied St John's: The Social History of a City at War 1939–1945* (Montreal and Kingston: McGill-Queen's University Press, 2010), 21–80.

2. C.A. Sharpe and A.J. Shawyer, *Sweat Equity. Cooperative House-building in Newfoundland, 1920–1974* (St. John's: ISER Books, 2016).

27

The Edge of Experience:
Coming to Newfoundland in the 1980s

Marilyn Porter

Gander airport is a dreary place at the best of times, and on a late August afternoon in 1980 it was not welcoming. All we could see out of the rain-speckled windows were stunted spruce, miles of them, and not much else. I looked nervously at my 10-year-old son. What benighted place was I bringing him to? But he had found some St. John's kids his own age, with the same taste in comics and games, and the common culture made him feel immediately at home. We went through some immigration procedures, of which I have no memory, and changed planes. We arrived in St. John's after dark and were immediately plunged into a departmental welcoming party. My son crashed out on a sofa somewhere and I did my jet-lagged, exhausted best to decode the sexual and intellectual tensions swirling round me. They put me to bed, finally, and the next morning I peered out of a small casement window down onto the harbour — and took in the boats, the South Side hills, the harbour entrance, the silvery light; things were looking up.

Like many people I came to Memorial by accident. After a bumpy divorce and sessional and less-than-sessional appointments, I had secured a tenure-track appointment in sociology at Manchester and moved, with my son, to Lancaster. It was a big, bustling, radical department with some key players in most areas of the discipline. There were three feminists — a radical feminist (Liz Stanley), a liberal feminist, a.k.a. a statistician (Alison Kelly), and me, holding the flag of Marxist feminist.[1] We got along famously and taught courses collectively and argumentatively, which must have been confusing for the students. Then came Thatcher and the first of the swingeing cuts to the universities. I was last-in-first-out and clearly doomed. But Peter Worsley (author of key sociology texts, pioneer in establishing sociology as an accepted discipline in the UK, and head of the Manchester department at the time) had visited Memorial on one of his academic wanderings; he made some connections and after the briefest vetting I was hired in the sociology department, albeit on a one-year appointment.

A few days after I arrived, I was hurtled into a full teaching schedule in a totally new academic and social environment. The students had come through a different school system, and had different knowledge and skills from the ones I had left behind in Manchester. They also had gaps in their knowledge that I first had to identify, then prioritize, and then plug. Was it really necessary for them to have heard of feudalism before I taught them Marx? My students were homogeneously bred in Newfoundland (not even Labrador) and they were deeply embedded in a uniquely different cultural and social background, about which I was woefully ignorant. I may, though I doubt it, have taught them some sociology in those early months, but undoubtedly they took me on a crash course in all things Newfoundland. I had not expected such strangeness, such richness, such difference from anything I had known before. They were deeply involved in large, complex, but close families and had the kind of deeply serious social and emotional knowledge that comes from living respectfully with different generations in isolated communities. Unlike UK students, who seemed to come detached from even their immediate families, Newfoundland students were helping with grandmothers with Alzheimer's disease and pregnant younger sisters, as well as having a depth of knowledge about weather, the ocean, fishing, surviving in the wilderness (and the city), and a sense of the history and culture of Newfoundland. They seemed both more grown up and less "knowing" than the rootless individuals I had been teaching. Some of those early students became, and remained, close friends and they certainly helped me to learn how to behave "in the field" and to understand what was being said to me.

I had been hired partly on my feminist credentials and was promptly allocated all the courses on or about women that sociology had on its list, a 3000-level course called Sex Roles and Social Change, and a 4000-level course called Gender and Social Theory. I found both courses over-subscribed and the students committed and enthusiastic. They were lively in class and contributed interesting papers. But none of them seemed to have any connection with the women's movement outside the university. This sense of separation between feminism inside and outside the university was an issue for other feminists who worked in both the university

and the community, and led to building and sustaining a strong link between Women's Studies in the university and feminism in the community
in the Women's Studies program when it developed. As in the universities where I had taught in the UK, the students' experience of the growing field of feminist scholarship was also limited because there were
only isolated courses in different departments on various aspects of
women's experiences. There was no opportunity for these courses to
come together in a coherent understanding and theory of women; and
similarly, teachers were unable to compare notes and develop a comprehensive program. There was a master's program in Sociology, which enabled me to continue to work with feminist students, but it was some
years before my department introduced a PhD program.

In any event, I arrived at Memorial convinced that Sociology at
Memorial, as in Manchester, would make a natural home for feminist
scholarship, and that sociology was, or should be, coterminous with radical activities and politically innovative thinking, and in many ways this
was the case. I had freedom to teach my courses as I saw fit and there
was money for both research and to go to conferences where I could
meet and build working relationships (and close friendships) with feminists from across Canada. But as a feminist I was a lone voice in the
department. There was one other woman on the faculty, but she was not
a feminist and not sympathetic to either my views or my research. It was
some years before the next feminist was appointed, and more years and
much resistance before we could build a critical number of feminists in
the department. Those who had opposed my appointment made it
abundantly clear that my ways were freakish and not entirely academically respectable, my political activities suspect, and the whole project of
feminism something of a sideshow. While I experienced support and
friendship from the faculty in my specialty of "political economy," as
well as from faculty in the Anthropology Department and, of course,
from the growing core of feminists in other departments, I was always
aware that there was a hostile strand in the department that would pre-
fer that I either conform or go. But I was also receiving encouragement
from feminists — in sociology and other disciplines — in the growing
feminist scholarly groups in the rest of Canada and was increasingly
able to apply my energies fruitfully outside the department.[2]

Memorial was a big university by UK standards and the faculty were drawn from a diversity of backgrounds and countries. Sociology had only recently parted from Anthropology, and Archaeology was some time away from going its own way. We all lived together in Queen's College, and coming, as I did, from a background in history and a Sociology Department heavily loaded with anthropologists (both at Bristol and at Manchester), I gravitated naturally to the anthropologists and to sociologists with an anthropological bias. In any case, the Sociology Department at the time was a divided house. The principal division was between the "theorists" and those they designated "mere empiricists." Fascinated by the new research possibilities all around me, I fell happily into the "mere empiricists" group, from whom I received consistent support. While the Institute of Social and Economic Research (ISER) had already set up a solid body of research on rural Newfoundland and Labrador, there was virtually no mention of women. A very few scholars, Ellen Antler and Bonnie McCay in particular, had done valuable work, but it was not widely known or recognized as important. Having scoured what there was and learned a good deal about the vibrant culture of women from my students, I set to work to begin to establish a feminist body of sociological research on women in Newfoundland and Labrador.

This research was immeasurably accelerated and enriched by the culture of generosity in both departments. Fellow researchers in my field willingly shared both their knowledge (data) and their connections (access), without which I would have been stalled for years. There was so much to do and so few of us to do it that developing our sociological understanding of Newfoundland and Labrador became something of a group project. I wrote excitedly to the British Sociological Association about faculty exchanging information about fish prices in the hallways and comparing notes about living in remote communities. ISER provided such small funds as I needed and in my first summer I was able to "piggyback" my preliminary research onto a much larger project with a site on the Southern Shore — "The Meaning of Work and the Reality of Unemployment," led by Bob Hill. I took the opportunity to carry out a small-scale project on women's economic lives in a rural community. Here I learned essential fieldwork lessons: that kids are a useful adjunct, that it's best to bring your own "healthy" foods, that letting your car escape "park" and roll into the ocean is the very best way to be accepted by the community, and so on.

That first year I had acquired an enormous and ancient gas guzzler and long before the summer research season I set about exploring as much of the island as I could. Luckily my son and the various friends who accompanied him were prepared to trade wandering round historic sites and chatting to locals for enough time for throwing endless stones into the ocean. We took coastal ferry trips to Labrador and along the south coast; drove to St. Anthony to see icebergs, which that year had failed to come south; went trout fishing and explored every cove along the northwest shore. We entered the sailing scene with an improbably racy but ancient sailboat (a Columbia 31) and trained an endless crew of my son's friends in how to tie bowlines. Living downtown meant a quick acquaintance with the cultural hotspots like the Ship Inn, the LSPU Hall (an innovative and energetic centre for the arts), George Street (in its calmer days), and the Friday night Memorial film series. I was settling in and had no intention of moving on, despite the difficulties of securing a tenure-track position and blandishments from the mainland.

Over the next 10 years I pursued my initial interests in mostly rural communities across the island (although not into Labrador, which I saw as requiring a whole other set of expertise). My principal vehicle was a quite large study of "Women's Experience of Their Economic Lives" (1988–92) in the contrasting communities of South East Bight, Grand Falls, and Catalina. This was buttressed by smaller-scale research in Burin and on the northeast coast that investigated women's historical economic contributions. In the late 1980s it was still possible for a single researcher to apply for and get the money to run such projects. I was able to employ three fieldworkers, although not to get release time to spend in the communities myself. Coming from a more ethnographic perspective I found it frustrating to be dealing with "second-hand data" collected by other people with different perspectives, who "saw" different things.[3] It also entailed a great deal of driving as I crisscrossed the island receiving progress reports, talking over the results, and delivering vital supplies such as green salads and wine. The social science research funding model in Canada changed shortly after this period. The universities and granting agencies began first encouraging and then insisting on the formation of interdisciplinary teams of researchers, focusing on topics that could be seen to have policy relevance and supporting and training numbers of graduate students. These teams were then encouraged to apply for ever larger sums of money. The resulting administrative apparatus and responsibility for complex finance had the side effect of detaching the lead researchers from the actual people they were studying. It is a tendency that has grown in recent years with a political atmosphere that is increasingly hostile to primary social science research (especially research critical of the status quo), and with teams that are now national and international, very large, and composed of diverse (and sometimes conflicting) interests.

Soon after I arrived some of the feminists teaching the scattered courses on women began to link their courses and come together to plan a properly constituted Women's Studies program at Memorial. Linda Kealey (a patient and exact historian), Roberta Buchanan (a pioneer in courses on women's writing and a strong presence in the feminist community), Joanne Prindiville (the anthropologist who introduced me to Indonesia), Cathy Penny (a psychologist interested in cognition), Ellen Balka (the first of the full-time coordinators, with a background in computer sciences), and many others were involved in the long process of manoeuvring through the complex university system of accreditation, beginning with the proposal to the Faculty of Arts for a Women's Studies minor. This process began in 1982, when I was back in the UK, and by the time I returned the committee, already formalized as the Women's Studies Council, was wrestling with deciding the lists of required and optional courses for a minor in Women's Studies from existing courses, as well as designing the overarching Women's Studies 2000 and Women's Studies 4000 courses that would attempt to be interdisciplinary (rather than merely cross-disciplinary), comprehensive, and pedagogically innovative. Much of this work was done by dedicated feminists on a volunteer basis, as it was all over Canada. The next development in the Women's Studies program was the institution of a graduate master's in Women's Studies in 1990, the first such program east of Montreal. We were more than ready for such an expansion, although desperately short of resources and faculty time, but in fact we were precipitated into it by the arrival of two Indonesian students as a result of a partnership program I had secured between Memorial and the University of Indonesia to help them develop their Women's Studies program. All this time, the program had been run by a Coordinator (with the exception of the years it was headed by Ellen Balka, released by various departments for a period of three years), a Council, and committees (all done on overload by numerous feminist faculty). Finally, an Academic Progress Review (2005) strongly recommended that the program be put on a more formal footing as a department; with a department head, specifically appointed faculty, and major, minor, and graduate programs. Thus Women's Studies became a fully recognized department in the university in 2006 and a new era began.

Since I began my research in the mid-1980s, many feminist scholars had been working on different aspects of women's lives, and Newfoundland women had begun examining their own lives and writing about it. By the mid-1990s, there was plenty of material in various genres by feminist scholars for Barbara Neis, Carmelita McGrath, and myself to put together a substantial anthology of scholarly work on Newfoundland and Labrador women's lives titled *Their Lives and Times*.[4] Coupled with a growing strength in Women's Studies at Memorial and a strong feminist presence in the community, knowledge about and analysis of women's lives increased and strengthened over the next decade. *Weather's Edge: A Compendium of Women's Lives in Newfoundland and Labrador*, another volume I co-edited, represented some of the diverse strands of writing by and about women's experiences that were developing in the new century.[5] An important aspect of both these collections was the insistence on collaboration between feminists in the community, especially recognizing the creative writers and feminists in the university. This project drew both on the increasing strength of Women's Studies at Memorial and on the growing number of lively women's centres that were established across the island and in Labrador.

Meanwhile, all this time I was also learning that there was a different politics and a different political history outside the university. The women's movement I encountered in St. John's was a startlingly different body from the one I had left behind in the UK. That one was fractious and divided, energetic and diverse, and much more explicitly "political." It did not usually trouble itself with the minutiae of legal reform, preferring to take its complaints to the streets. The women's movement in St. John's was closely related with a Canadian women's movement that had a very different history and relationship with government and the wider society. The national organization of women, the NAC — National Action Committee on the Status of Women — would have been far too liberal for the UK women's movement, but they were undertaking hard and practical work lobbying and organizing for legal changes around key issues such as property rights for women in marriage; violence against women; women's health, especially reproductive rights; gay and lesbian rights; child care; and the sexual abuse of children. The NAC included representatives from all the feminist (and para-feminist) groups in Canada, and representatives from Newfoundland and Labrador were very active in its work at the national level. At the local level the St. John's Women's Centre was started by the Newfoundland Status of Women Council, who organized the purchase of the house on Military Road that became the longest-running women's centre in Canada. When other women's centres were started in Corner Brook and Labrador, we changed the name to the St. John's Status of Women Committee. The Provincial Advisory Council on the Status of Women was appointed by the provincial government and came much later, as did the Women's Policy Office, urged on by politicians such as Lynn Verge, Minister of Justice, and Ann Bell. So the decade of the 1980s was an exciting period in the Newfoundland and Labrador women's movement, and, in many ways, we seemed to lead the country in both organization and accomplishments. But such activity and such broad alliances did come with a cost. Newfoundland feminists wanted to work together and not to critique the differences between them. This atmosphere of consensus led to very little political discussion in the women's movement or analysis of the directions we were going in. Individual feminists from the university were active in the community of feminists, but before Women's Studies in the university became organized, feminism in the community was largely separated from the work of feminists in the university, which partly explains why the first students I was teaching were largely unaware of all the activity going on around them in the community.

It was well into the fall of my first year when I realized that I had never been to "Canada," i.e., the mainland. Canada was an obscure and misty presence, whose political and social contours were fuzzy but apparently not entirely friendly to my new identity as a Newfoundland resident. I can't remember my first visit to this strange land. It was most likely to Halifax, which was recognizably similar to St. John's and where I was already making friends in the vibrant community of sociologists who, at the time, were organized through the Atlantic Association of

Sociologists and Anthropologists. They held extremely lively and support-ive meetings, usually in intolerable weather, which entailed us getting to know each other even better. This organization and the networks it sup-ported perished in the 1990s, mostly because of lack of funding for travel. It is one of the many losses that came when the funding dried up, for surely the need is still there for such regional networks. In these confer-ences, and in my growing involvement with the Canadian Research Institute for the Advancement of Women (CRIAW), the Canadian Sociology and Anthropology Association (CSAA, now CSA), as well as in the more political field of the New Democratic Party, I became in-creasingly aware of both my commitment to my new home (and my new knowledge about it) and my responsibility to ensure that New-foundland's interests were heard and its identity recognized. It is impos-sible to "speak for" a place, especially if you are not "from there," but it is possible to speak loudly and clearly on behalf of the things you know are true about a place and that are often ignored.

I arrived at Memorial in August 1980 for a one-year appointment. It took me the next three years to convert that into a full-time tenure-track position. I retired formally in 2010, although I use my Emerita status as a way to stay actively involved in research and writing. These are random reflections from my very early days at Memorial. Since then, my research has taken me in various directions, mostly towards issues of women in development and the experiences of women in countries of the Global South, including Indonesia, Pakistan, Tanzania, and Kenya. My political activities also changed and moved into new areas, as did my specifically feminist interests and involvements. I got a bigger boat, later a smaller boat, and a place in the country. My son grew up and moved to Halifax, as so many Newfoundland youngsters do. But the contours of my life in Newfoundland were set that first year: the integrated nature of my involvement with both Memorial and the community outside; the underlying commitment to feminism and to a radical understanding of the world; and above all, a commitment to "this place" and a respon-sibility to defend the unique and sometimes fragile nature of it.

Notes

1. A grossly simplified account of the various feminist "currents" at the time would be that radical feminists thought that men were the problem, Marxist feminists/socialist feminists (the terms were interchangeable in the UK at the time) thought that capitalism was the problem, and liberal feminists (the dominant strand in Canada) thought the problem could be solved within the existing system by legal changes and political pressure.

2. In broader terms I have discussed this in several papers, for example: "Call Yourself a Sociologist — and you've never even been arrested?" *Canadian Review of Sociology and Anthropology* 32, 4 (Nov. 1995); "Cuckoos in the Nest? Feminists in Sociology," in G. Finn, ed., *Limited Edition: Voices of Women, Voices of Feminism* (Halifax: Fernwood, 1993).

3. Marilyn Porter, "Second-hand Ethnography: Some Problems in Analyzing a Feminist Project," in R. Burgess and A. Bryman, eds., *Analyzing Qualitative Data* (London: Routledge, 1993).

4. Carmelita McGrath, Barbara Neis, and Marilyn Porter, eds., *Their Lives and Times — Women in Newfoundland and Labrador: A Collage* (St. John's: Creative Press, 1995).

5. Carmelita McGrath, Linda Cullum, and Marilyn Porter, eds., *Weather's Edge: A Compendium of Women's Lives in Newfoundland and Labrador* (St. John's: Killick Press, 2006).

28

Married Bachelor in the Department of Sociology

Stephen Harold Riggins

The Real Indiana

When a conversation with a stranger turns to the topic of our origins, I usually mention that my childhood was spent in the scenic part of Indiana. The hilly, forested southern counties are the northern extreme of Appalachia. To me, this is the real Indiana. The state is made up of two regions: the flat northern two-thirds, which non-Hoosiers are likely to see as they drive through Indiana on interstate highways; and the southern third, which I appreciate. The beauty of the landscape continually draws me back.

In some photographs, taken *circa* 1880, my maternal grandfather, Ellis Niblack Ledgerwood, playfully exaggerated the stereotype of hillbillies.[1] There are pictures of my father, Harold Riggins, 80 years later, in which he also pretended to be a hillbilly. Some of the women among my ancestors were passionate about quilting, a quintessential rural handicraft.[2] I have had the same experience of my ancestors as the poet Thom Gunn: "The surprising thing about one's dead is that your relationship with them can change over time. Even after they've been dead for years, you still find your feelings about them changing or growing. And that makes them seem to alter, too."[3]

Loogootee, Indiana, where I grew up, had one stoplight. The population was about 3,000. On grandmother's next-door property, which we owned, was a large vegetable garden, a raspberry patch, two cherry trees, a grape arbour, bantam chickens in a hen house, a cage of pet raccoons, and a small two-storey barn sheltering my father's restored Model-T Ford. My parents' home faced the huge vegetable garden of the high school agriculture teacher. There was a large Amish community nearby and every day they passed through town in horse-drawn buggies.

One unusual childhood experience is the amount of time I spent with older adults as a consequence of my parents being married for 17 years before their only child was born. They were over 40 when I was born. Mother's father was over 50 when she was born. Consequently, the normal span of five generations was closer to three in Mother's family. My mother, Eithel (Ledgerwood) Riggins, worked as a dental assistant. Her boss also owned a small savings and loan company and was a local leader of the American Red Cross. So Mother — ahead of her time with respect to gender — was simultaneously dental assistant, bookkeeper, and secretary for the Red Cross. My father operated a tiny factory behind the house that specialized in the first stage of manufacturing buttons from White River mussel shells. When plastic replaced shell in the 1940s, he became a carpenter sanding hardwood floors in houses and gymnasiums. The biggest indulgence in my parents' lives was spending money on my education.

I had substitute grandparents, Reba and Guy Chandler, who were neighbours. My appreciation of nature comes from the Chandlers. Reba was a great storyteller and devotee of crossword puzzles and teaching Sunday school. Guy was a retired veterinarian. In 1924 he had led a parade without a hood,[4] but by the 1960s his views on race and religion were too unpopular to influence me. So I consider that, in general, the influence on my life of my older-than-average parents and substitute grandparents was a blessing. But it encouraged a perspective that is, arguably, a liability for a mainstream career in sociology. My vision was more consistent with a career as a historian, folklorist, or anthropologist.

Indiana University

If I had not experienced the student activism of the 1960s counterculture, I doubt that I would have majored in sociology at Indiana University.[5] Accidents saved me from the excesses of the counterculture. I was academically oriented and saw student politics as a distraction. Research shows that first-generation university students tend to be less inclined to sacrifice their time in socializing and student politics. Spending my junior year in Germany at the University of Munich interrupted my involvement in student politics. Left-wing student activists at the Bloomington campus of Indiana University were militant heterosexuals. For some students this was a barrier to full participation in the movement.

The Indiana University sociologist I remember the most fondly is the underappreciated Francis Joseph Schneider. A graduate of the University of California at Berkeley, he was an anarchist, socialist, pacifist, and a marginal person within a quantitatively oriented department. Schneider was one of the pioneers of the sociology of war and peace but published too little to be professionally recognized. He claimed that abolishing war should be easier than abolishing crime. While crime is a reflection of people's innate anti-social tendencies, this is not true for war. Despite a rather gruff exterior, Joseph Schneider attracted an enthusiastic following among intellectually ambitious students and activists.[6]

On the 4th and 5th of April 1968 in Louisville, Kentucky, I completed my physical examination for the military draft. Martin Luther King Jr. was assassinated on the first day of my examination, and his death was celebrated with cheers by some of the men completing their physical examination with me. I was interviewed by an FBI agent because I belonged to suspect left-wing organizations (the Socialist Workers Party and Students for a Democratic Society) and had visited Prague and East Berlin. I had planned to become a conscientious objector but the agent persuaded me that this was unnecessary. Thus I was classified 4-F, unfit for military service. The reason was my sexual orientation. It was the easy way out. I cannot know what the FBI agent was thinking when he gave me advice. But I assume he was actually concerned about my welfare and was urging me to avoid a decision that would unnecessarily complicate my life.[7] In 1968, my knowledge of pacifism came primarily from Schneider's course on the sociology of war. My knowledge of Marxism was mostly from undergraduate social theory courses.

You Can't Sell Your Parents on the Greatness of Canada

Disappointed with American politics and the decay of inner cities, and looking for adventure, I moved to Toronto. New York seemed too dangerous, California too distant. The critic of city planning and author of *The Life and Death of Great American Cities*, Jane Jacobs, resided in Toronto. She was one of my heroes. I knew no one in Toronto and had visited the city for only a few hours, but migrating to Canada was often in the news due to war resisters fleeing the US to escape the draft. I drove my red Ford Mustang to Toronto in late August 1969. It was then very easy for Americans to immigrate to Canada. The border agent encouraged me to declare social work as my occupation because that knowledge gave me more points in the ranking system for immigrants. I have never taken a single social work course.

Within a month of arriving in Toronto I met an authentic French structuralist at the St. Charles Tavern, a bar on Yonge Street where one would least expect to spot a student of Claude Lévi-Strauss. Paul Bouissac was an aspiring novelist, semiotician, and Professor of French at the University of Toronto. He became *the* anthropological authority on the circus. My career has been profoundly influenced by Paul. Without his support, I could not have led such an impractical early career, most obviously in writing the PhD thesis "Institutional Change in 19th-century French Music" for a degree in Sociology.[8]

In one sentence I would describe my conflicts with my parents as a clash between my baby-boomer, post-materialist values and Mother's preoccupation with money, so typical of her generation. For my parents a university education was a route to a financially secure future. They had married in September 1929, a month before the stock market crash. Because my education stretched into my thirties, this long adolescence was a very foreign experience to them. They did not understand the 1960s idealization of individualism, authenticity, and recreational deviance.

At home there was opposition to my move to Canada. On 26 September 1969 this message arrived from Mother. "I don't know just how to say this so you will understand. It seems all we do is yell at each other on the telephone." Mother continued:

> I can see now that we were so old when you came along and we were so glad we just loved you too much to let you learn to grow up and learn how to manage and stand on your own feet. But it's too late to correct that I am sure.
>
> You have always lived very well and still want to but we realize your salary isn't enough to live on that scale. Since your dad won't be working anymore for several months after his eye surgery, we know you must live on whatever your salary is going to be. We would be glad if you were close enough to visit us once in a while. But if you are happy and can make enough money to pay your bills, we will try and quit yelling each telephone call.

> . . . You are associating with salaried people who can afford those things. I hope you can get something so you can live as you like. How can you go to school and work swing shift? Please try and do something with your sociology.
>
> Sorry we can't see things your way. We have to live on our salary and certainly not the way we would prefer.
>
> . . . Where did you meet the Mr. Bouissac?
>
> Forgive us for not seeing things your way. Most parents and children don't see things alike. Generation gap.

A year later, 24 November 1970, not much progress had been made in resolving our conflicts about Canada. Mother wrote:

> In that article you sent home it seemed most of the brains were people who had gotten their education in the US and also worked and got their experience here in the States. It used to be the land of quick work, getting a job, but too many your age have gone to Canada. Most people in the US just aren't interested in Canada and no matter how well you like it, you can't sell them on the greatness of Canada, not even us, your parents. . . . I held down four jobs to put you through college so naturally I hoped you could get a good job. Anyway, you can use the education if you ever make up your mind that you really want to make money.

Mother did work three or four jobs some years, if part-time work is included. Supporting me in college was not the sole reason. The added income helped build up her pension.

The Long Trek to Tenure

Most people are not aware of the sacrifices academics have to make, especially in periods of precarious employment, in order to obtain a secure teaching position. The start of my career coincided with the worst period (*circa* 1975–95) to begin teaching at the university level since the Great Depression. Two years elapsed after completing my PhD at the University of Toronto before I landed a job. In the interval my activities included working as a reporter for the *Toronto Native Times*, published by the Native Centre in Toronto. Ultimately, volunteering at the Centre was more important for my career than my PhD thesis. I would advise all undergraduate students to augment their resumés by volunteering at non-profit organizations. At Memorial, I created an internship course in order to give Sociology majors course credit for volunteering. My story about the *Toronto Native Times* when it was on the verge of bankruptcy led to an invitation to edit a 1983 issue of *Anthropologica* titled Native North Americans and the Media: Studies in Minority Journalism; then to broader topics, such as editing the book *Ethnic Minority Media: An International Perspective*, and finally *The Language and Politics of Exclusion: Others in Discourse*. Indigenous or First Nations print media have a weak organizational structure. This results in some content being a poor reflection of Indigenous values. My most controversial conclusion was that the dominant discourse in articles about environmental politics in some prominent Indigenous newspapers was inconsistent with traditional ecological knowledge.[9]

In the middle of October 1982, I was appointed by Laurentian University in Sudbury, Ontario, to replace a professor who had become ill, Czech-Canadian sociologist Bedrich Baumann. There was absolutely no time to prepare. Given my weak knowledge of mainstream sociology, I needed far more preparation time than an average graduate. I was also painfully shy. The night before I had to teach my first two-hour class, I thought I would rather throw myself in one of the lakes on campus than lecture about classical social theory. That first year of teaching was the most difficult experience in my entire life. I had a nearly constant headache for the first three weeks. It is so stressful to walk to class giving no thought to the looming lecture because you are worried you have nothing for tomorrow. At the end of a year in which courses lasted from September to April I vowed that if every year was this stressful I would rather live on welfare than teach at a university. I commuted between downtown Toronto and Sudbury while at Laurentian. Round-trip, this was 500 miles on a bus every weekend. Friday evenings, Paul waited in downtown Toronto beside the Park Plaza Hotel for the return bus as it came down Avenue Road. He was sometimes mistaken for one of the impoverished men who sold newspapers on the sidewalk.

After three years at Laurentian University (1982–85), a year at

Memorial as a Visiting Professor (1985–86), three years of teaching at the University of Alberta in Edmonton (1986–89), and one year at the University of Toronto (1989–90), I returned to Memorial to accept a position as Assistant Professor. Teachers in the early stages of a university career have to be willing to move. By 1990 I had acquired the experiences that enabled me to credibly teach courses on mass media, sociological theory, deviance, ethnicity, and the sociology of the arts. My edited book, *Beyond Goffman: Studies on Communication, Institution, and Social Interaction*, was on the verge of appearing.

The department at Memorial University was more sociable than many sociology departments in Canada. Professor Larry Felt attributed the collegiality to the quality of life in St. John's. The Avalon Peninsula is an exceptionally beautiful landscape. St. John's is one of the unique cities in Canada, and a good place to raise children. Several sociologists came to Memorial after unpleasant experiences elsewhere. "If you really like a place," Felt once said to me, "you try to make it work." But to be frank, we did have our village soap operas. There is no pill for that, unfortunately.

In the mid-1980s two factions began to emerge whose members had *somewhat* different concepts of sociology and university service. The factions were generally good at accommodating each other. They existed until approximately 2005. They could lie dormant for a while but were likely to flare up again as soon as a decision had to be made about hiring. In addition, some members of the faculty were independents or crossovers. The factions were jokingly called "theory" and "fish." I like these humorous labels because they suggest children arguing on a playground. The fish faction consisted of Canadian come from aways and British immigrants. They specialized in research about socio-economic development, usually in Newfoundland. The theory faction, skeptics of the neo-Marxism popular among their colleagues studying socio-economic development, engaged in research about theoretical issues or rooted in geographical areas outside Canada. The intellectually eclectic theorists were American or European. The one exception was born in Malaysia to English and Canadian parents. The key person in the theory faction was Volker Meja, an internationally recognized specialist in the sociology of knowledge. In the fish faction the main person was Peter Sinclair, who served as department head longer than anyone else and published theoretically informed research about the social organization of the fishing industry.

The sense of community in the department gradually eroded. After a few years of residence in St. John's, some Memorial professors found that because of the small size of the university they had exhausted the possibilities for intellectual renewal (and romance). Local intellectual exchanges also occurred more often before the Internet and e-mail. Finally, university budgets became less generous in providing places on campus where faculty could socialize. When I was department head (2005–08), one of my concerns was recreating a sense of community. Consequently, I founded, edited, and subsidized the department newsletter, *Sociology on the Rock*; organized the first group portrait of Memorial sociologists in nearly 50 years; and began writing a history of the department.[10]

Research on Ethnicity, Culture, and the History of Higher Education

As a scholar who studies mass media, I specialize in the discourse analysis of print media. My models are linguists and I try to replicate their close reading of texts. My focus is on the subtle bias of front-page news stories about ethnic conflicts that appear in the most highly regarded newspapers, typically *The New York Times* and *The Globe and Mail*. My aim is to show the ways in which these stories are less objective than the current model of value-free journalism. To provoke class discussion, my students and I dissect news stories in class. For the most part, I think these exercises have contributed to a multicultural outlook among my students. Only occasionally did I hear the plea "but I didn't want to major in English!" I have also explored the common-sense knowledge embodied in anecdotes. The fact that these micro-narratives are memorable, spread quickly, and contain some proverb about the essence of a group or individual indicate that a minor literary genre — and social ritual — is more significant than it appears to scientifically oriented social scientists looking for quantitative information.[11]

In his exposé of the harsh life of tenant farmers in 1930s Alabama, *Let Us Now Praise Famous Men*, the novelist and film critic James Agee discussed the shape, colour, location, size, and aesthetics of their possessions.[12] The exhaustiveness of his descriptions was a political act. Humble things were accorded the attention normally reserved for the fine arts. "Fieldwork in the Living Room," in my edited book *The Socialness of Things: Essays on the Socio-semiotics of Objects*, is my attempt to provide a systematic methodology for descriptions of interior decoration. One set of categories represents the features of individual artifacts. The other is about the way objects are displayed and perceived in relation to each other. My interviews begin with a prominent object likely to attract attention and then proceed systematically around the room. Photographs, which are essential because I do not assume residents are authorities on their own homes, need to be made in the same manner. This is a very invasive methodology which, given the present concern about research ethics, requires that interviewees be treated as co-authors. Stories about objects often serve as an excuse for talking about the people and social occasions they symbolize. This makes the study of domestic objects relevant to the sociology of families as well as the study of consumption.[13]

Although my research is primarily curiosity-driven, some publications have a political dimension and applied value. Scholars who stress our social obligations to the public may not be happy — and for good reasons — with my continuing research on southern Indiana. At first glance, criticism might seem to be nitpicking because my work is about inconsequential events in one of the smallest counties in one American state. I think I am contributing to working-class history by giving people, who are usually overlooked, a sort of afterlife — to the extent that this is possible. The writings are a rebellion against the great-man theory of history.[14] In my research I tend to imagine a community spirit I am not able to find in my own life. My focus is on the years when socializing was more intense, not the years since 1950 when modernization undermined neighbourhood and family. My writings tend to have a nostalgic edge. They could have a political impact that is the opposite of my personal commitment to globalization. Ironically, I am contributing to rural identity although I am not able to live in a rural environment. The folklore I gather about anonymous actors on the stage of history is perhaps the intellectual equivalent of gay men safeguarding culture by preserving historic buildings and antiques.[15]

There is, however, a more serious problem with my writings about Indiana. No one learns from my articles that the largest inland naval facility in the entire United States is in the county I study because I concentrate on the era of family farming. The base was established during World War II and is still thriving. Tiny Martin County is financially dependent on the military-industrial complex. In Toronto, Paul and I live on Richmond Street West, a rare one-way street in the downtown area. The rumour is that years ago Richmond Street West was made one-way in order to facilitate the evacuation of Toronto in case of a nuclear attack. I should be writing about the sociology of war and peace.

Married Bachelors

The book I am most proud of, and that took over 30 years of part-time work, is *The Pleasures of Time: Two Men, a Life*. It makes sense to view these stories about me and Paul Bouissac living in France as an odd mix of realist and impressionist ethnography, although they were written as an escape from sociology. In a realist tale the author is like a fly on the wall noticing everything. Nothing in the text calls attention to the author as witness. An impressionist tale is so sketchy it is barely a story but it is evocative and conveys a certain mood about a brief moment in time. My original intention was to write about "little people." I made compromises. Commercial publishers were not interested in little people. The distinguished Alberta sociologist Susan McDaniel recommended *The Pleasures of Time*:

> It is a sociological book that defies categorization. It is an examination of the intertwined lives of two men, of the birth and growth of cultural studies over a critical historical period, of Bouissac's and Riggins' wondrous encounters with the unexpected . . . intellectually and personally, of their amazing personal intersections with Lévi-Strauss, Foucault (who Riggins interviewed — a rare event indeed!), Sartre, and de Beauvoir, John Cage, Brian Ferneyhough, Allan Bloom (the list goes on), and of an era of tumult, politically and socially. It is also very much a personal history, a kind of auto-ethnography, of a committed gay relationship and of the transforming and transformative gay world in the late 20th century. And it is anthropological ethnography as well. It is, in sum, an extraordinary book, a

significant book and a book that touches the reader's heart
as well as the reader's mind.[16]

Although the People's Republic of China once seemed the most
desolate place on earth, it re-emerged on the world stage, and unexpectedly in the 1980s I became interested in East Asian cultures. One aspect
of my teaching at Memorial that I enjoyed the most was introducing
our students to East Asian cultures. I did this in the context of courses
on race and ethnicity. Justification for such content is the fact that the
Chinese are the largest visible minority in Canada. In addition to assigning some standard publications about the sociology of race and ethnicity, I assigned, depending on the year, either the *Tao de Ching* or
Thomas Merton's translation of Chuang Tzu. There were also lectures
about philosophical Taoism and a lecture or two stolen from Daisetz T.
Suzuki's *Zen and Japanese Culture*. This philosophical content is unusual
for a sociology course.

Male Chinese immigrants in North America in the early twentieth
century were sometimes called married bachelors.[17] Many were married
and had fathered children in China, but they lived in Canada in a society
of bachelors because of racism. They were not allowed to bring their families to Canada. Obviously, their experiences were more oppressive than
mine. But given Memorial's geographical location, it is not unusual for
members of our faculty to be in commuting relationships resembling the
austere lifestyle of married bachelors. ("Married bachelor" suggests a
range of experiences, not all of which are bleak.) The university has lost
several faculty members because of commuting relationships and the expense of two residences. I am told that Memorial is one of the Canadian
pioneers in facilitating spousal appointments. Memorial University administrators, however, cannot guarantee a spousal appointment. The relevant department must voluntarily accept the husband or wife. The
administration also has little power over hiring outside the university.

Teaching in St. John's required that I sacrifice my personal life, although no one in the department expected me to hide it. Commuting is
a cruel existence. To be middle-aged and hope that time will pass as
quickly as possible is really sad. I coped by resolutely refusing to think
about my unhappiness and by reminding myself that my professional
life outweighed the sacrifices. Commuting between St. John's and Toronto

meant that my experience of Newfoundland was odd. I taught at Memorial for a dozen years before I spent a summer on the island and discovered to my surprise that St. John's is full of lilac bushes and laburnum trees. They look too delicate to survive Newfoundland gales. As I prepare for retirement, drivers in downtown St. John's still stop to let pedestrians jaywalk across the street; the passengers on city buses still thank the driver or say goodbye as they leave. In winter pedestrians have to confront cars by walking in the street because the sidewalks are not properly cleared of snow. It is for me a quintessential St. John's experience. Piano lessons, Taoist Tai Chi, and photographing St. John's changed my relationship to the city. You cannot dislike a place when you stalk heritage buildings searching for the precise moment of the day when they look their best.

A longer version of this autobiography will be published in Canadian Sociology in the First Person, *edited by Stephen Harold Riggins and Neil McLaughlin.*

Notes

1. Stephen Harold Riggins, "'If Work Made People Rich': An Oral History of General Farming," *Midwestern Folklore* 17, 2 (1991): 73–109.

2. Stephen Harold Riggins, "Shoofly Quilts and Poetry," *The Globe and Mail*, 18 July 2005, A14. At: http://www.theglobeandmail.com/incoming/shoofly-quilts-and-poetry/article18240981/.

3. Gunn, as quoted in Wendy Lesser, *The Amateur: An Independent Life of Letters* (New York: Vintage, 2000), 263.

4. "Had Big Crowd — with Thousands of Visitors Law, Order, and Peace Observed and Protected in Loogootee," *Martin County Tribune*, 1 May 1924, 1; Stephen Harold Riggins, *The Pleasures of Time: Two Men, a Life* (Toronto: Insomniac Press, 2003), 196–98.

5. Mary Ann Wynkoop, *Dissent in the Heartland: The Sixties at Indiana University* (Bloomington: Indiana University Press, 2002).

6. Joseph Schneider, "On the Beginnings of Warfare," *Social Forces* 31, 1 (1952): 68–74; Schneider, "Is War a Problem?" *Journal of Conflict Resolution* 3 (1959): 353–60.

7. Stephen Harold Riggins, Unpublished statement made to the FBI, 5 Apr. 1968. A copy can be found in Special Collections, Archives of Victoria

University, Toronto, E.J. Pratt Library, Fond 50.

8. Stephen Harold Riggins, "Institutional Change in Nineteenth-century French Music," *Current Perspectives in Social Theory* 6 (1985): 243–60.

9. Stephen Harold Riggins, "Environmental Ethics and Indigenous Identity in *Wawatay News*," *Journal of Applied Journalism & Media Studies* 4, 1 (2015): 131–52.

10. Stephen Harold Riggins, "'A Square Deal for the Least and the Last': The Career of W.G. Smith in the Methodist Ministry, Experimental Psychology, and Sociology," *Newfoundland and Labrador Studies* 27, 2 (2012): 179–222; Riggins, "Memorial University's First Sociologist: The Dilemmas of a Bureaucratic Intellectual," *Newfoundland and Labrador Studies* 29, 1 (2014): 47–83; Riggins, "Sociology by Anthropologists: A Chapter in the History of an Academic Discipline in Newfoundland during the 1960s," *Acadiensis* 46, 2 (2017): 119–42.

11. Stephen Harold Riggins, "The Value of Anecdotal Evidence," in Lorne Tepperman and Harley Dickinson, eds., *Reading Sociology: Canadian Perspectives* (Toronto: Oxford University Press, 2007), 11–13.

12. James Agee and Walker Evans, *Let Us Now Praise Famous Men* (Boston: Houghton Mifflin, 1960; originally published 1941).

13. Stephen Harold Riggins, "The Natural Order Is Decay: The House as an Ephemeral Art Project," in Anu Kannike and Patrick Laviolette, eds., *Things in Culture, Culture in Things* (Tartu, Estonia: University of Tartu Press, 2013), 36–57.

14. See, for example, Stephen Harold Riggins, "The Spirit of Commerce in the Journalism of Carlos McCarty," *Indiana Magazine of History* 84, 3 (1988): 262–81.

15. Will Fellows, *A Passion to Preserve: Gay Men as Keepers of Culture* (Madison: University of Wisconsin Press, 2004).

16. Susan McDaniel, *Canadian Review of Sociology*, online book reviews (2004). At: https://www.csa-scs.ca/files/www/crs/documents/reviews/archives/pdf/200408RIGGINS.pdf.

17. "The Bachelor Society," Library and Archives Canada. At: http://www.collectionscanada.gc.ca/eppp-archive/100/205/301/ic/cdc/generations/immigration/bachelors.html.

V
GROWING PAINS

Language labratory. (Photo from *Memorial University of Newfoundland and its Environs: A Guide to Life and Work at the University in St. John's,* courtesy of Memorial University Libraries.)

Faculty Women: The Struggle for Equality

Roberta Buchanan

It didn't take me long as a young woman in England to realize that there was systemic discrimination against women in patriarchal society. Except that we hadn't heard of the word "systemic," and "patriarchal" was not part of our vocabulary. We had no analysis, as later feminists would say. But even I could see that there was something wrong when I was an undergraduate in the 1950s and obtained a summer job in a local factory. I was paid four pounds a week; a male student was paid seven pounds — almost double — for doing exactly the same job.

If you questioned this blatant injustice, the reason given was always the same: men were the breadwinners and had to support their families. (The male student and I were both single.) But what if women were the breadwinners? What if a single woman had to support an aged parent — or herself? What if a widow supported her children? These objections were never answered, but merely brushed aside. It was assumed that single women ("spinsters") would get married. If they didn't, it was their own fault; they were "left on the shelf" because of some defect in themselves. Many married women in the factory worked because their husbands did not make a decent living wage. That was not discussed either.

Terms and Conditions

When I arrived in St. John's in 1964, feminism was not much in evidence. When I was appointed to the post of Lecturer in the English Department, I was given an eight-page booklet entitled "Terms and conditions of appointment, tenure, service and employment of the teachers of the University." There was a special rule in Section VI, "Suspension and Termination of Employment," which applied only to women:

> Upon the marriage of a female teacher, her employment
> shall terminate, but the Board of Regents, on the recom-

mendation of the President, *may* continue her employment on a *temporary* basis for such period as the Board may determine and may further continue such employment *from time to time* on the same basis.[1]

Rule VI.18 was devastating to the careers of academic women. If they married, they could lose their jobs or be demoted to the lowly rank of part-time "sessional," rehired or "let go" from semester to semester, year to year, according to the vagaries of enrolment or the whim of the head of department. The woman academic's income dropped drastically, and she lost all the privileges of a full-time academic: the paid non-teaching third research term; paid sabbatical leave for research after seven years of teaching; the pension and other benefits. Worse, the sessional often did not know (and still does not) until after student registration whether she will be employed for the next academic term. This is always an anxious time for the head of department. How many courses will go ahead? Will extra sections of courses have to be suddenly added? The sessional may get a call the night before lectures begin, or even after they have begun, and has to scramble to get her textbooks and teaching schedules in order. It was/ is a miserable and uncertain existence for many women.

As to the paid third research term that full-time professors enjoyed, it was pointed out to me that married women didn't need it. They had to look after their husbands and children, they had no time for research! Women professors suffered a substantial drop in their income once they got married, even though they were teaching the same number of courses as before — there was a ready answer for *that*. They didn't need the money! They had husbands to support them. They worked just for amusement, for pin money.

So it was that there was an underclass of underpaid married women in the English Department, whom the full-time professors looked down upon with pity. They all taught the same courses: first-year English, with the biggest classes and the most marking, looked upon as drudgery work. Even in that, they had no choice as to the texts they would teach. It was "The Elements of Pitteracy," as we called it, by David Pitt, whose wife Marion was one of the sessionals. (Copies of David G. Pitt, *The Elements of Literacy*, are in the Centre for Newfoundland Studies.) It had little exercises for the students to test and expand their vocabulary, such as "What is the adjective for 'of the elbow'?" (Answer: cubital, "of the forearm;" cubit, "an ancient measure of length, approximately equal to the length of a forearm," from the Latin word for "elbow," *cubitum*: *Canadian Oxford Dictionary*.)

While I shared a spacious office with Dr. Elizabeth Orsten, medievalist, a gaggle of married women were lumped together in one office: Mrs. Pratt, Mrs. Frecker, Mrs. Pitt, Mrs. Wareham, Mrs. Eaton . . . . Mrs. Pratt belonged to a wealthy business family; Mrs. Frecker was wife of the provincial Minister of Education in the Smallwood government, and lived in a large mansion on Circular Road. Obviously these women didn't need the money, and it would be greedy of them to expect it, according to the views of the day. The fact that the Freckers had a large family of eight children to support and educate was never considered. The married women in the English Department seemed, to us younger, unmarried academics, to live in their own rarefied milieu — cocktail parties, the social round of the St. John's wealthy elite — a remote distant world from the one we lived in. The married women talked to each other. We talked to our academic colleagues.

I remember being at a meeting — was it the Faculty Association? — at which Mrs. Frecker stood up and asked indignantly, "Do they think women lose their minds once we get married?" Helena Frecker had the distinction of being the first woman to graduate from Memorial University College, in 1926. She went on to get a degree in English and History at the University of Toronto, and returned to teach English and Latin at Memorial College before her marriage. A devout Roman Catholic, she was a devotee of Sir (Saint) Thomas More, now known chiefly as the author of *Utopia* and for being beheaded by Henry VIII. Helena was embarking on an ambitious research project on More: to document all the authors he referred to in his voluminous writings, which would provide an interesting insight into the reading of one of the leading intellectuals of his day. However, she didn't count as a scholar by the university administration — she was only a married woman.[2]

Two cases in particular illustrate the blatant discrimination of Rule VI.18. Case A was another graduate of Memorial College. She was the first Newfoundland woman in the English Department to get a doctorate (from an English university). She got married and came back to teach in the English Department. A concession was made: she was given the rank of Assistant Professor, but she was still a sessional, with no pension, until 1969 when that inequity was stopped and she was able to pay into the pension fund. She became the first woman full professor in the English Department, a witty, popular, and much beloved teacher. But we, the other women, noticed that at English Department meetings she was always referred to as *Mrs.* A, never as Doctor A, while the men with doctorates were always called Dr. Pitt or Dr. Story or Dr. Francis; the women always Miss or Mrs., as if in their case the doctorate didn't count. When Dr. Bernice Schrank, from New York and the University of Wisconsin, joined the department, she wasn't having any of that! A formidable presence, she was a woman to be reckoned with. Some of us who defined ourselves as feminists took a certain glee in correcting our colleagues by referring pointedly to *Doctor* A, or *Doctor* Schrank, with emphasis.

Averil Gardner was another woman affected by Rule 18. Averil and her husband Philip were teaching at different Japanese universities when they were both offered positions in the English Department in the early 1960s. Averil was hired as a "university wife" Lecturer, with a lower salary than her husband and no pension. While still in Japan she became pregnant. When she wrote to inform the head of department of her pregnancy, and that Philip was willing to take over her classes for the few weeks when she could not teach, she was told that her job was "in abeyance." To combine marriage with pregnancy was another strike against a female academic. The university seemed to have a horror of pregnant women in the classroom. When she arrived in St. John's, she was told that she hadn't got a job; Moses Morgan, then Dean of Arts and Sciences, had cancelled it. After she had her baby, at the new academic year in September she was appointed as Sessional Lecturer, with no benefits, and employed for only nine months of the year.

When Patrick O'Flaherty, of the English Department, became President of the Memorial University of Newfoundland Faculty Association (MUNFA), Averil had been a Lecturer long enough to be promoted and he took it up as a faculty association matter. In 1970 she was promoted to Assistant Professor, with tenure, pension, and benefits, even though this was opposed by the then Vice-President of Finance.

Shocking as the treatment of married women was at Memorial University, it had its roots in the attitude adopted by the Board of Governors of Memorial University College in a March 1940 directive to

President Hatcher that it was "inadvisable at present to add any more married women to the staff." Historian Malcolm MacLeod is baffled as to what caused the Board to make this "momentous, sexist decision" in 1940, at a time when hitherto closed doors in employment were being opened to women during World War II. This policy persisted for 20 years, well beyond the establishment of Memorial University in 1949.[3] The University Act of 1949 was silent on the question of women faculty, although clause 47 permitted women to be members of the Board and the Senate.[4]

With the expansion of the 1960s, the university discovered there were "recruiting advantages" to hiring married couples. MacLeod comments: "the sex-liberalization in MUN's hiring policy was a by-product of necessity and convenience," and not due to "lofty ideas about gender equality. Lifting the ban on married women was done without fanfare; there was no announcement."[5] MacLeod, however, seems to be referring only to women hired to tenure-track positions rather than to the numerous underclass of lowly paid faculty women hired per course or per semester, without job security and deprived of benefits and pensions. This large group of faculty women is ignored by MacLeod.

The Struggle for Equal Pay

One of the causes feminists (both female and male) at Memorial fought for was equal pay for work of equal value. This was part of a wider ferment for change in Canada. The Royal Commission on the Status of Women in Canada was established in 1967 by Prime Minister Lester B. Pearson, responding to pressure by a coalition of women's organizations, led by the president of the Canadian Federation of University Women, Laura Sabia. The Commission's Report was published in 1970; a federal Minister responsible for the Status of Women followed in 1971.

In the late 1960s the Canadian Association of University Teachers (CAUT) started to publish annual summaries and analyses of salaries at Canadian universities, by rank and region, noting male–female differentials and the exclusion of women from the higher-paying ranks of full professor, dean, vice-president, and other administrative positions. It was easy to see, from the statistics CAUT published, and that our Faculty Association publicized, that my pay was well below the average for someone in my rank and years of experience. True, there was a system of "merit pay," but this was decided, in the English Department, by a committee of the full professors (all men) who of course voted themselves the highest merit pay, leaving the scraps for the rest of us.

What could we do to redress the situation? If only, we thought, we could get on the committees that influenced these decisions, we could undermine the patriarchy from within and change the system of discrimination! In 1973 I ran for Vice-President of MUNFA and was elected. I joined a lively and active executive, with Charles Preston of Psychology as President. There was a general dissatisfaction with the university administration. Salaries were the big issue, and economist Bill Schrank was instructed to "pursue the Male vs Female salary study"; David Hart was to prepare recommendations for a promotions and tenure appeals procedure.[6] This was part of a wider discontent in the university, which included the strike of maintenance workers and the students' strike when they occupied the President's office and took over the Arts and Administration Building.[7]

Cathy Penney and David Hart revamped the *MUNFA Newsletter*, printed as an attractive booklet with coloured covers. The next step was that four feminist academics — Dell Texmo, Merrily Sterns, Elena Hannah, and myself — volunteered to work on the newsletter. We knew each other well because we were in the same consciousness-raising group, where we discussed and debated women's issues. Dell Texmo, in Junior Division English, was a real activist who was not afraid to live her beliefs. She soon organized her own pioneer women's studies course in Junior Division, given as an Extension course. She scandalized the conservative administration by living openly with her partner without being married, and having no intention of doing so, even after she became pregnant.[8] Merrily Sterns was an American who had come to Memorial with her husband, and was thus relegated by the university to "faculty wife" status as a part-time sessional in the English Department. Elena Hannah, in Psychology, was well known as a leader in the local La Leche League, encouraging women to breastfeed their babies. A colleague complained to the authorities that she brought her baby to her office where she breastfed her. Scandalous! Elena taught childhood development and delighted her students by bringing her baby to class. In 2002, Elena edited *Women in the Academic Tundra: Challenging the Chill*, in which she described her experience of teaching at Memorial:

In my twenty-eight years as a faculty member in the Psychology Department . . . I have held a full-time, tenure-track position (eight years), a part-time, per course position (eight years), a full-time, non-tenure-track, contractual position (ten years), and a full-time, sessional position (two years). Apart from a few months' maternity and sick leave, and a year when I followed my then husband for his sabbatical in another province (where I also taught two full terms), I have always taught here. However, despite my twenty-eight years as an academic member of this university, I have no job security, a below poverty level income, no health insurance, no vacation pay — no benefits at all. I never know, from one term to the next, what my income will be or if, indeed, I will have one.[9]

Elena worked at Memorial from 1970 until she retired in 2013, 43 years in all.

The first issue of the *MUNFA Newsletter* produced by this feminist collective was published in November 1973. Dell had the inspired idea of putting a satirical cartoon on the coloured cover, which would reflect in an amusing way on one of the issues being discussed, and she found the perfect cartoonist in Bill Mahoney, a medical student. Our "editorial principles" were to provide "a forum for debate on issues relevant to faculty," and we appealed for "contributions, criticisms, and letters to the editors"; also for volunteers to join our editorial staff. We encouraged debate by having an editorial and a "Counter-Editorial." The controversy was over whether the MUNFA executive acted improperly at a faculty association meeting by awarding $700 to the striking maintenance personnel when the meeting did not have a quorum. Dell supported the decision; Elena, in her counter-editorial, argued against it.

The cover cartoon depicted the Red Queen from *Alice in Wonderland* shouting at a small and defiant Alice: "OFF WITH HER HEAD!!"The recently appointed President of the university, Moses Morgan, was facing a drop in enrolment, and wanted to discuss with the President of MUNFA several proposals about the classes of faculty who might be considered first for redundancy: for example, married women, both with and without tenure. Dr. Preston "told Mr. Morgan that under no circumstances would MUNFA agree to sex or marital status being used as a criterion for redundancy," and the principle of tenure should not be violated.[10] President Morgan must not have realized that most of the MUNFA executive had spouses who taught in the university and who were committed to their careers: Bernice Schrank, for instance, and Helen Jones both taught in the English Department. Anne Hart worked in the university library. Dell Texmo's partner, Keith Storey, taught in the Geography Department. The sexist assumption that women academics are dispensable, no matter what their qualifications, was not acceptable.

As Vice-President, I wrote a rousing editorial drawing attention to our issues of concern: the exploitation of part-time faculty, overwhelmingly female ("<u>PART-TIMERS: ARE YOU HAPPY?</u>"); the lack of paid maternity leave ("<u>MATERNITY LEAVE WITH PAY: WHAT ABOUT IT?</u>"); women being held back from promotion ("<u>PROMOTIONS: NOW IS THE HOUR</u>"). I ended with an attack on Morgan's proposal that married women should be the first to be fired, which "shows how very far this university is from considering women faculty as equal members of the scholarly community. Women faculty must not lie down under this threat but rather stand up and speak out for the principle of equality."[11] Not only was the tone of the article confrontational, but I sent President Morgan a copy of the newsletter and invited his response.

To our surprise and delight, President Morgan responded almost immediately to the November newsletter with a two-page letter. This we published at the front of the next *MUNFA Newsletter* (March 1974), listed in the table of contents as "A Letter from M.O.M." – the President's initials, Moses Osbourne Morgan. Morgan argued that he was not discussing "proposals" but merely questions "that might be raised both within and without the University" should reduction of faculty become necessary. "One of the questions was whether married women should be retained on the faculty, with two incomes going into the home, while the only income earner, in another home, was being released." The administration welcomed the MUNFA study on the status of women and wished "to rectify any possible discrimination that may exist."[12]

These were fine sentiments but, unfortunately, the day after the newsletter appeared in November 1973, three faculty women were fired — "or, in official terminology, 'reminded' that their contracts were due to expire in August."[13] We encouraged the three women to appeal; and

Gordon Jones, who had taken over from Charles Preston as President of MUNFA, and I asked to see President Morgan to protest the firing. From what I remember of the conversation, Morgan said that people in the town had objected to married couples being employed at the university, and earning two salaries, while some (men? Newfoundlanders?) were deprived of work. Also, from the university's point of view, married women provided a convenient pool of highly qualified persons who could be hired on a part-time basis and let go as registration fluctuated. (This is still true today, in 2017, over 40 years later, but now includes men as well as women.) I reminded the President that one of the women in question was unmarried, and, further, was a veteran. (Memorial University was founded to honour Newfoundlanders who served in the Great War of 1914–18.) She was given a job on the Memorial University *Gazette*. Later, student enrolment improved, and the other two women were rehired.

In my riposte to the President's letter, I pointed out that, although the three women in question had "excellent records as teachers, male faculty hired in the same department at the same time or after them have been appointed on 'regular' two-year contracts. If this is not discrimination against women, what is?" I reminded the administration that they had endorsed the policy statement of equal opportunity for women academics to similarly qualified men, and commented indignantly, "That does not mean giving women 'irregular' one-year contracts because they are women or 'faculty wives,' and giving men 'regular' contracts." All women faculty were advised to look at Table II of the February 1974 MUNFA salary brief, which had been circulated to all faculty, to check whether their salaries were below the average for their qualifications, rank, age, and experience. If it was, they should write to their head of department and Dean asking for "appropriate adjustments" to be made. President Morgan had told the Faculty of Arts Council that "the first slice of the salary pie" would go towards the rectification of inequities. I couldn't resist quoting Morgan's own words as published in the Memorial University *Gazette* from his address to convocation at Queen's University on 24 November 1973:

> I think we will all recognize that there is a time and place
> for protesting against what we know is evil or unjust. For it

is incumbent upon us all to take positive action to rectify
wrongs that are committed, to protest against injustices
that occur, so that those in whose power the remedy lies,
may be aware of the situation.[14]

This time, Morgan did not reply. And those of us who wrote a letter to
the administration citing Table II of the MUNFA salary brief as evidence of our lower pay received no answer or acknowledgement.

Some members of the MUNFA executive disliked the free expression of opinions in the newsletter and wanted all articles to be vetted
and approved by the board. In my view, it was not up to the executive to
censor the views of the faculty. They are only elected to carry out the
wishes of the faculty. I resigned from the editorial collective. In the next
issue, November 1974, the new President of MUNFA, Peter Fisher,
declared that communication between faculty and MUNFA executive
would be better served by issuing "information bulletins" at intervals.[15]
The lively *MUNFA Newsletter* with its amusing cartoon covers ceased to
be, replaced by dreary one-page bulletins issued by faceless committees.

After I left the *MUNFA Newsletter* in 1974, I moved on to become
Memorial's "corresponding member" of the CAUT Status of Academic
Women Committee. The first meeting of the Atlantic provinces representatives was in Halifax. What an eye-opener! The committee was
chaired by a male, and another male representative (a department head
from a Nova Scotia university) stated at the meeting that he would never
employ a woman in his department because there were "certain words"
you could not say in front of a woman. So it was for this trivial reason
that women were excluded from university teaching! Nothing to do with
her academic qualifications. That this outright sexism was expressed at a
meeting concerned with the status of academic women astounded me.

In 1974 we set up our own Status of Academic Women Committee
at Memorial, as part of MUNFA. The eight committee members were
drawn from a wide range: two co-chairs, Dell Texmo, English, and Jean
Tague, Mathematics; Penny Allderdice, Medical School; Hilary Bates
and Karen Lippold, both librarians; Ruth Pierson, History; Jill Snowden,
Education; and myself. Penny Allderdice was a pioneer in research into
genetically transmitted diseases in Newfoundland; Ruth Pierson, historian and poet, taught the first course on the history of women at the

university; Jill Snowden, actor, was a specialist in educational drama and was active in starting ACTRA (Alliance of Canadian Cinema, Television and Radio Artists) in Newfoundland.[16] Karen Lippold, an advocate for maternity leave for faculty women and librarians, made an impression on Moses Morgan, who referred to her as "that Lippold woman."[17]

The purpose of the committee was "to stimulate and initiate activities which will improve the conditions under which women academics and professionals work at Memorial University and to implement the recommendations of the report on the Royal Commission on the Status of Women." Paragraph 234 of its Report (1970) focused specifically on academic women, a study the Royal Commission had initiated "to find out whether women are being discriminated against in Canadian universities." Based on data supplied by the Canadian Association of University Teachers for 1965–66, it found that women received an average salary of $2,262 less than men, or 77 per cent of what a male academic earned (male academics' average salary: $10,960; female academics' average salary: $8,428). We intended to collect comparative information at Memorial on the status of women and men in the areas of salary, promotions, health benefits, leaves, and conference opportunities. We urged the 115 women faculty and 14 women librarians on campus to report if their salaries were below average, so that we could make recommendations to the administration to correct any existing inequalities for *specific* women.[18]

The Schrank Reports

This ad hoc collection of information was far from satisfactory. We needed a serious study comparing salaries of male and female faculty. This had already been set in motion when, on 9 April 1973, a general meeting of the membership of MUNFA had passed a resolution asking for such a study to be made. Dr. C.F. Preston and Dr. G.P. Jones, successive Presidents of MUNFA, negotiated with the then Vice-President (Academic), Moses Morgan, who agreed to allow economist Dr. W.E. Schrank to have access to the relevant university files, the data to be treated with strict confidentiality. Schrank worked under a watchdog committee consisting of one member of the administration — Arnold Betz, director of the university's Operational Statistics Unit — and one member of the MUNFA executive, Dr. Catherine Penney. The study was confined to full-time, tenure-track faculty only and excluded the Medical School.

It took five months to collect the data, and there was much anticipation when the report was finally released to the faculty in September 1974. Here at last was statistical, factual data of discrimination against Memorial women faculty. Some of it was in highly technical language, giving the formulas used in the statistical analysis. (The next cover of the *MUNFA Newsletter*, November 1974, showed a witch-like woman in a flowing black robe trying to calculate her salary by means of the esoteric formula she was muttering.) But the conclusions of the study were clear enough: that women faculty were paid less than men with identical qualifications and experience to do the same job; and that women were systematically discriminated against in promotions to senior academic rank and to administrative appointments. No surprises there. Schrank's calculation of the average discrimination by sex was $530, which rose to an average of $1,357 when lack of promotions of women to senior academic rank and administrative positions was taken into account.[19]

There were also anomalies in men's pay: Faculty of Science men were paid more than Faculty of Arts men, but less than men in other faculties. Men in Junior Division were paid less than their equivalently qualified colleagues in other faculties. To my surprise, the male faculty I talked to were more concerned about the *men* who were being discriminated against than they were about the women!

We waited expectantly to see what would happen. MUNFA had recommended that the salaries of faculty women should be adjusted by a total of $70,447.[20] The administration responded by doing its own review of faculty salaries, and paid out just $64,000 in adjustments. The bulk of it went to the women in the underpaid School of Nursing and to Junior Division. But 42 per cent of the total sum went to the *men* in Junior Division.[21] I was pleased that the nurses were adequately compensated, but why was so much given to the men? What about the other underpaid women?

Schrank received some queries about his methodology, which led him to make some revisions in the analysis of the data. His first report provided data on faculties, but not on individual departments within faculties. He now treated Commerce, Nursing, and Social Work as separate entities, and divided Junior Division English from the rest of the English Department. This revealed some new differences: science salaries, except for the Psychology Department, were now equal to the higher-paid faculties: the faculties of Education, Engineering, and Physical Education were the highest paid in the university. In Physical Education the men were very well paid, but the women "are very heavily penalized for their sex."[22] In the English Department, women were paid slightly more than most members of the Faculty of Arts, but "far below" their equivalent male colleagues.

The university administration had really made no effort to address the problem of sex discrimination in our salaries across the board. Glaring anomalies still existed. Schrank's published version in the *Canadian Journal of Economics* two years later had an even higher sex differential: an average of $705 per woman when ranks were excluded, $1,766 when ranks were taken into account.[23] After 10 years had elapsed, had anything changed? We demanded a further survey.

Accordingly, Dr. Schrank was asked to do a second salary survey, based on 1982–83 figures. The results were disturbing. No adjustment had been made in the lower-paid Faculty of Arts. There was a bias against older women. Some of the findings were ludicrous and even comic. There was the "married women effect" in the Faculty of Science: married women were not only paid on the average nearly $2,363 less than their married male peers, but were paid $864 less than their unmarried male and female peers. The acquisition of a doctorate actually counted against women in the Faculty of Education: "The sex term appears as a downward differential of $4,412 against women with the doctorate . . . the doctorate makes a difference for men, but not for women."[24] I found Schrank's exoneration of Memorial's administrators hard to take:

> [T]here is not necessarily an implication that the administration acted *consciously* to establish the patterns . . . . the presence of statistically significant discrimination against women need not imply that any particular administrators acted *intentionally* to keep the salaries of women low with respect to those of men.[25]

In a satiric poem on the Schrank report, "$alary Discrimination at MUN: A Found Poem," I commented:

> Yes, I clearly
> see
> these decisions are made by
> nobody[26]

To be fair, Schrank does go on to say:

> But salaries are determined by administrators and it is assumed that in setting salaries they use the information which is available to them. The obverse of this argument is that administrators cannot be expected to use information which is not available to them.[27]

This assumes that administrators are free from bias in favour of the male sex and from assigning a lower value to the female.[28] And they had the information of the first Schrank report available to them.

I could not resist poking fun at the more extreme forms of bias against women revealed in the Schrank Report:

> Faculty of *Science:*
> Women scientists! Stay single
> If you want to hear your money jingle!
> Oh Madame Curie
> If you worked at MUN today
> What would your salary be? ...

> Faculty of *Education:*
> Women! don't bust your gut
> to get that doctorut:
> it doesn't make
> a damned bit
> of difference to your take
> home pay.

Women educators! Take no spouse
If you want money in your house.
Marry and you'll rue the day.
A husband means a cut in pay.[29]

The poem was a great success as a performance piece. Laughter is the best assault against the infection of prejudice.

Unionization

The MUNFA salary brief of February 1974 noted that the unionized workers in the university had achieved progress towards an adequate salary, while the faculty was lagging behind, with lower pay than the schoolteachers of the province. After much debate, in 1987 the faculty unionized and negotiated its first contract with the university in 1989. The sticking point was salaries. In the year 2000 we went on strike. A deal was struck: the university would bring the lower-paid faculty members up to par with their colleagues, but not address the general problem of Memorial University salaries being lower than those at other Canadian universities.

So it was that one day I opened the annual letter stating my pay for the next academic year. I couldn't believe my eyes! My salary had doubled, and I also got some back pay. I was in a state of shock. I was speechless. I had always wondered how my colleagues managed to live in fancy houses and support children while I struggled to pay my bills at the end of the month. I was suddenly rich!

Then I became very angry at all those who had made the decisions as to my pay: the successive heads of departments, some of whom were my friends, the deans of arts, not to mention the university administration, who had allowed this injustice of economic discrimination against women to go on for years.

What did I do with this sudden wealth? I went to the Avalon Mall and splurged on two winter coats. Then I flew to Malta especially to look at the huge statues of the Mother Goddess. Naturally I stayed at the best hotel.

The Goddess rules!

One individual cannot change "systemic" discrimination. It takes the combined efforts of many over many years. Our struggles at Memorial were part of a wider process taking place in universities all over North America, and expressed in several collections of memoirs by academic women. Among them are *A Fair Shake: Autobiographical Essays by McGill Women*, edited by Gillett and Sibbald; *Gender and the Academic Experience: Berkeley Women Sociologists*, edited by Orlans and Wallace; and *Women in the Canadian Academic Tundra*, edited by Hannah et al.[30] I am grateful to those academics who devoted time to gathering and analyzing statistics from Statistics Canada for the Canadian Association of University Teachers, and to those members of our Faculty Association, who went through the process of unionization, and spent hours, days, weeks, and even years negotiating our salaries. I should also be grateful to Presidents Morgan and Harris, for agreeing to give Bill Schrank open access to university files relating to salary, and to Bill for doing the painstaking analysis that ultimately led to my amazing increase in pay. Thanks to them, when I retired in 2003 I received a decent pension and can live in comfortable retirement in my declining years. The story had a happy ending.

For me. And for other full-time tenured faculty members. The part-timers, who now make up a large portion of the teaching staff, still languish in the purgatory of the underprivileged: poor pay, no job security, no medical benefits, and no pension.

Acknowledgements: Thanks to Melvin Baker, Archives of Memorial University; Tony Chadwick; Averil Gardner; Philip Gardner; Elena Hannah; Dorothy Milne; Patrick O'Flaherty; Brian Payton; Georgina Queller, and members of the Newfoundland Writers' Guild; Stephen Riggins; Joan Ritcey and the staff of the Centre for Newfoundland Studies, Queen Elizabeth II Library; Joan Scott for information and comments; Steven Wolinetz.

Notes

1. Memorial University of Newfoundland, *Terms and conditions of appointment, tenure, service and employment of the teachers of the University* (St. John's: Memorial University of Newfoundland, 22 Ap. 1959), VI.18; my emphasis. In Memorial University Archives.

2. Roberta Buchanan, "From Helena's Box," *Newfoundland Quarterly* 89, 4 (1995): 15–16.

3. Malcolm MacLeod, *A Bridge Built Halfway: A History of Memorial University College, 1925–1950* (Montreal and Kingston: McGill-Queen's University Press, 1990), 92.

4. *Statutes of Newfoundland*, 1949, No.55, Memorial University Act.

5. Malcolm MacLeod, "Crossroads Campus: Faculty Development at Memorial University of Newfoundland, 1950–1972," in Paul Stortz and E. Lisa Panayotidi, eds., *Historical Identities: The Professoriate in Canada* (Toronto: University of Toronto Press, 2006), 141.

6. "Executive Joint Committee," *MUNFA Newsletter* 2, 2 (July 1973): 2.

7. "MUNFA Initiates Negotiations between Board of Regents and Striking Students," *MUNFA Newsletter* 2, 1 (1973): 1.

8. Dell defied the university's threat of firing her if she did not get married; a compromise was reached and she was given a leave of absence to have her baby. She quit the university to start her own business and became a successful entrepreneur. She related her experiences with the university and the feminist movement in an interview in "Let's Teach about Women: The Women's Movement in Newfoundland and Labrador 1970 to 1989," at: www/teachaboutwomen.ca. Dell Texmo passed away in 2012 at age 68; an obituary, by Joan Sullivan, appeared in *The Globe and Mail*, 14 Apr. 2012.

9. Elena Hannah, "Doing the Tango in the Canadian Academic Tundra: Keep Those Feet Moving Fast," in Elena Hannah, Linda Paul, and Swani Vethamany-Globus, eds., *Women in the Canadian Academic Tundra: Challenging the Chill* (Montreal and Kingston: McGill-Queen's University Press, 2002), 98.

10. "MUNFA Says No to Sexual Discrimination," *MUNFA Newsletter* 3, 1 (1973): 5.

11. Roberta Buchanan, "The Status of Faculty Women at MUN: MUNFA VP Speaks Out," *MUNFA Newsletter* 3, 1 (1973): 12.

12. M.O. Morgan, "A Letter from M.O.M.," *MUNFA Newsletter* 3, 2 (1974): 2–3.

13. Roberta Buchanan, "MUNFA Vice President Comments," *MUNFA Newsletter* 3, 2 (1974): 4–6.

14. Quoted ibid.

15. Peter Fisher, "Report from the President," *MUNFA Newsletter* 4, 1 (1974): 13–15.

16. "Status of Academic Women Committee," *MUNFA Newsletter* 3, 2 (1974): 27–28.

17. Steven Wolinetz, personal communication, 2014.

18. "Status of Academic Women Committee."
19. William E. Schrank, "A Report on Sex Discrimination in Faculty Salaries at Memorial University of Newfoundland, 1973–74," Submitted to the President of Memorial University and the Executive Committee of the Memorial University of Newfoundland Faculty Association, 27 Sept. 1974, QEII Library, Centre for Newfoundland Studies, pp. 39–40.
20. William E. Schrank, "Sex Discrimination in Faculty Salaries at Memorial University: A Decade Later," A Report Submitted to the President of Memorial University and the Executive Committee of the Memorial University of Newfoundland Faculty Association. 8 Apr. 1985, QE II Library, Centre for Newfoundland Studies, p. 2.
21. William E. Schrank, "Sex Discrimination in Faculty Salaries at Memorial University of Newfoundland, 1973–74: A Further Analysis," 16 Apr. 1975, QE II Library, Centre for Newfoundland Studies, p. 1.
22. Ibid., p. 7.
23. William E. Schrank, "Sex Discrimination in Faculty Salaries: A Case Study," *Canadian Journal of Economics* 10, 3 (1977): 431.
24. Schrank, "Sex Discrimination in Faculty Salaries at Memorial University: A Decade Later," p. 48.
25. Ibid., pp. 4–5 (my emphasis).
26. Roberta Buchanan, *I Moved All My Women Upstairs.* Newfoundland Poetry Series (St. John's: Breakwater, 1989), 49.
27. Schrank, "Sex Discrimination in Faculty Salaries at Memorial University: A Decade Later," p. 5.
28. This bias is, of course, essential to the power structure of the patriarchal system. President Hatcher of Memorial College wrote to the Board of Regents about appointments that "Lecturer (man)" was paid at a higher rate than "lecturer (woman)": MacLeod, *A Bridge Built Halfway*, 92 and n. 22.
29. Buchanan, *I Moved All My Women Upstairs*, 47–48.
30. Margaret Gillett and Kay Sibbald, eds., *A Fair Shake: Autobiographical Essays by McGill Women* (Montreal: Eden Press, 1984); Katherine P. Meadow Orlans and Ruth A. Wallace, eds., *Gender and the Academic Experience: Berkeley Women Sociologists* (Lincoln: University of Nebraska Press, 1994); Elena Hannah, Linda Paul, and Swani Vethamany-Globus, eds., *Women in the Canadian Academic Tundra: Challenging the Chill* (Montreal and Kingston: McGill-Queen's University Press, 2002).

The 1972 Occupation of the Arts and Administration Building: What Happened and Why

30

Steven B. Wolinetz

Towards the end of the 1972 fall semester, Memorial University students occupied the Arts and Administration Building. That this occurred at all was a surprise: MUN students were typically rather apathetic about campus politics. At issue were finances of the Council of the Students' Union (the acronym was then CSU; now MUNSU, the Memorial University of Newfoundland Student Union) and the autonomy of the CSU. The CSU wanted to purchase three houses where students could live. To do this it needed funds advanced from the dues that the university collected on its behalf. President and Vice Chancellor, Lord Stephen Taylor of Harlow, not only objected but also argued that the CSU spent too much of its annual budget (about $140,000) on administration and salaries. Rather than respecting the autonomy of the student union, Lord Taylor wanted to inspect its books, a demand refused by the CSU's financial officer, Dennis (Doc) O'Keefe (who was later to become Mayor of St. John's). Finances were not the only point of contention: there had been a breakdown in relations between the CSU and Lord Taylor. The CSU had withdrawn from the Student Advisory Committee, nominally attached to the Board of Regents.[1]

Impetus for the occupation was the Board of Regents' decision of 9 November 1972 to end the automatic deduction of student union dues from student fees. Although the decision was made by the Board of Regents, it was undoubtedly at the behest of Lord Taylor — the Board rarely acted on its own — who took over and served as chief protagonist. Lord Taylor insisted that student union membership should be voluntary rather than compulsory. This had implications for the Council of the Students' Union and its finances: ending compulsory deductions would deprive the CSU of a predictable revenue stream on which it relied. Instead, the CSU would have had to persuade its students — invariably short of cash — to join and pay their dues voluntarily. Few expected that this would happen.

The Board's decision did not go down well, but nothing happened until the following week. Remembrance Day and mid-term break intervened. Back on campus, students organized a meeting in the Thomson Student Centre — then little more than a large gymnasium, still on the ground floor, with two cafeterias attached. The event ended with a call to occupy the Arts and Administration Building so phlegmatic that those of us who went to see what was happening thought nothing would come of it. A couple of hours later we learned that the Arts and Administration Building had been occupied.[2]

That an occupation happened was not a surprise: student protests on American campuses and on mainland Canadian campuses had become increasingly virulent. At Cornell and Yale from 1961 to 1970, I witnessed a rising tempo of activism that began with the civil rights movement and morphed into the anti-war movement when the Vietnam War escalated. University campuses became hotbeds that engulfed some but by no means all of their students. I was only a bit player but I marched on Washington in 1963, took part in anti-war demonstrations in the late 1960s, and joined efforts to dislodge Democratic Party regulars who endorsed the war and politics as usual. In the Netherlands for dissertation research from 1968 to 1969, I witnessed student occupations and teach-ins in Leiden and Amsterdam. Back at Yale from 1969 to 1970, it was difficult not to notice that politically quiescent Yale had turned into a hotbed of political activity. In 1970 members of the Chicago Seven were tried in the federal courthouse on New Haven Green. Demonstrators flooded into Yale's residential colleges. Stores bordering the campus were boarded up. National Guard troops lined familiar streets. In 1970 demonstrators at Kent State University were shot and killed by National Guard troops called out to keep the peace. Nor was Canada immune: demonstrations and occupations took place on several Canadian campuses and the computer centre at Sir George Williams University (now Concordia) was occupied and trashed in 1969.

In contrast, the occupation of the Arts and Administration Building was a low-key affair. Students met, talked, baked bread in the second-floor Common Room, and held larger meetings in the Little Theatre (now the Reid Theatre). Had a similar occupation taken place elsewhere students would have divided into competing factions camped in separate corners. Memorial University's student newspaper, *The Muse*, and the *Evening Telegram* covered the occupation in considerable detail. Their accounts describe a gentle occupation: students organized themselves, setting up cleaning and security details; held teach-ins; and debated strategy and tactics. The occupation began on 14 November 1972 and ended 10 days later. There are other stories about students arranging for food, formulating demands, and negotiating with university officials such as the Dean of Student Affairs, J. Douglas Eaton. Although night classes were disrupted and students and professors barred the next morning, the main doors were later opened. Classes continued elsewhere on campus and resumed in the Arts and Administration Building when Commerce students protested that they would be disadvantaged because all their classes were held there.[3] One of the editors of this volume, Roberta Buchanan, recalls being given a pass that allowed her to enter the Arts and Administration Building.

Student occupiers took breaks to attend classes. Administrators decamped to the Junior Common Room, while department heads with offices in the Arts and Administration Building set up shop in seminar rooms in other buildings. Lord Taylor was prevented from entering his office or remaining in the Arts and Administration Building. Rumours flew, suggesting that the RCMP (I am not sure why it was not the Royal Newfoundland Constabulary, which had jurisdiction) was going to retake the building, but nothing like that took place. Newspaper reports indicate that neither the Constabulary nor the RCMP had any intention of intervening unless violence erupted.[4] It didn't and they didn't.

Students sought a way out as soon as the occupation began. Once selected, leaders proposed a compromise: CSU representatives would return to the Student Advisory Committee. However, Lord Taylor rejected this. Sensing they needed a broader mandate, the occupiers accepted a Graduate Student Union (GSU) offer to mediate and organize a referendum. The question was:

> *Resolved*: The President of the University and the Board of Regents do not have the right to unilaterally alter or interfere with the structure of the student body, and that Board of Regents should rescind its decision of Thursday, No-

vember 9, 1972, and that the decision should be made by
the student body.[5]

Lord Taylor was not amused. Rather than seizing a solution that
might have ended the occupation, he attacked referenda as undemocratic
and the three-part question as biased (it wasn't). According to Lord
Taylor: "Never in my life have I seen a more loaded question. It is rem-
iniscent of Hitler at his silliest. My advice to the university community
is to have nothing whatever to do with it."[6]

One can quibble with the wording of a survey or ballot question but
few social scientists would have characterized this question in the way
that Lord Taylor did. Nor — and here I speak as a political scientist
who taught European politics and insisted that history mattered —
have I ever heard Adolf Hitler described as silly.

The referendum took place on 17 November 1972. According to the
Evening Telegram, 4,121 of 6,790 undergraduate students (some 60 per
cent) voted. Of these, 3,775 voted yes (91 per cent of those voting), 328
voted no, and 18 cast spoiled ballots. Occupation leaders regarded this
as a strong mandate. CSU Vice-President Wayne Hurley argued that 60
per cent was a good turnout. The referendum had been held on eight
hours' notice and polls were open for only seven hours on a Friday when
students may have left early to go home for the weekend. Balloting
normally took place over two days.[7]

Since their numbers were dwindling, the 75–100 occupiers had to
go to residences every evening to recruit students to reinforce their
numbers. The occupiers used the weekend to assess their options. These
were grim: Lord Taylor had indicated that he would be willing to meet
with students if they vacated the building, but doing so meant capitulat-
ing without resolving the underlying issues. Gordon Winter, the Chair
of the Board of Regents, backed Lord Taylor. Sympathetic faculty
members — I was one — had intimated that faculty would back the
students when the Memorial University of Newfoundland Faculty Association (MUNFA) met. However, that support did not materialize.
When MUNFA met on 20 November 1972, it voted to remain neutral
and mediate between the two sides. Disappointed, the occupiers adopted
a wait-and-see stance. In the interim, they received support from the
Human Rights Association, the New Labrador Party, and the (Liberal)

opposition education critic, Fred Rowe. On 21 November, Ricky Cashin, President of the Newfoundland Food, Fisheries, and Allied Workers (NFFAW), delivered a rousing speech to 500 students who crammed the Little Theatre.[8]

Although Lord Taylor was unwilling to compromise, others were. Several things happened. Students living in campus residences organized a mass rally in the Thomson Student Centre. Three thousand students attended. Out of that meeting came the idea of a mass strike. At the same time, the university position changed. Although Lord Taylor insisted that there had been no disruption to the normal operations of the university — a point that students disputed — others were ready to bring the conflict to an end. A meeting on 23 November was arranged between negotiating teams from each side. Chaired by labour lawyer Robert Wells, this took place at the Holiday Inn. The Board Chair, Gordon Winter, attended but Lord Taylor did not. Out of it came a settlement: students were to vacate the building, leaving it in the condition they found it. The Board was to rescind its 9 November decision and continue the mandatory collection of CSU dues pending the outcome of the referendum to be held during the winter semester. There were to be no reprisals; university officials were to request Senate to recommend academic leniency in instances in which students were unable to complete assigned work. Cancelled for the day, classes were to resume on Monday. However, the occupation was not without fallout. Lord Taylor announced his resignation and was conspicuously absent from Senate in December 1972 and gone by June 1973.[9]

MUNFA organized the referendum. According to *The Muse* the campaign that preceded it was lacklustre. The *Evening Telegram* lost interest. Neither the referendum campaign nor the meetings that the CSU organized on how the Union might be restructured aroused much interest.[10] The referendum took place on 22 and 23 February 1973. Only 2,700 (36 per cent) of the CSU's members cast votes. Of these, 1,436 (53 per cent) voted for compulsory dedication of union dues. However, 1,272 (47 per cent) were opposed.[11] I was asked to help with the count. Supervising it was Dick Middleton, a Professor of Anatomy. Ballot boxes were brought to his workspace, the anatomy room in the temporary buildings. Although the turnout was lower and the margin narrower, students voted to retain the automatic check-off. As a political scientist with some knowledge of voting behaviour, I can report that students who voted in tunnels saved the compulsory deduction of fees and, with it, the CSU. There were five ballot boxes in different locations. The four located above ground returned majorities opposed to the check-off, but the fifth, located in the main tunnel next to the Thomson Centre entrance, had sufficient votes in favour to offset the others. Whether students who spent time underground — in those days the tunnels seemed so crowded that you wondered whether they lived there — voted differently is another matter: it is more likely that the intersection — a choke point — was a convenient place for many students to vote.

The CSU's finances had become uncertain when the outcome of the second referendum was not known. The CSU limped through January and February, barely able to act. Occupying the Arts and Administration Building, students saved the Student Union. Had students not voted yes in February 1972, it is likely that the CSU would have collapsed.

What was the occupation really about? On the surface, it was an argument about the CSU and the compulsory and automatic deduction of dues. Deeper down, something else was underway: Lord Stephen Taylor became President in 1967. From 1958 to 1972 the power to name Memorial's President rested not with the Board of Regents but rather with the Premier, Joseph R. Smallwood. The President from 1953 to 1967, Raymond Gushue, was stepping down. According to *The Book of Newfoundland,* Smallwood threw himself into the selection process. Travelling to England, he met with prominent politicians and academics and came up with a physician, Lord Stephen Taylor, who had a distinguished career behind him. Active in public health and preventative medicine, Taylor had been a Labour Party MP and a minister in the post-war Attlee government. There he participated in the creation of the National Health Service. Rewarded with an appointment to the House of Lords — Taylor was one of the Labour Party's first life peers — Taylor took Harlow as his seat.[12] Invited to assume Memorial's presidency, he declined three times and accepted only after he visited the province.[13] What is striking about the process is that it did not involve faculty, staff, or students, as it would today, or even the Board of Regents. At Memorial, many thought the job should have gone to M.O. (Mose) Morgan, the Dean of Arts and Science. Instead, Morgan became Vice-President (Academic). It would be wrong to suggest that Morgan engineered the occupation. However, it is likely that he allowed it to run its course. No one bothered to restrain Lord Taylor or prevent him from railing about the undemocratic qualities of referenda. Instead, he was allowed to work himself out of a job. Its power to appoint the President restored by the Moores government, the Board of Regents appointed M.O. Morgan as President and Vice-Chancellor.

My evidence for this is scant but compelling: Morgan had run the university as Dean of Arts and Science and Vice-President (Academic). Known for hands-on control, Morgan was nowhere to be seen during the occupation. He also made sure that a young assistant registrar was closeted in his office when he was supposed to be reading a speech by Lord Taylor, because Taylor had laryngitis. Nor was there any interest in calling the police and clearing the building. Students occupying the Arts Building were also told that they had support from the administration. Had such a message been sent, it is likely that it would have been delivered by Doug Eaton, the Dean of Students. It is too late to ask either about the roles they played, but I suspect that Doug Eaton, a consummate storyteller, would have told me a great deal. In contrast, Mose Morgan might have smiled but said little or nothing. In retrospect, it is no surprise that the occupation was allowed to run its course.

One final word: Aside from the fleeting involvement of the later Mayor of St. John's, Dennis O'Keefe, I've said nothing about the dramatis personae. Some of those involved were people whose names are so familiar that they count as usual suspects. Leading the occupation were Bob Buckingham, CSU President following the resignation of Charlie Green; Earl McCurdy and his late brother, Dave McCurdy, editor of *The Muse*; as well as others, such as CSU Vice-President Wayne Hurley and Geoff Hunt, whose names I recall because they were Political Science majors. Of these, Bob Buckingham and Earl McCurdy are still frequently in the news, the former because he practises criminal law, the latter because he succeeded Ricky Cashin as President of the Fisheries Union and was leader of the provincial NDP from 2015 to 2017. Stantec consultant, Mark Shrimpton, was Vice-President of the Graduate Student Union and active on its behalf.

Notes

1. *Evening Telegram,* 10 Nov. 1972.
2. Ibid., 15 Nov. 1972.
3. Ibid., 15, 16 Nov. 1972.
4. Ibid., 15, 16 Nov. 1972.
5. Ibid., 17 Nov. 1972.
6. Ibid.
7. Ibid., 18 Nov. 1972.
8. Ibid., 20, 21 Nov. 1972.
9. Ibid., 23, 24, 25 Nov. 1972.
10. *The Muse,* 16, 26 Feb. 1973.
11. *The Muse,* 26 Feb. 1973; *Evening Telegram,* 24 Feb. 1973.
12. Stephen Taylor (Lord Taylor of Harlow), *A Natural History of Everyday Life: A Biographical Guide for Would-be Doctors of Society* (London: British Medical Journal, 1988).
13. James R. Thoms, "We Begin to Build a Great University," in Joseph R. Smallwood, ed., *The Book of Newfoundland,* vol. 4 (St. John's: Newfoundland Book Publishers, 1967), 118–23.

Student occupation of the Arts and Administration Building. (Photo from *Celebrate Memorial: A Pictorial History of Memorial University of Newfoundland,* originals held at Memorial University Library Archives and Special Collections.)

My Fifty Years at Memorial University

Joan Scott

31

I arrived in Newfoundland in 1962, a young mother with a two-year-old son, Nicholas. My husband John had recently completed a PhD in Chemistry. Canada was turning out too few scientists, and we were part of an infusion of scientist researcher-teachers meant to bring Prime Minister John Diefenbaker's program of university expansion to life. John's appointment to the Chemistry Department at Memorial was his fourth position since we married in 1955. Before that he had a two-year National Research Council Fellowship in Ottawa; then we moved back to England for a year; then to Stamford, Connecticut, where John worked in industry at American Cyanamid. Here I gave birth to Nicholas, cared for him, and began some college-level courses.

I had always assumed I would work outside the home. I had a teaching diploma, taught Grades 5 and 6 in Ottawa, then in a comprehensive school in Harlow New Town when we returned to England. In Connecticut I was assigned an alien's card, which meant that I could not do paid work. I had looked forward to the move to Newfoundland. I expected to feel freer and more at home in this Canadian university town than I had in the United States. Here I would no longer be denied paid work. Perhaps because I was now a mother, I craved that feeling of belonging to a place and the stability I had once enjoyed in my home town of Ipswich.

We lived in St. John's in a rented house on University Avenue. This was our ninth house in seven years of marriage. I was an old hand at setting up a new home and connecting with new dentists, doctors, etc. I was also getting tired of moving. The arrival of our furniture was delayed by two weeks. When it arrived I had shingles, probably due to stress.

As my husband got stuck in the long hours of his work, our lives were enriched by social activities with his colleagues and their families. Every Friday at five in the afternoon, we looked forward to the family swim time at the Memorial pool. It was easy to make new friends, among them several women, also "from away," around my own age and with young children.

Soon after arrival in St John's I went to the Confederation Building to find a teaching job. I was ignorant of the denominational school system. I saw five offices along a corridor, each with a flag-like sign indicating a Christian denomination: Anglican, Roman Catholic, United, Salvation Army, and Pentecostal. Having belonged to the Methodists as a teenager in England, I felt that the United Church (which included the former Methodist Church of Canada) was the best place to start. I knocked on that door.

Early in the interview I was asked if I was a believer, and I admitted that I was not. "How can you aspire to be a teacher if you have no moral code?" Hmm. There was no point in arguing. I left to seek my fortune elsewhere. The next most likely fit seemed to be the Anglicans. I thought I was ready for anything but was shocked by the incredibly low salary. This would be my first job since becoming a mother and I wanted to pay my sitter something respectable from my earnings. (I was still naive enough to see her as "my" sitter, as opposed to ours.) That would be impossible given the figures quoted, regardless of the denomination, so the most worthwhile thing to do was to go back to school. Somebody else would have to pay for the sitter.

There were virtually no daycare centres, although there was a good supply of experienced women, in town and out, willing to do this work. Nicholas and I became grateful for them. In the newspaper, the live-in help-wanted ads often said "Outport replies awaited."

I joined a non-credit university course in creative writing taught by Dr. Aldus of the English Department. There my fellow students included the wonderful Newfoundland writers Bernice Morgan, Helen Porter, and Gerry Rubia. Also, I had time for lots of reciprocal coffee mornings with my neighbours. I was proud of my ability to keep both my son and myself involved with all kinds of projects.

Especially for a stay-at-home mom the St. John's winter weather was important. Staying indoors was often unavoidable. I found it generally tolerable; although walking home once from a nearby neighbour's house at night in a blizzard with whiteouts had challenged my sense of direction. I was scared when the wind made our two-storey house creak and groan. Roofs *did* blow off houses; and picture windows *were* blown in. That winter a woman died in a snowbank and was not found until there was a thaw.

As February wore on I had expectations of better weather, but they were not realized. By then, bulbs were blooming everywhere else I had lived, but not here. Later I learned to appreciate the longer, brighter days of late February, the real signs of spring, but then getting the most out of life, for Nicholas and myself, became challenging and I wanted to go away. Flying was expensive. That left driving. I did not have the courage to deal with possible storms and getting stranded. I was trapped. I had a precious young child. This was my first year in St. John's and I had no experience with this kind of winter weather, let alone of driving in it. I feared the highway that crossed the island. It was not fully paved until 1965. That "spring" was one of the blacker periods of my life.

Then I became aware that I was pregnant. My life was unfolding the way I had intended. Good-weather days occurred more frequently. The crocuses came out in gardens, and my son and I could go out more often. I began to look ahead.

At first all I had intended was to do "some courses," but this changed to doing a degree. A prerequisite for all students was Norman Brown's philosophy course, which he taught in the evenings. I was pregnant with Kitty, my second child, and in the afternoons I might walk while Nicholas, nearly three years old, rode his tricycle. One evening I fell asleep in class, but still somehow I passed. I expected my second child to be my last, and after I was over the birth and life with her had settled into a routine, I began to think about my long-term future. I collected together the necessary documentation.

From ages 18 to 20, in 1953–55, I had taken a two-year diploma in primary education from Philippa Fawcett College, which was affiliated with London University. There was a shortage of teachers in the UK and the Diploma in Education was then the normal and complete qualification for teaching in elementary schools. In the early 1960s I thought a degree would improve my pay in any job. A Biology degree was on my personal list of things I wanted to do. Also, I hoped it might get me out of the classroom.

Although I enjoyed some aspects of teaching, it was never my passion: so a reader might wonder why I got into the classroom in the first place. When I was at grammar school, I passionately wanted to be a BBC announcer or a veterinarian. However, I was discouraged from pursuing these careers at school. BBC announcers were chosen, I was told, "from the typing pool." But typing was to be avoided by any young woman who had "passed the scholarship."

This was not simply academic snobbery. There was some wisdom in it, which applied on both sides of the Atlantic. If a woman could type, she might never be offered a better job regardless of higher qualifications. This point was made in 1977, by two Carleton University professors, Jill McCalla Vickers and June Adam, in their book *But Can You Type? Canadian Universities and the Status of Women.*

As for being a vet, I was told that farm animals were too big for little women. Caught up by a romantic vision of rural England and farming, based on stories my granddad told me as a child and the rural memoirs I found on the school library shelves, I sent to Rothamstead Experimental Station for application forms. This was and is the leading UK government agricultural research establishment, founded in 1843, one of the oldest in the world. Rothamstead offered courses and diplomas for which I could qualify; but my father, whose own father had been a horseman on a farm — at the time when the horse was king — strongly discouraged me. The status of horsemen fell when the tractor took over, and my granddad then seemed like an ordinary farm labourer. Dad said that I should choose a "real" job and confine milking cows to my holidays.

My school did not help me to be true to myself either. There was a strict division between arts and sciences. At age 16, we took up to eight courses for the school certificate and were encouraged to take English and math and then specialize in either arts or sciences. For the next stage, up to age 18, we took up to four courses, which had to be in one camp or the other. My interests lay in botany, zoology, and English. They crossed the two camps. However, I was assigned to do sciences: botany, zoology, and chemistry. I came out of this stage of schooling with only two sciences, not three, and therefore was not eligible for a Borough Major Scholarship, which would have permitted me to enter university. So going to university was not an option, but I was eligible for a Borough Minor Scholarship for teacher's college. Indeed, I was overqualified. I was accepted by all the colleges I applied to, including Philippa Fawcett in London, the city where my boyfriend, later husband, was working on his PhD. So love was another of the contingencies that brought me into teaching. Also, I had heard that the National Union of Teachers (the so-called NUTs) had won equal pay, which sounded like a very good thing. I wanted to have children and as a teacher I could have my summers off with them. Teaching, if not a perfect career for me, was achievable and had its perks. Once in teaching I realized that I could do it even though the fit was less than perfect.

In Newfoundland, the conditions to do a degree were in place. To get into Memorial University as a mature student in the early 1960s, I first had to meet with the Registrar, Harry Renouf. I sought credits for several compulsory first- and second-year courses. He said I would get credit for the first French course only if I passed the second. He made it clear that he thought I had a swelled head for expecting to get credit for both courses. I felt rather inadequate as it had been 10 years since I last took French.

Susan Jackson, a more established faculty wife who had taught French, agreed to coach me in the second French course so that I might take one course and get both credits. The professor was Terry Mellor, who was also an artist and had an exhibition at the university art gallery around the same time. Such was the quality of French in the schools in those days that when students answered in class, they often spelled their answers. I was shocked and saw my own French classes in a state school in Britain, complete with their young Mam'selles who gave us conversational French in small groups, in a new light. In Terry's course we read *Candide* in a textbook that had the French on one page and the English opposite. With help from Susan Jackson, I passed this hurdle.

I agreed with my husband that the math course would be a good test of whether or not I would go for the degree. It was a summer course, and perhaps we got by without a sitter, with my husband filling in for me. I enjoyed the math professor, Ben Gardner, and my fellow students. Some, like Dorothy Wyatt, who later became the famous, headband-wearing Mayor of St. John's, were nurses upgrading their hospital-based registered nursing qualifications to the new university-based Bachelor in Nursing. Another student in the class was her friend Ms. Elton, who ran the parts department of the Colonial Garage, her family's business. This was a time when wigs were in vogue purely for the fun of radically changing our appearance. I had one and Dorothy had several. I watched Dorothy as she made her entrance after each weekend to see which one she would be wearing. A 1969 photograph of Dorothy shows her as one of the four women in the first BN graduating class.[1] I believe she is wearing a wig. I passed the scary math course and went on to tackle the organic chemistry course, which I also passed.

The many biology courses took a lot of time, but they were really interesting. Two of my professors specialized in beautiful marine invertebrates: Fred Aldrich, the imaginative American who built the Ocean Sciences Centre to match the shape of a sea anemone, and who also successfully sought out physical examples of the close-to-mythical Kraken or giant squid; and John Evans, from McGill, who had studied boring clams on the US west coast. This may sound weird but there really is a group of clams that bore into cliffs. In the 1970s John Evans became Mr. Humus Toilet as he introduced what were then advanced notions of organic farming and composting to all who would listen.

One biology course, Boreal Ecology, looked into ecological relationships, i.e., between the non-living (climate and soils) and living organisms such as trees, lichens, moose, rabbits, caribou, and humans in the boreal zone, the zone just south of the Arctic. It was a very special course because it covered material relevant to this province and we had really fun field trips such as to Terra Nova National Park in the winter snow. We studied the productivity of the tiny voles and found it better than that of farmed animals. We live-trapped, weighed, marked, and released the voles; and with reference to existing data on their reproduction, etc., we were able to estimate how many grams of vole meat they produced per unit of territory and compared it with such animals as cattle.

Dr. Bill Pruitt, who taught that course was, like the others, a bit of a chauvinist but also admirable. His classes were lively and, more importantly, he really lived his beliefs. An American, he had been fired by the University of Alaska for leading a group of faculty members who resisted a proposal to use a nuclear bomb to construct an artificial harbour on the North Slope of Alaska, a harbour that would be ice-free for only a few months in the year. Although widely supported at the time (1958), this was the unbelievable "Project Chariot," championed by Edward Teller, known as the "father of the hydrogen bomb." The story is told by Dan O'Neill in *The Firecracker Boys*.[2] He argues that Pruitt's campaign is one of the roots of the modern environmental movement.

My neighbour, friend, and Memorial English Professor, Gill Sandeman, whose children played with mine, taught a memorable English course. I was fascinated by the mirror structure of Emily Bronte's *Wuthering Heights*. Last but not least, Milton Freeman, along with Robert Paine, taught a sociology/anthropology course in human ecology. This was my one discretionary course in the degree. Freeman's research included sticklebacks of the eastern Hudson Bay area, and he was later famous for studies of Inuit land use on which land claims were partly based. He also invited us to join small tutorial groups to discuss specific issues. Paine was famous for his work on the way of life of the Sami or Lapps in Scandinavia. At home, after their bedtime stories, I popped my little kids into bed at seven and got on with reading my daily quota of pages. I graduated in 1968 with a BSc Hons.

Next, as part of my project to avoid the classroom I accepted a job as "invertebrate pathologist" in the Biology Department. (Dr. Laird was the new head of the Biology Department who was away travelling a great deal. "Yes Virginia, there is a Dr. Laird" was famously written on one Memorial bathroom wall.) Despite my impressive title it turned out to be a very boring job. I had to examine slides of bird blood from around the world for microscopic signs of bird malaria. Most were clear of the parasite, but I had to spend 20 minutes systematically scanning each microscope slide before I could declare a slide free of it. A lot of biological research is monotonous like this. At the end of the month when the similarly microscopic cheque arrived, I quit. My excellent but expensive sitter, a Miss Lake, was giving my kids a fabulous time exploring St. John's in the summer, but it did not make sense for me to be indoors and earning so little.

At the careers office, then in the Physical Education Building, I sought some rewarding work in exchange for my long hours of study, but outside of schoolteaching I was offered nothing. This probably reflected both an actual shortage of such positions plus the backward thinking of all concerned, who in those days offered women only a narrow range of job opportunities. In 1968–69 my fate was to teach at Holy Heart, an all-girls Catholic high school. It was easy getting the job. At Holy Heart nobody asked me if I believed in God or even whether I was a Catholic. In 1968, in the Newfoundland Christian denominational system, a brand new Memorial University BSc Hons. trumped those issues.

In 1969–70 my husband spent a sabbatical year in Calgary to work with his old boss from Ottawa days, Ross Robertson. I was soon teaching biology at Viscount Bennett High School in Calgary. There I discovered that a colleague, who was teaching the same biology courses, did not teach the evolution chapter because, she said, "it's only a theory, there is no proof." I never came across this phenomenon in St. John's, although in my early years here students frequently asked "when does life begin?" The question was, of course, a veiled exploration of what I might say regarding when abortion is morally acceptable. As a biology teacher, my answer was a simplified version of the following. I said that life began long ago when conditions on our planet were very different than they are today. The planet does not now offer the conditions necessary for the chemical and physical processes we call life to begin. Nowadays the thread of life does not begin. It either continues or comes to an end, dies. Of course, my answer did not engage with the abortion issue, which perhaps was just as well.

The most significant aspect of teaching in Calgary for my Memorial University life was that I taught some Grade 12 students, large guys indifferent to academics but of great value to the school's football team. When I returned to St. John's in 1971, Dr. Art Sullivan was setting up the new Junior Division to help Grade 11 students from small rural schools make a better transition to the large first-year classes of the university. The professors were often from away and had little appreciation of the schooling their students had experienced, and typically, had not completed any courses in education. With no Grade 12 in the schools, too many students were failing Memorial's first year. Junior Division inserted a pre-first year taught by experienced high school teachers as a bridge. I heard the call of Memorial University's Junior Division via a public service announcement on a Sunday afternoon on the CBC. My husband was most enthusiastic about me following this up and I did. He advised me before going to the interview not to accept any position that was not full-time from the start. With my experience teaching Grade 12 in Calgary, I joined Junior Division and was teaching the equivalent of Grade 12 within days. At the same time I found that I was pregnant with my third child.

In Junior Division we former high school teachers, of all disciplines, started with classes of no more than 33 in purpose-built classrooms in the temporary buildings. Very lively meetings of the whole faculty were held monthly. Very soon, due to the university expansion of the early 1960s in Canada, many people with PhDs were competing for our jobs. We who had recently been hired for our high school teaching experience were pressed to become more qualified for our university positions.

This is when I started an MSc in Biology. The coursework went well but the fieldwork, or rather pond work, did not. The species of gnat larva I was studying died out in the original pond. The cause was unclear. I was taking very few specimens and so my activities were not the cause, but perhaps someone had sprayed an insecticide there. Since I had collected some data on it I wanted to continue to use the same organism. The only other place I could find the larva was in a pond that required me to use a boat (and a helper) because of the greater depth of the water. I could not find a helper. My supervisor was sympathetic and explained that biology grad students typically helped each other. I was not a member of those groups and anyway had no spare time to give to others, and no other quid pro quo was available from this older and married woman with children. So after excellent marks in all my coursework, the first of my three tries to get a master's degree fizzled out.

For a while the Junior Division process was highly documented, perhaps to justify its existence. I had completed a statistics course as part of my master's, and I used a huge calculating machine, a relic of one of my husband's research projects, to produce some of the data for biology. Perhaps our stats did not support continuing the Junior Division at the university, which with its small classes must have been expensive, although it was much cheaper than the better alternative of offering Grade 12 to school students regardless of their intentions of going on to university. Whatever the reasons, our classes got bigger every year, and we were pressured to join our parent departments. In the case of Biology, our "parent" at first rejected us. After all, teaching first year was traditionally a despised activity and they had got rid of it. But pressure from above was relentless, and soon our parent was approaching us to join them. Junior Division ceased to exist, and we former Junior Division people really had to get traditional university qualifications. We took various paths to achieving them. Some went to the north campus to do medicine and others to biology grad courses, while I gave up on the Biology master's and headed to the Faculty of Education.

This was a hectic time for me. I tried to hold on to my vision of myself as superwoman, able to successfully fulfill simultaneously the traditional roles of mother and wife, plus those of professor and graduate student. The role of wife was sacrificed as the existing cracks in my marriage gave way under the strain.

The second wave of feminism was making good sense to me. I

wanted to do a feminist master's, i.e., to choose a topic arising from the first tenet of feminism that in this society women in general are oppressed. It was thinkable to choose to explore whether and how women were oppressed through education and employment. I could have chosen to explore whether women are oppressed in this society through their biology, but politically that was and still is unacceptable to me.

I looked specifically to my earlier qualifications in education. The new discipline of Women's Studies was being taught in the US, so why not eventually in St. John's? I would be qualified for that when it happened and, in theory at least, would be able to step sideways into a Women's Studies teaching position. From my academic and personal experiences I saw a difference between the inequalities that existed and the ideal of equal access to science education and employment for qualified women and men. Why and how was this happening? This gave me a research problem that I knew was well worth exploring. I proposed to study women and science, starting at their numbers and grades at the high school levels, and questioning the validity of the general view that women were few in science because women could not do the science courses. When I revealed/declared my proposed research problem, I ran into a brick wall. My thesis topic was rejected.

I felt painted into a corner and wondered if I really was "crazy," as some people said. However, Dr. Jeff Bulcock, an Education Professor and a thoughtful man of few words, gave me access to some punch-carded data and showed me how to use it. Among other information, such as family size and birth order, it included the high school science subject choices and marks of the whole cohort of the students of this province, by sex, who were born in one year in the late 1950s. Thank you, Jeff, for a truly empowering opportunity! I ran with it, and with this unofficial help produced a paper built on the structure of an earlier well-received education thesis. I hoped that my paper would be accepted as a master's thesis. However, it was not.

But I'd like to assure Jeff, who has now passed on, that even if it was not defined as a thesis this piece of writing had quite a life. First it became a paper, which I gave at a CRIAW (Canadian Research Institute for the Advancement of Women) conference. I had been to lots of conferences and listened to many papers, but this was the first paper I had written and presented myself.

The paper elided little details like the fact that I did not understand the math that the machine (and Jeff) was doing for me, although of course I did understand the findings. The data showed that the girls of our province were doing more of the harder math courses than were the boys, and they were doing better in them. These are gatekeeper subjects. For instance, good math marks give access to many other rewarding courses such as physics. Thus, girls in Newfoundland schools should have been doing more physics courses, but they were not. I saw this as an example of females being subtly excluded from advancement. Perhaps other under-represented groups were being similarly excluded.

When presented at the CRIAW conference, the audience for the paper included Drs. Margrit Eichler and Dorothy Smith, two prestigious professors in sociology of education at the Ontario Institute for Studies in Education (OISE). They were happy because I was that rare commodity, a feminist academic from the sciences. When my presentation was over, these two high-powered women came over to chat with me. Heady stuff. I was not crazy after all, and would fit in at OISE, which according to Dr. Florence Howe, founder of The Feminist Press in the United States, was offering the best feminist courses in North America. So I started my third master's degree.

As I am writing this many years later, I want to draw attention to this use of the word, "crazy." It was used in a derogatory way against me, to discourage me from pursuing what I recognized as a problem from my experience. In a society that under-educates all of us about mental illness and under-serves all of the sufferers, I do not wish to seem to be trivializing illnesses that are frequently fatal.

Meanwhile my marriage came to an end. I was granted a sabbatical year. I moved to Toronto with my nine-year-old daughter, to do graduate work at OISE, now the Graduate Department of Education, in the sub-department of Sociology in Education, in the University of Toronto. I was able to stay longer than the sabbatical year because the Newfoundland Education Department introduced Grade 12 into the schools (a better solution than Junior Division to Memorial's high first-year failure rate), which meant that for one year there would be practically no intake of students at Memorial University. That resulted in me being funded to stay away longer, enabling me to spin out my stay at OISE for a total of four years, living on one-third of my salary for each of the last three. Thus I was able to begin to work on my PhD. The Toronto OISE experience enriched my life enormously, teaching me more about the world of reading, writing, and ideas, and building hugely on what I had learned from science. Science answers simple questions with very reliable answers, whereas sociology deals with more complex questions and finds answers that are not so reliable.

The women informants for my 1994 thesis — Joan Pinner Scott, *Women's Distinctive Careers in Academic Science: Discrimination or Ordinary Practices?* — whose own names are not used, were truly amazing people. I often wish I had not signed contracts with them to ensure confidentiality. Their stories deserve to be well known.

In 1983 Women's Studies (now Gender Studies) finally went on stream at Memorial University. I felt very ready to fall into teaching a course immediately, but some of the leading women were not so convinced. Admittedly, at that time I still had no PhD and they still saw me as a Junior Division biology teacher. However, I was eventually called on to co-teach the introductory course (Women's Studies 2000). Co-teaching, which was the WS 2000 norm, is not a bad idea although I am not clear now about the justification for it at that time. Perhaps it was because the course was interdisciplinary and faculty members were "borrowed" from their main departments, whether Biology, History, English, Psychology, Sociology, etc. Perhaps it was because we gloried in our interdisciplinarity. Co-teaching with Roberta Buchanan was a joy. She used student-centred methods to which I had been introduced during the previous four years. Co-teaching did not last long. Eventually half of my load was in Women's Studies and the opportunity arose to write my own course, Women and Science (WS 2001). I was at last shaping my work the way I wanted. I especially chuckled over the number I had chosen for it, which was the title of the movie *2001, a Space Odyssey*. The course gave me a chance to attack the subject of Women and Science in three ways. One part was about women "greats" in science, such as Marie Curie, the physicist who won two Nobel Prizes but was seen as an exception who proved the rule rather than one of a cavalcade of outstanding women in science. I brought all the historic greats together in a slide show with brief biographies and wonderful old black-and-white images. Another part of the course concerned the history of women's science education and achievements more widely. I also had a chance to expose the students to some misuses of science, such as using imprisoned men of colour for medical experiments, and to the kind of science (hormones, brains, sexual development, etc.) that has been used to "prove" that women and other disadvantaged groups could not do science. I enjoyed teaching this original course, which was one of very few in Canada.

In these years before my retirement in 2001 several events occurred that were all major for me, although not especially related to Memorial University.

In 1988, I had been hired at the Canadian Advisory Council on the Status of Women (CACSW) in Ottawa, while taking a two-year leave of absence from my Memorial position. I applied for the job because I was interested in the work, thought I would enjoy living in Ottawa again, and the pay was close to double what I was receiving at Memorial. In the 1980s, I was privileged to meet or hear many of the leaders of the feminist movement in Canada, the US, and even some from Europe. Among them were Adrienne Rich, Kay McPherson, Nancy Riche, Lynn Macdonald, Rose Sheinin, Sunera Thobani, and Judy Rebick. Sunera Thobani led the National Action Committee for the Status of Woman (NAC) and is now a Professor at the Institute for Gender, Race, Sexuality and Social Justice at the University of British Columbia. She has a long list of controversial, ground-breaking publications. Rose Sheinin was a strong supporter of my work. She put me in touch with Dr. Cannie Stark-Adamec, who put together a special issue of *The International Journal of Women's Studies* devoted to women and science, which included my paper on female achievement in Canadian high schools.[3] Rose Sheinin was a senior scientist, a Fellow of the Royal Society of Canada, famous for her early conviction regarding the connection between cancer and viruses. She was also the daughter of a communist milkman. It is impossible to do her life justice here.[4]

Also in 1988 my grandson Elliott Zane Scott Coen was born.

In 1994, I added the title of Doctor to my professional identity.

Back in Newfoundland with the thesis finally behind me, I became involved in politics. In 1997, I was the candidate for the federal election in the riding of Humber, St. Barbe, Baie Verte for the New Democratic Party. Although there was little in the way of party resources, it was exhilarating to work with supportive people to try to reach as many voters as possible in that extensive and lovely part of the world. My results were respectable given that I was parachuted in and that it was a first try. Gerry Byrne won and later became a provincial MHA. Although asked to run in following elections, I did not have what it takes to run again.

The main reason was that, in 1998, my son Nicholas took his life. I was tempted not to mention this as I do not want to make people sad, but saying or writing his name and talking about him is good for me; and also good for all readers who have been touched by this or related experiences. Mental illness and suicide are not reasons for shame and should not be hidden. This loss is my hardest and that ache will be with me for the rest of my life.

Being among the last group to have been compulsorily retired from Memorial University (in 2001), I resolved to enjoy my retirement, while watching slightly younger former colleagues soldier on. I continue my connections to Memorial through my pension, of course, and the physical and mental stimulation of The Works, the university athletic centre, and the library, and most valuably through friendly contacts such as the Memoirs Group of the Pensioners' Association. These years are bittersweet as we wrinkle and crumble. I am still well enough to walk to a distant pond and swim on a summer day, or trek into the woods for fungi, yet must watch as others reach the end. Before I moved to Newfoundland, my husband's colleague Ross Robertson warned, "Joan will not be happy there." But he was wrong. I have been a Memorial University faculty wife, a Memorial University student, a Memorial University faculty member in Junior and Senior Divisions, and now a Memorial University retiree; and for me it was a largely happy period, and Memorial University was certainly the key.

Notes

1. *Newfoundland Quarterly* (Winter 2012–13): 5.
2. Dan O'Neill, *The Firecracker Boys* (New York: St. Martin's Griffin, 1994; revised 2007).
3. Joan Scott, "The Determinants of Science: Subject Choice and Achievement of Females in Canadian High Schools," *The International Journal of Women's Studies* 4 (Sept.–Oct. 1981).
4. See the obituary of Rose Sheinin in *The Globe and Mail*, 10 Apr. 2009.

Another Viking Invades Newfoundland: The Music School

Kjellrun Hestekin

Birth of a Notion

One of Dr. M.O. Morgan's objectives for his tenure as President of Memorial University was the establishment of a School of Music.[1] Don Cook, a local teacher, entertainer, and church organist and choir director, was appointed as head of the new Department of Music within the Faculty of Arts. In 1975 he began the task of developing a program, recruiting students and hiring faculty. In the fall of 1976, the Department of Music became a reality.

Serendipity

Early in 1976 I was finishing up my master's degree. I had initially planned to go back to teaching high school, but friends had convinced me to look for a "college" job. Figuring it wouldn't hurt to try, and to get my friends off by back, I made a few visits to the university's placement office. There were a few schools with a theory position to fill, but nothing that got my heart racing. In some cases the location was unattractive: a huge city or somewhere in the Deep South (two years as an undergraduate in Kansas had convinced me that I was not made for warm weather). In other cases the position was combined with a second area like jazz studies or harpsichord in which I had no expertise. The comfortable high school job was looking better and better.

Then I spotted a copy of *University Affairs* — a great title! And there was an ad for three new positions in the Department of Music at Memorial University in St. John's, Newfoundland, Canada. I had no idea where Newfoundland was, but three new positions sounded intriguing: either the department was growing fast or, could it be, a brand new program?! The possibility that it was a dysfunctional unit that had to replace several of its members never entered my mind. I posted my application with fingers crossed.

The winter term progressed with courses to complete, comprehensive exams to prepare for, and a thesis to write. And the "thanks, but no thanks" letters started coming in. "Your CV looks good, but we're looking for someone with experience" became an all too familiar refrain. The application to Memorial faded from memory. Spring break was looming, but I decided I could afford neither the expense nor the time of taking a holiday and so stayed in Madison. I was sitting in my room, plugging away at my thesis, when the phone call came: could I travel to St. John's for an interview next week?

The next few days were a blur, but somehow, at the appointed date and time, I was on a plane headed east. Waaay east. I had looked at a map and found Newfoundland, so I had a vague idea of where I was going, and how far it was. I had never thought of Canada as being a distant country. Our family had vacationed there often; you could easily drive there in a day, but that was Thunder Bay or "The Soo." This was something else again, but it was a real, live interview, so I went. There was no danger of getting the job anyway; I still had no university-level experience and besides, they'd want to hire a Canadian, wouldn't they? I was pretty relaxed, knowing this was basically a practice exercise.

If I had been nervous, the trip to St. John's would have done me in. Remember, this was spring break. March. And I was flying to Newfoundland. We did manage to land at a place called Gander, where we all climbed aboard a vintage yellow school bus. My map study hadn't been terribly extensive; I had no idea where Gander was in relation to St. John's, so I climbed aboard, trusting we'd soon be there. After hours of travel through grey flannel, we stopped for a break in a place called Clarenville. I actually got off the bus and crossed the road to try to get some idea of what this place looked like. (In retrospect, not the wisest move, but fortunately, traffic was light — at least I didn't see any cars.)

Eventually, we arrived in St. John's and a short little fellow in a salt-and-pepper cap greeted me and identified himself as Don Cook, head of the new Department of Music. He brought me to a small motel near the university; now the Guv'nor Inn, then about half as large, much seedier, and with a restaurant restricted both in its operating hours and in its menu offerings. We chatted over a bowl of pea soup and Don explained that this was, indeed, a brand new Department of Music. He had wanted to have the positions filled the previous fall, but a postal strike had meant he couldn't get the notices out till winter. Had he had his way, the position would have been filled before I even started looking. And had I been off on holidays when he called, he most likely would have gone on to the next name on the list. Don gave me a run-down of the next day's schedule, now only a few hours away, and disappeared into the fog.

The next two days were a whirlwind of meetings: President Morgan; Dean Bruce with his ever-present pipe; search committee members; Doreen Coultas in Music Education; and the Music School staff, Deryck Harnett and Maria Crane. The planned tour of the area with trips to Signal Hill and Cape Spear was scrubbed, not so much because of time constraints but because there really was no point; you still could barely see across the street.

The tour around campus was sobering, though. I was used to large campuses with beautiful grounds. The University of Wisconsin lies on a 13.25 acre (5.36 ha.) lake and boasts its own sailing club. Even my hometown university, the same size as Memorial University at the time, faced the banks of the beautiful Chippewa River and was bisected by a beautiful little stream. It had its own arboretum and backed on to the cliffs of Putnam Heights. I wasn't sure if Memorial's campus of nondescript brick boxes, with very little in the way of vegetation, would look better or worse in the sun. The dingy little student union was a far cry from Madison's palatial building with its theatres, Rathskeller, and dining areas featuring campus-made ice cream and other dairy treats.

And then there was the Music Building. A big cardboard box perched on concrete blocks. No washrooms. No water of any kind. To say the least, I was pretty ambivalent as I returned to Gander in the yellow school bus, enveloped in unrelenting grey. It was a relief to get back to Wisconsin. And spring. With sun and flowers and trees in leaf.

But when Don called a few weeks later to offer me the job, he was a consummate salesman. Starting a brand new department was just too tempting to turn down. And there was this eerie coincidence of the timing of it all; maybe it was meant to be. Besides, Memorial seemed to be the only university that was willing to take a chance on a rookie. So, despite my misgivings, and to my mother's great distress, I took the job. After all, it wouldn't be forever. I'd stay for two or three years, get some experience, and then find a job closer to home.

The rest of the spring and summer was a flurry of activity: writing exams, finishing the thesis, and getting ready to move while preparing a whole year's worth of new courses. Even more daunting, I soon learned, was dealing with government red tape. There were endless forms to fill out, but instead of a package being sent, one form would arrive. I would fill it out, send it in, and wait for the next one. By midsummer, I was getting anxious. Time was running short and the paperwork was still creeping along. Finally, just days before my departure date, I had all my documentation.

As I drove off in my overloaded green-gold Pinto, reality began to loom large. Being responsible for the theory program all by myself with almost no experience wasn't an issue — I was far too wet behind the ears to realize how daunting that should have been. Nor was I particularly worried about the week-long trip. I had never had to drive in big city traffic, not for any more than two or three hours at a stretch, so I had absolutely no idea what might lie ahead. But the fact that it would take most of a week to get there became a sobering reality — this was really far away! I said my last goodbyes in Madison and cried all the way to Chicago.

Evensdottir's Newfoundlanding

I made landfall at Argentia in mid-August. The trip had been a mishap-free adventure. I had managed, for the most part, to find accommodations for less than $30 a night, essential as my meagre grad student income was fading in the rear-view mirror while the first paycheque from Memorial University glimmered faintly somewhere in the foggy future. I had boarded the *Ambrose Shea* (which I kept calling the *Andrea Doria*, an Italian ocean liner that sank off the coast of Massachusetts in 1956, adding to my mother's anxiety, I'm sure) in North Sydney without having booked a cabin. Fortunately, I had my camping gear with me, so I followed the lead of the locals and bedded down comfortably on the floor with rows of empty seats keeping rigid vigil.

I got down to the business of trying to find accommodations in a town with a less than 1 per cent vacancy rate. The university would put us up at the Kenmount Motel for one week, then we were on our own. The fact that there was a baseball tournament going on and the loudest teams were apparently lodged at our motel added to the urgency. The promised assistance from the school with house-hunting never materialized. Murray Charters, the new cellist and musicologist, and his wife Judy managed to find a nice basement apartment just blocks from the university, their elderly landlady instantly falling in love with two-year-old Owen. My efforts weren't so fruitful. There were few apartment listings in the paper and more often than not, by the time an apartment was listed, it was already rented. (Being unfamiliar with the area, I thought the listing for an "apartment in Paradise" was a bit over the top!) St. John's streets that changed names every few blocks presented a particular challenge. One evening I was so confused, I thought I was going to have to spend the night in the car and try to find my way back to the motel in daylight. It turned out I was in the right place, but the street name had changed at the intersection and there was no sign indicating the new name. But the biggest problem turned out to be a gender issue. People would not rent to a single female. As one gentleman told me, "My daughter's a nurse and I wouldn't even rent to her!"

I finally managed to rent one of the new row houses on top of "Walton's Mountain." The road wasn't paved yet, and they were still adding the finishing touches to the homes, but it was clean and available. My meagre furnishings were still in storage somewhere — they were so few that the moving company would only bring them out when they could piggyback them with another load. My camping gear came in handy again! The apartments included a stove and fridge. Murray and Judy's apartment had a washer and dryer, so they loaned me theirs — Murray nearly burned out his car's transmission trying to get them up the "mountain."

Meanwhile we were busy planning for the new fall term. We got settled into our new offices in the Music Building: a cardboard box tucked between the Thomson Student Centre and the Arts and Administration Building. We had planning meetings — meetings with faculty, staff, library personnel, and administration. We would begin with a student body of 16, five second-year students and 11 first-years. The second-years were "townies" Don had recruited away from Mount Allison and St. Francis Xavier. In fact, all of our original students were from inside the overpass; recruiting would become a big part of our jobs.

Over the Labour Day weekend, we initiated a wonderful tradition: the faculty/staff blueberry outing. The whole tribe, including Paul Bendza, the third new music musketeer, and his family, recently arrived from Ontario, packed delicacies for a potluck dinner and drove out the CBS highway to Colliers to pick berries. It didn't take long to fill our buckets with the biggest, sweetest wild berries we had ever seen; then on to Brigus for a boil-up. It was a great get-to-know-you time, and (exactly as Don had planned, I'm sure) the start of a deep love of this unique and beautiful province.

Ready or Not

September of 1976 marked the official opening of the Department of Music at Memorial. Don Cook had taught a few courses to a few students the previous year, and had enticed a few others to come back home after first-year studies on the mainland. In addition to Don, there were three tenure-track faculty members. Murray Charters taught musicology and cello and conducted the chamber orchestra; Paul Bendza taught woodwinds and instrumental conducting and led the jazz ensemble; I taught theory, aural skills, keyboard harmony, and brass. In the second year I also took over the fledgling wind band from Paul. In addition to his administrative duties, Don directed the Festival Choir, instructed the organ majors, and taught some of the music history courses. For the first few years sessional instructors taught the piano and voice students, as well as some of the instrumentalists.

Our weeks were quite full. Classes ran the usual nine to five, Monday through Friday. In addition, each ensemble had a three-hour rehearsal one night a week. Faculty members were also expected to teach in the Saturday Preparatory School, our own little feeder system. School-aged students as well as adults could get private instruction on band and orchestral instruments, theory classes, and ensemble playing experience. The department ran weekly recitals at three on Sunday afternoons, featuring student and faculty performers. Sunday nights found Murray, Paul, and me at rehearsals of the St. John's Symphony Orchestra, as the Newfoundland Symphony Orchestra was then called. I'm sure if he thought he could get by with it, Don would have had us singing in his Cathedral Choir on Sunday mornings.

Being a small group in close quarters for long hours could have been problematic. Fortunately, the excitement of being pioneers, fanned by Don's boundless enthusiasm and seemingly inexhaustible energy, drew us into a close-knit group. It wasn't unusual for a group of students and faculty to go out for a few lines of bowling on Fridays (after the weekly 3–5 p.m. faculty meeting, of course). Faculty recital extravaganzas were held to raise money for our scholarship fund. After a few years we added a champagne brunch at the Holiday Inn. Faculty served (but did *not* cook) and played chamber music à la Palm Court Trio. Patrons could make a donation to request a favourite tune. If requests were slow, the trio would play a particularly grating number, repeatedly if necessary, until the patrons paid them to stop.

For their part, in the first year the students formed the Student Music Society, still active today. The Society organizes social events and raises money for their own scholarship fund. One of their earliest projects was a new phenomenon to me — a turkey tea. I couldn't imagine the size of the flow-through bag, let alone the cup that a turkey would require! Another lasting tradition was the welcome weekend for incoming students. This culminated in a scavenger hunt, with teams comprised of a mix of new and returning students plus a faculty or staff member. Don, the consummate townie, would make up a set of cryptic clues ultimately leading to the secret locale for a potluck dinner. An emergency number was provided for teams who were hopelessly lost by the 5 p.m. finish time. It was a great way to introduce students from "beyond the overpass" (as well as CFA faculty) to St. John's — and each other.

There were few school bands and almost no school orchestras in the province in the mid-1970s. Furthermore, there were strong ties in the musical communities to the Maritime universities, so recruitment was essential to our long-term success. Faculty and selected students travelled beyond the overpass to play recitals to both school and community audiences. Faculty also went out to do school workshops and clinics, often spending as much time giving first aid to derelict instruments as to teaching eager young students. Paul and I made a memorable trip to the Burin Peninsula. We rode out in one of the rural "taxis" — a van crammed with passengers and luggage of every size and shape. Not far down the road one of the passengers began to heartily sing songs of her own making. What a privilege to witness this very personal aspect of the folk tradition!

Adjudicating music festivals was another means of outreach and a wonderful opportunity to travel around the province. There were a few well-established music programs in places like Grand Falls and Corner Brook, where I heard fine bands and instrumentalists. I even learned to deal with solo and choral speech, doing my best to give helpful commentary to brightly beaming kindergarten classes earnestly chanting "The Three Lit-tle Kit-tens. By. Eliza. Lee. Follen." But the most interesting events were in the smaller communities. I heard (and adjudicated!) Girl Guide troops singing campfire songs, a melodica band, and a Salvation Army timbrel corps (all in the same class — pick the winner!), an adult ukulele ensemble, and a guitar and bagpipe duo. But my all-time festival favourite was a class in one smaller community called "Rhythm in Music": three junior high girls' gym classes executing bouncing basketball routines to "Mack the Knife." A bit hard to give constructive criticism, but in all cases easy to applaud the desire to get as many kids (or adults) as possible involved in the festival.

Late August was time for the summer music camp at Salt Pond, Burin. Memorial had been running a summer music camp for schoolchildren for several years and we began our official duties there. It was a chance to meet some of the local instrumental music teachers and get a first-hand look at (and listen to) the level of music instruction in the province's schools. The camp was held at the trades college, as they had not only adequate instructional space but residential and dining facilities, featuring french fries three meals a day — four if you counted the evening snack time. We had full days of rehearsals, sectionals, private lessons, and theory instruction. Evenings were for recreation, though, including the annual students versus faculty soccer match. There was one special rule for this event: no matter what the score, the faculty always won. I became acutely aware that the Burin Peninsula is a hotbed of soccer talent when I was nearly decapitated by a shot on goal whistling by, millimetres from my head.

The wind band and Festival Choir made occasional concert trips to communities around the island. The Chamber Choir and Brass Quintet were able to travel more extensively. While most of their travel was also restricted to the island portion of the province, more ambitious travel was occasionally possible. In 1978 the student brass quintet played for Her Majesty Queen Elizabeth and Prince Philip at the sod-turning ceremonies for the QE II Library, then left for a month-long trip along the Northern Peninsula and down the Labrador as far as Nain. The Chamber

Choir made a pilgrimage to England in 1983, the 400th anniversary of Sir Humphrey Gilbert's claiming Newfoundland for England. They spent a week as choir-in-residence at Exeter Cathedral, Gilbert's home parish.

Life in a Cardboard Box

For its first nine years, the Department of Music was housed in a "temporary" building located between the original Arts and Administration Building and the Thomson Student Centre (now the site of the Bruneau Centre). T-11 had served for many years already as the graphics lab, and looked it.

Offices were arranged around the outer perimeter of the west and north sides of the building with practice rooms along the other two sides. The window in my office was aligned with a narrow passageway between the Student Centre and another temporary building. This was a popular location for certain small business transactions and, often, sampling of the goods.

The centre area of T-11 was divided into two rooms, a classroom large enough to hold about 20 students and a Music Resource Centre with scores, recordings, and several turntables (remember LPs?) with headphones. This arrangement worked for the first few years, but a growing student body meant the Music Resource Centre was needed for a second teaching area. The scores and recordings would have to be housed in the library until the Music Department moved to a larger facility. This arrangement ultimately led to a bit of a turf war. The main library, seeing possession as nine-tenths of the law, was not interested in returning the scores and recordings to the care of the School of Music when we moved into the Morgan Building in 1985. We, on the other hand, argued that these materials were classroom resources, not unlike chemicals for the Chemistry Department, and it was unreasonable to expect faculty to have to go from one end of campus to the other to pick up scores and recordings for daily classroom use. The School of Music won most of its case; scores, recordings, and listening posts are back in the Morgan Building, with journals and videos housed in the QE II Library.

Space limitations were not the only shortcomings of T-11. We called it a cardboard box for good reason. Outer walls were made of plywood; inner walls were simple sheets of gyprock. Sound insulation was non-existent. My office happened to back on to a room that housed a small practice organ. I always knew when one particular student, re-nowned for his aggressive pedal technique, was rehearsing; the loud thudding sent me off to seek a quieter place to work for an hour or two. The two inner rooms shared a ventilation duct and, at times, lectures. Normal professorial droning wasn't problematic, but keyboard harmony and aural skills classes had to be scheduled carefully. The arrival of a new musicologist also added a challenge. He maintained that to hear the music properly the volume had to be set on "bust." No other classes could be scheduled at the same time as his lectures. But, as the saying goes, there's no cloud without a silver lining. As we could easily hear our students' efforts in the practice rooms (there was a gap of at least an inch between the practice room doors and the floor) we knew exactly what issues to focus on when they came for their weekly studio lessons.

The building construction afforded a few other adventures. Unlike many of the other temporary buildings, T-11 did not have a permanent foundation; rather, it rested on concrete blocks. Unfortunately, this led to some rather undesirable basement tenants. Rats eventually drew cats, which drew stray dogs. The final straw came when one distraught ses-sional fled her studio refusing to teach there any longer because there was a furious dog-and-cat fight going on just beneath her feet. The SPCA was called and the Maintenance Department left poison and traps for the rats. All was calm for a few days until a nasty smell began to seep up through the floorboards. The "remedy" was to spray the place with some overwhelmingly cloying substance that took weeks to subside.

T-11 also had a drop ceiling of acoustical tiles as a feeble attempt at sound abatement. A group of students discovered this one evening and went exploring. This feature, of course, gave them access to all the teaching studios and even the main office. They were eventually found out when they misjudged a joist and fell through onto Doug Dunsmore's desk.

Because of its purported temporary status, T-11 had no plumbing. When nature called, or if we simply wanted a drink of water, we had to go to the Arts and Administration Building or the Thomson Student Centre. On weekdays, this was simply an inconvenience. Working late at night or on weekends, this issue became more serious as the Arts and Administration Building would be closed. Most dreaded were Satur-days, when we offered the preparatory school program. We, and our school-aged students, had to pick our way through broken glass and the stench of stale beer and cigarette smoke, remains of the weekly Friday night beer bashes, to get to a washroom or drinking fountain. Small wonder that the prep school only lasted a few years!

But despite all these hurdles (or perhaps because of them), we managed to build a strong, cohesive unit, and the students from these early days seem to have the fondest memories of their time at Memorial.

Note

1. The Department of Music was elevated to the School of Music in 1985 and housed in its own new building, named in honour of M.O. Morgan: Melvin Baker and Jean Graham, *Celebrate Memorial!* (St. John's: Memorial University of Newfoundland, 1999), 74.

Inside the Henrietta Harvey Library. (Photo from *Memorial University of Newfoundland and its Environs: A Guide to Life and Work at the University in St. John's*, courtesy of Memorial University Libraries.)

Suggested Reading about Memorial University and Education in Newfoundland

Baker, Melvin, and Jean Graham. *Celebrate Memorial! A Pictorial History of Memorial University of Newfoundland*. St. John's: Memorial University of Newfoundland, 1999.

Carew, S.J., ed. *J. L. P. — A Portrait of John Lewis Paton by His Friends*. St. John's: Memorial University of Newfoundland, Paton College, 1968.

Colton, Glenn David. *Newfoundland Rhapsody: Frederick R. Emerson and the Musical Culture of the Island*. Montreal and Kingston: McGill-Queen's University Press, 2014.

Gough, Ruby L. *Robert Edwards Holloway: Newfoundland Educator, Scientist, Photographer, 1874–1904*. Montreal and Kingston: McGill-Queen's University Press, 2005.

Hawkin, David J. *Pilgrims in a Barren Land: A Novel.* [Raleigh, N.C.]: Lulu, 2010.

Joyal, Mark. 2001. "Classics at Memorial, 1925-2000: A Brief History." In Mark Joyal, ed., *In Altum: Seventy-five Years of Classical Studies in Newfoundland*, 3–38. St. John's: Memorial University of Newfoundland, 2001.

MacLeod, Malcolm. *A Bridge Built Halfway: A History of Memorial University College, 1925–1950*. Montreal and Kingston: McGill-Queen's University Press, 1990.

———. "Crossroads Campus: Faculty Development at Memorial University of Newfoundland, 1950–1972." In Paul Stortz and E. Lisa Panayotidis, eds., *Historical Identities: The Professoriate in Canada*, 131–57. Toronto: University of Toronto Press, 2006.

———, ed. *Crossroads Country: Memories of Pre-Confederation Newfoundland*. St. John's: Breakwater, 1999. (Includes interviews with David Pitt, Moses O. Morgan, Leslie Harris, Helena McGrath Frecker, and Ian Rusted.)

———. "Parade Street Parade: The Student Body at Memorial University College, 1925–49." In Paul Axelrod and John G. Reid, eds., *Youth, University and Canadian Society: Essays in the Social History of Higher Education*, 51–71. Montreal and Kingston: McGill-Queen's University Press, 1989.

Mathews, Larry. *The Artificial Newfoundlander: A Novel.* St. John's: Breakwater, 2010.

————. *An Exile's Perfect Letter.* St. John's: Breakwater Books, 2018.

McCann, Phillip, ed. 1982. *Blackboards and Briefcases: Personal Stories by New-foundland Teachers, Educators and Administrators.* St. John's: Jesperson Press, 1982.

————.*Schooling in a Fishing Society: Education and Economic Conditions in New-foundland and Labrador, 1836–1986.* St. John's: Institute of Social and Economic Research, 1994.

Poole, Cyril F. *Mose Morgan: A Life in Action.* St. John's: Harry Cuff Publications, 1998.

Roberts, Gildas. *Chemical Eric.* St. John's: Belvoir Books, 1974.

Rowe, Frederick W. *The Development of Education in Newfoundland.* Toronto: Ryerson Press, 1964.

————. *Education and Culture in Newfoundland.* Toronto: McGraw-Hill Ryerson, 1976.

Steele, D.H., ed. *Early Science in Newfoundland and Labrador.* St. John's: Avalon Chapter of Sigma Xi, 1987.

Taylor, Stephen James Lake, Lord Taylor of Harlow. *A Natural History of Everyday Life: A Biographical Guide for Would-be Doctors of Society.* Memoir Club Series. [London:] British Medical Journal, 1988. (Autobiography, including his experience at Memorial and his views on M.O. Morgan and Leslie Harris.)

Webb, Jeff A. *Observing the Outports: Describing Newfoundland Culture, 1950–1980.* Toronto: University of Toronto Press, 2016.

List of Contributors

Raoul Andersen was born in Chicago, Illinois. He completed a PhD in Anthropology at the University of Missouri, Columbia, and taught in the Memorial Department of Anthropology, serving as chair. Raoul has written about Newfoundland's First Nations population and about the fishery industry.

Melvin Baker is Archivist-Historian for Memorial University (President's Office). A native of Catalina, NL, he completed BA and MA degrees (Newfoundland history) from Memorial and a PhD (Canadian history) from the University of Western Ontario. He has written extensively on the history of Newfoundland and Labrador.

James G. Barnes joined the Department of Commerce in 1968 and retired 41 years later. He was appointed Director of the School of Business Administration and Commerce and became the first Dean of Business Administration. A native of St. John's, he holds degrees in Commerce and Economics from Memorial, an MBA from Harvard Business School, and a PhD from the University of Toronto.

Norman John Peppin Brown (1922–2014), BPhil (Oxon), MA, BA, became the founding member of Memorial University's Philosophy Department. Born in Dover, England, he received his degrees from Christ Church, Oxford. While in St. John's, he was active in music at the Basilica and St. Patrick's Glee Club and broadcasting at the CBC. He left Memorial in 1965 to teach philosophy at Queen's University in Kingston, Ontario.

Roberta Buchanan was born in Uitenhage, South Africa, and educated in England. She received her PhD from the Shakespeare Institute, University of Birmingham. Roberta immigrated to St. John's in 1964 to teach English literature. She was a founding member of the Women's Studies program. Publications include *I Moved All My Women Upstairs* (poetry); with Anne Hart and Brian Greene, *The Woman Who Mapped Labrador: The Life and Labrador Expedition Diary of Mina Hubbard*.

Sharon Buehler was born in Jacksonville, Illinois. In 1967 she came to Memorial with her husband, who was appointed in Folklore. Sharon was a research assistant and later received a PhD in epidemiology. She spent the next 18 years in undergraduate and graduate teaching in Community Medicine.

Born in Stoke-on-Trent, *Tony Chadwick* was appointed Lecturer in French at Memorial in 1967. He was heavily involved for 10 years with amateur theatre, especially the Open Group's productions, as actor, stagehand, and director.

Born in Seoul, Korea, *Chung-Won Cho* received his PhD in Physics from the University of Toronto. He joined Memorial as an Assistant Professor of Physics in 1958, later serving as department head. He was the first non-white person appointed at Memorial to a tenure-stream position.

Howard and *Leila Clase* were keen naturalists and gardeners who had an association with the Memorial University Botanical Garden from its earliest days. Howard was born in England and has a PhD in Chemistry from Cambridge. Leila was born and educated in Finland, receiving a Fil. Kand. (master's) degree from Helsinki University. They came to St. John's in 1968, where Howard taught inorganic chemistry. Leila earned a master's degree in linguistics from Memorial and taught courses in linguistics and Russian. She died in 2014.

Born in Farnham, Surrey, UK, and having taught in England for several years, *Michael Collins* came to Memorial in 1969 as a Lecturer in Junior Studies (biology). He was Director of the Division of General Studies from 1988 to 1994. A pioneer in the development of computer-based education, he developed Memorial's first web-based course. He received a 3M Teaching Fellowship, Canada's highest award for university teaching. He served as Associate Vice-President (Academic), Acting Vice-President (Academic), and Pro-Vice Chancellor.

Sandra Djwa is a biographer, cultural critic, editor. Born in St. John's, she took first-year Education at Memorial University and received BEd and PhD degrees from the University of British Columbia. Sandra has taught Canadian literature at Simon Fraser University, where she was chair of English. She co-edited the collected and selected works of E.J. Pratt. Her biography of P.K. Page won the Governor General's Award for non-fiction. She has also published biographies of F.R. Scott and Roy Daniells.

Pearl Herbert obtained nursing training at Southlands Hospital in Shoreham-by-Sea, West Sussex, England, and trained in midwifery in England before immigrating to Canada. At Dalhousie University, she completed studies in public health nursing, education, and health education. She moved to St. John's in 1979. She taught in the midwifery part of Memorial's Outpost Nursing Program. When the Memorial University midwifery program was discontinued, she taught maternal and child health courses and other nursing courses.

Kjellrun K. Hestekin (1948–2015) was born in Eau Claire, Wisconsin. She completed a BA in music at the University of Kansas, MA in music at the University of Wisconsin, and was awarded a diploma by the Faculty of Fine Arts in Music from the University of Calgary. She came to Memorial in 1976, and was one of the first three faculty members who established the School of Music.

Born in Leicestershire, England, *John Hewson* completed a BA in Classics at

University College, London, and a PhD at Laval. In 1960 he was appointed as a linguist in the French Department. John founded the MUN Linguistics Department and served as head. He has been a University Orator, University Research Professor, and Henrietta Harvey Professor. He has published a score of books and over 200 articles and chapters.

Lin (Francis Lindbergh) Jackson was born on Bell Island in 1928 and educated in St. John's. After employment as a flight planner-meteorologist, Lin took up studies at Memorial College, completing MAs in psychology and philosophy at Dalhousie, Utrecht, and Toronto. Invited in 1965 to help found Memorial's Philosophy Department, he served as department head and on the university Senate.

Ralph Matthews is a former President of the Canadian Sociological Association (CSA) and former editor of the *Canadian Review of Sociology*. He is a recipient of the CSA Outstanding Career Award and the UBC Killam Research Prize. The author of five books and over 100 professional papers and reports, he has also served as President of the Research Committee on Sociology of Science and Technology of the International Sociological Association. Born and raised in Newfoundland, he holds a BA (Hons.) from Memorial University and MA and PhD degrees from the University of Minnesota. He is currently a Professor Emeritus of Sociology at McMaster University and Professor of Sociology at the University of British Columbia.

Born and raised in Montreal, *Dorothy Milne* graduated from Brown University with a PhD in cell biology. Having studied and taught at five universities in Canada and the United States, she came to Memorial in 1980. She was the Science Collections Librarian at the Queen Elizabeth II Library for 26 years.

Born in London, England, *Brian Wallace Payton* (1930–2014) was a physician and Professor of Physiology. His PhD was in Pharmacology. In 1965 he went to the US to work at Columbia University, Yeshiva University, and the Woods Hole Biological Laboratory. Dr. Payton was one of the first three faculty members in Memorial's Faculty of Medicine.

David George Pitt (1921–2018) was born in Musgravetown, NL, and attended several outport schools around the island, Memorial College in St. John's, Mount Allison University, and the University of Toronto (PhD). In 1949 he was appointed to the English Department at Memorial University, where he served as department head. His publications include fiction and several scholarly editions and collections. He is best known for his biographical research on the Newfoundland-born poet E.J. Pratt. He received honorary degrees from Mount Allison and Memorial.

Marilyn Porter spent her childhood in Wales. Her PhD is from the University of Bristol. Radicalized in the 1960s, she turned to sociology and studied working-class women's class consciousness. After a year teaching at a progressive school in Botswana and sessional posts at Bristol, Memorial, and Manchester universities, she secured a tenure-stream position in sociology at Memorial in 1980, where she served out her academic career.

Stephen Harold Riggins, PhD, University of Toronto, taught sociology at Memorial University for 25 years, first as a Visiting Professor and in a tenure-stream position beginning in 1990. He has served as department head. Stephen has edited four books about ethnic minority media, sociological theory, and material culture studies. He is the author of the autobiographical book *The Pleasures of Time: Two Men, a Life*. Stephen was born in southern Indiana.

Neil V. Rosenberg is from the western United States. He has a PhD degree in Folklore from Indiana University and is a recipient of the Marius Barbeau Medal for lifetime achievement from the Folklore Studies Association of Canada, and is a member of the International Bluegrass Music Hall of Fame. He won a Grammy Award for his album notes for the Smithsonian/Folkways reissue of Harry Smith's *Anthology of American Folk Music*. His *Bluegrass Generation: A Memoir* was published in 2018.

Joan Scott came to Newfoundland from Ipswich, UK, in 1962, with her husband, who was appointed in Chemistry. She obtained a BSc at Memorial and taught Junior Studies biology. She completed a PhD at the Ontario Institute for Studies in Education, Toronto, and taught Women's Studies and biology at Memorial. She has filled several roles: faculty wife, student, graduate student, and professor.

Robert Sexty was born and raised in Alberta and joined the Department of Commerce as an Assistant Professor in 1968 and retired in 2007. He has a PhD from the University of Colorado, and taught in the Strategic Management and Business Ethics areas at Memorial.

Bruce Shawyer, born in Kirkcaldy, Scotland, completed a PhD degree at the University of St. Andrews. After teaching at the University of Nottingham and the University of Western Ontario, he came to Memorial in 1985 to head the Department of Mathematics and Statistics.

Jo Shawyer, who grew up on a farm in southern Ontario, has a PhD in Geography from the University of Nottingham. Her landscape studies include: farm structure; township history; urban neighbourhoods in London, Ontario; the history of agriculture in Newfoundland; community museums as community health; a policy analysis of C.A. Pippy Park in St. John's; and cooperative housing in Newfoundland and Labrador.

Born in London, Ontario, *Don H. Steele* (1932–2013), marine biologist, was awarded a PhD by McGill University. He taught biology at Memorial University from 1962 to 1998. Don was an authority on the natural history of Newfoundland and Labrador, and edited *Early Science in Newfoundland and Labrador*.

Jeff Webb is a Professor of history at Memorial University who has written on radio broadcasting and the history of scholarship. His most recent book, *Observing the Outports: Describing Newfoundland Culture, 1950–1980*, is a study of the early social science and humanities literature on Newfoundland that was conducted at Memorial. He is past editor of the journal *Newfoundland and Labrador Studies*.

Elizabeth Willmott was born in Indianapolis, Indiana, and spent her childhood in Toledo, Ohio, and Washington, DC. She completed an MA in Psychology at the University of Michigan. Her art is in the collections of Canadian and European museums. In St. John's her mentor was the sculptor Hans Melis, remembered locally for his busts of Premier Smallwood and the founders of Memorial University. Elizabeth is the wife of Donald Willmott, the first sociologist at Memorial. Elizabeth and Donald lived in St. John's from 1956 to 1959.

Steven B. Wolinetz is Professor Emeritus in Political Science. He grew up in New York and Long Island, and completed graduate degrees at Yale. His research focuses on political parties and the politics of smaller democracies, particularly the Netherlands and Newfoundland. He came to Memorial in 1971.

Index